USERNAME: REGENERATED

THE RETURN OF THE **SUGG SQUAD**!

D1621834

MINDY LOPKIN IS RESPONSIBLE FOR ALL THE COOL SPEECH BUBBLES, EFFECTS AND LETTERING.

AMRIT BIRDI IS THE GUY BEHIND THE INCREDIBLE ILLUSTRATIONS IN THE USERNAME SERIES.

JOE SUGG CREATED THE STORYLINE AND CHARACTERS AND DIRECTED THE PROJECT TO MAKE THE BEST GRAPHIC NOVEL SERIES POSSIBLE.

MATT WHYMAN IS THE PERSON WHO TOOK THE STORY AND CREATED A GRIPPING NARRATIVE TO ACCOMPANY THE ARTWORK.

JOAQUIN PEREYRA BROUGHT THE IMAGES TO LIFE WITH HIS AMAZING COLOURING.

TO EVERY KEITH I'VE EVER MET
OR WILL MEET IN THE FUTURE...
CURRENTLY ON ZERO.

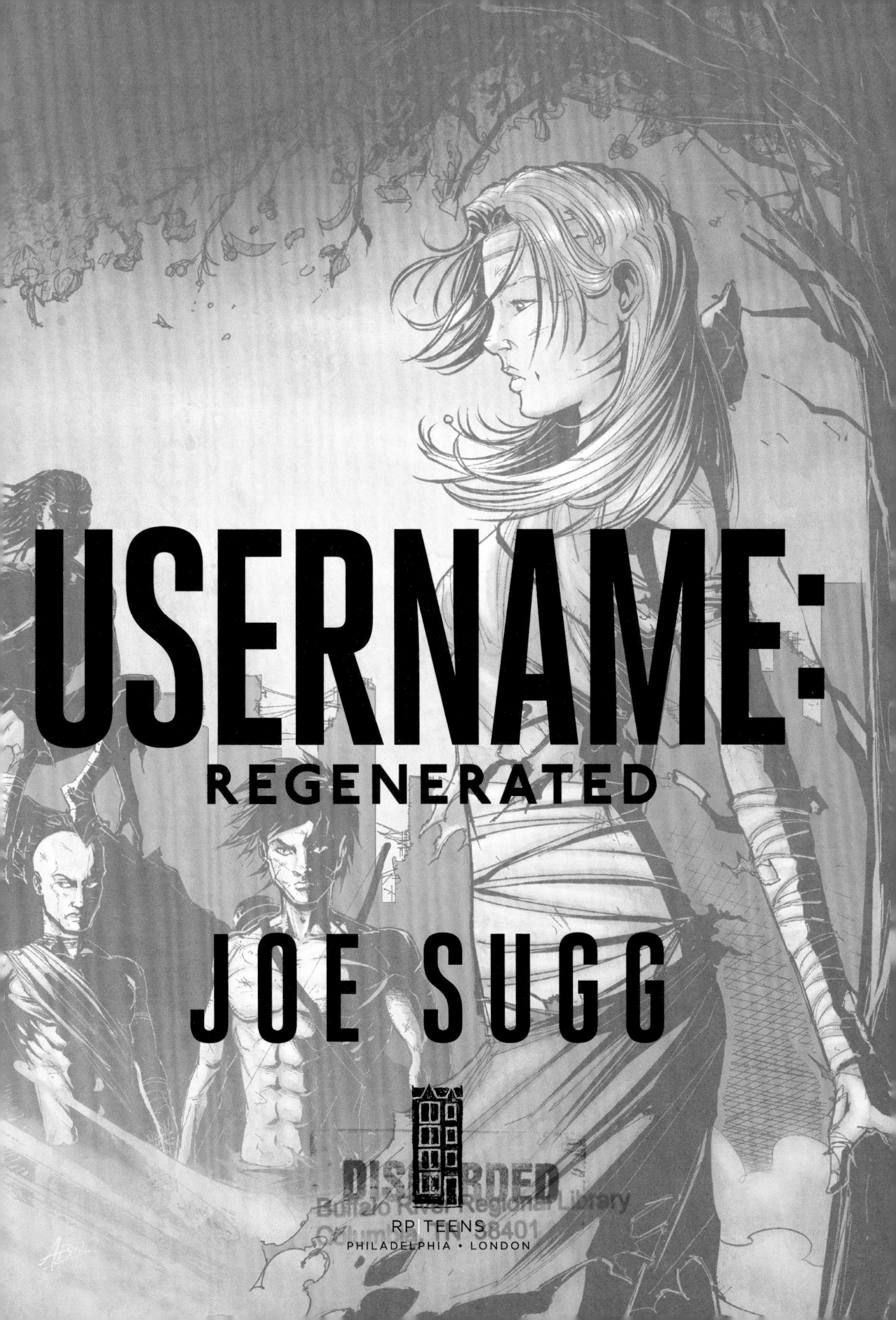

USERNAME:

REGENERATED

JOE SUGG

RP|TEENS
PHILADELPHIA • LONDON

Books published by Running Press are available at special discounts for bulk purchases in the United States by corporations, institutions, and other organizations. For more information, please contact the Special Markets Department at the Perseus Books Group, 2300 Chestnut Street, Suite 200, Philadelphia, PA 19103, or call (800) 810-4145, ext. 5000, or e-mail special.markets@perseusbooks.com.

ISBN 978-0-7624-6150-9
Library of Congress Control Number: 2016949130

E-book ISBN 978-0-7624-6151-6

9   8   7   6   5   4   3   2   1
Digit on the right indicates the number of this printing

With thanks to Matt Whyman
Artwork produced by Amrit Birdi & Co.
Illustrator: Amrit Birdi
Colorist: Joaquin Pereyra
Letterist: Mindy Lopkin
Art Assistant: Lisamaria Laxholm

Running Press Book Publishers
2300 Chestnut Street
Philadelphia, PA 19103-4371

Visit us on the web!
www.runningpress.com/rpkids

HELLO AGAIN

I NEVER QUITE THOUGHT I WOULD BE SAYING THIS BUT HERE IT IS..! BOOK TWO IN THE USERNAME SERIES! AND JUST LIKE THE LAST TIME I'M SO EXCITED FOR YOU TO READ AND ENJOY THE STORY AND LET ME KNOW WHAT YOU THINK.

ONCE AGAIN I HAVE YOU GUYS TO THANK FOR MAKING THIS POSSIBLE. YOU MIGHT BE WONDERING, 'JOSEPH, WERE YOU SURPRISED BY THE SUCCESS OF YOUR FIRST GRAPHIC NOVEL, USERNAME: EVIE?', AND THE ANSWER IS, 'YES I FLIPPIN' WELL WAS!'. I'VE BEEN OVERWHELMED BY JUST HOW AMAZING THE RESPONSE WAS – FROM REVIEWS ONLINE, THE REACTION TO SIGNINGS (I MET OVER 5,000 OF YOU) AND COMMENTS ACROSS MY CHANNELS. I STILL CAN'T BELIEVE EVERYTHING WE'VE ACHIEVED TOGETHER WITH USERNAME: EVIE.

BUT WHAT WAS EVEN BETTER TO ME WAS THAT SO MANY OF YOU HAVE SAID USERNAME:EVIE WAS THE FIRST GRAPHIC NOVEL YOU'D READ AND HOW MUCH YOU HAD ENJOYED THIS KIND OF BOOK, WHICH WAS REALLY IMPORTANT TO ME RIGHT FROM THE START. AS YOU KNOW I'VE ALWAYS BEEN INTO COMICS AND GRAPHIC NOVELS SINCE WAY BACK AND TO INTRODUCE NEW READERS TO THE GENRE IS SOMETHING I NEVER EXPECTED BUT AM SO PROUD OF. YOU LOT ARE THE BEST AND I'M SO HAPPY YOU ENJOYED EVIE'S FIRST ADVENTURE.

QUESTION IS ARE YOU READY FOR THE NEXT ONE?

SO WHAT CAN YOU EXPECT FROM USERNAME: REGENERATED? WELL FOR A START THERE'S PLENTY OF FAMILIAR FACES, BUT TIME HAS PASSED AND ALTHOUGH YOU MIGHT RECOGNISE THE GANG FROM U:E (THAT'S A HANDY ABBREVIATION ISN'T IT?) THEY'VE DEFINITELY DONE A LOT OF GROWING UP. AND OF COURSE THERE'S A WHOLE CAST OF NEW CHARACTERS FOR YOU TO GET TO KNOW. THERE'S ADVENTURE, DANGER, EVEN REVISITING THE PAST! UNEXPECTED FRIENDSHIPS AND A TWISTY PLOT TO KEEP YOU ON YOUR TOES.

I'VE LIVED WITH THESE CHARACTERS SINCE WAY BACK BEFORE EVEN THE RELEASE OF U:E AND FOR THIS BOOK I REALLY WANTED TO DEVELOP THEM AND THEIR STORIES – GIVING THEM MORE DEPTH AND SHOWING DIFFERENT SIDES TO THEM AND THEIR WORLD (OR SHOULD THAT BE WORLDS). AND I'LL LET YOU INTO A LITTLE SECRET...I'D ALWAYS IMAGINED THERE TO BE MORE THAN ONE BOOK SO WHAT YOU'RE ABOUT TO READ IS LIKE ANOTHER EPISODE IN THE USERNAME SERIES!

ONCE AGAIN THANKS TO EVERY ONE OF YOU WHO TAKES THE TIME OUT TO WATCH MY VIDEOS, READ MY BOOKS AND SUPPORT ALL THE AMAZING THINGS I GET TO DO. I HOPE YOU GET AS MUCH OUT OF THE THINGS I MAKE AS I DO CREATING THEM. YOU LOT ARE MY BIGGEST INSPIRATION AND NONE OF THIS WOULD BE POSSIBLE WITHOUT YOU – THANKS FOR COMING ON THIS CRAZY RIDE WITH ME.

SO SIT BACK, RELAX, AND ENJOY THE RIDE THAT IS USERNAME: REGENERATED.

ALL THE BEST

JOE

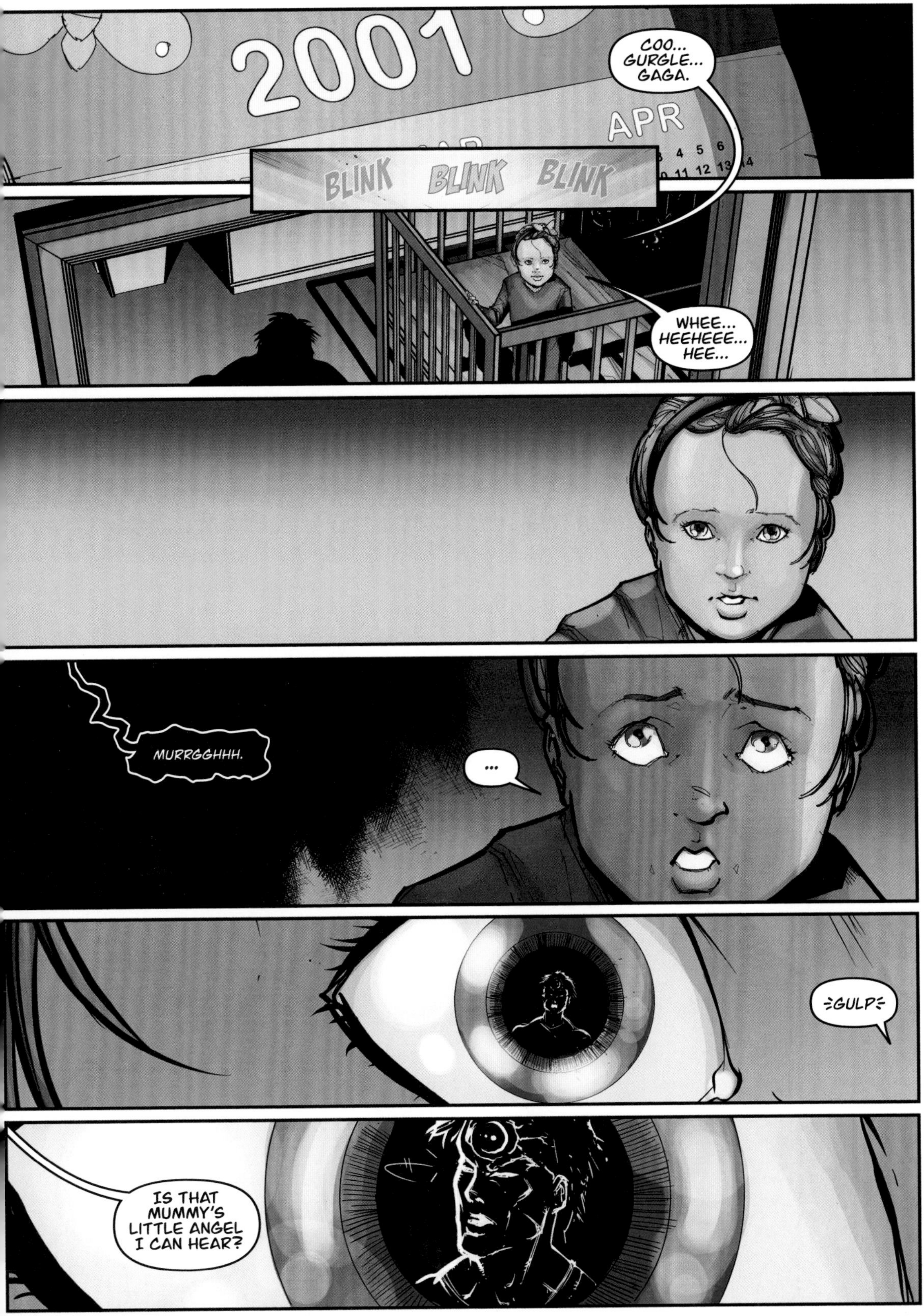
2001
APR
COO... GURGLE... GAGA.
BLINK BLINK BLINK
WHEE... HEEHEEE... HEE...
MURRGGHHH.
...
GULP
IS THAT MUMMY'S LITTLE ANGEL I CAN HEAR?

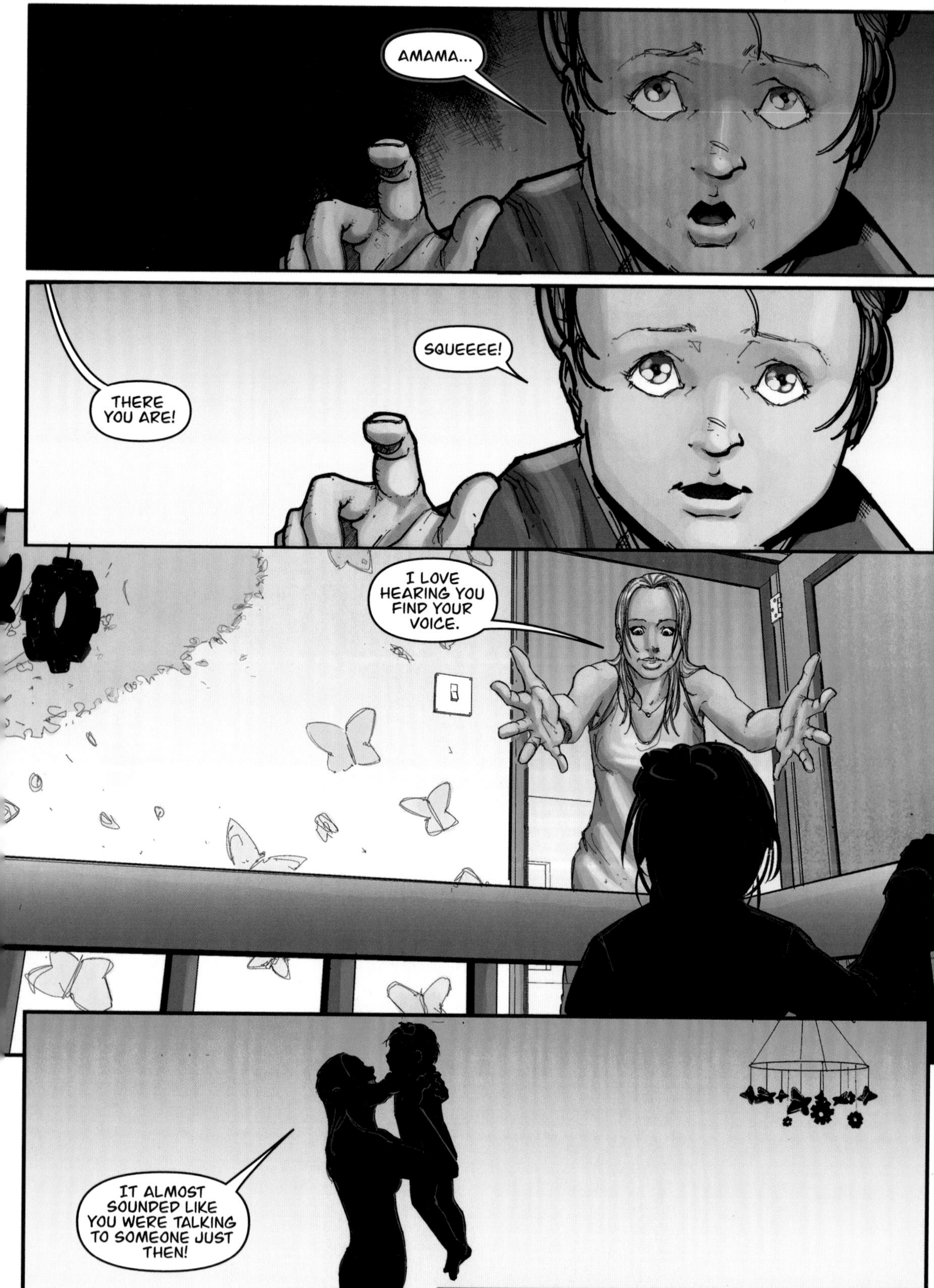
AMAMA...
SQUEEEE!
THERE YOU ARE!
I LOVE HEARING YOU FIND YOUR VOICE.
IT ALMOST SOUNDED LIKE YOU WERE TALKING TO SOMEONE JUST THEN!

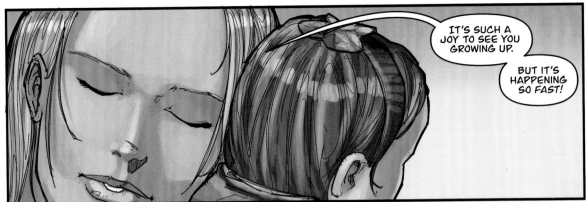

IT'S SUCH A JOY TO SEE YOU GROWING UP.

BUT IT'S HAPPENING SO FAST!

WHATEVER LIFE HAS IN STORE FOR YOU, EVIE, YOU'LL ALWAYS BE MY BABY.

AMAMAM... MA...

≑GASP≑ EVIE! CAN YOU SAY THAT AGAIN?

AMA... MUMA!

I JUST WISH YOUR FATHER WERE HERE TO WITNESS THESE MOMENTS.

3

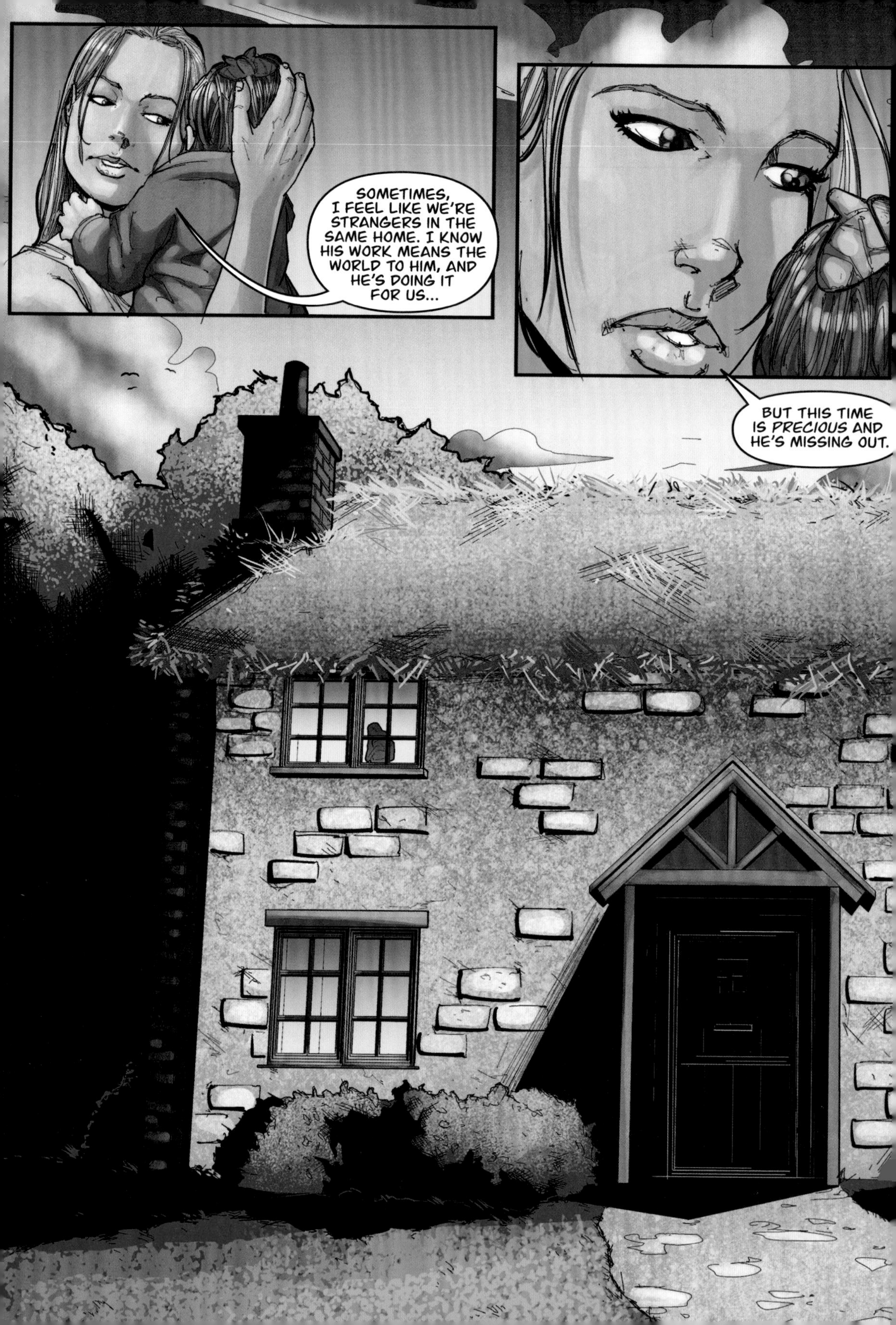
SOMETIMES, I FEEL LIKE WE'RE STRANGERS IN THE SAME HOME. I KNOW HIS WORK MEANS THE WORLD TO HIM, AND HE'S DOING IT FOR US...
BUT THIS TIME IS *PRECIOUS* AND HE'S MISSING OUT.

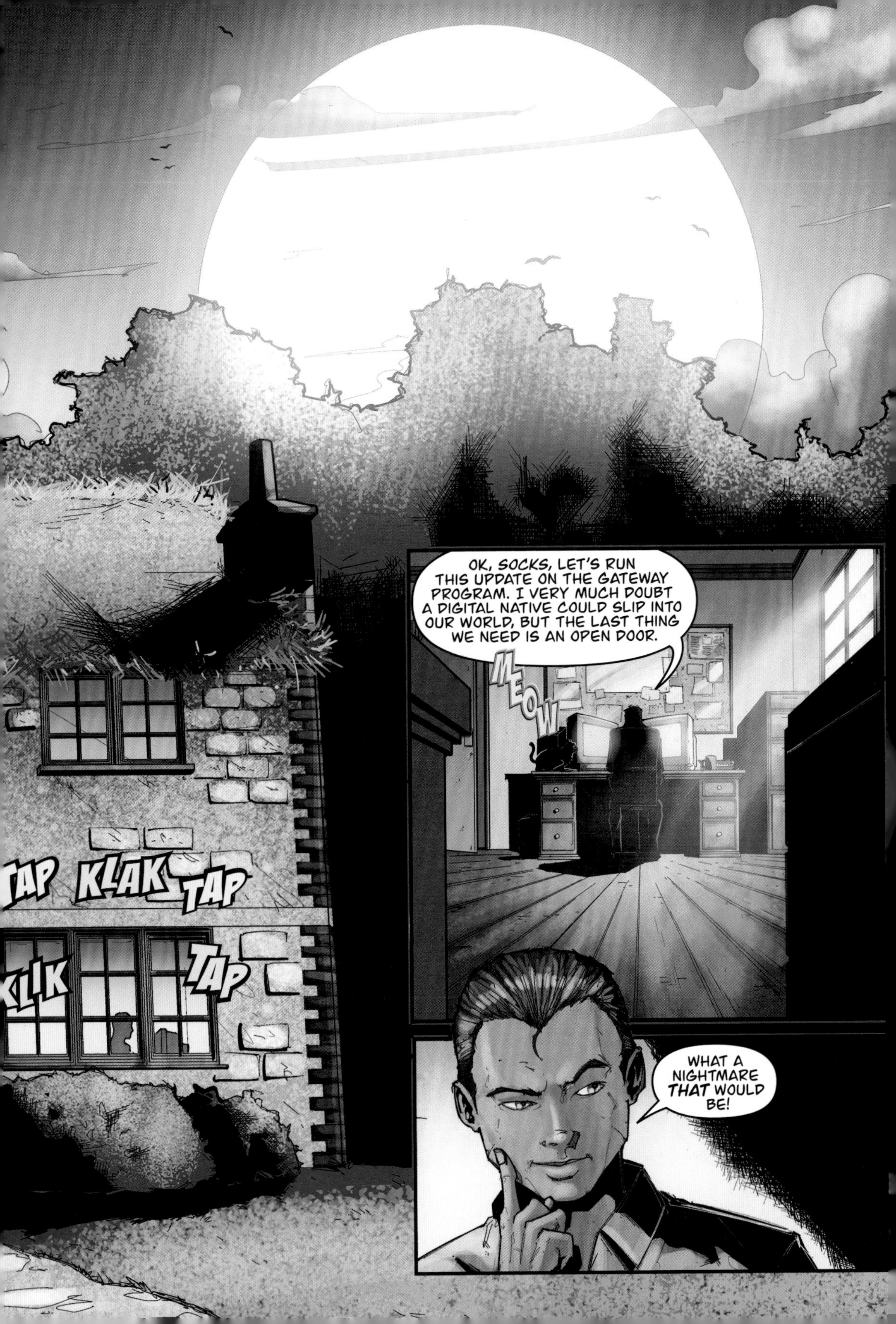
TAP KLAK TAP
KLIK TAP
OK, SOCKS, LET'S RUN THIS UPDATE ON THE GATEWAY PROGRAM. I VERY MUCH DOUBT A DIGITAL NATIVE COULD SLIP INTO OUR WORLD, BUT THE LAST THING WE NEED IS AN OPEN DOOR.
MEOW
WHAT A NIGHTMARE *THAT* WOULD BE!

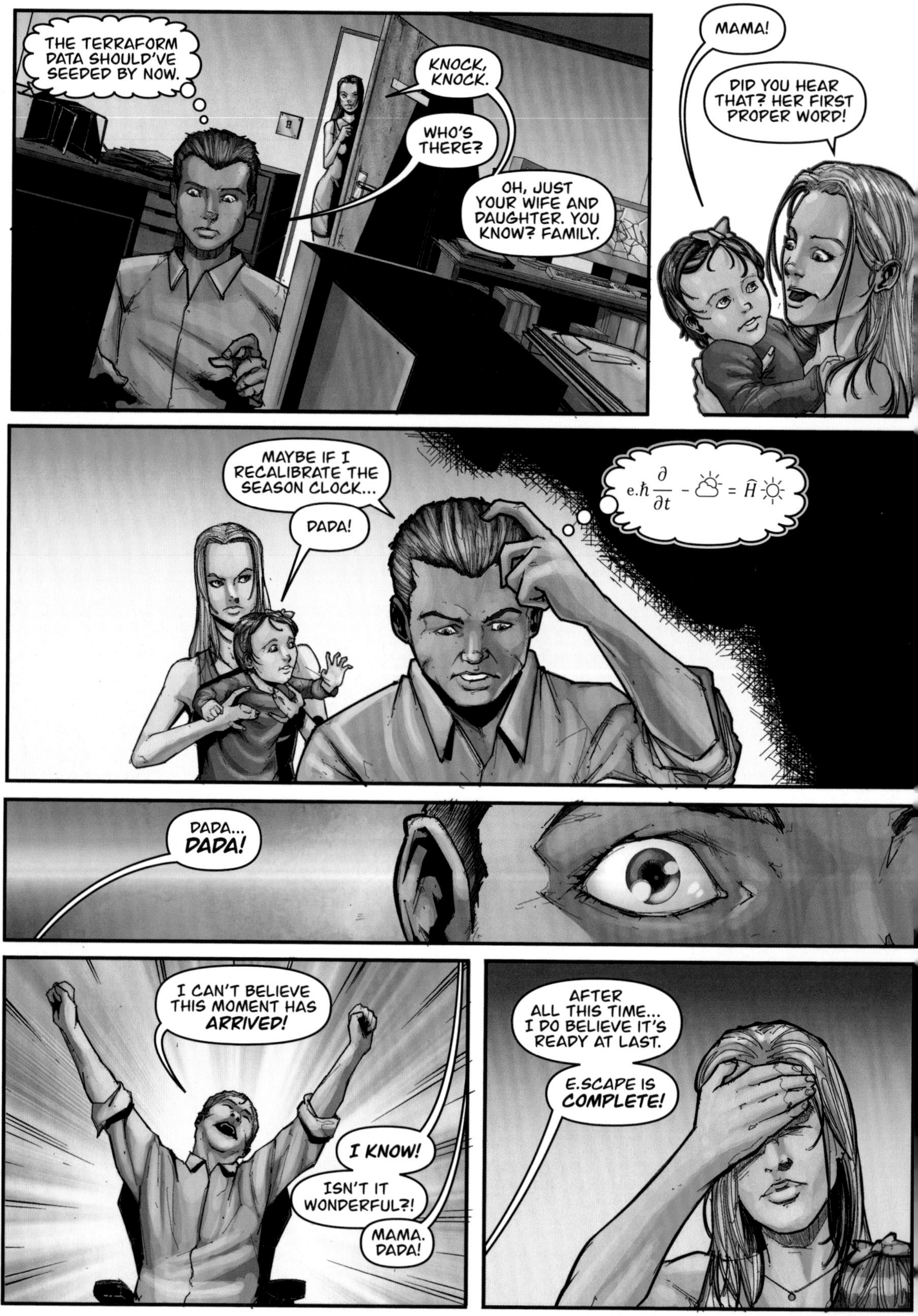
THE TERRAFORM DATA SHOULD'VE SEEDED BY NOW.
KNOCK, KNOCK.
WHO'S THERE?
OH, JUST YOUR WIFE AND DAUGHTER. YOU KNOW? FAMILY.
MAMA!
DID YOU HEAR THAT? HER FIRST PROPER WORD!
MAYBE IF I RECALIBRATE THE SEASON CLOCK...
DADA!
$\mathrm{e}.\hbar \frac{\partial}{\partial t} - \quad = \hat{H}$
DADA... **DADA!**
I CAN'T BELIEVE THIS MOMENT HAS **ARRIVED!**
I KNOW!
ISN'T IT WONDERFUL?!
MAMA. DADA!
AFTER ALL THIS TIME... I DO BELIEVE IT'S READY AT LAST.
E.SCAPE IS **COMPLETE!**

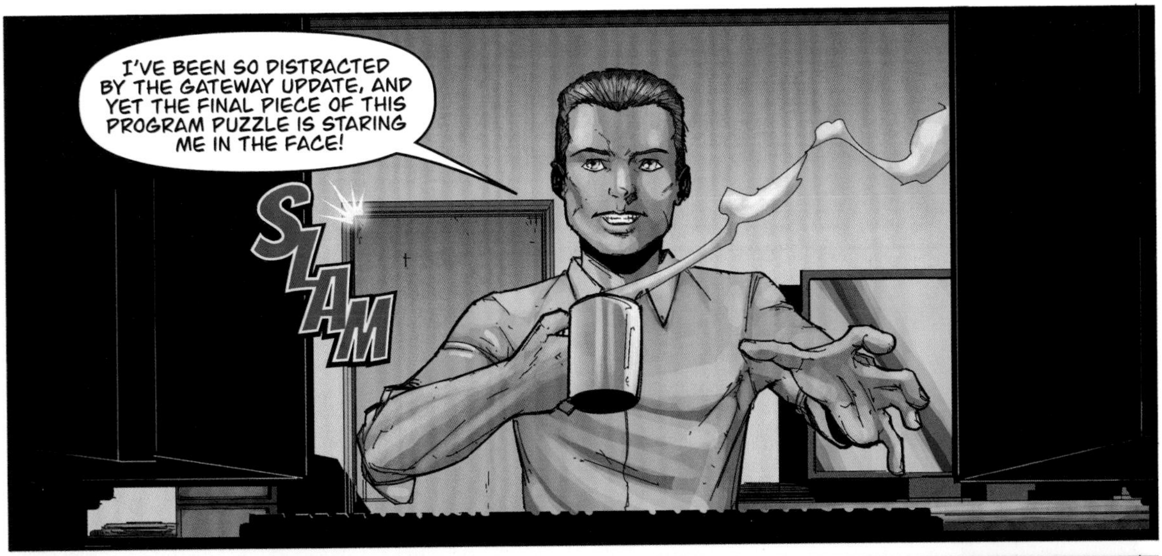
I'VE BEEN SO DISTRACTED BY THE GATEWAY UPDATE, AND YET THE FINAL PIECE OF THIS PROGRAM PUZZLE IS STARING ME IN THE FACE!
SLAM
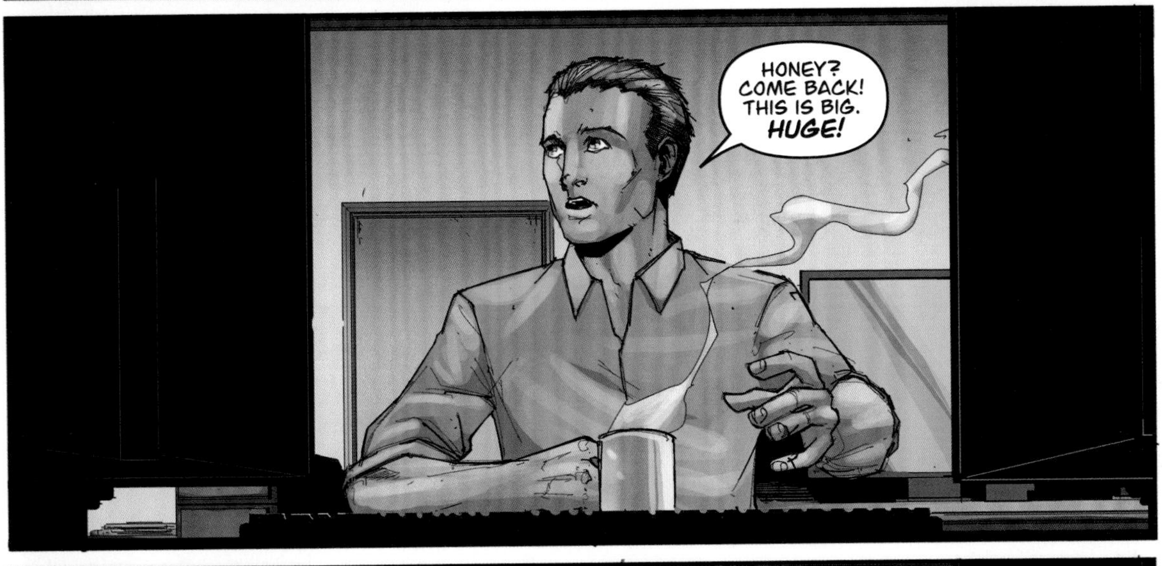
HONEY? COME BACK! THIS IS BIG. HUGE!
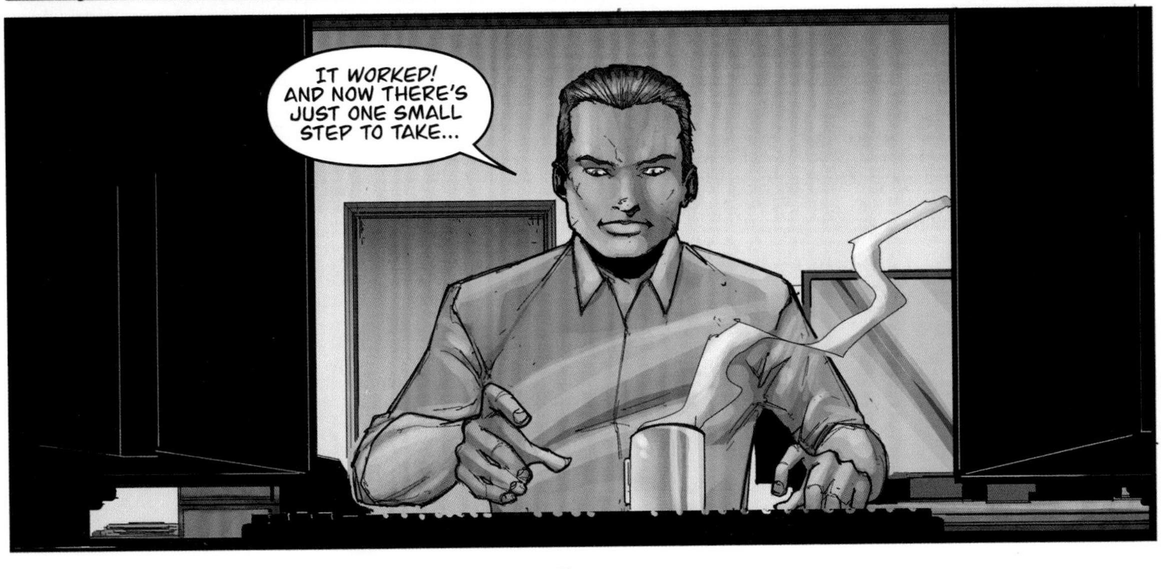
IT WORKED! AND NOW THERE'S JUST ONE SMALL STEP TO TAKE...

LATER...

MAYBE YOU'D LIKE TO SETTLE EVIE IN HER COT. THAT'S IF YOU CAN REMEMBER WHERE THE NURSERY IS.

HONEY, WHAT ELSE CAN I SAY? IT WAS A BIG MOMENT FOR ME... A BIG MOMENT FOR US ALL.

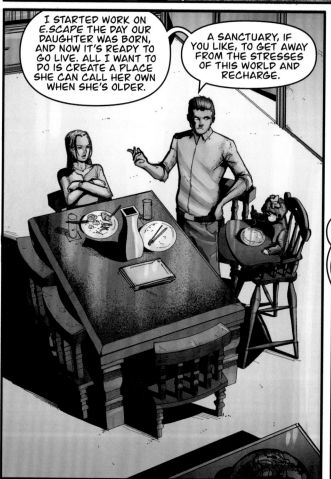

I STARTED WORK ON E.SCAPE THE DAY OUR DAUGHTER WAS BORN, AND NOW IT'S READY TO GO LIVE. ALL I WANT TO DO IS CREATE A PLACE SHE CAN CALL HER OWN WHEN SHE'S OLDER.

A SANCTUARY, IF YOU LIKE, TO GET AWAY FROM THE STRESSES OF THIS WORLD AND RECHARGE.

BUT IT'S JUST A STRING OF CODE.

OH, IT'S **SO** MUCH MORE THAN THAT.

E.SCAPE IS YEARS AHEAD OF ITS TIME.

A VIRTUAL WORLD THAT FEELS **COMPLETELY** REAL. IT'S PROGRAMMED TO REFLECT EVIE'S PERSONALITY AND CONNECT WITH HER IN **EVERY** WAY.

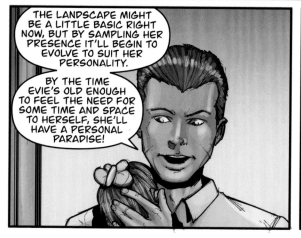

THE LANDSCAPE MIGHT BE A LITTLE BASIC RIGHT NOW, BUT BY SAMPLING HER PRESENCE IT'LL BEGIN TO EVOLVE TO SUIT HER PERSONALITY.

BY THE TIME EVIE'S OLD ENOUGH TO FEEL THE NEED FOR SOME TIME AND SPACE TO HERSELF, SHE'LL HAVE A PERSONAL PARADISE!

OR A USELESS REMINDER OF HOW HER CRAZY FATHER TURNED HIS BACK ON THE FIRST YEAR OF HER LIFE.

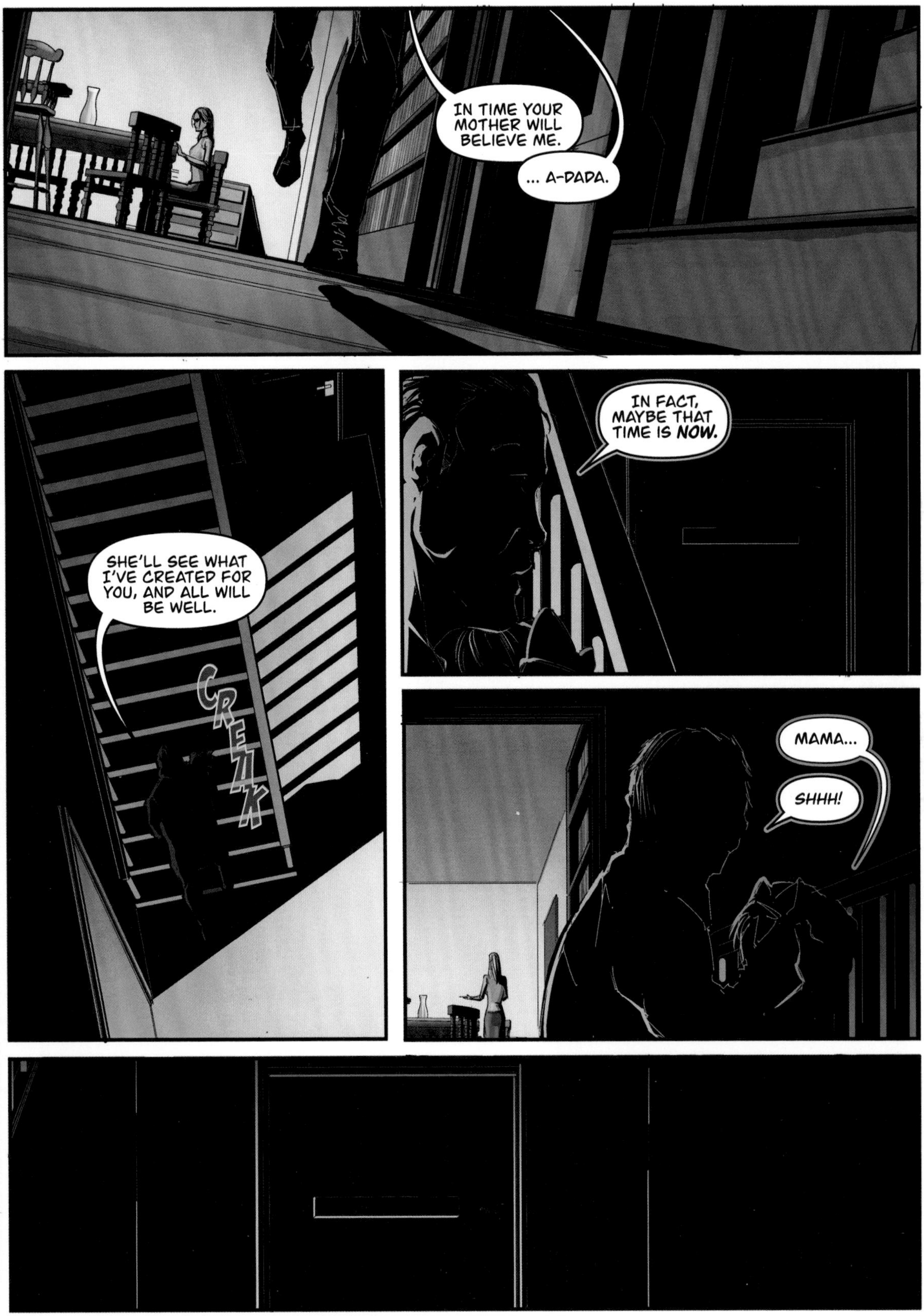
IN TIME YOUR MOTHER WILL BELIEVE ME.
... A-DADA.
SHE'LL SEE WHAT I'VE CREATED FOR YOU, AND ALL WILL BE WELL.
CREAK
IN FACT, MAYBE THAT TIME IS **NOW.**
MAMA...
SHHH!

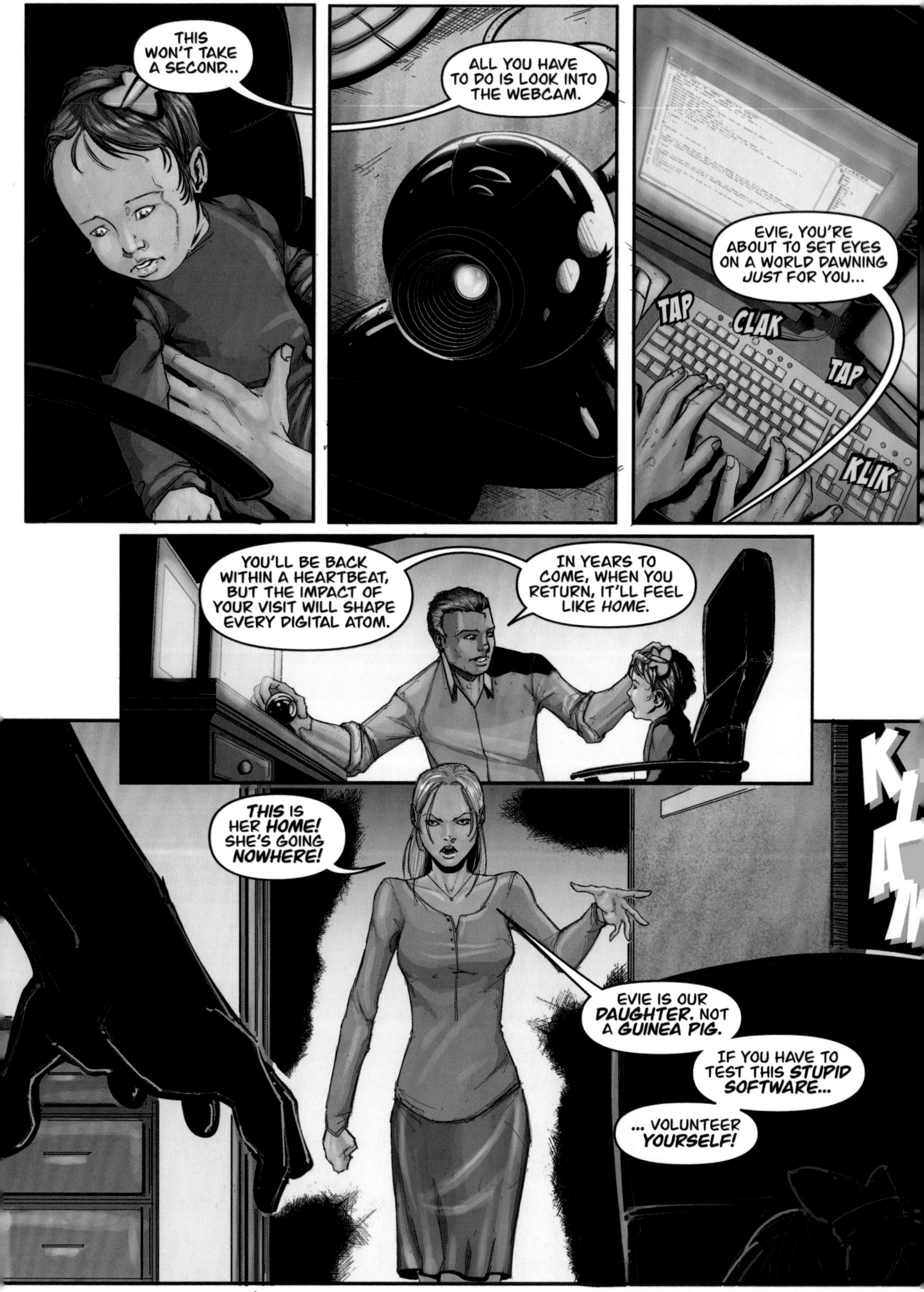
THIS WON'T TAKE A SECOND...
ALL YOU HAVE TO DO IS LOOK INTO THE WEBCAM.
EVIE, YOU'RE ABOUT TO SET EYES ON A WORLD DAWNING JUST FOR YOU...
TAP
CLAK
TAP
KLIK
YOU'LL BE BACK WITHIN A HEARTBEAT, BUT THE IMPACT OF YOUR VISIT WILL SHAPE EVERY DIGITAL ATOM.
IN YEARS TO COME, WHEN YOU RETURN, IT'LL FEEL LIKE HOME.
THIS IS HER HOME! SHE'S GOING NOWHERE!
EVIE IS OUR DAUGHTER. NOT A GUINEA PIG.
IF YOU HAVE TO TEST THIS STUPID SOFTWARE...
... VOLUNTEER YOURSELF!

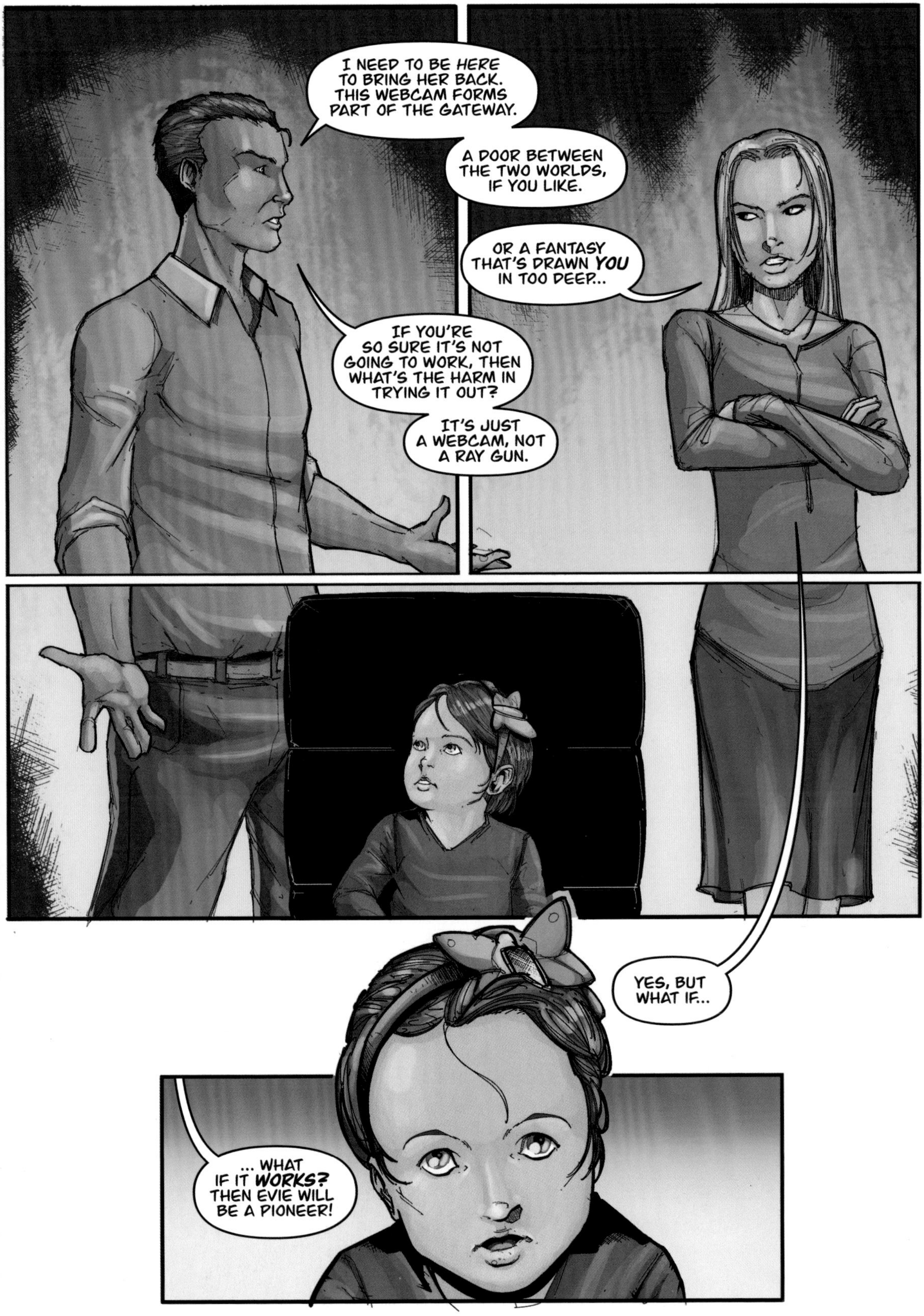

I NEED TO BE HERE TO BRING HER BACK. THIS WEBCAM FORMS PART OF THE GATEWAY.
A DOOR BETWEEN THE TWO WORLDS, IF YOU LIKE.
OR A FANTASY THAT'S DRAWN ***YOU*** IN TOO DEEP...
IF YOU'RE SO SURE IT'S NOT GOING TO WORK, THEN WHAT'S THE HARM IN TRYING IT OUT?
IT'S JUST A WEBCAM, NOT A RAY GUN.
YES, BUT WHAT IF...
... WHAT IF IT ***WORKS?*** THEN EVIE WILL BE A PIONEER!

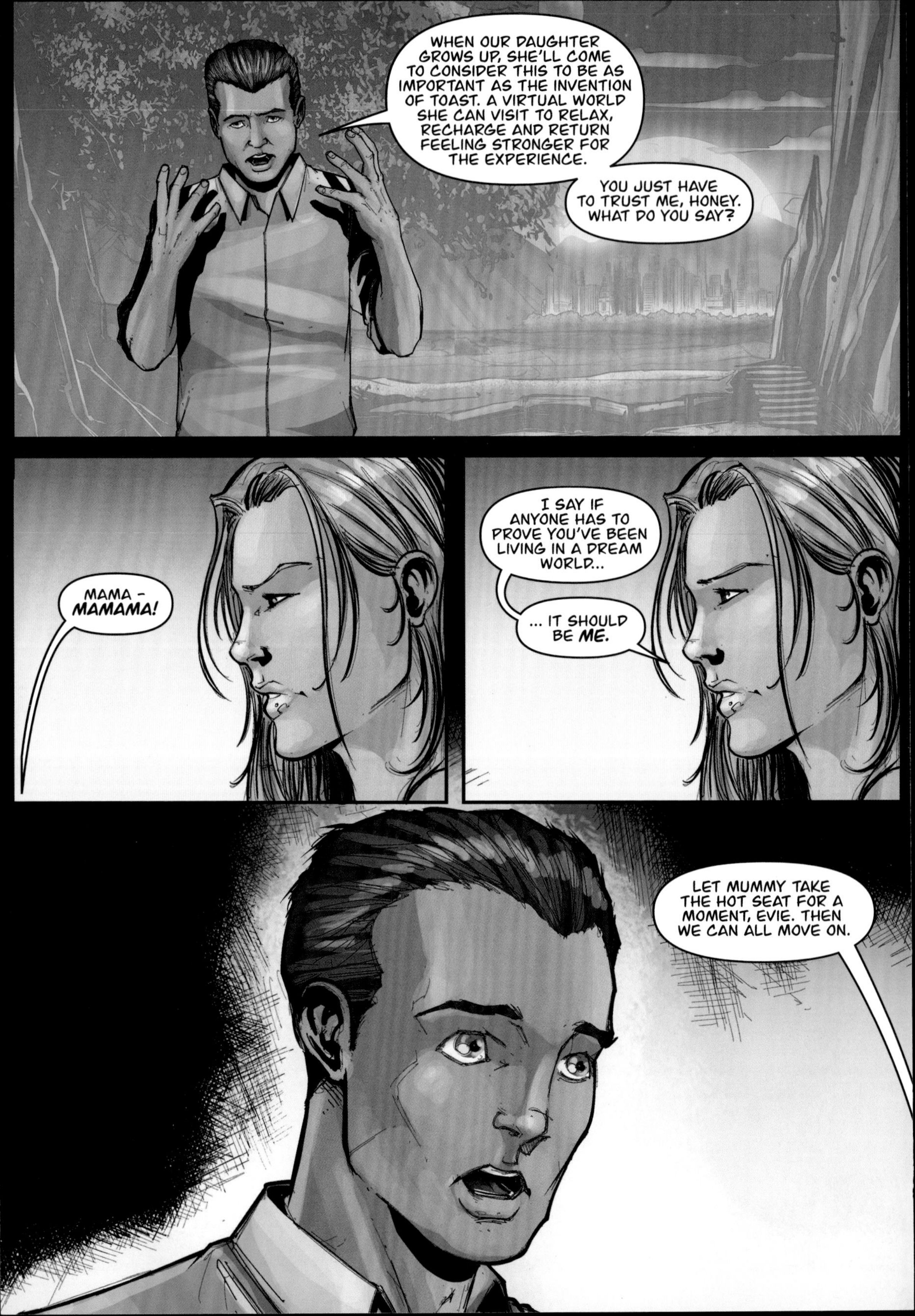
WHEN OUR DAUGHTER GROWS UP, SHE'LL COME TO CONSIDER THIS TO BE AS IMPORTANT AS THE INVENTION OF TOAST. A VIRTUAL WORLD SHE CAN VISIT TO RELAX, RECHARGE AND RETURN FEELING STRONGER FOR THE EXPERIENCE.
YOU JUST HAVE TO TRUST ME, HONEY. WHAT DO YOU SAY?
MAMA - *MAMAMA!*
I SAY IF ANYONE HAS TO PROVE YOU'VE BEEN LIVING IN A DREAM WORLD...
... IT SHOULD BE *ME.*
LET MUMMY TAKE THE HOT SEAT FOR A MOMENT, EVIE. THEN WE CAN ALL MOVE ON.

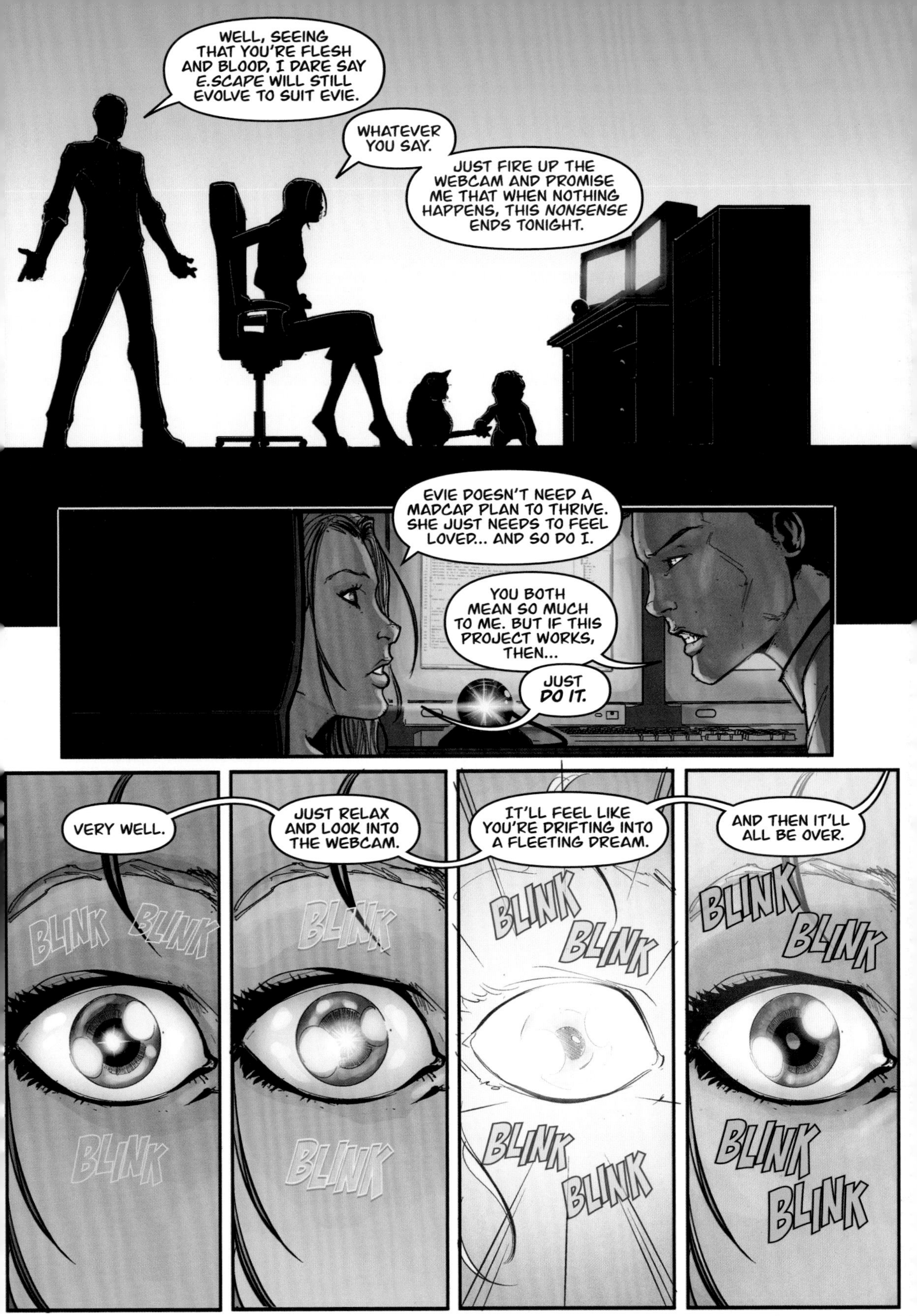
WELL, SEEING THAT YOU'RE FLESH AND BLOOD, I DARE SAY E.SCAPE WILL STILL EVOLVE TO SUIT EVIE.
WHATEVER YOU SAY.
JUST FIRE UP THE WEBCAM AND PROMISE ME THAT WHEN NOTHING HAPPENS, THIS NONSENSE ENDS TONIGHT.
EVIE DOESN'T NEED A MADCAP PLAN TO THRIVE. SHE JUST NEEDS TO FEEL LOVED... AND SO DO I.
YOU BOTH MEAN SO MUCH TO ME. BUT IF THIS PROJECT WORKS, THEN...
JUST DO IT.
VERY WELL.
BLINK BLINK
BLINK
JUST RELAX AND LOOK INTO THE WEBCAM.
BLINK
BLINK
IT'LL FEEL LIKE YOU'RE DRIFTING INTO A FLEETING DREAM.
BLINK BLINK
BLINK BLINK
AND THEN IT'LL ALL BE OVER.
BLINK BLINK
BLINK BLINK

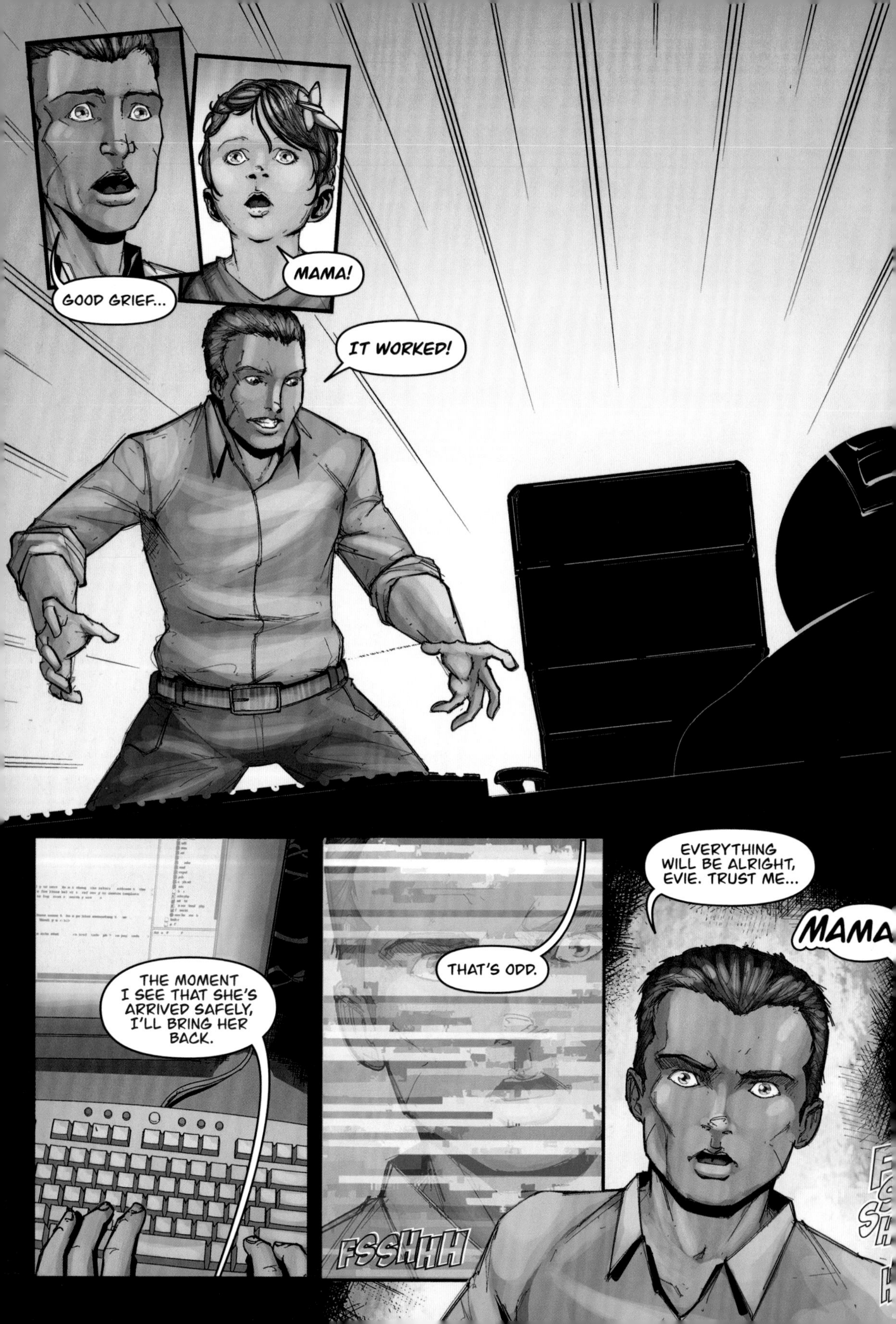
GOOD GRIEF...
MAMA!
IT WORKED!
THE MOMENT I SEE THAT SHE'S ARRIVED SAFELY, I'LL BRING HER BACK.
THAT'S ODD.
FSSHHH
EVERYTHING WILL BE ALRIGHT, EVIE. TRUST ME...
MAMA

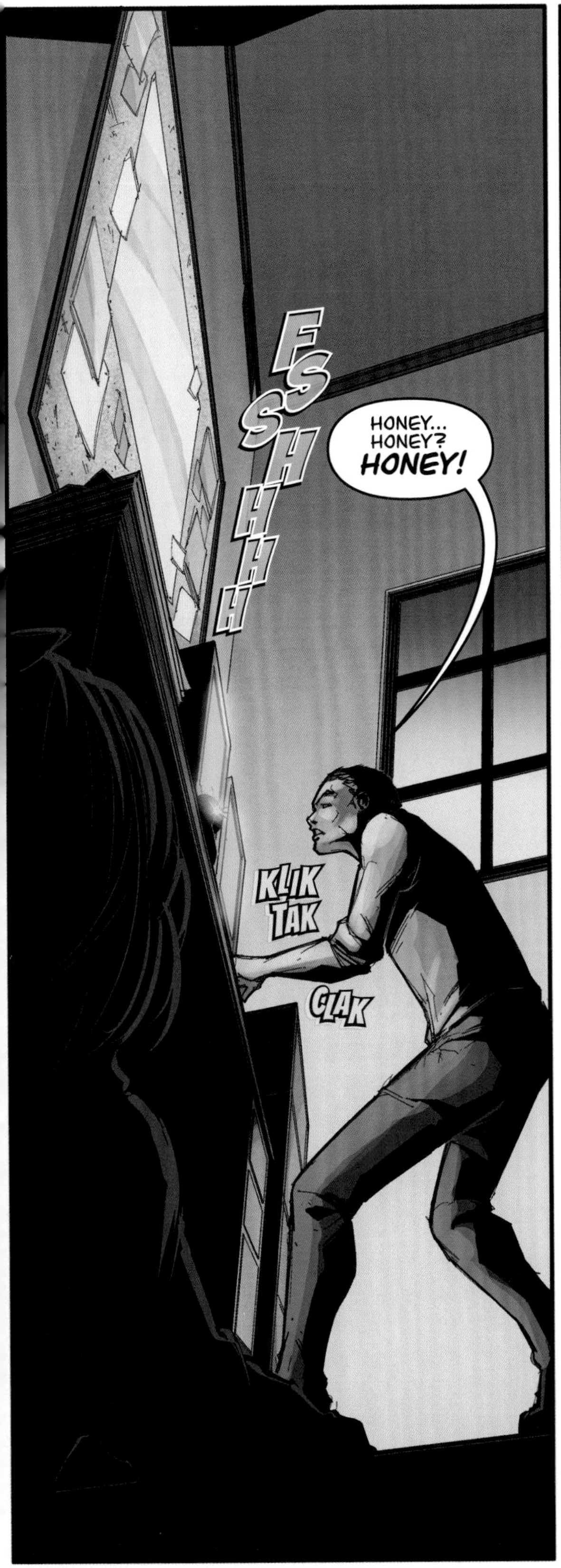
FSSHHHHH
HONEY... HONEY? HONEY!
KLIK TAK
CLAK

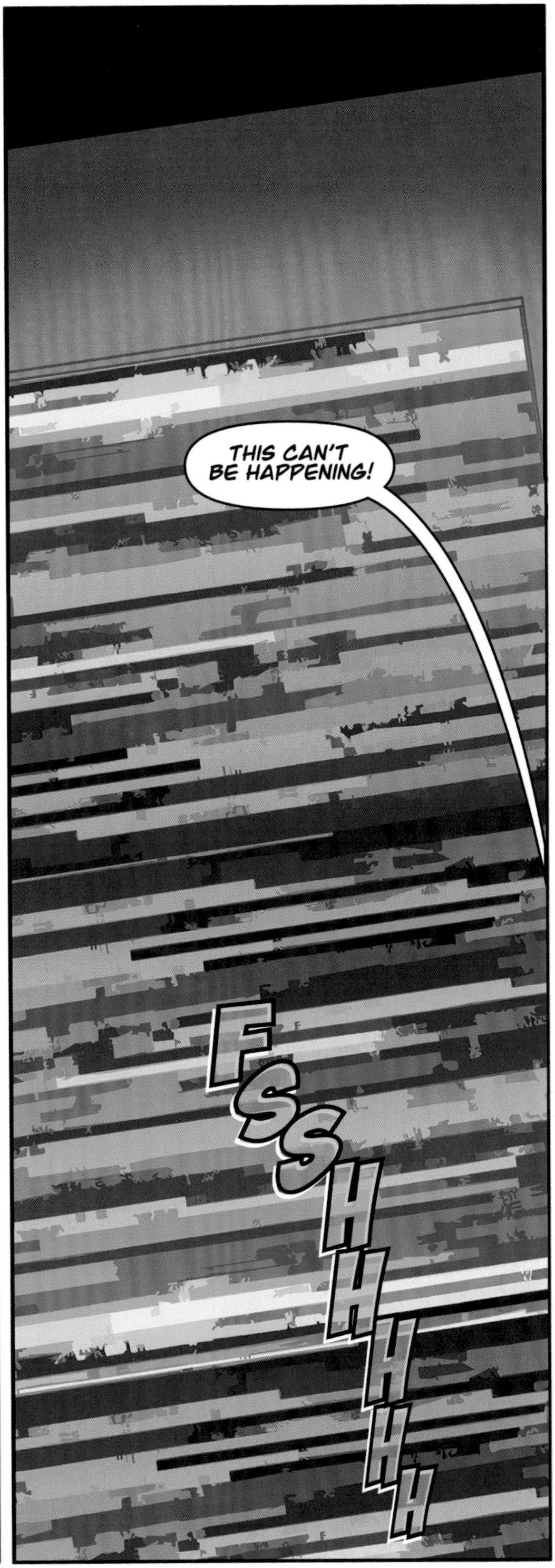
THIS CAN'T BE HAPPENING!
FSSHHHHH

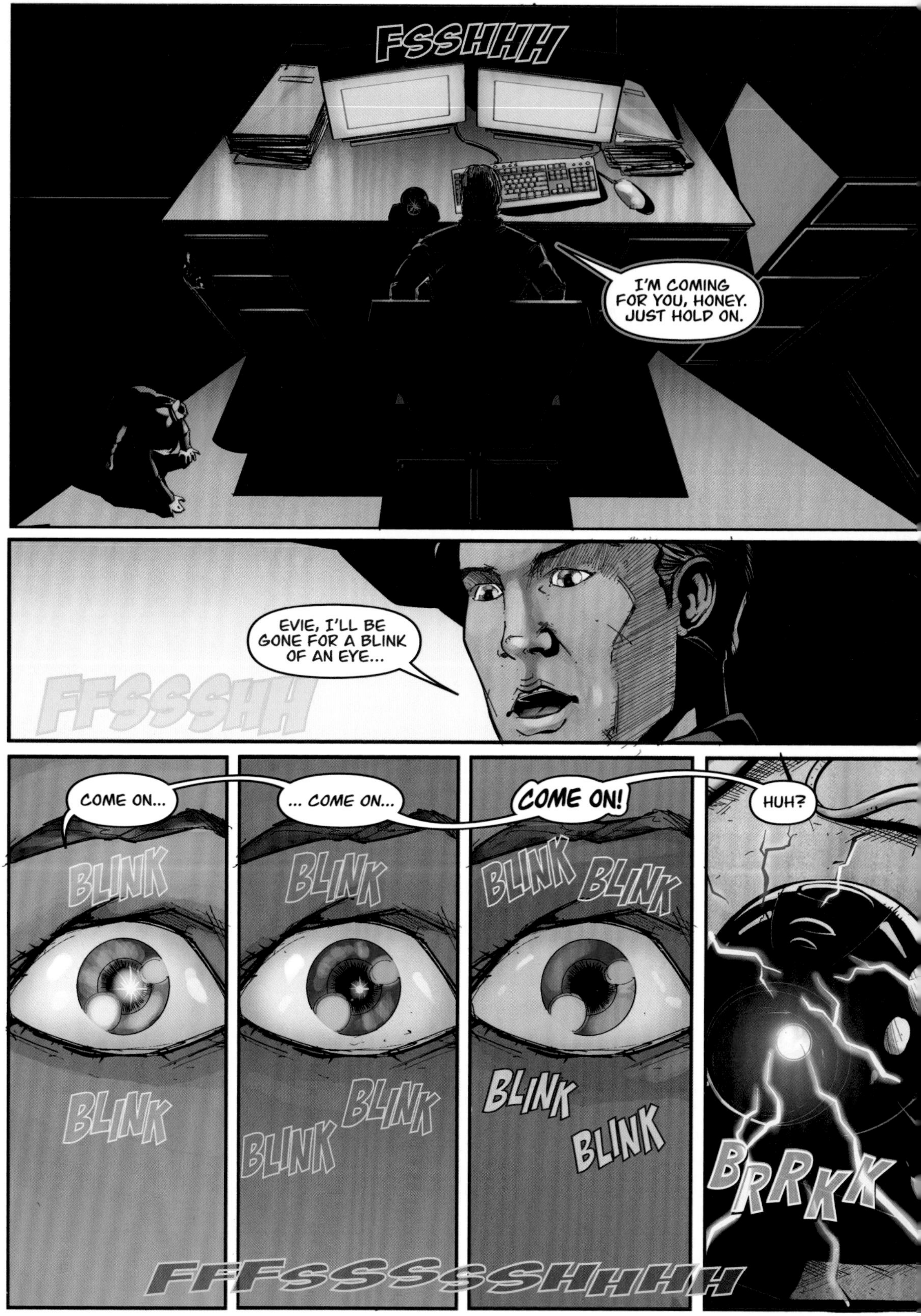
FSSHHH
I'M COMING FOR YOU, HONEY. JUST HOLD ON.
EVIE, I'LL BE GONE FOR A BLINK OF AN EYE...
FFSSSSHH
COME ON...
BLINK
BLINK
... COME ON...
BLINK
BLINK
BLINK
COME ON!
BLINK
BLINK
BLINK
BLINK
HUH?
BRRKK
FFFSSSSSSHHHHH

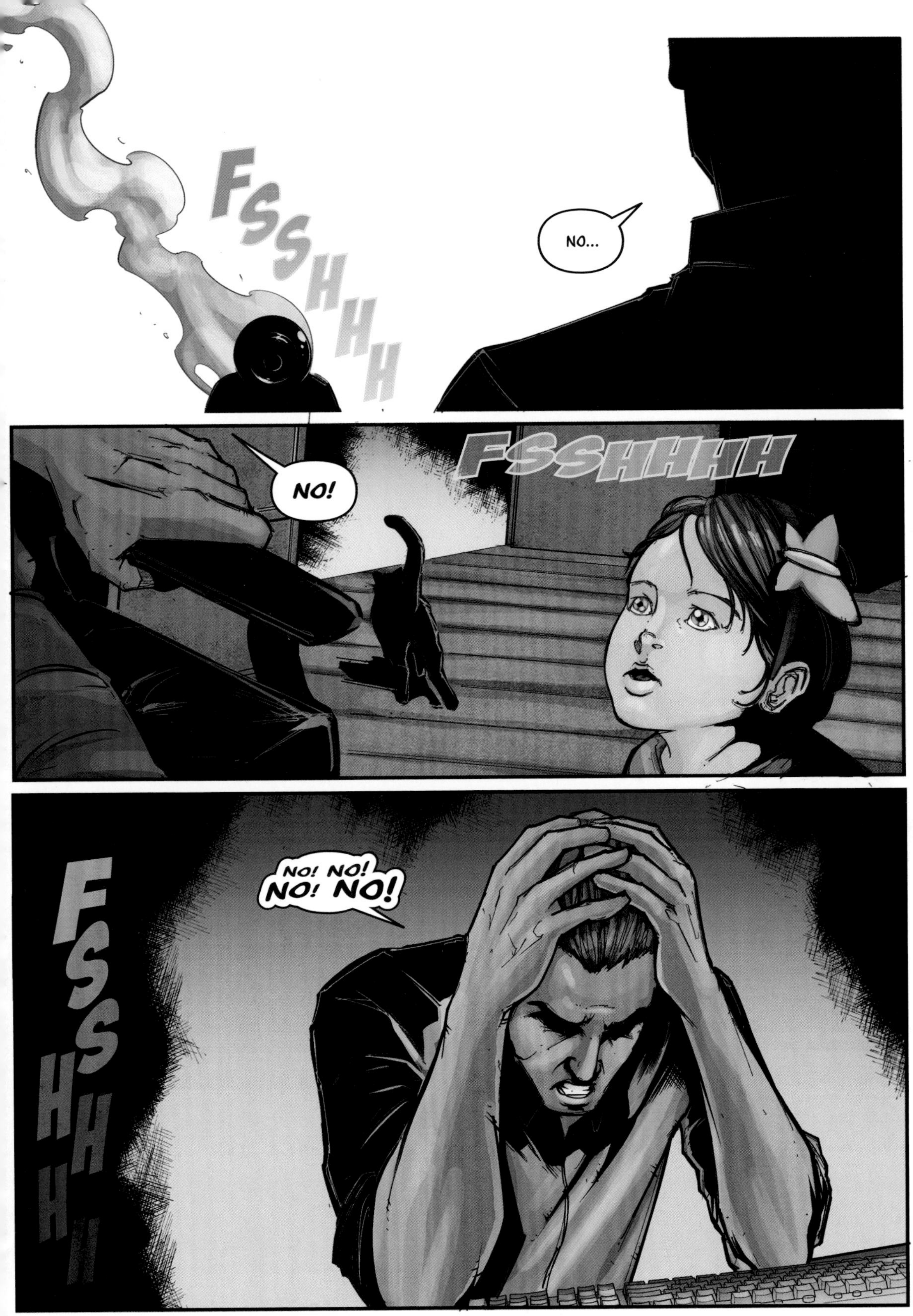
FSSHHHH
NO...
NO!
FSSHHHH
NO! NO!
NO! NO!
FSSHHHH

THE HABITAT SYSTEM SEEMS STABLE. NO GLITCHES OR BUGS REPORTED.

SO, IT CAN ONLY BE A PROBLEM WITH... THE GATEWAY.

FFSSSHHHH

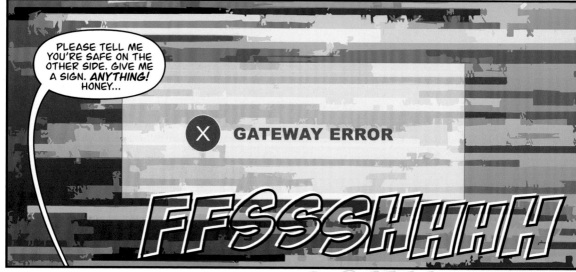

PLEASE TELL ME YOU'RE SAFE ON THE OTHER SIDE. GIVE ME A SIGN. *ANYTHING!* HONEY...

✕ GATEWAY ERROR

FFSSSHHHH

FFSSSHHHH

I'M SORRY. SO SORRY!

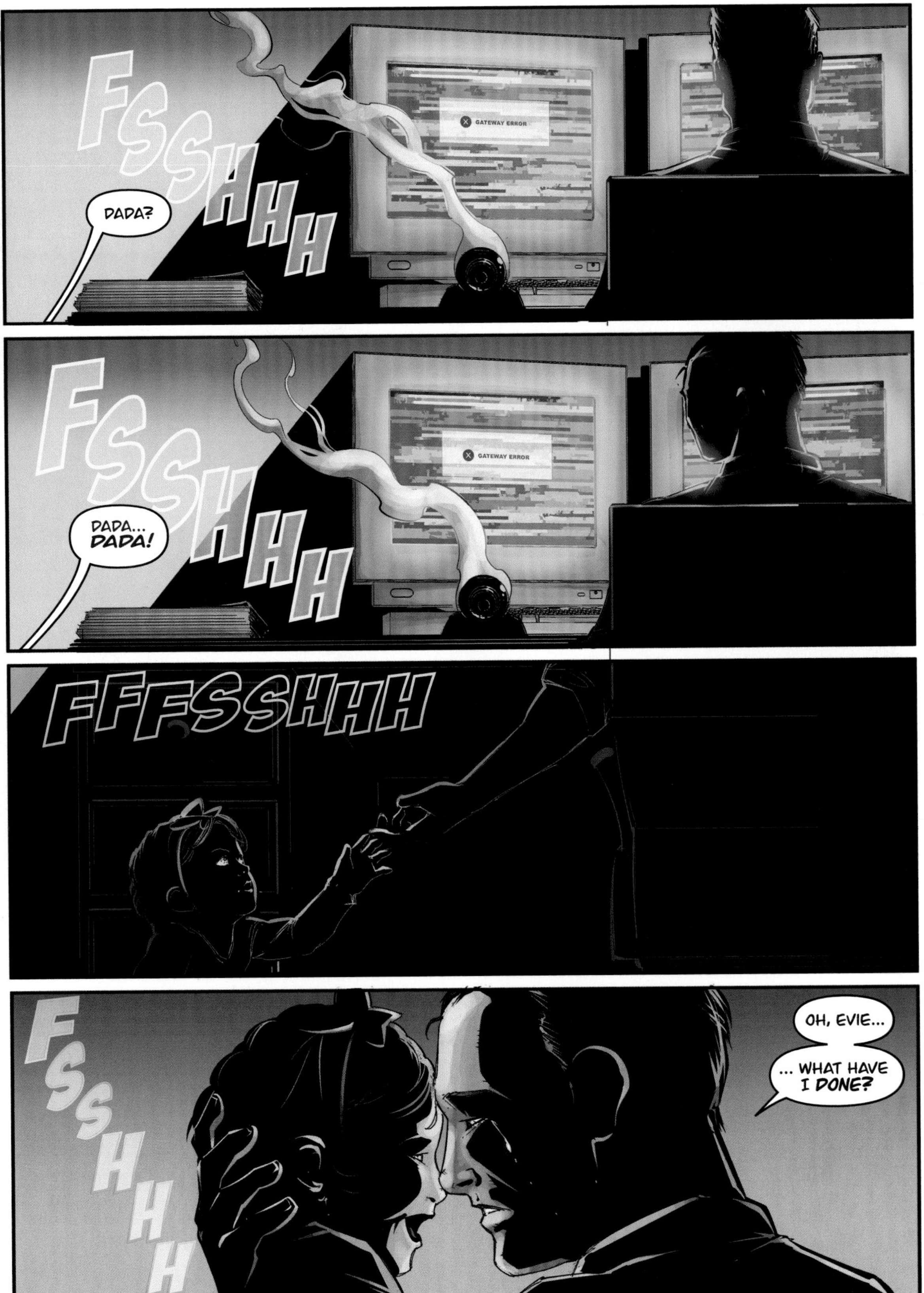
FSSHHHH
GATEWAY ERROR
DADA?
FSSHHHH
GATEWAY ERROR
DADA... DADA!
FFFSSHHH
FSSHHH
OH, EVIE...
... WHAT HAVE I DONE?

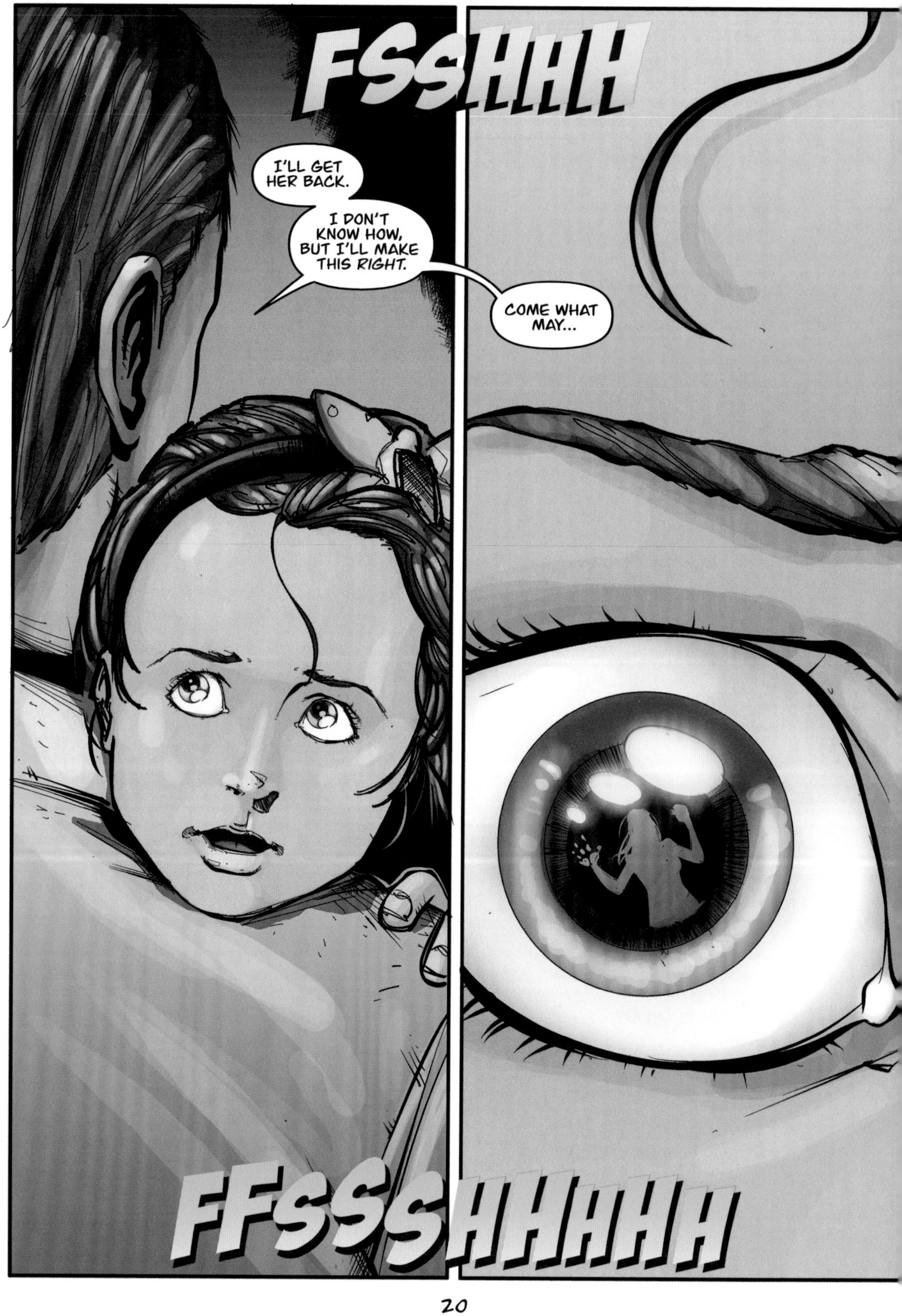
FSSHHH
I'LL GET HER BACK.
I DON'T KNOW HOW, BUT I'LL MAKE THIS RIGHT.
COME WHAT MAY...
FFSSSHHHHH

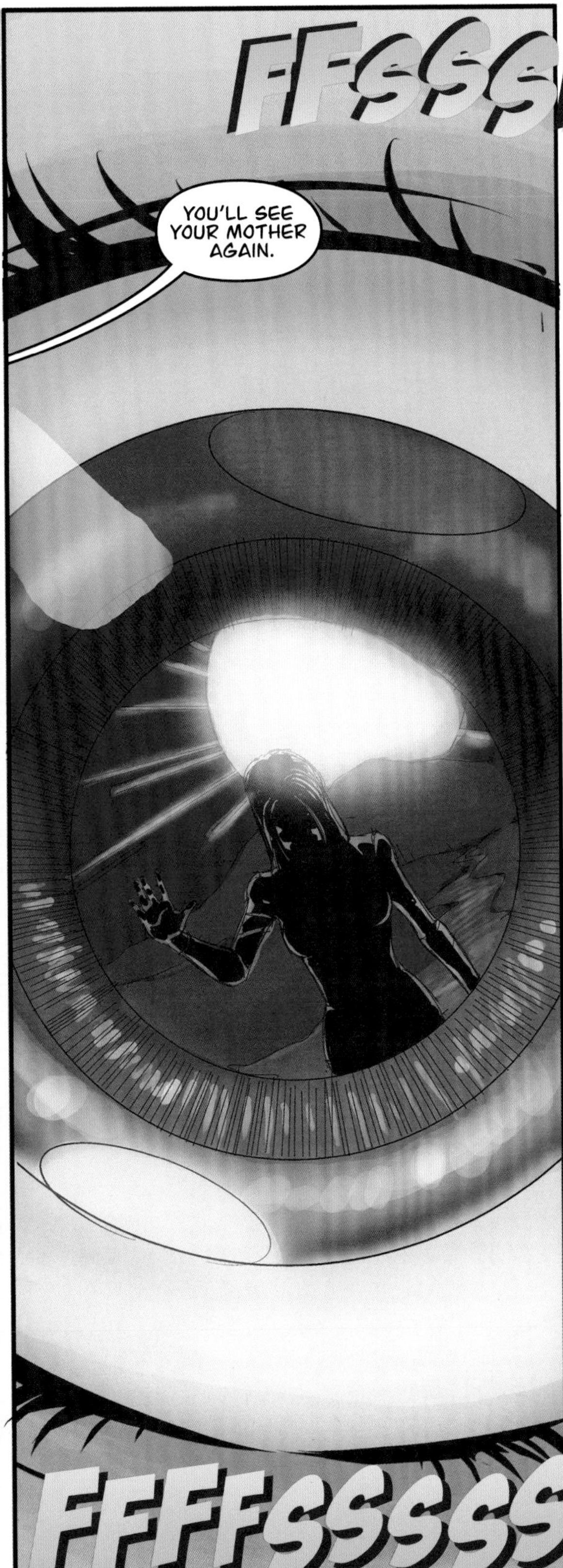
FFSSSHHHHHH
YOU'LL SEE YOUR MOTHER AGAIN.

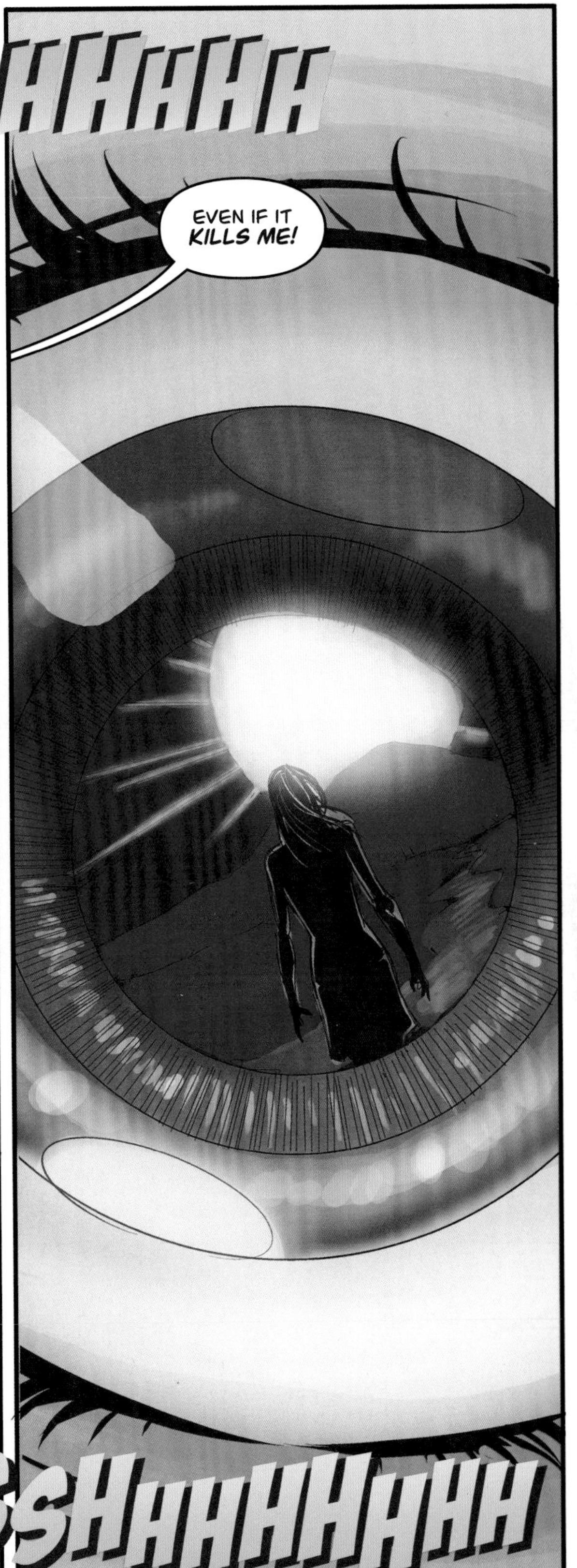
EVEN IF IT KILLS ME!
FFFFSSSSSSSHHHHHHHHH

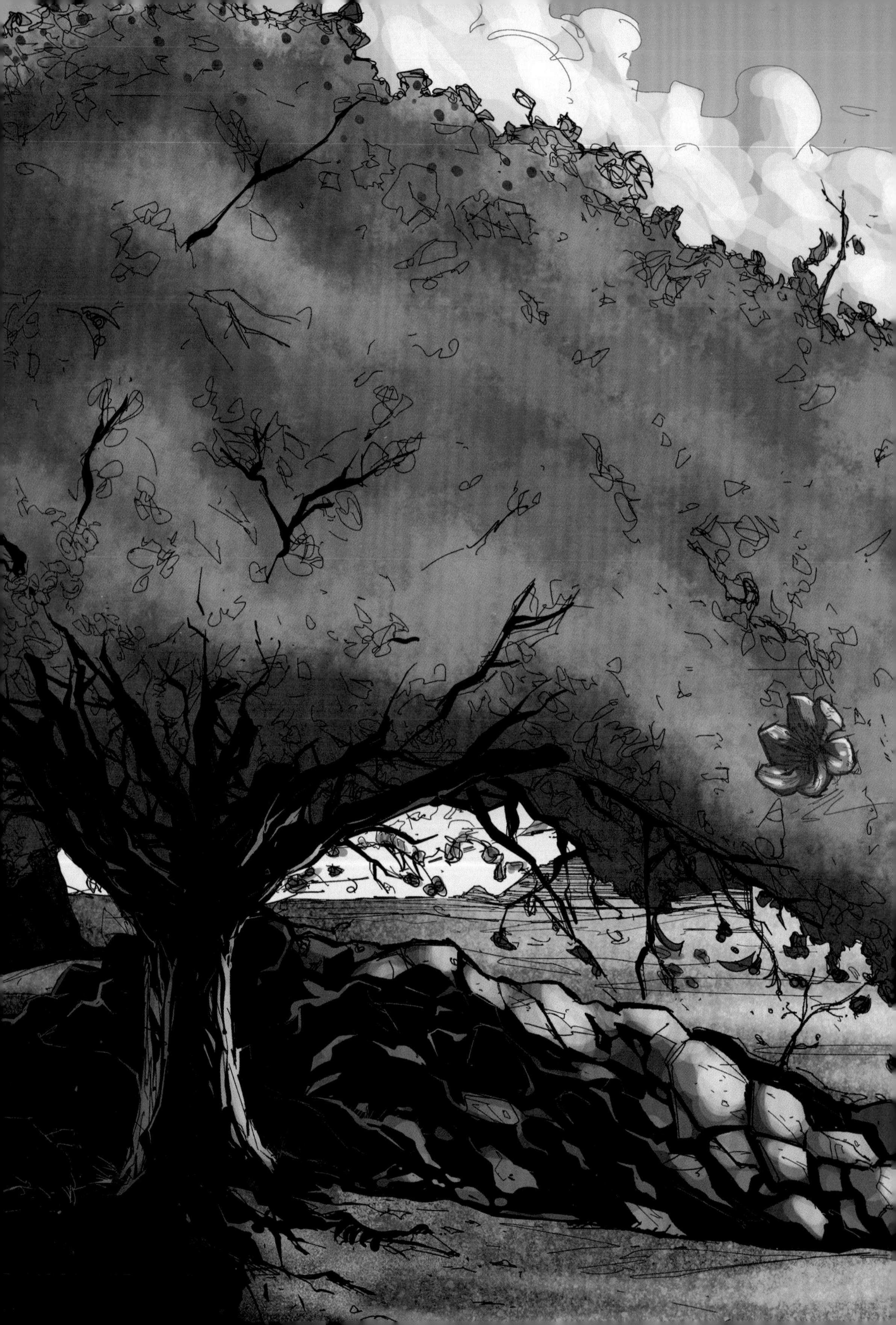

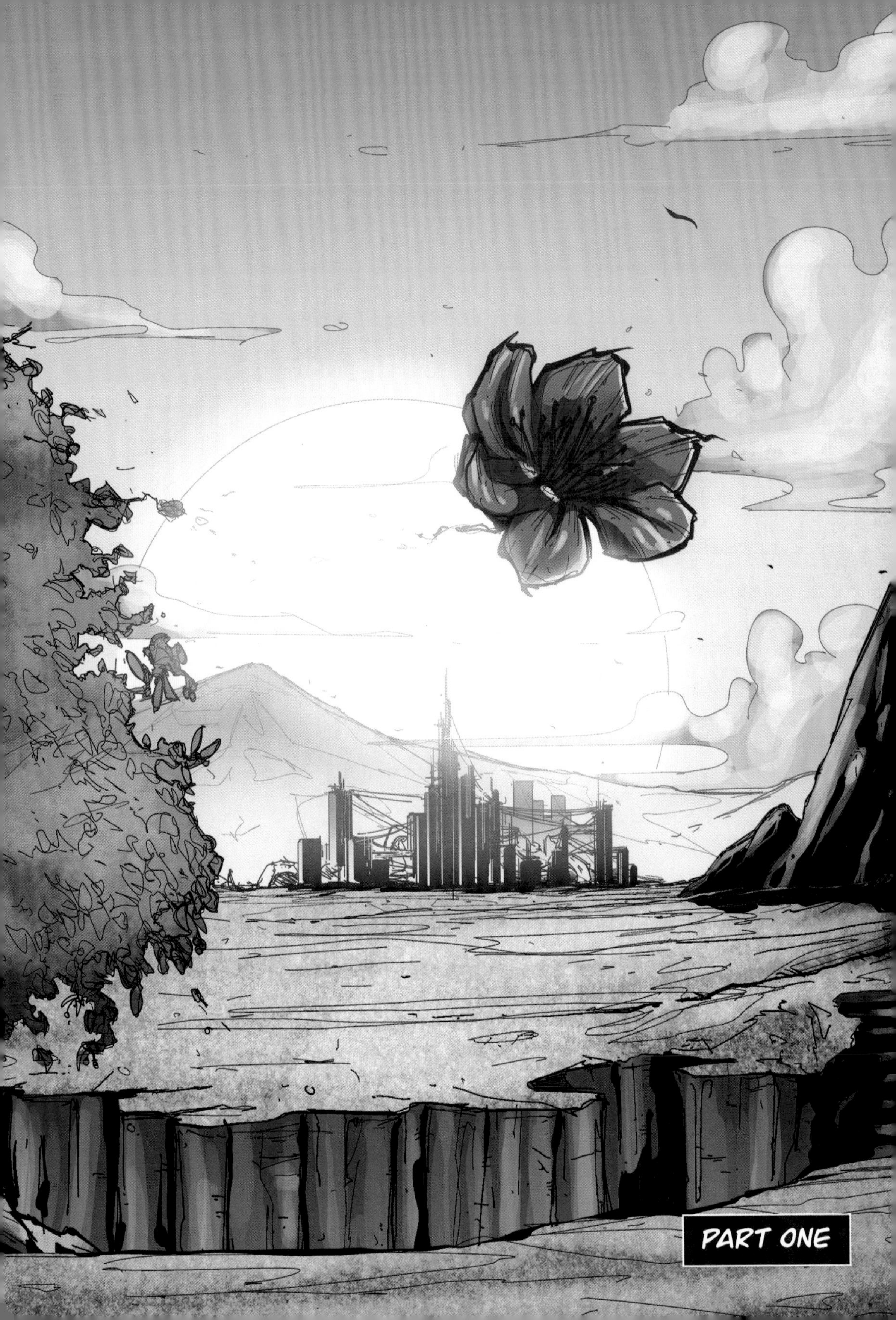
PART ONE

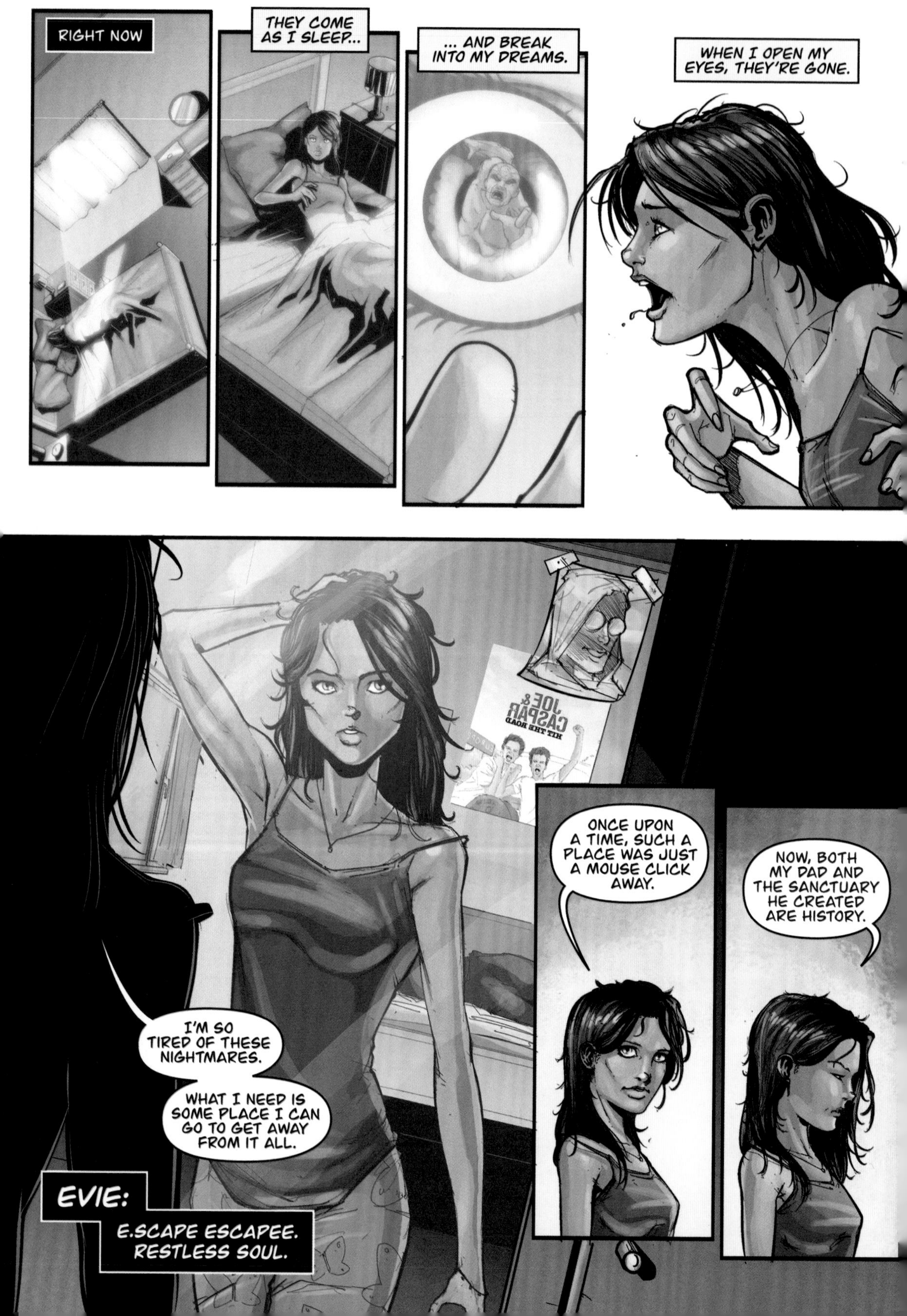
RIGHT NOW
THEY COME AS I SLEEP...
... AND BREAK INTO MY DREAMS.
WHEN I OPEN MY EYES, THEY'RE GONE.
JOE & CASPAR HIT THE ROAD
I'M SO TIRED OF THESE NIGHTMARES.
WHAT I NEED IS SOME PLACE I CAN GO TO GET AWAY FROM IT ALL.
EVIE:
E.SCAPE ESCAPEE. RESTLESS SOUL.
ONCE UPON A TIME, SUCH A PLACE WAS JUST A MOUSE CLICK AWAY.
NOW, BOTH MY DAD AND THE SANCTUARY HE CREATED ARE HISTORY.

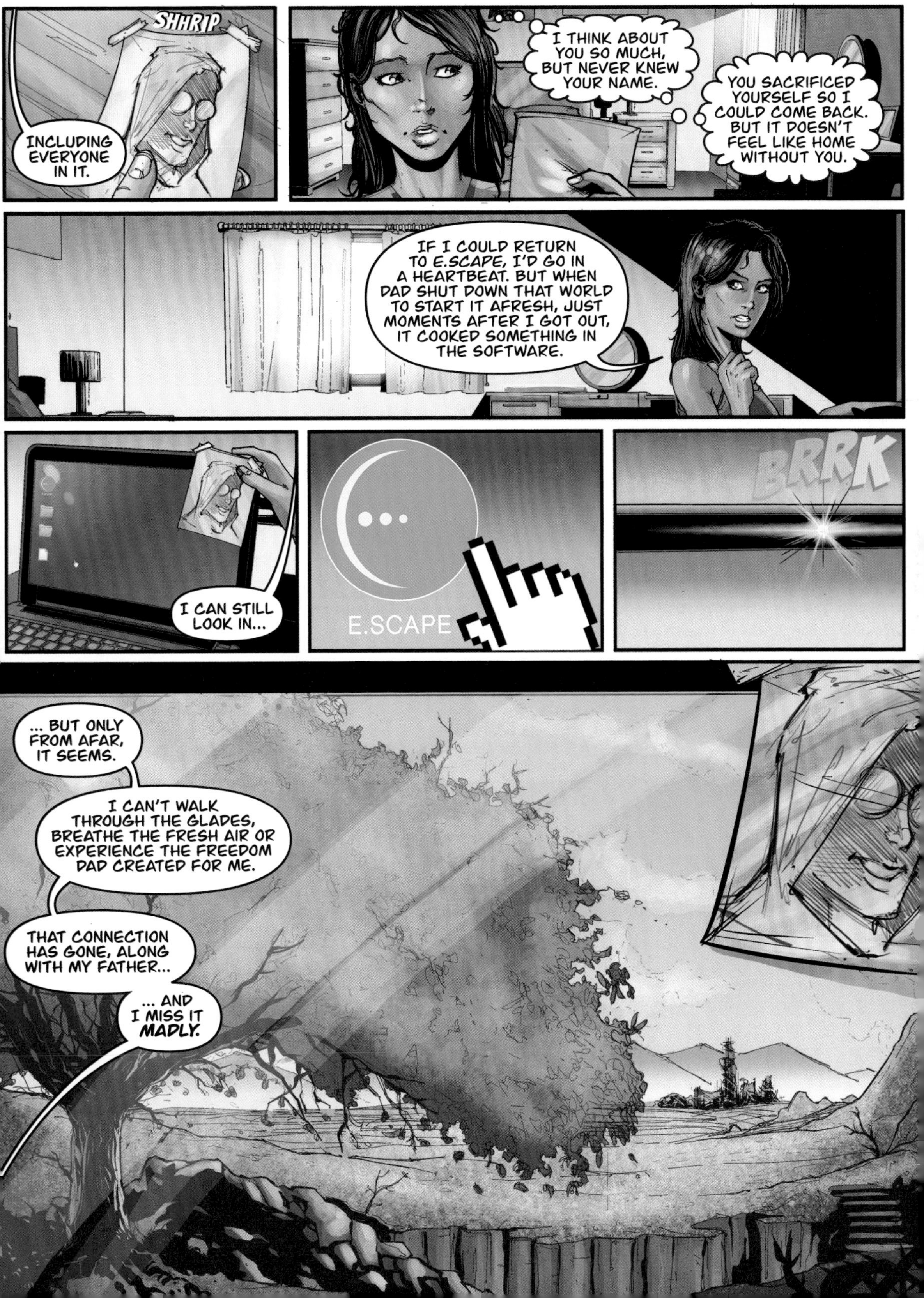
SHHRIP
INCLUDING EVERYONE IN IT.
I THINK ABOUT YOU SO MUCH, BUT NEVER KNEW YOUR NAME.
YOU SACRIFICED YOURSELF SO I COULD COME BACK. BUT IT DOESN'T FEEL LIKE HOME WITHOUT YOU.
IF I COULD RETURN TO E.SCAPE, I'D GO IN A HEARTBEAT. BUT WHEN DAD SHUT DOWN THAT WORLD TO START IT AFRESH, JUST MOMENTS AFTER I GOT OUT, IT COOKED SOMETHING IN THE SOFTWARE.
I CAN STILL LOOK IN...
E.SCAPE
BRRK
... BUT ONLY FROM AFAR, IT SEEMS.
I CAN'T WALK THROUGH THE GLADES, BREATHE THE FRESH AIR OR EXPERIENCE THE FREEDOM DAD CREATED FOR ME.
THAT CONNECTION HAS GONE, ALONG WITH MY FATHER...
... AND I MISS IT *MADLY.*

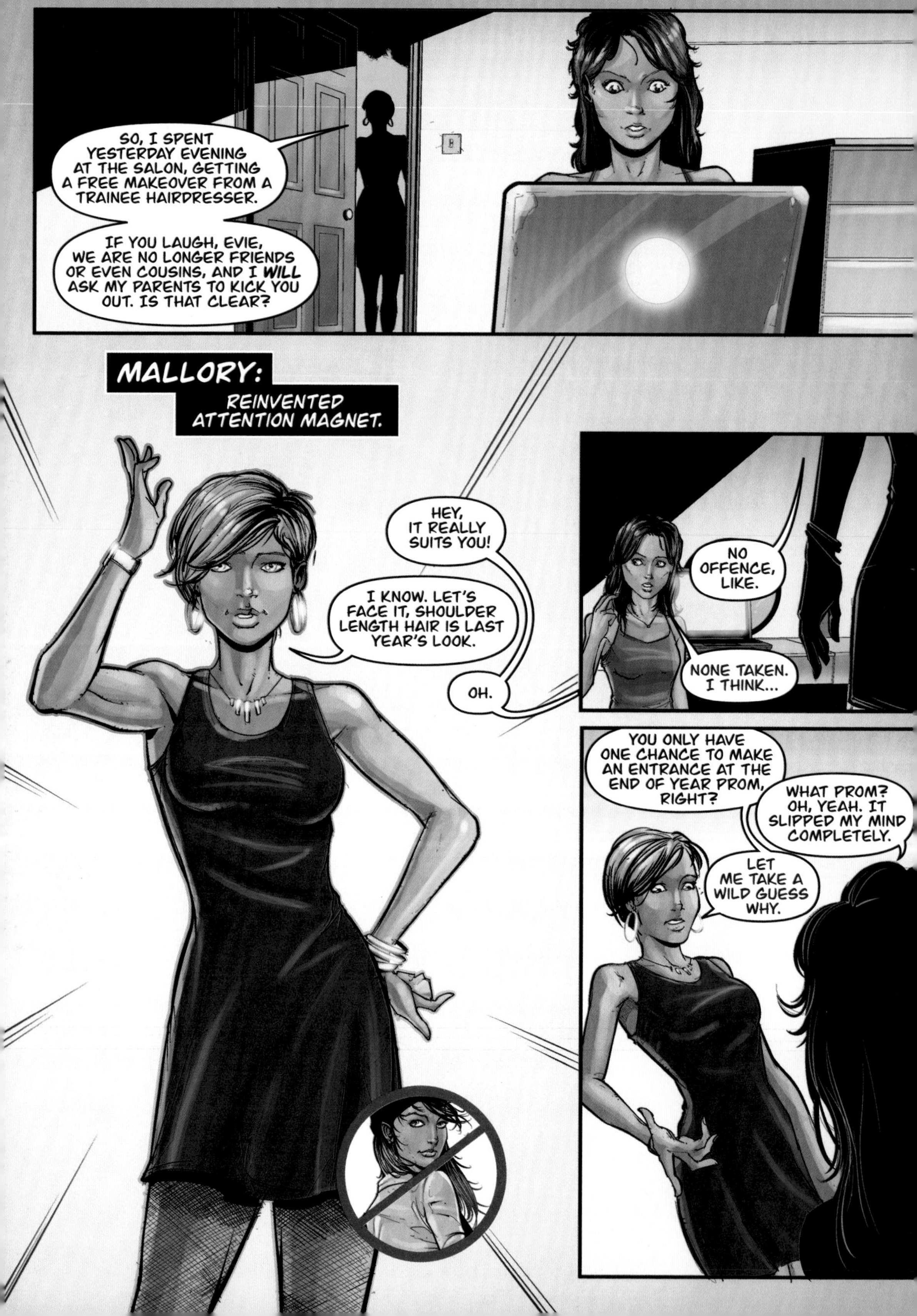
SO, I SPENT YESTERDAY EVENING AT THE SALON, GETTING A FREE MAKEOVER FROM A TRAINEE HAIRDRESSER.
IF YOU LAUGH, EVIE, WE ARE NO LONGER FRIENDS OR EVEN COUSINS, AND I WILL ASK MY PARENTS TO KICK YOU OUT. IS THAT CLEAR?
MALLORY:
REINVENTED ATTENTION MAGNET.
HEY, IT REALLY SUITS YOU!
I KNOW. LET'S FACE IT, SHOULDER LENGTH HAIR IS LAST YEAR'S LOOK.
OH.
NO OFFENCE, LIKE.
NONE TAKEN. I THINK...
YOU ONLY HAVE ONE CHANCE TO MAKE AN ENTRANCE AT THE END OF YEAR PROM, RIGHT?
WHAT PROM? OH, YEAH. IT SLIPPED MY MIND COMPLETELY.
LET ME TAKE A WILD GUESS WHY.

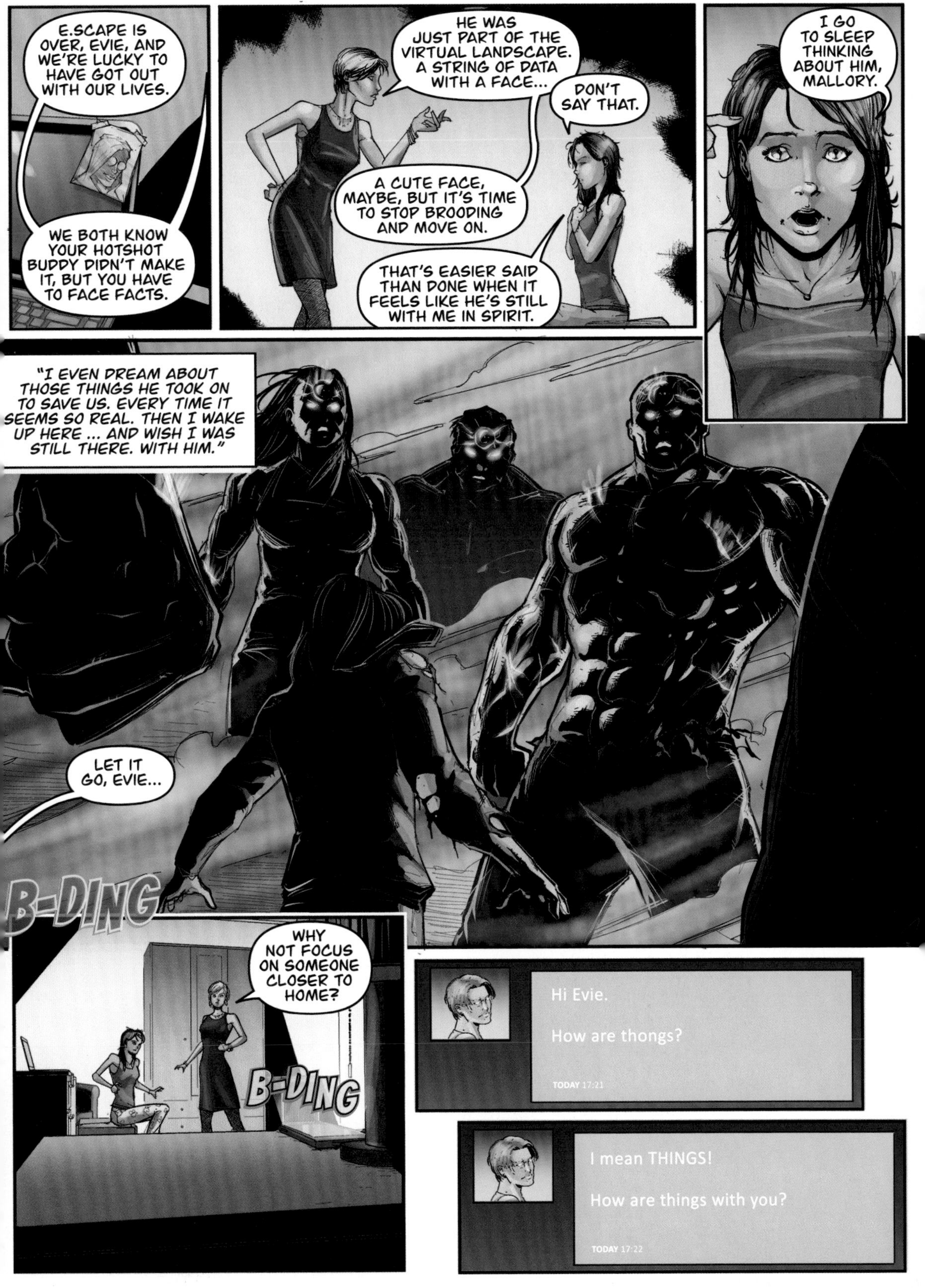
E.SCAPE IS OVER, EVIE, AND WE'RE LUCKY TO HAVE GOT OUT WITH OUR LIVES.
WE BOTH KNOW YOUR HOTSHOT BUDDY DIDN'T MAKE IT, BUT YOU HAVE TO FACE FACTS.
HE WAS JUST PART OF THE VIRTUAL LANDSCAPE. A STRING OF DATA WITH A FACE...
DON'T SAY THAT.
A CUTE FACE, MAYBE, BUT IT'S TIME TO STOP BROODING AND MOVE ON.
THAT'S EASIER SAID THAN DONE WHEN IT FEELS LIKE HE'S STILL WITH ME IN SPIRIT.
I GO TO SLEEP THINKING ABOUT HIM, MALLORY.
"I EVEN DREAM ABOUT THOSE THINGS HE TOOK ON TO SAVE US. EVERY TIME IT SEEMS SO REAL. THEN I WAKE UP HERE ... AND WISH I WAS STILL THERE. WITH HIM."
LET IT GO, EVIE...
B-DING
WHY NOT FOCUS ON SOMEONE CLOSER TO HOME?
B-DING
Hi Evie.
How are thongs?
TODAY 17:21
I mean THINGS!
How are things with you?
TODAY 17:22

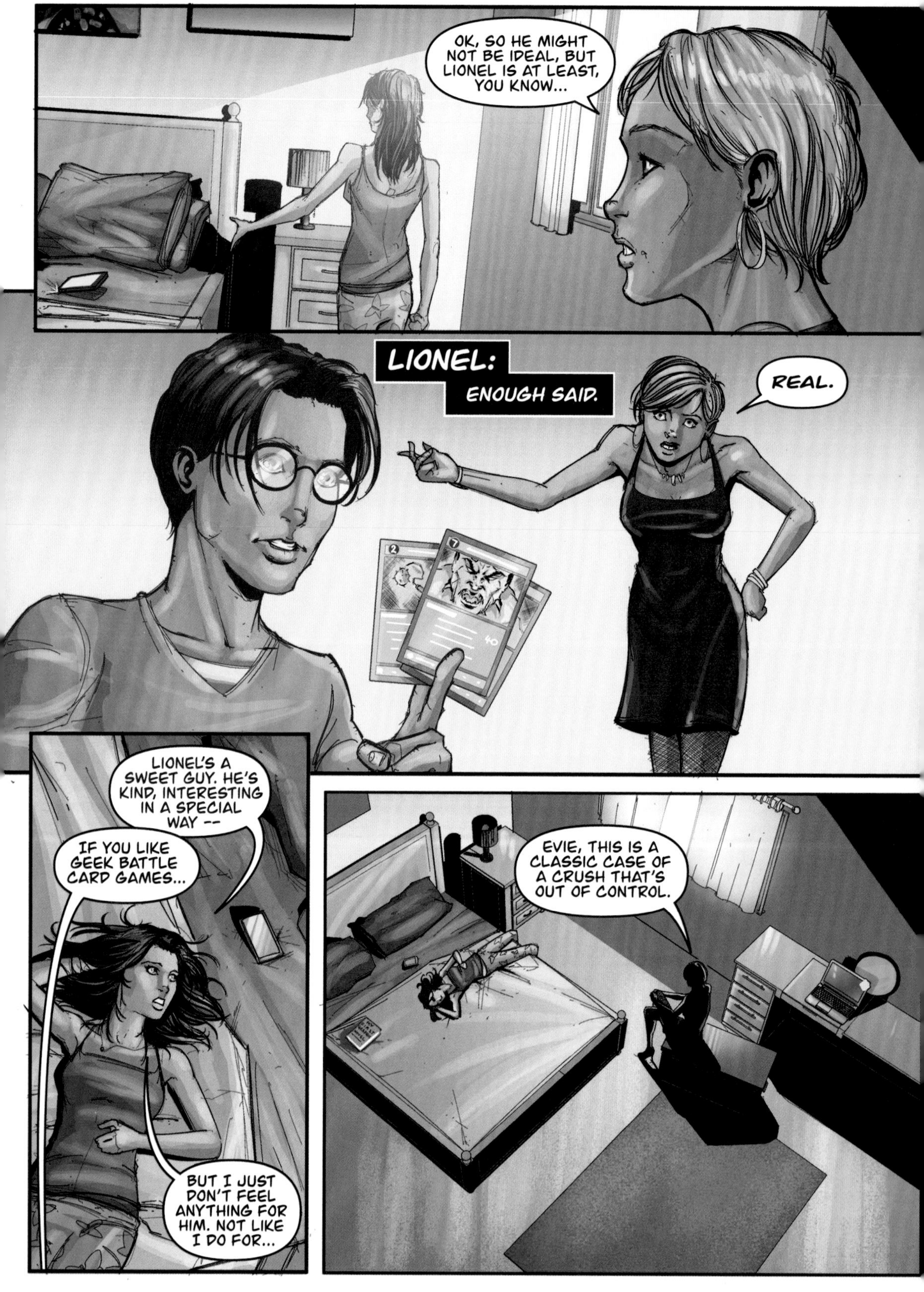
OK, SO HE MIGHT NOT BE IDEAL, BUT LIONEL IS AT LEAST, YOU KNOW...
LIONEL:
ENOUGH SAID.
REAL.
LIONEL'S A SWEET GUY. HE'S KIND, INTERESTING IN A SPECIAL WAY --
IF YOU LIKE GEEK BATTLE CARD GAMES...
BUT I JUST DON'T FEEL ANYTHING FOR HIM. NOT LIKE I DO FOR...
EVIE, THIS IS A CLASSIC CASE OF A CRUSH THAT'S OUT OF CONTROL.

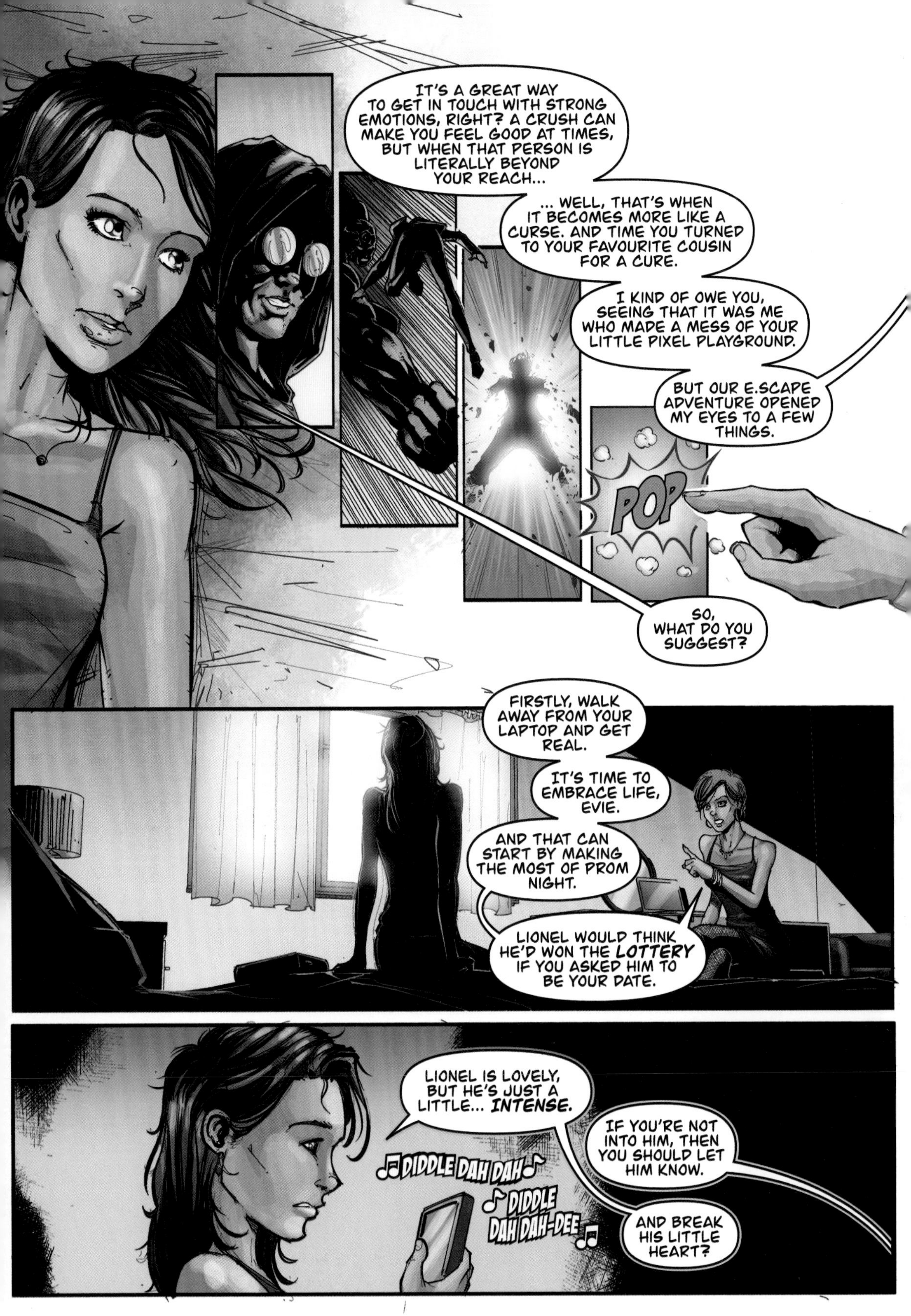
IT'S A GREAT WAY TO GET IN TOUCH WITH STRONG EMOTIONS, RIGHT? A CRUSH CAN MAKE YOU FEEL GOOD AT TIMES, BUT WHEN THAT PERSON IS LITERALLY BEYOND YOUR REACH...
... WELL, THAT'S WHEN IT BECOMES MORE LIKE A CURSE. AND TIME YOU TURNED TO YOUR FAVOURITE COUSIN FOR A CURE.
I KIND OF OWE YOU, SEEING THAT IT WAS ME WHO MADE A MESS OF YOUR LITTLE PIXEL PLAYGROUND.
BUT OUR E.SCAPE ADVENTURE OPENED MY EYES TO A FEW THINGS.
POP
SO, WHAT DO YOU SUGGEST?
FIRSTLY, WALK AWAY FROM YOUR LAPTOP AND GET REAL.
IT'S TIME TO EMBRACE LIFE, EVIE.
AND THAT CAN START BY MAKING THE MOST OF PROM NIGHT.
LIONEL WOULD THINK HE'D WON THE *LOTTERY* IF YOU ASKED HIM TO BE YOUR DATE.
LIONEL IS LOVELY, BUT HE'S JUST A LITTLE... **INTENSE.**
DIDDLE DAH DAH
DIDDLE DAH DAH-DEE
IF YOU'RE NOT INTO HIM, THEN YOU SHOULD LET HIM KNOW.
AND BREAK HIS LITTLE HEART?

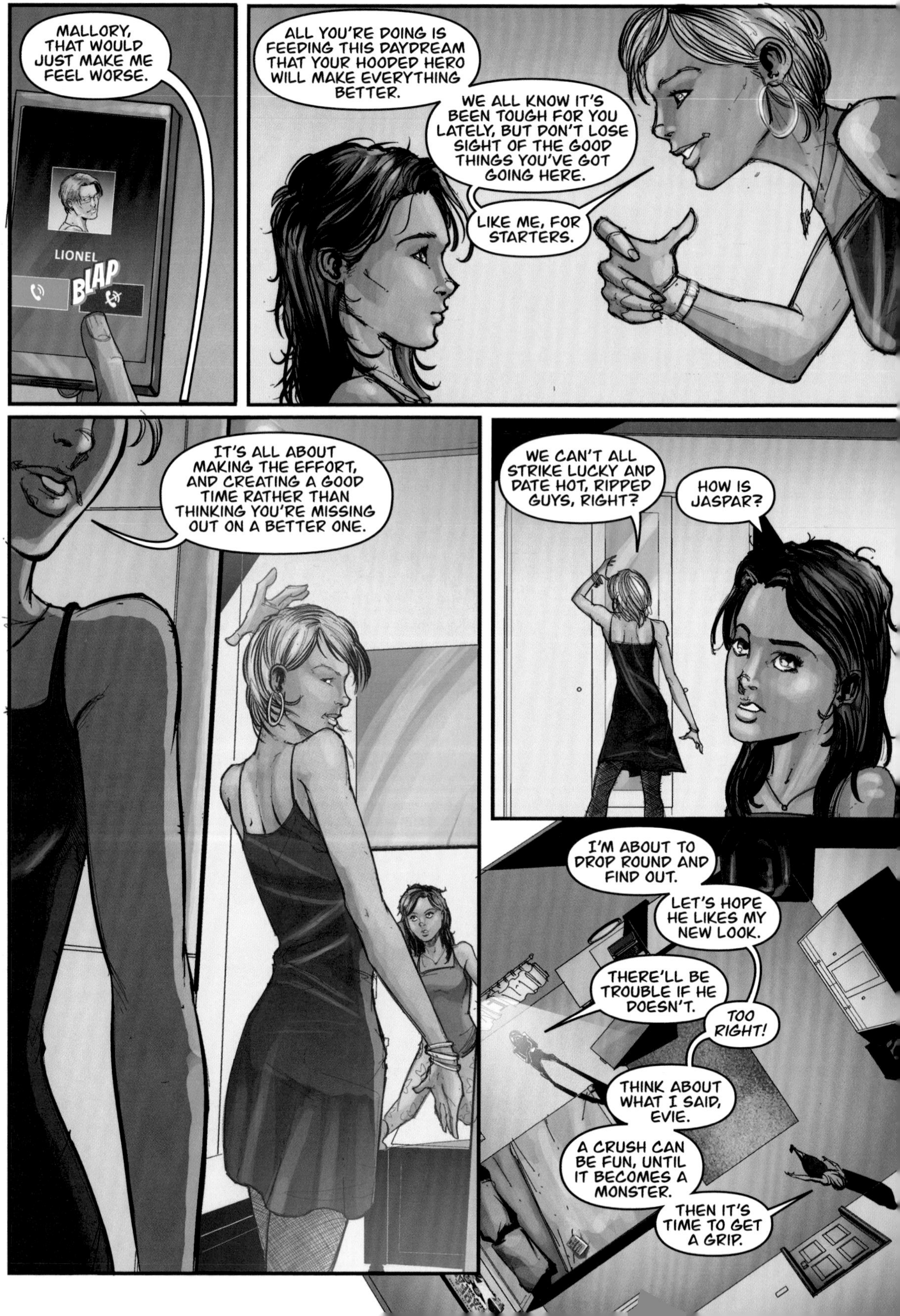
MALLORY, THAT WOULD JUST MAKE ME FEEL WORSE.
LIONEL
BLAP
ALL YOU'RE DOING IS FEEDING THIS DAYDREAM THAT YOUR HOODED HERO WILL MAKE EVERYTHING BETTER.
WE ALL KNOW IT'S BEEN TOUGH FOR YOU LATELY, BUT DON'T LOSE SIGHT OF THE GOOD THINGS YOU'VE GOT GOING HERE.
LIKE ME, FOR STARTERS.
IT'S ALL ABOUT MAKING THE EFFORT, AND CREATING A GOOD TIME RATHER THAN THINKING YOU'RE MISSING OUT ON A BETTER ONE.
WE CAN'T ALL STRIKE LUCKY AND DATE HOT, RIPPED GUYS, RIGHT?
HOW IS JASPAR?
I'M ABOUT TO DROP ROUND AND FIND OUT.
LET'S HOPE HE LIKES MY NEW LOOK.
THERE'LL BE TROUBLE IF HE DOESN'T.
TOO RIGHT!
THINK ABOUT WHAT I SAID, EVIE.
A CRUSH CAN BE FUN, UNTIL IT BECOMES A MONSTER.
THEN IT'S TIME TO GET A GRIP.

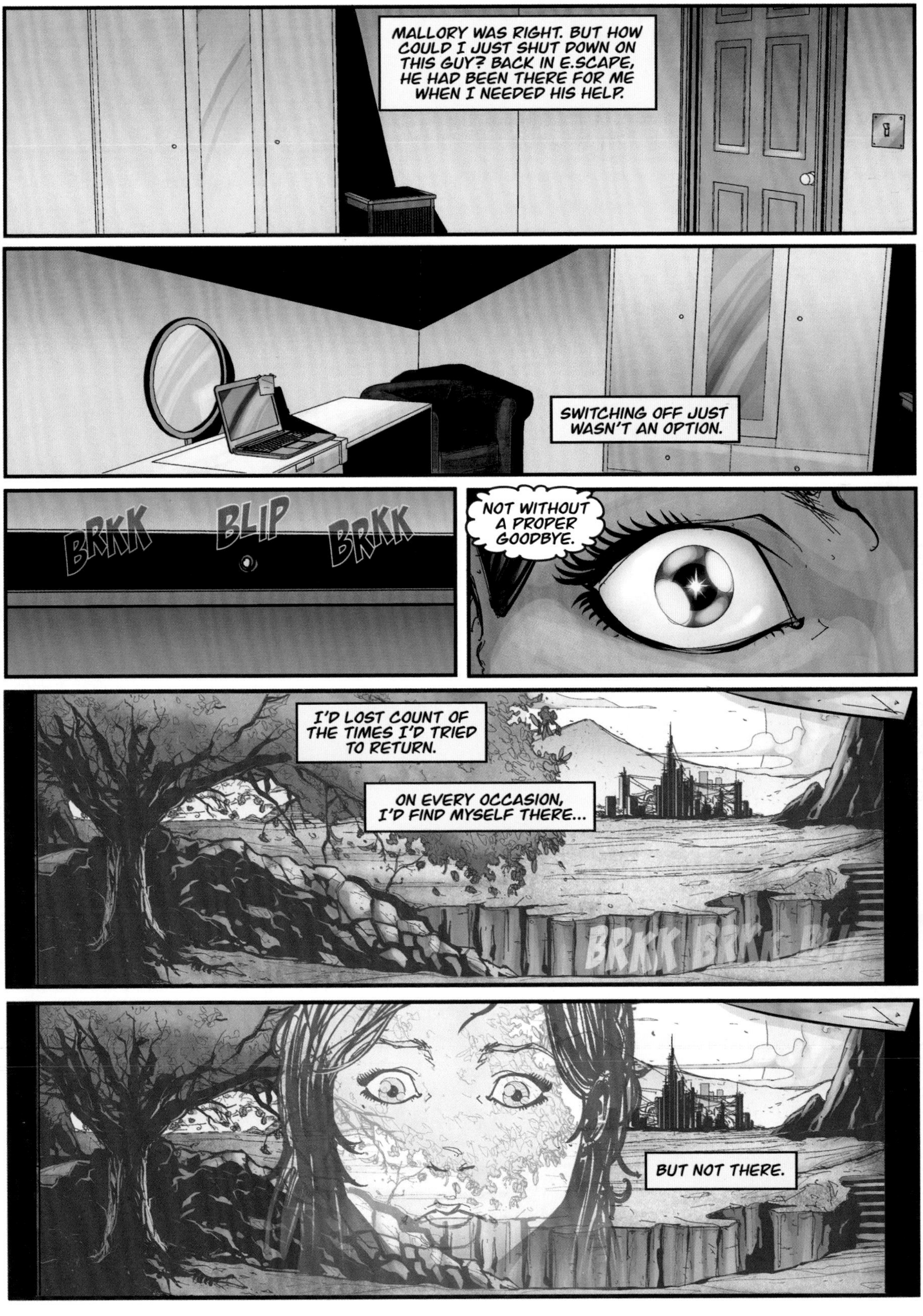
MALLORY WAS RIGHT. BUT HOW COULD I JUST SHUT DOWN ON THIS GUY? BACK IN E.SCAPE, HE HAD BEEN THERE FOR ME WHEN I NEEDED HIS HELP.
SWITCHING OFF JUST WASN'T AN OPTION.
BRKK
BLIP
BRKK
NOT WITHOUT A PROPER GOODBYE.
I'D LOST COUNT OF THE TIMES I'D TRIED TO RETURN.
ON EVERY OCCASION, I'D FIND MYSELF THERE...
BRKK BRKK
BUT NOT THERE.

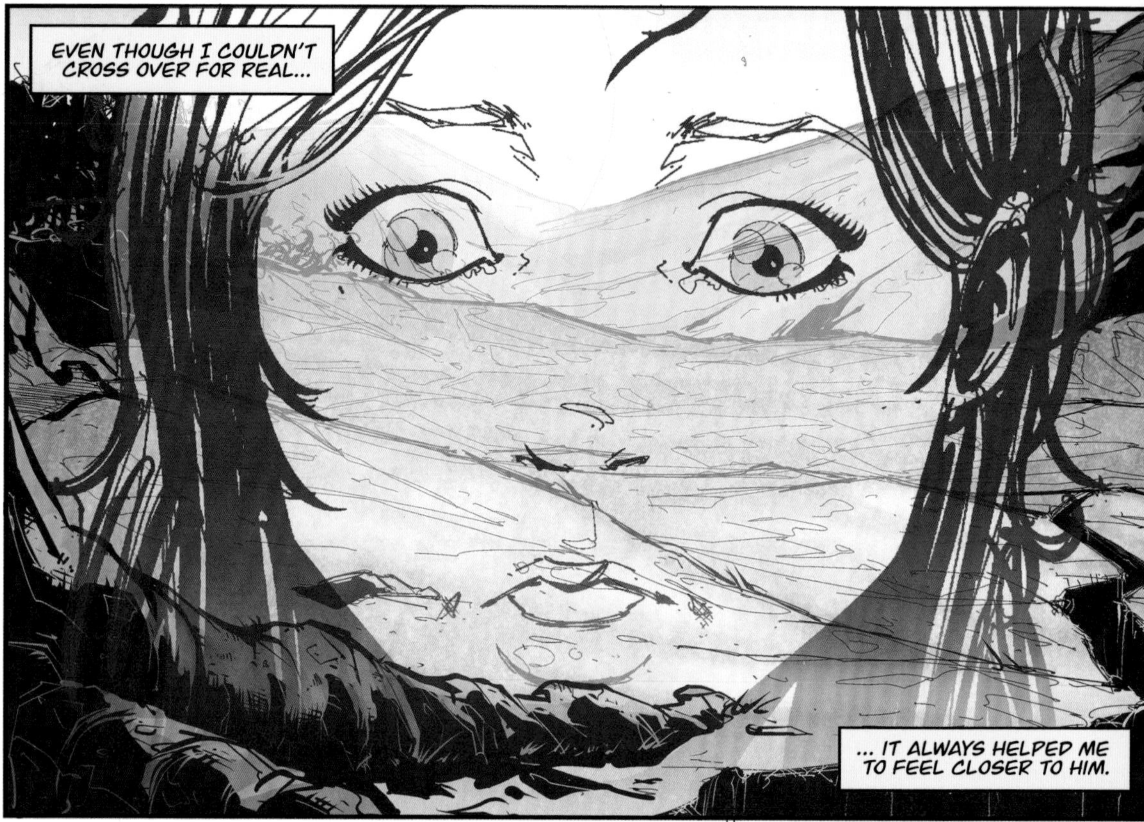
EVEN THOUGH I COULDN'T CROSS OVER FOR REAL...
... IT ALWAYS HELPED ME TO FEEL CLOSER TO HIM.

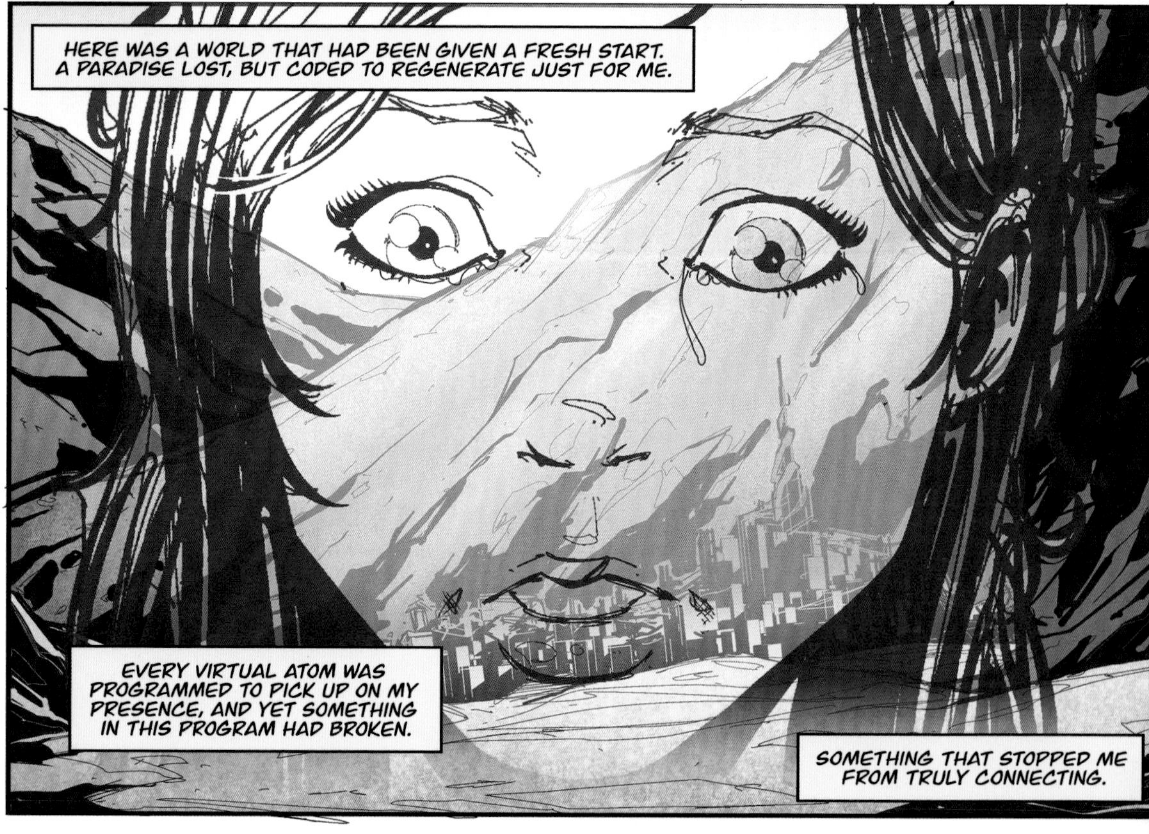
HERE WAS A WORLD THAT HAD BEEN GIVEN A FRESH START. A PARADISE LOST, BUT CODED TO REGENERATE JUST FOR ME.
EVERY VIRTUAL ATOM WAS PROGRAMMED TO PICK UP ON MY PRESENCE, AND YET SOMETHING IN THIS PROGRAM HAD BROKEN.
SOMETHING THAT STOPPED ME FROM TRULY CONNECTING.

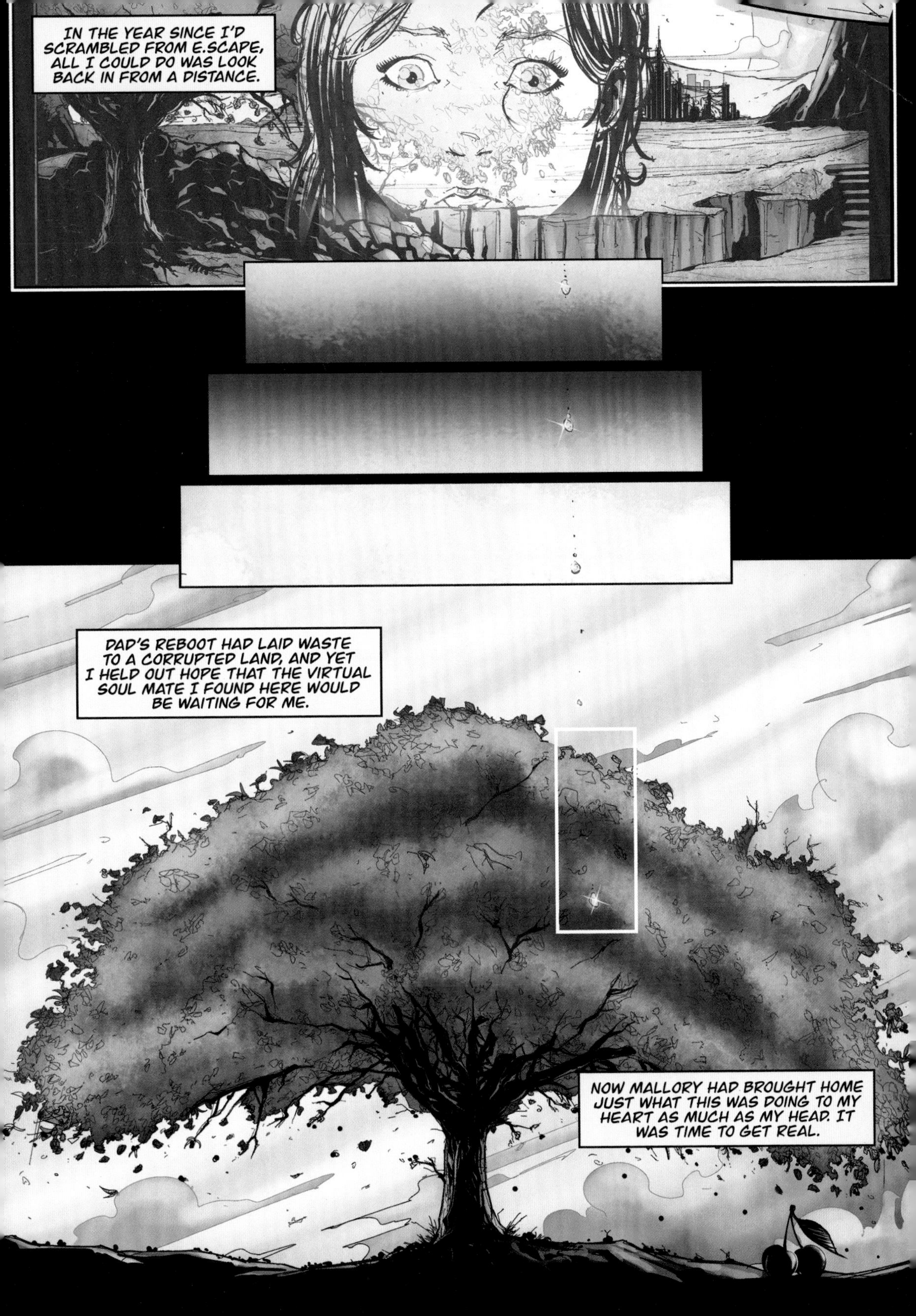
IN THE YEAR SINCE I'D SCRAMBLED FROM E.SCAPE, ALL I COULD DO WAS LOOK BACK IN FROM A DISTANCE.
DAD'S REBOOT HAD LAID WASTE TO A CORRUPTED LAND, AND YET I HELD OUT HOPE THAT THE VIRTUAL SOUL MATE I FOUND HERE WOULD BE WAITING FOR ME.
NOW MALLORY HAD BROUGHT HOME JUST WHAT THIS WAS DOING TO MY HEART AS MUCH AS MY HEAD. IT WAS TIME TO GET REAL.

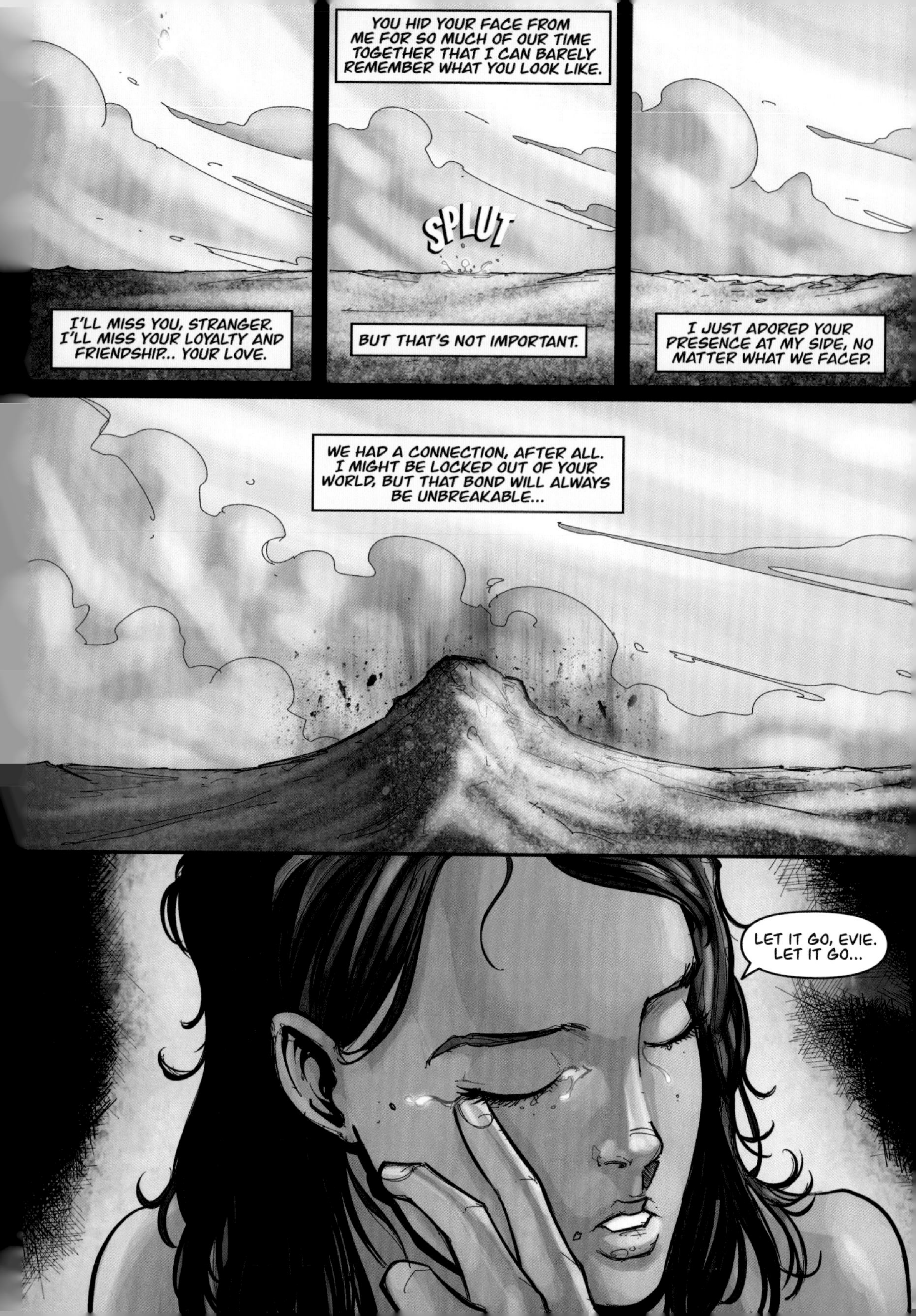
YOU HID YOUR FACE FROM ME FOR SO MUCH OF OUR TIME TOGETHER THAT I CAN BARELY REMEMBER WHAT YOU LOOK LIKE.
I'LL MISS YOU, STRANGER. I'LL MISS YOUR LOYALTY AND FRIENDSHIP... YOUR LOVE.
SPLUT
BUT THAT'S NOT IMPORTANT.
I JUST ADORED YOUR PRESENCE AT MY SIDE, NO MATTER WHAT WE FACED.
WE HAD A CONNECTION, AFTER ALL. I MIGHT BE LOCKED OUT OF YOUR WORLD, BUT THAT BOND WILL ALWAYS BE UNBREAKABLE...
LET IT GO, EVIE. LET IT GO...

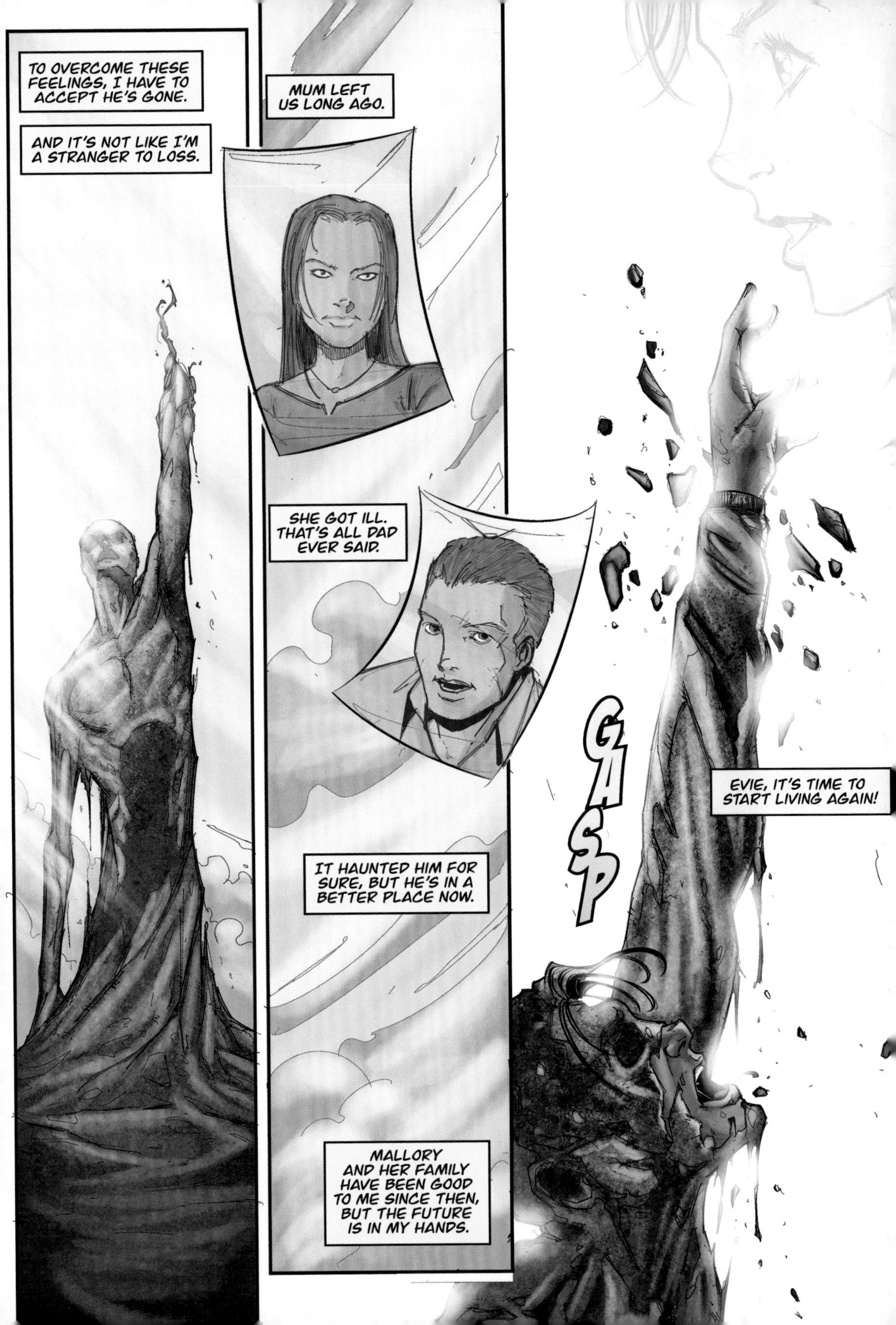
TO OVERCOME THESE FEELINGS, I HAVE TO ACCEPT HE'S GONE.
AND IT'S NOT LIKE I'M A STRANGER TO LOSS.
MUM LEFT US LONG AGO.
SHE GOT ILL. THAT'S ALL DAD EVER SAID.
IT HAUNTED HIM FOR SURE, BUT HE'S IN A BETTER PLACE NOW.
MALLORY AND HER FAMILY HAVE BEEN GOOD TO ME SINCE THEN, BUT THE FUTURE IS IN MY HANDS.
GASP
EVIE, IT'S TIME TO START LIVING AGAIN!

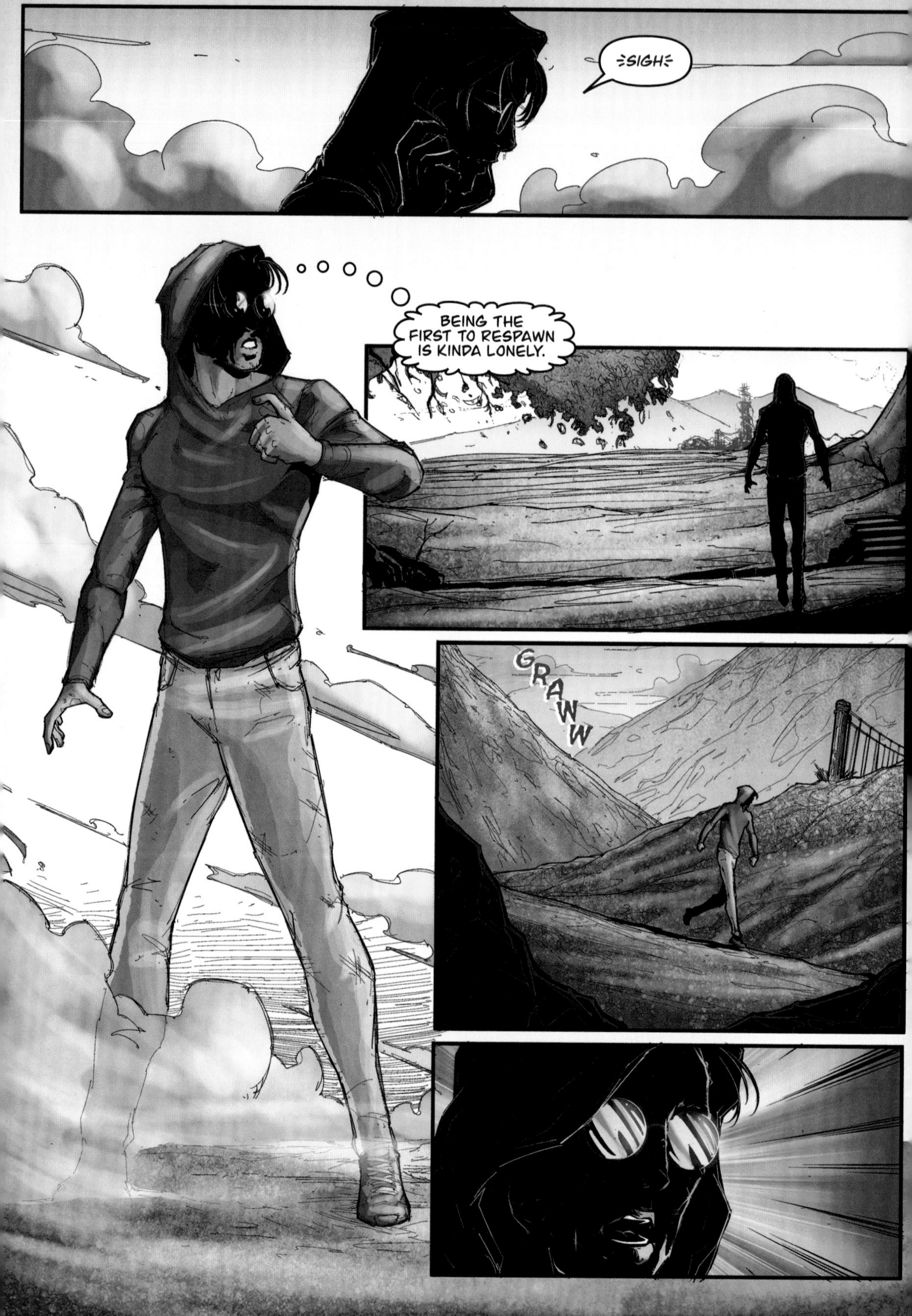
SIGH
BEING THE FIRST TO RESPAWN IS KINDA LONELY.
GRAWW

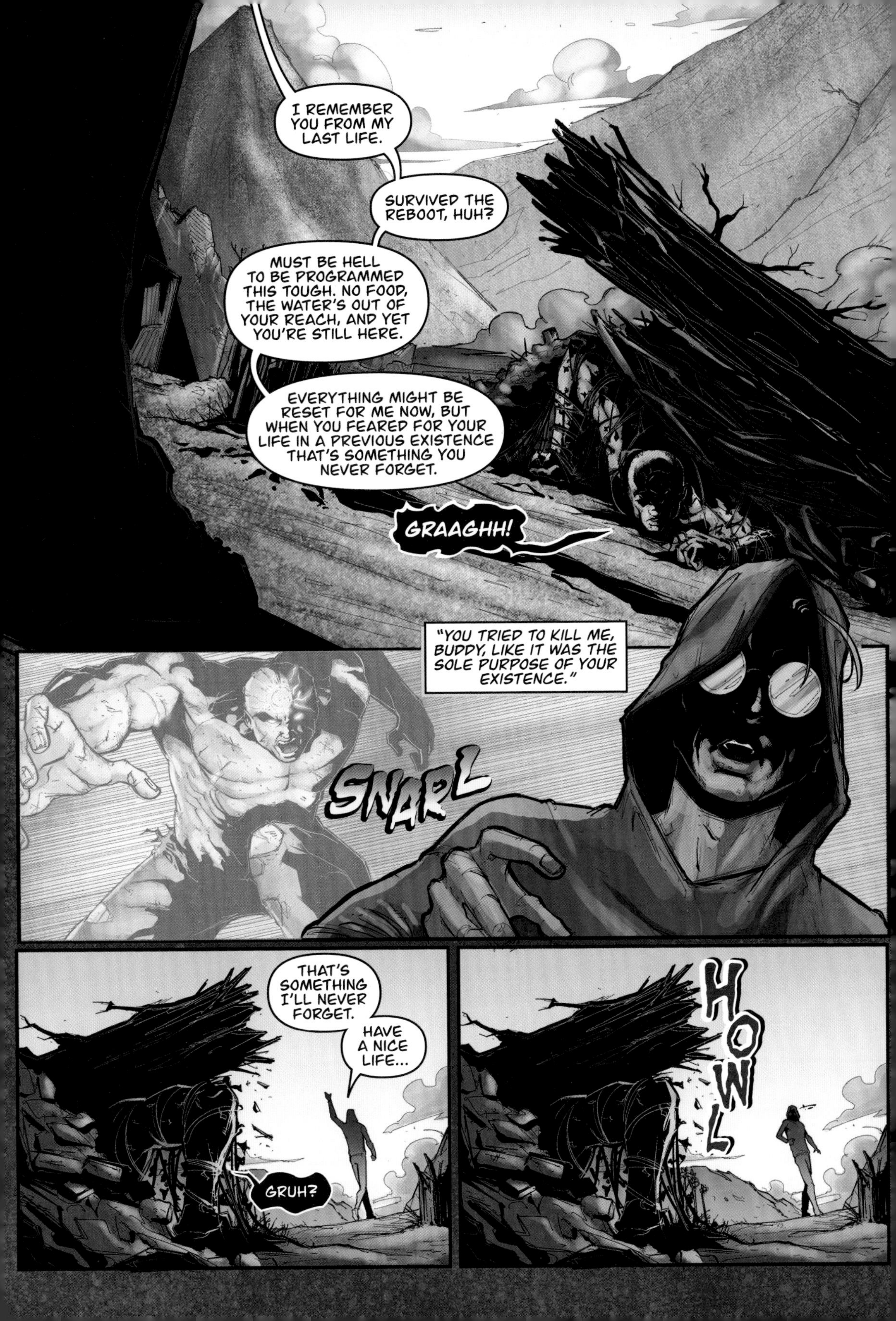
I REMEMBER YOU FROM MY LAST LIFE.
SURVIVED THE REBOOT, HUH?
MUST BE HELL TO BE PROGRAMMED THIS TOUGH. NO FOOD, THE WATER'S OUT OF YOUR REACH, AND YET YOU'RE STILL HERE.
EVERYTHING MIGHT BE RESET FOR ME NOW, BUT WHEN YOU FEARED FOR YOUR LIFE IN A PREVIOUS EXISTENCE THAT'S SOMETHING YOU NEVER FORGET.
GRAAGHH!
"YOU TRIED TO KILL ME, BUDDY, LIKE IT WAS THE SOLE PURPOSE OF YOUR EXISTENCE."
SNARL
THAT'S SOMETHING I'LL NEVER FORGET.
HAVE A NICE LIFE...
GRUH?
HOWL

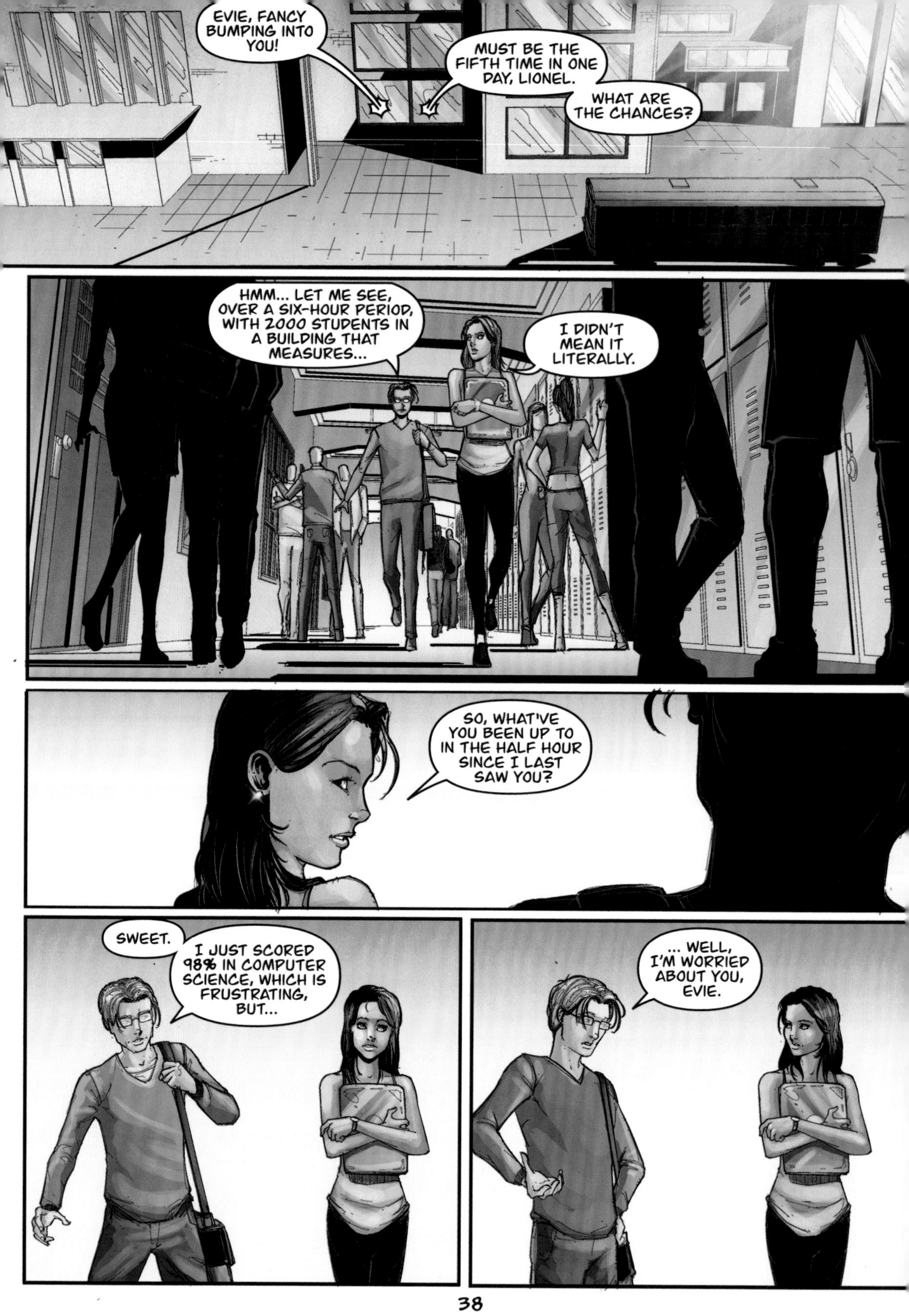
EVIE, FANCY BUMPING INTO YOU!
MUST BE THE FIFTH TIME IN ONE DAY, LIONEL.
WHAT ARE THE CHANCES?
HMM... LET ME SEE, OVER A SIX-HOUR PERIOD, WITH 2000 STUDENTS IN A BUILDING THAT MEASURES...
I DIDN'T MEAN IT LITERALLY.
SO, WHAT'VE YOU BEEN UP TO IN THE HALF HOUR SINCE I LAST SAW YOU?
SWEET.
I JUST SCORED 98% IN COMPUTER SCIENCE, WHICH IS FRUSTRATING, BUT...
... WELL, I'M WORRIED ABOUT YOU, EVIE.

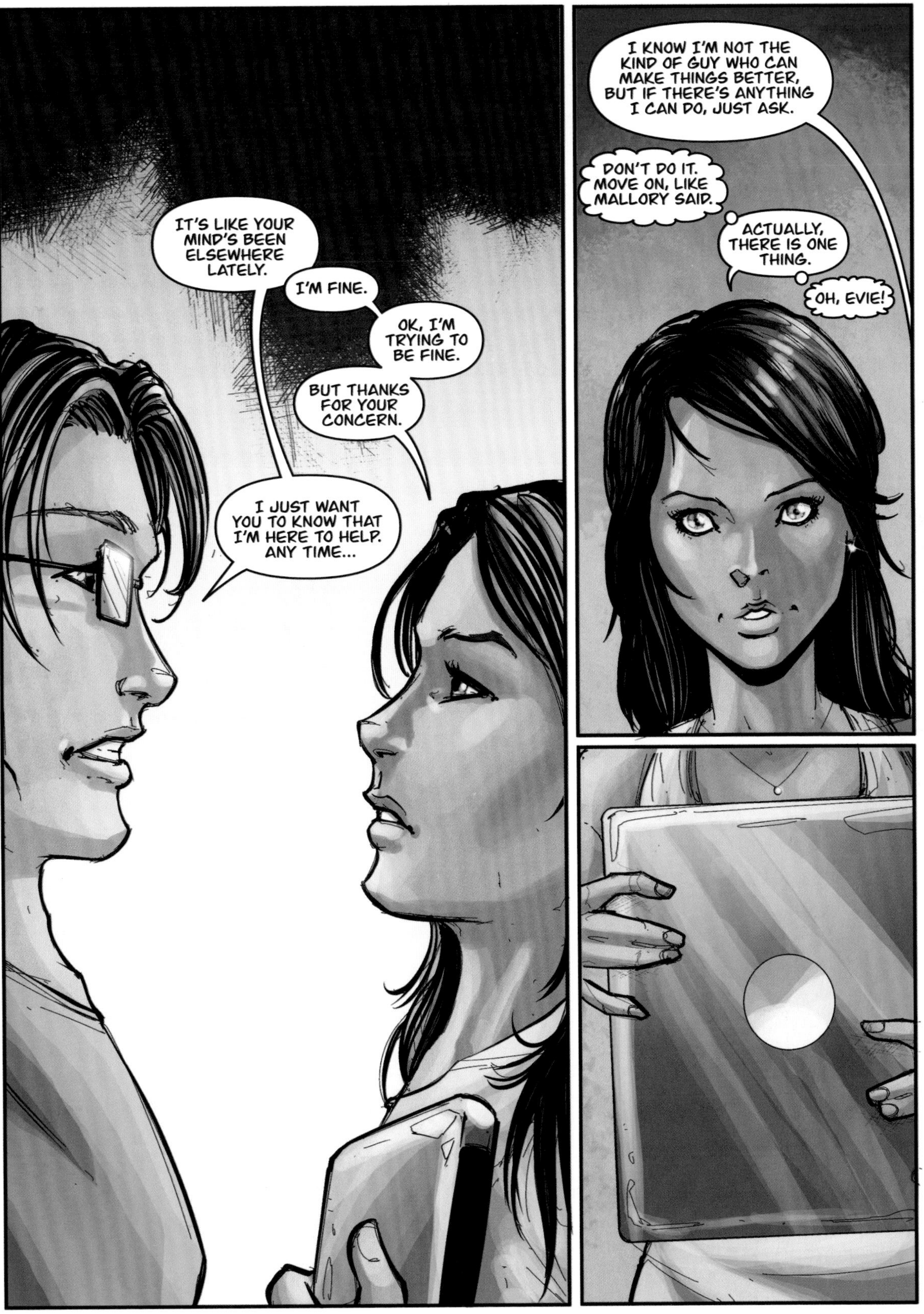
IT'S LIKE YOUR MIND'S BEEN ELSEWHERE LATELY.
I'M FINE.
OK, I'M TRYING TO BE FINE.
BUT THANKS FOR YOUR CONCERN.
I JUST WANT YOU TO KNOW THAT I'M HERE TO HELP. ANY TIME...
I KNOW I'M NOT THE KIND OF GUY WHO CAN MAKE THINGS BETTER, BUT IF THERE'S ANYTHING I CAN DO, JUST ASK.
DON'T DO IT. MOVE ON, LIKE MALLORY SAID.
ACTUALLY, THERE IS ONE THING.
OH, EVIE!

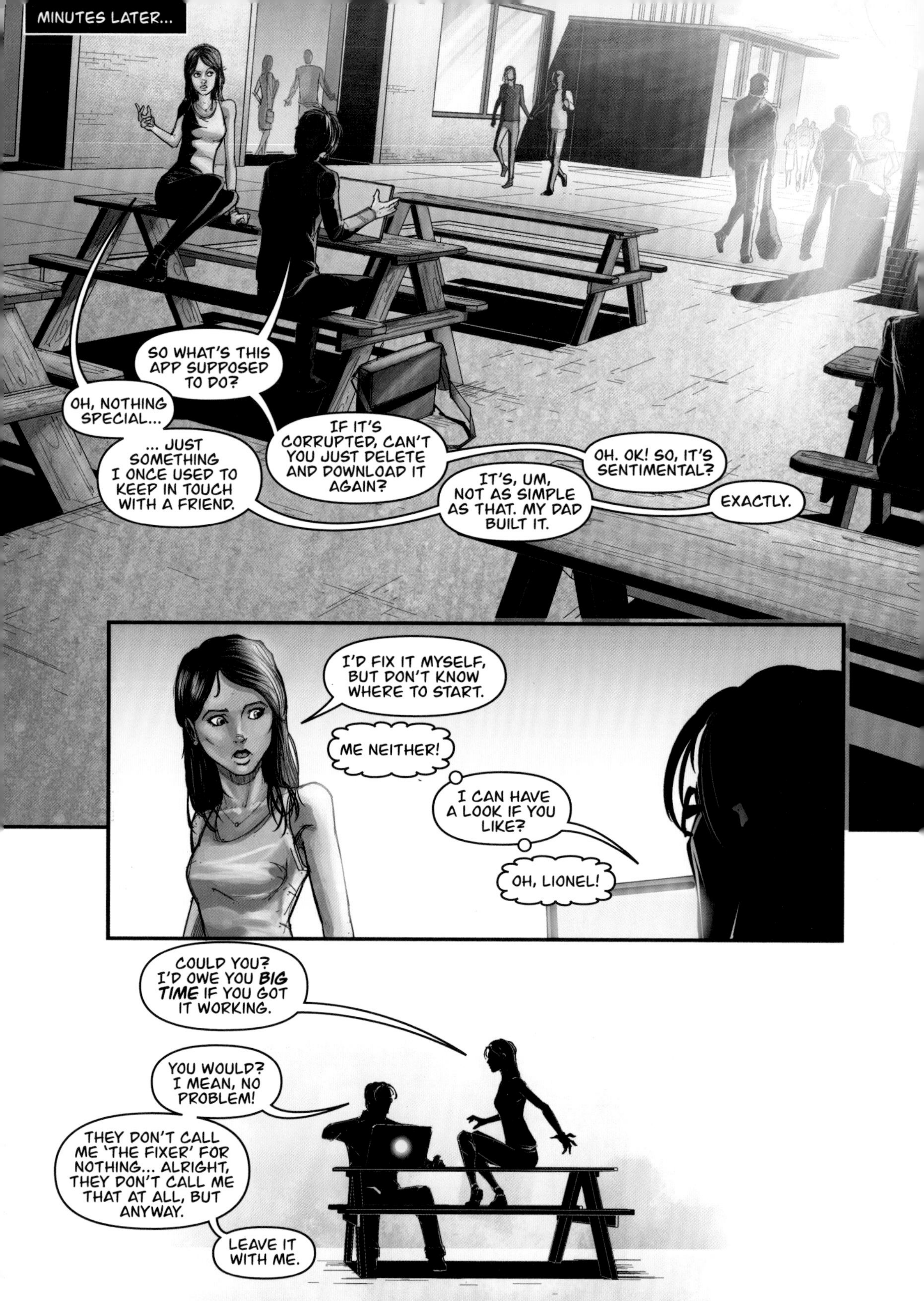
MINUTES LATER...
SO WHAT'S THIS APP SUPPOSED TO DO?
OH, NOTHING SPECIAL...
... JUST SOMETHING I ONCE USED TO KEEP IN TOUCH WITH A FRIEND.
IF IT'S CORRUPTED, CAN'T YOU JUST DELETE AND DOWNLOAD IT AGAIN?
IT'S, UM, NOT AS SIMPLE AS THAT. MY DAD BUILT IT.
OH. OK! SO, IT'S SENTIMENTAL?
EXACTLY.
I'D FIX IT MYSELF, BUT DON'T KNOW WHERE TO START.
ME NEITHER!
I CAN HAVE A LOOK IF YOU LIKE?
OH, LIONEL!
COULD YOU? I'D OWE YOU **BIG TIME** IF YOU GOT IT WORKING.
YOU WOULD? I MEAN, NO PROBLEM!
THEY DON'T CALL ME 'THE FIXER' FOR NOTHING... ALRIGHT, THEY DON'T CALL ME THAT AT ALL, BUT ANYWAY.
LEAVE IT WITH ME.

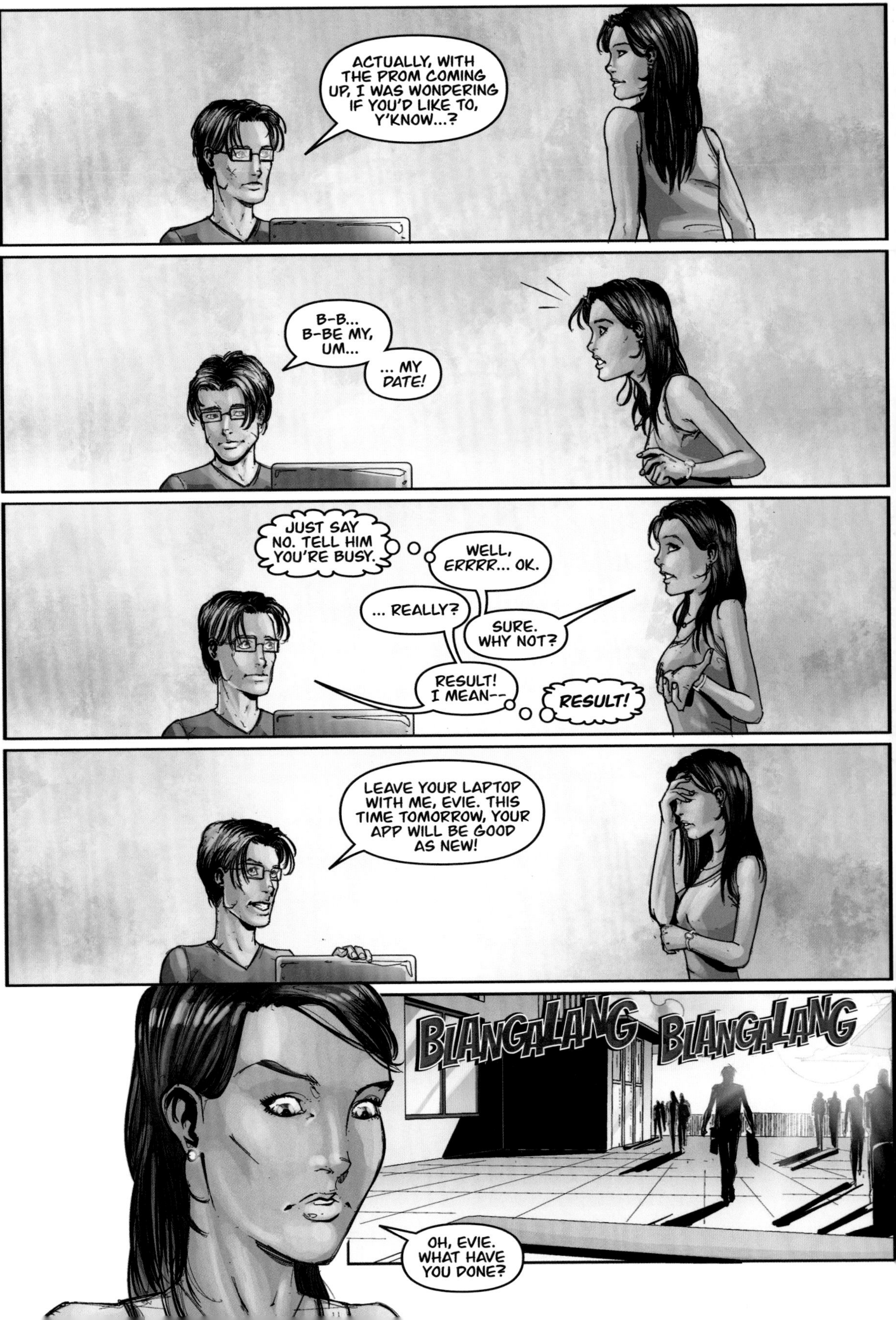
ACTUALLY, WITH THE PROM COMING UP, I WAS WONDERING IF YOU'D LIKE TO, Y'KNOW...?
B-B... B-BE MY, UM...
... MY DATE!
JUST SAY NO. TELL HIM YOU'RE BUSY.
WELL, ERRRR... OK.
... REALLY?
SURE. WHY NOT?
RESULT! I MEAN--
RESULT!
LEAVE YOUR LAPTOP WITH ME, EVIE. THIS TIME TOMORROW, YOUR APP WILL BE GOOD AS NEW!
BLANGALANG
BLANGALANG
OH, EVIE. WHAT HAVE YOU DONE?

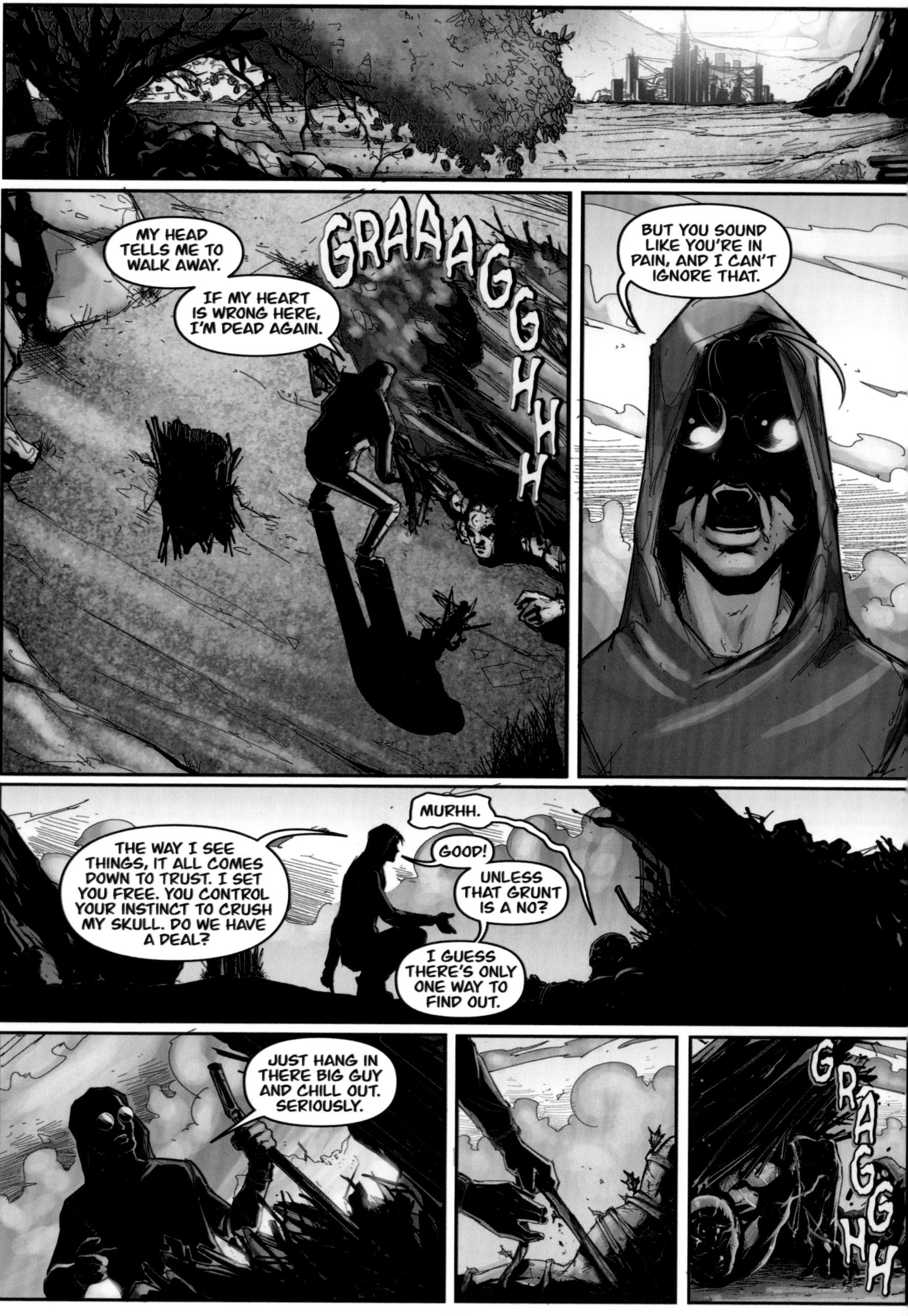
MY HEAD TELLS ME TO WALK AWAY.
IF MY HEART IS WRONG HERE, I'M DEAD AGAIN.
GRAAAGGHHH
BUT YOU SOUND LIKE YOU'RE IN PAIN, AND I CAN'T IGNORE THAT.
THE WAY I SEE THINGS, IT ALL COMES DOWN TO TRUST. I SET YOU FREE. YOU CONTROL YOUR INSTINCT TO CRUSH MY SKULL. DO WE HAVE A DEAL?
MURHH.
GOOD!
UNLESS THAT GRUNT IS A NO?
I GUESS THERE'S ONLY ONE WAY TO FIND OUT.
JUST HANG IN THERE BIG GUY AND CHILL OUT. SERIOUSLY.
GRAGGHH

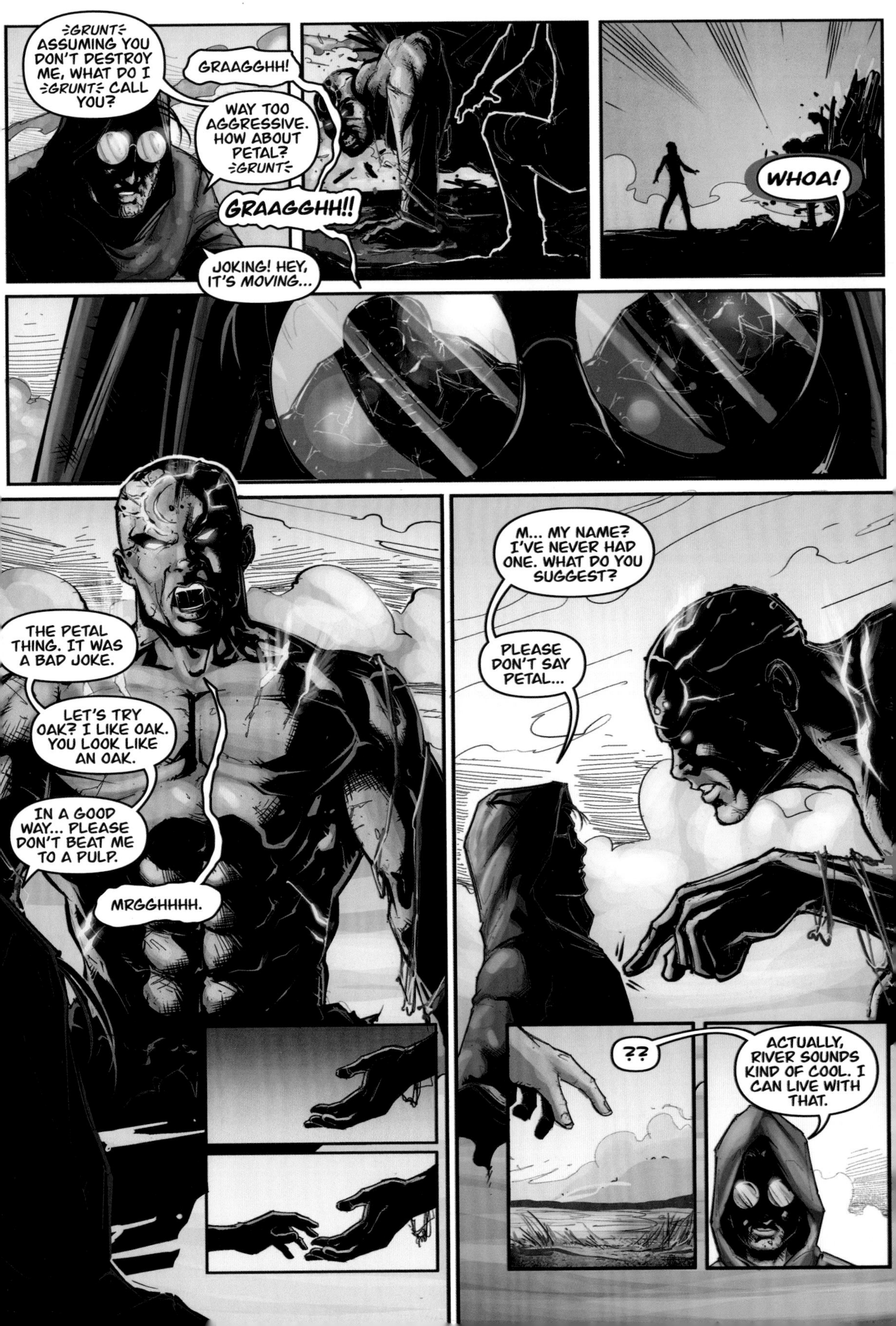

GRUNT ASSUMING YOU DON'T DESTROY ME, WHAT DO I GRUNT CALL YOU?
GRAAGGHH!
WAY TOO AGGRESSIVE. HOW ABOUT PETAL? GRUNT
GRAAGGHH!!
JOKING! HEY, IT'S MOVING...
WHOA!
THE PETAL THING. IT WAS A BAD JOKE.
LET'S TRY OAK? I LIKE OAK. YOU LOOK LIKE AN OAK.
IN A GOOD WAY... PLEASE DON'T BEAT ME TO A PULP.
MRGGHHHH.
M... MY NAME? I'VE NEVER HAD ONE. WHAT DO YOU SUGGEST?
PLEASE DON'T SAY PETAL...
??
ACTUALLY, RIVER SOUNDS KIND OF COOL. I CAN LIVE WITH THAT.

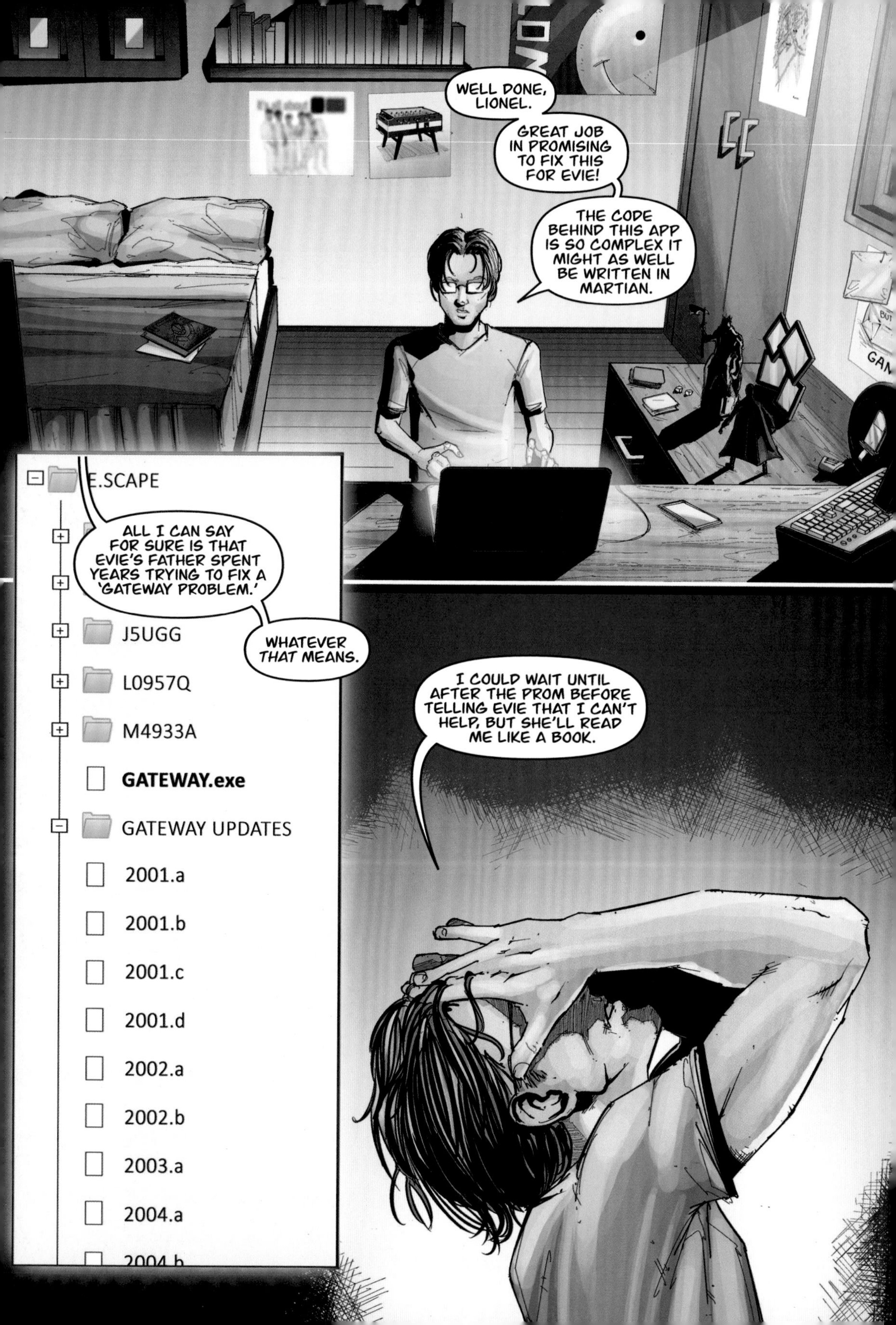
WELL DONE, LIONEL.
GREAT JOB IN PROMISING TO FIX THIS FOR EVIE!
THE CODE BEHIND THIS APP IS SO COMPLEX IT MIGHT AS WELL BE WRITTEN IN MARTIAN.
E.SCAPE
ALL I CAN SAY FOR SURE IS THAT EVIE'S FATHER SPENT YEARS TRYING TO FIX A 'GATEWAY PROBLEM.'
WHATEVER THAT MEANS.
J5UGG
L0957Q
M4933A
GATEWAY.exe
GATEWAY UPDATES
2001.a
2001.b
2001.c
2001.d
2002.a
2002.b
2003.a
2004.a
I COULD WAIT UNTIL AFTER THE PROM BEFORE TELLING EVIE THAT I CAN'T HELP, BUT SHE'LL READ ME LIKE A BOOK.

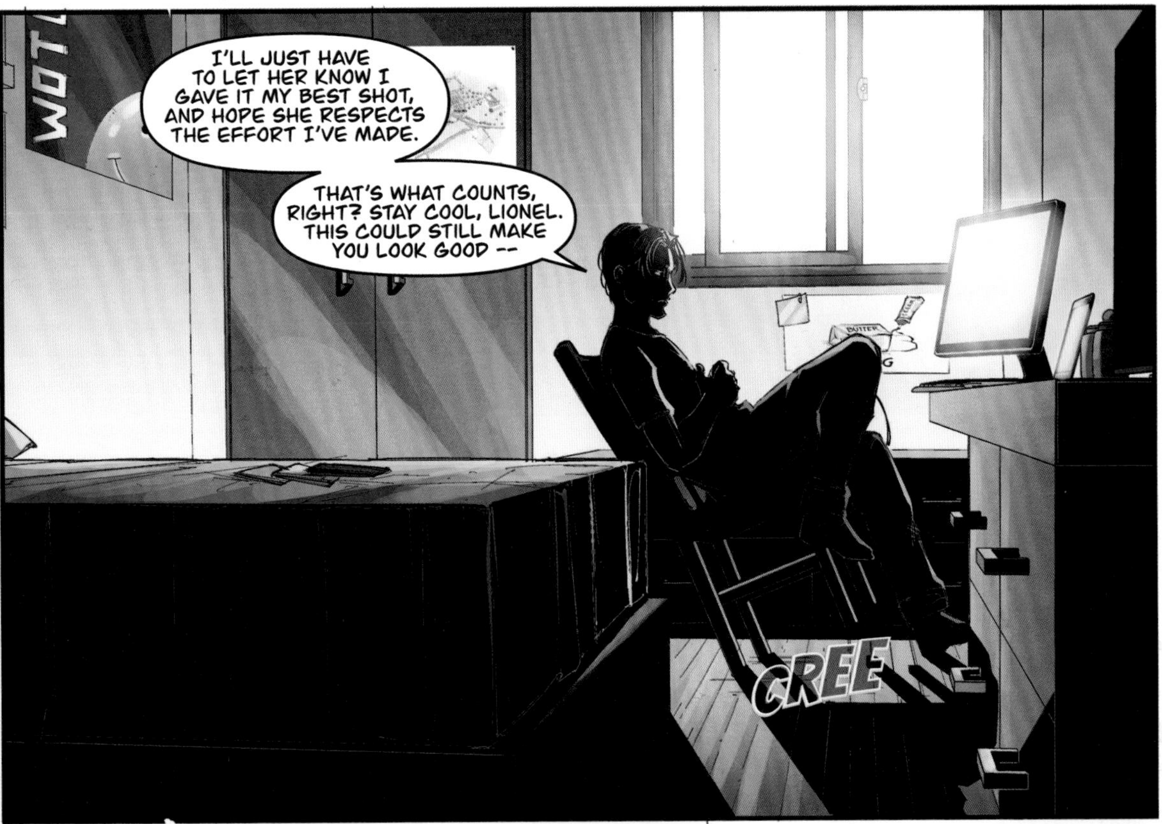
I'LL JUST HAVE TO LET HER KNOW I GAVE IT MY BEST SHOT, AND HOPE SHE RESPECTS THE EFFORT I'VE MADE.
THAT'S WHAT COUNTS, RIGHT? STAY COOL, LIONEL. THIS COULD STILL MAKE YOU LOOK GOOD --
CREE

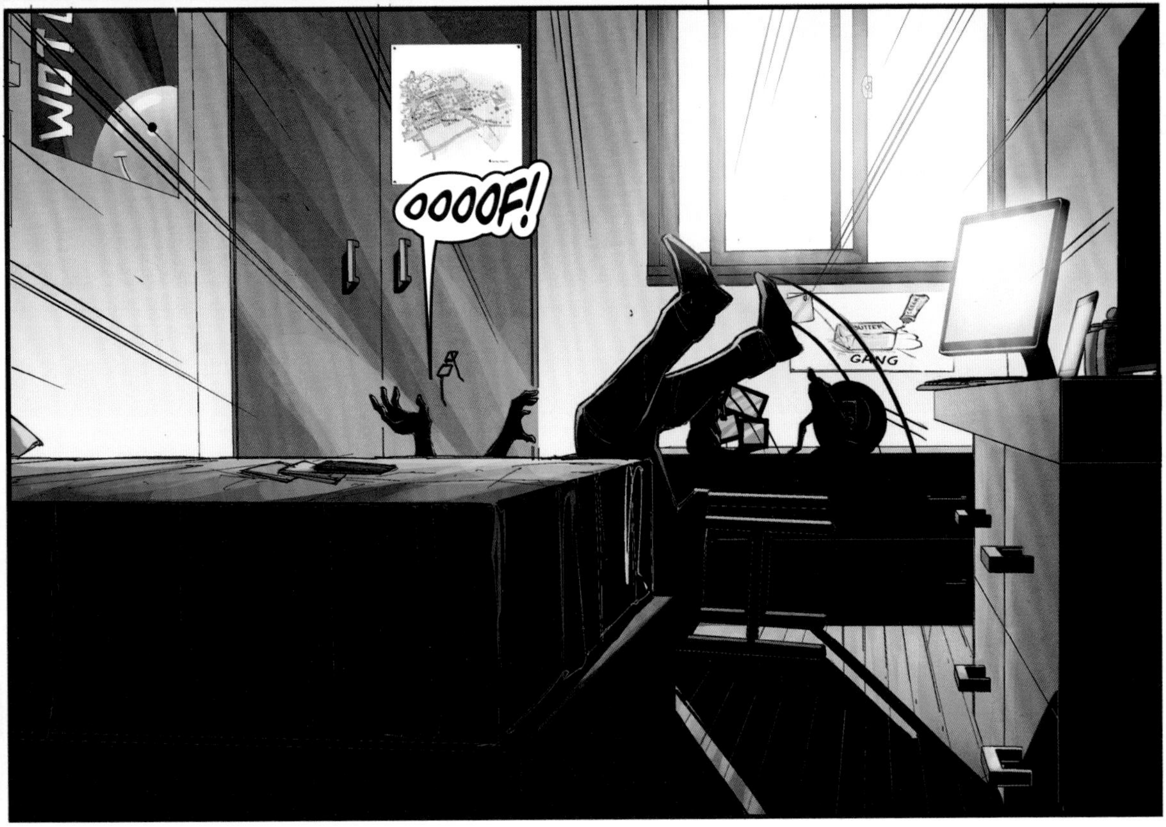
OOOOF!
BUTTER
GANG

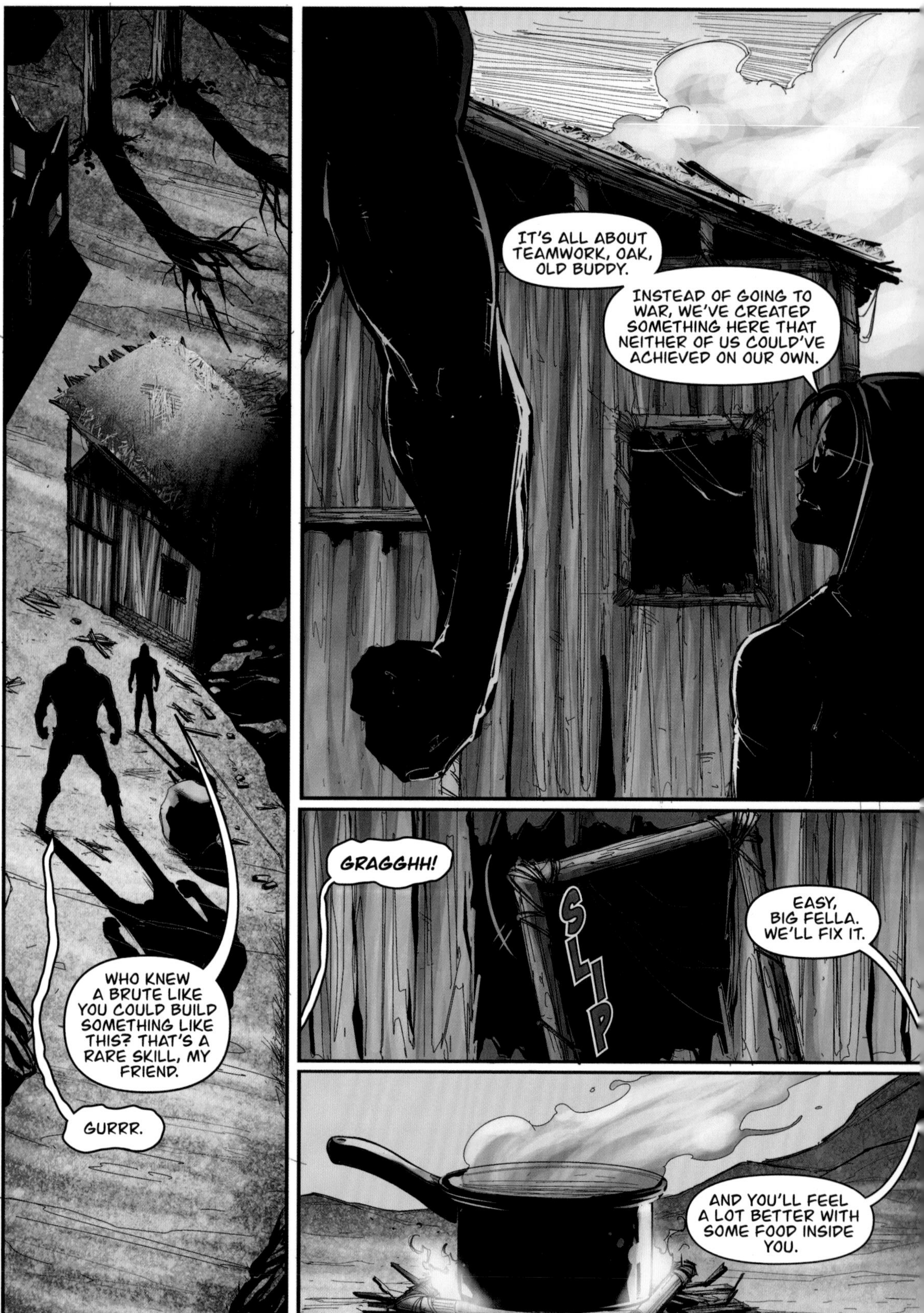
WHO KNEW A BRUTE LIKE YOU COULD BUILD SOMETHING LIKE THIS? THAT'S A RARE SKILL, MY FRIEND.
GURRR.
IT'S ALL ABOUT TEAMWORK, OAK, OLD BUDDY.
INSTEAD OF GOING TO WAR, WE'VE CREATED SOMETHING HERE THAT NEITHER OF US COULD'VE ACHIEVED ON OUR OWN.
GRAGGHH!
SLIP
EASY, BIG FELLA. WE'LL FIX IT.
AND YOU'LL FEEL A LOT BETTER WITH SOME FOOD INSIDE YOU.

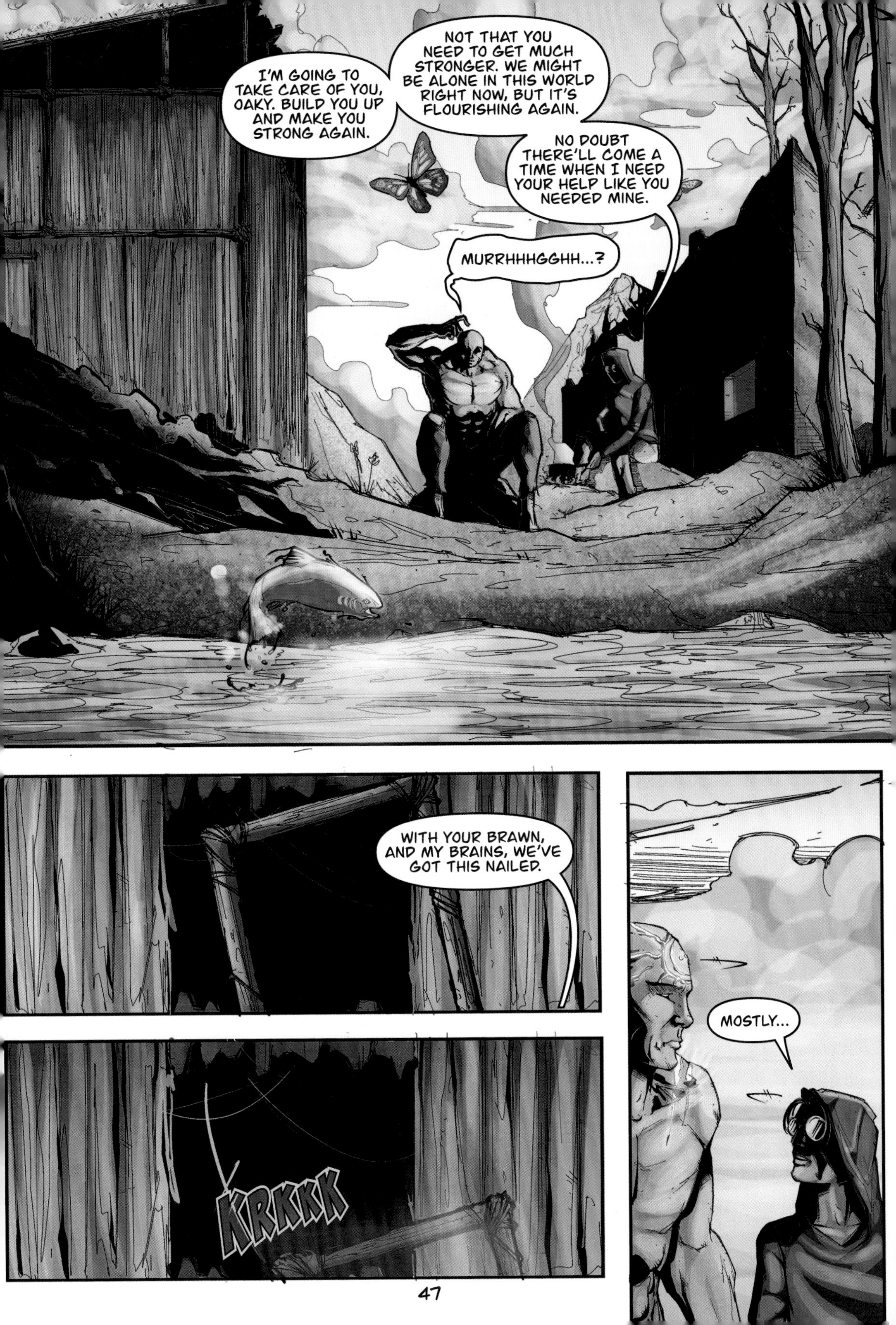
I'M GOING TO TAKE CARE OF YOU, OAKY. BUILD YOU UP AND MAKE YOU STRONG AGAIN.
NOT THAT YOU NEED TO GET MUCH STRONGER. WE MIGHT BE ALONE IN THIS WORLD RIGHT NOW, BUT IT'S FLOURISHING AGAIN.
NO DOUBT THERE'LL COME A TIME WHEN I NEED YOUR HELP LIKE YOU NEEDED MINE.
MURRHHHGGHH...?
WITH YOUR BRAWN, AND MY BRAINS, WE'VE GOT THIS NAILED.
KRKKK
MOSTLY...

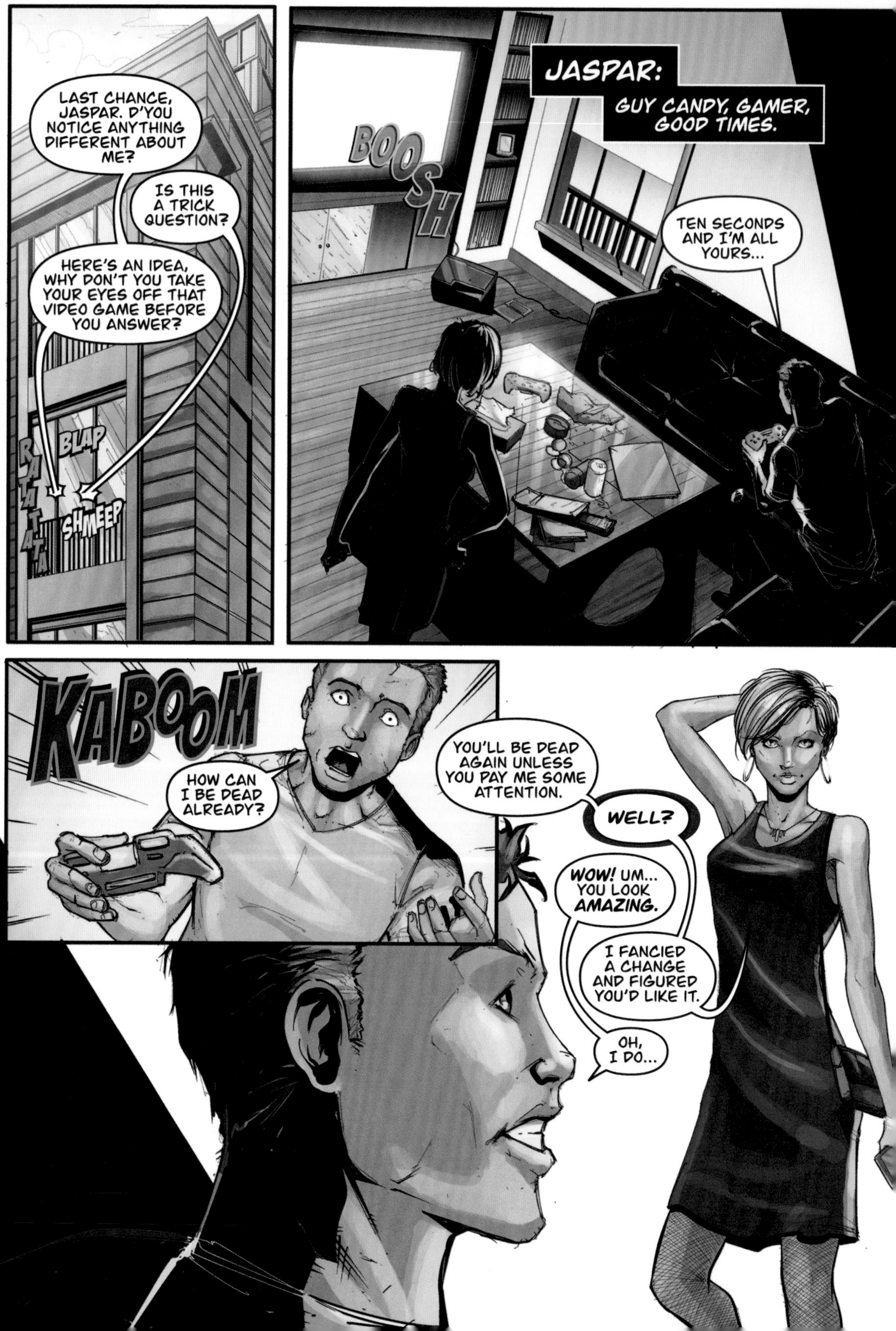
LAST CHANCE, JASPAR. D'YOU NOTICE ANYTHING DIFFERENT ABOUT ME?
IS THIS A TRICK QUESTION?
HERE'S AN IDEA, WHY DON'T YOU TAKE YOUR EYES OFF THAT VIDEO GAME BEFORE YOU ANSWER?
BLAP
RATATATATA
SHMEEP
BOOSH
JASPAR:
GUY CANDY, GAMER, GOOD TIMES.
TEN SECONDS AND I'M ALL YOURS...
KABOOM
HOW CAN I BE DEAD ALREADY?
YOU'LL BE DEAD AGAIN UNLESS YOU PAY ME SOME ATTENTION.
WELL?
WOW! UM... YOU LOOK AMAZING.
I FANCIED A CHANGE AND FIGURED YOU'D LIKE IT.
OH, I DO...

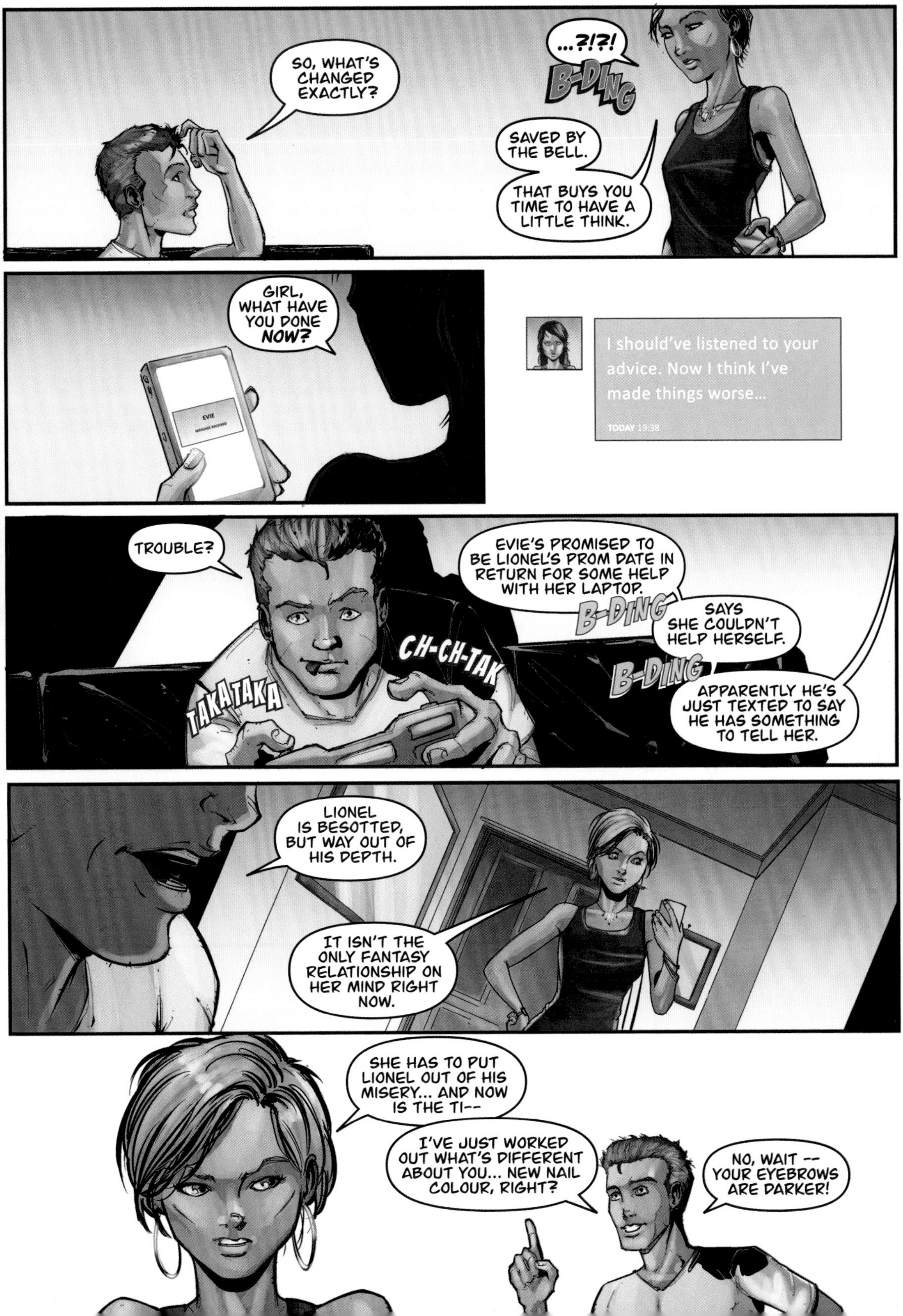
SO, WHAT'S CHANGED EXACTLY?
...?!?!
B-DING
SAVED BY THE BELL.
THAT BUYS YOU TIME TO HAVE A LITTLE THINK.
GIRL, WHAT HAVE YOU DONE NOW?
EVIE
I should've listened to your advice. Now I think I've made things worse...
TODAY 19:38
TROUBLE?
EVIE'S PROMISED TO BE LIONEL'S PROM DATE IN RETURN FOR SOME HELP WITH HER LAPTOP.
B-DING
SAYS SHE COULDN'T HELP HERSELF.
B-DING
APPARENTLY HE'S JUST TEXTED TO SAY HE HAS SOMETHING TO TELL HER.
CH-CH-TAK
TAKATAKA
LIONEL IS BESOTTED, BUT WAY OUT OF HIS DEPTH.
IT ISN'T THE ONLY FANTASY RELATIONSHIP ON HER MIND RIGHT NOW.
SHE HAS TO PUT LIONEL OUT OF HIS MISERY... AND NOW IS THE TI--
I'VE JUST WORKED OUT WHAT'S DIFFERENT ABOUT YOU... NEW NAIL COLOUR, RIGHT?
NO, WAIT -- YOUR EYEBROWS ARE DARKER!

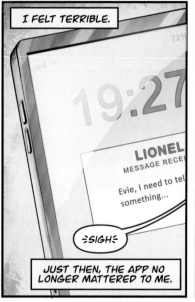

I FELT TERRIBLE.
19:27
LIONEL
MESSAGE RECEI
Evie, I need to tel
something...
SIGH
JUST THEN, THE APP NO LONGER MATTERED TO ME.
MALLORY HAD JUST SPELLED IT OUT TO ME: YES, I WAS ABOUT TO MAKE LIONEL FEEL BAD...
MALLORY
REPLY
DELETE
LIONEL
REPLY
DELETE
Evie, I need to tell you something...
TODAY 19:39
I have something to tell you, too.
TODAY 19:39
BUT IF I SAID NOTHING, WENT AHEAD WITH THE DATE AND HE WORKED OUT I WAS USING HIM TO FIX E.SCAPE, THAT WOULD JUST MAKE THINGS WORSE.
LIONEL
REPLY
DELETE
Evie, I need to tell you something...
TODAY 19:39
IT WAS NOW OR NEVER...
LIONEL
REPLY
DELETE
I have something to tell you, too.
TODAY 19:39
This isn't an easy thing for me to say...
B-DING
MALLORY
MESSAGE RECEIVED
Have you done the deed?
TODAY 19:39
IF MALLORY WOULD JUST GIVE ME A MOMENT.
This isn't an easy thing for me to say...

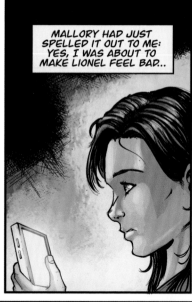

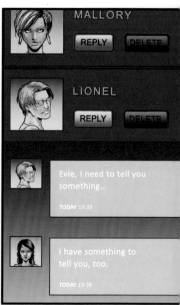

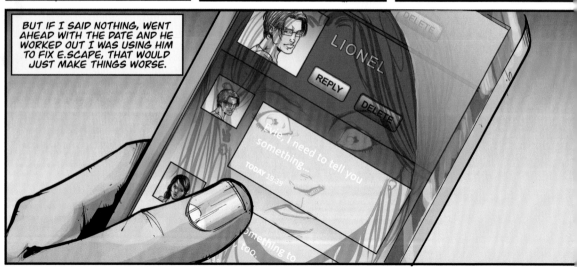

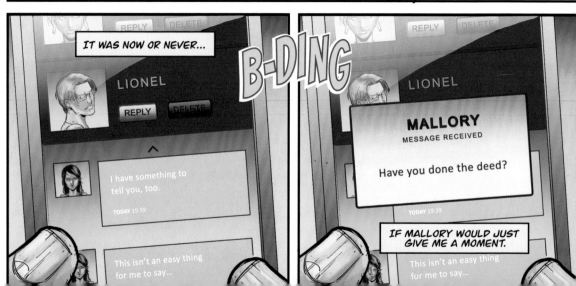

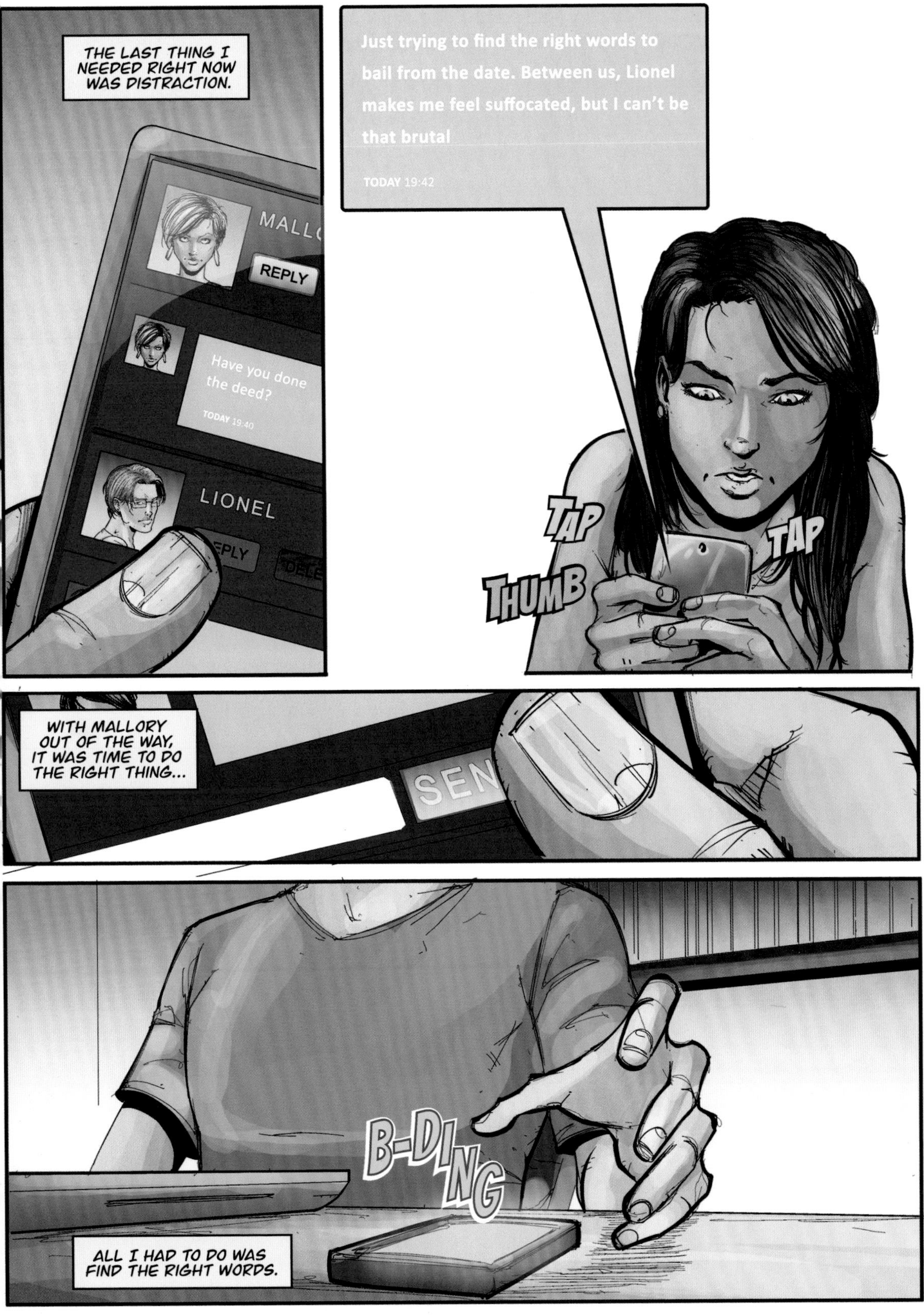
THE LAST THING I NEEDED RIGHT NOW WAS DISTRACTION.
MALLO
REPLY
Have you done the deed?
TODAY 19:40
LIONEL
EPLY
DELE
Just trying to find the right words to bail from the date. Between us, Lionel makes me feel suffocated, but I can't be that brutal
TODAY 19:42
TAP
TAP
THUMB
WITH MALLORY OUT OF THE WAY, IT WAS TIME TO DO THE RIGHT THING...
SEN
B-DING
ALL I HAD TO DO WAS FIND THE RIGHT WORDS.

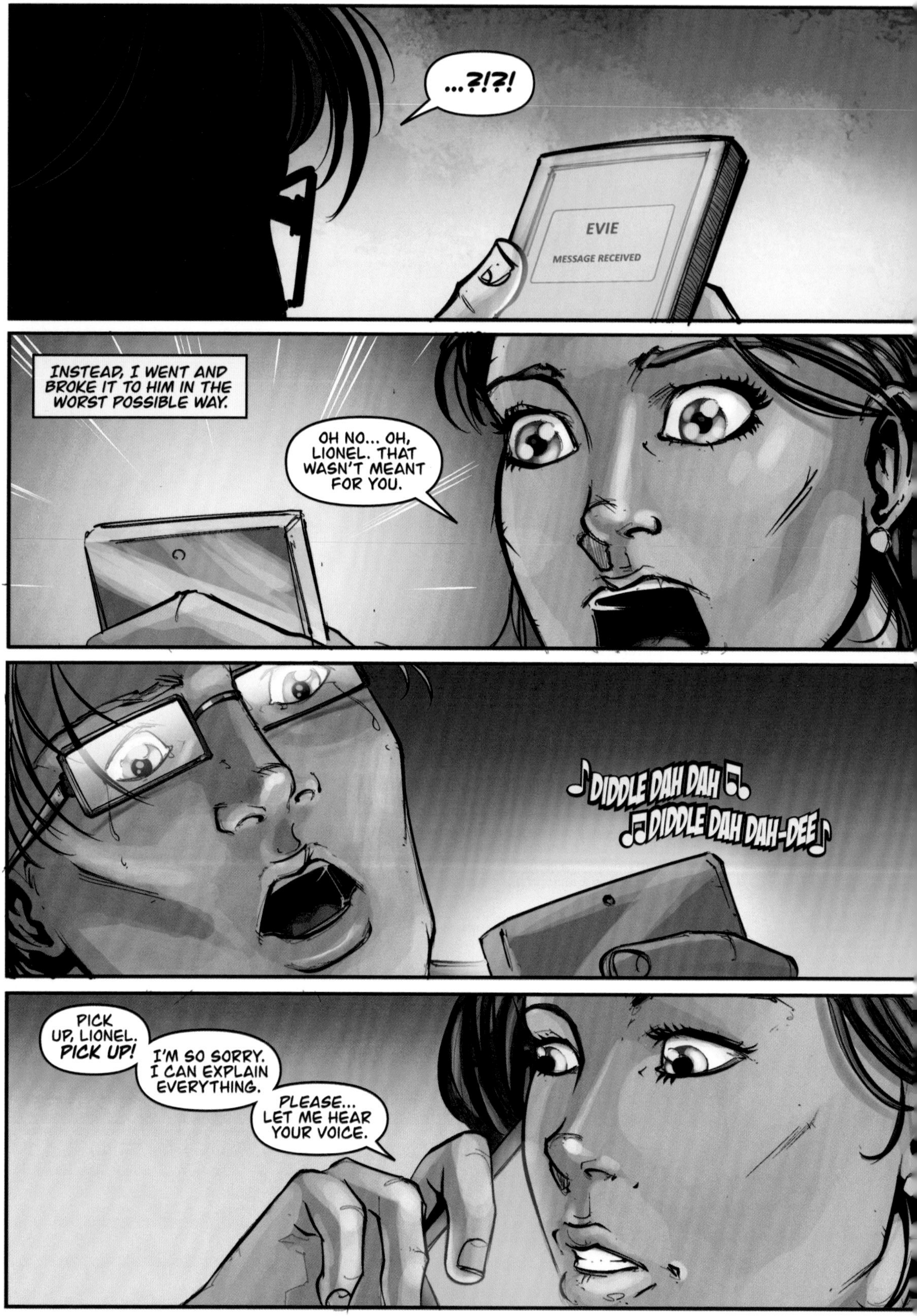

...?!?!
EVIE
MESSAGE RECEIVED
INSTEAD, I WENT AND BROKE IT TO HIM IN THE WORST POSSIBLE WAY.
OH NO... OH, LIONEL. THAT WASN'T MEANT FOR YOU.
DIDDLE DAH DAH
DIDDLE DAH DAH-DEE
PICK UP, LIONEL. PICK UP!
I'M SO SORRY. I CAN EXPLAIN EVERYTHING.
PLEASE... LET ME HEAR YOUR VOICE.

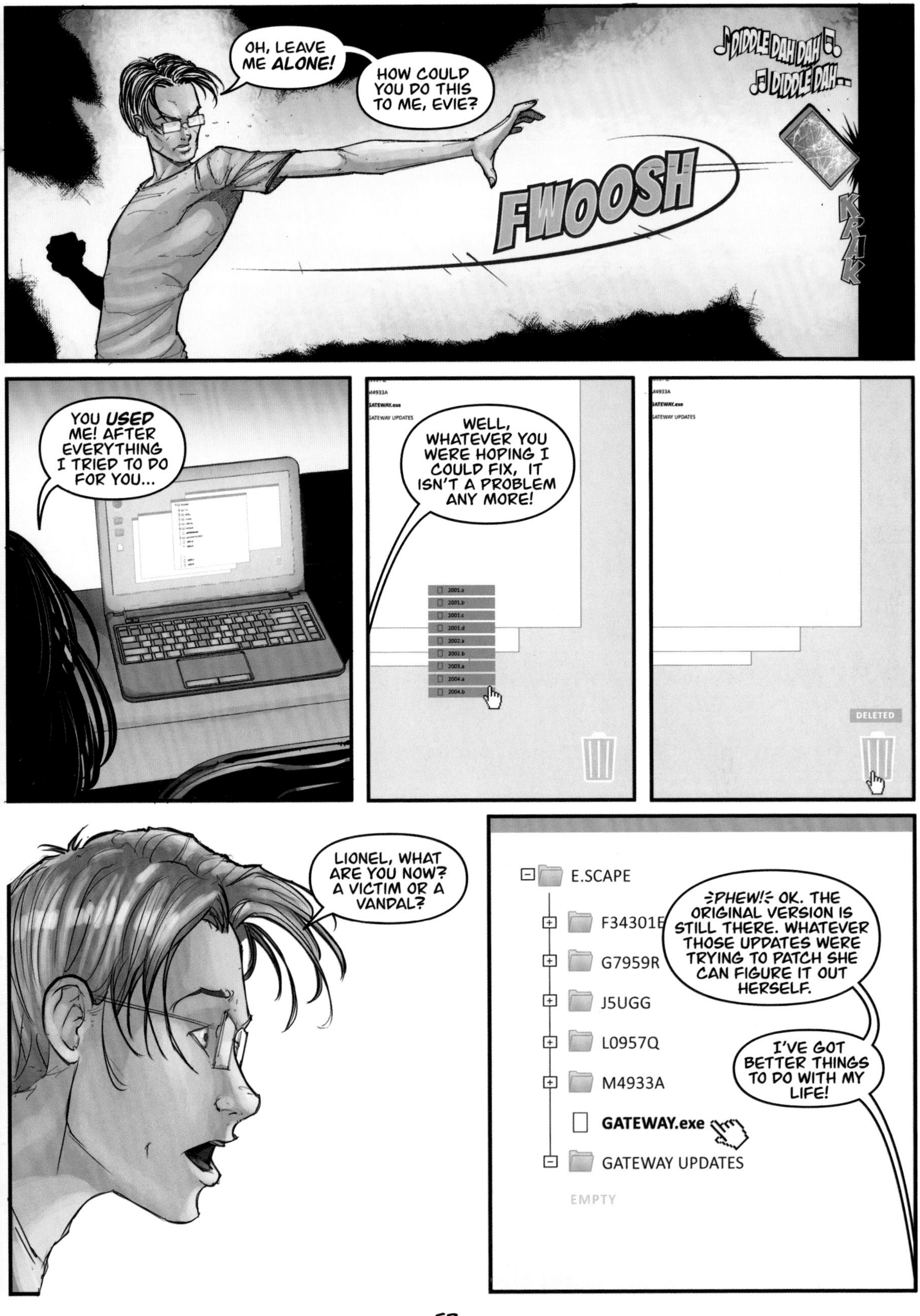
OH, LEAVE ME ALONE!
HOW COULD YOU DO THIS TO ME, EVIE?
DIDDLE DAH DAH DIDDLE DAH...
FWOOSH
KRAK
YOU USED ME! AFTER EVERYTHING I TRIED TO DO FOR YOU...
M4933A
GATEWAY.exe
GATEWAY UPDATES
WELL, WHATEVER YOU WERE HOPING I COULD FIX, IT ISN'T A PROBLEM ANY MORE!
2001.a
2001.b
2001.c
2001.d
2002.a
2002.b
2003.a
2004.a
2004.b
DELETED
LIONEL, WHAT ARE YOU NOW? A VICTIM OR A VANDAL?
E.SCAPE
F34301E
G7959R
J5UGG
L0957Q
M4933A
GATEWAY.exe
GATEWAY UPDATES
EMPTY
PHEW! OK. THE ORIGINAL VERSION IS STILL THERE. WHATEVER THOSE UPDATES WERE TRYING TO PATCH SHE CAN FIGURE IT OUT HERSELF.
I'VE GOT BETTER THINGS TO DO WITH MY LIFE!

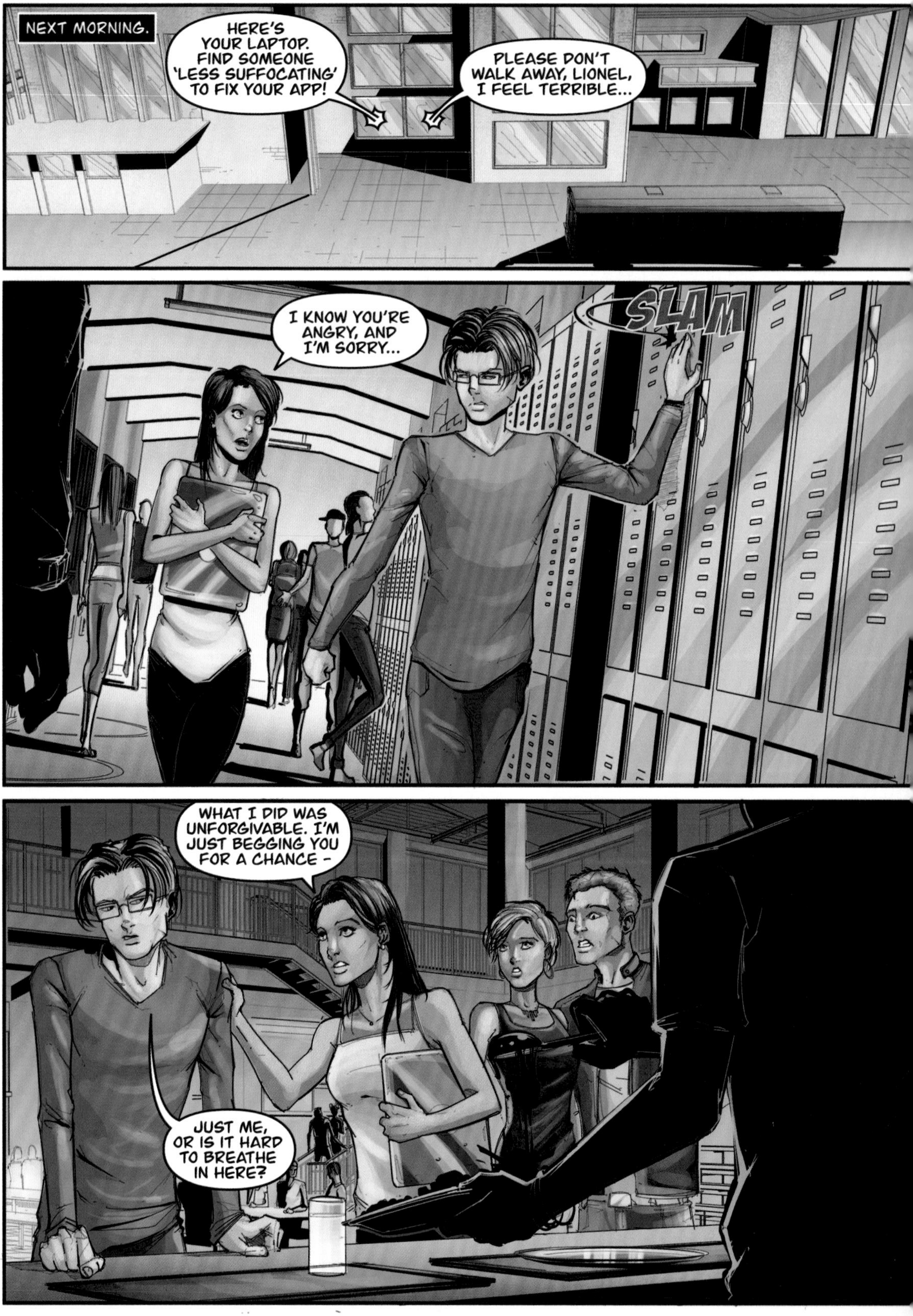
NEXT MORNING.
HERE'S YOUR LAPTOP. FIND SOMEONE 'LESS SUFFOCATING' TO FIX YOUR APP!
PLEASE DON'T WALK AWAY, LIONEL, I FEEL TERRIBLE...
I KNOW YOU'RE ANGRY, AND I'M SORRY...
SLAM
WHAT I DID WAS UNFORGIVABLE. I'M JUST BEGGING YOU FOR A CHANCE -
JUST ME, OR IS IT HARD TO BREATHE IN HERE?

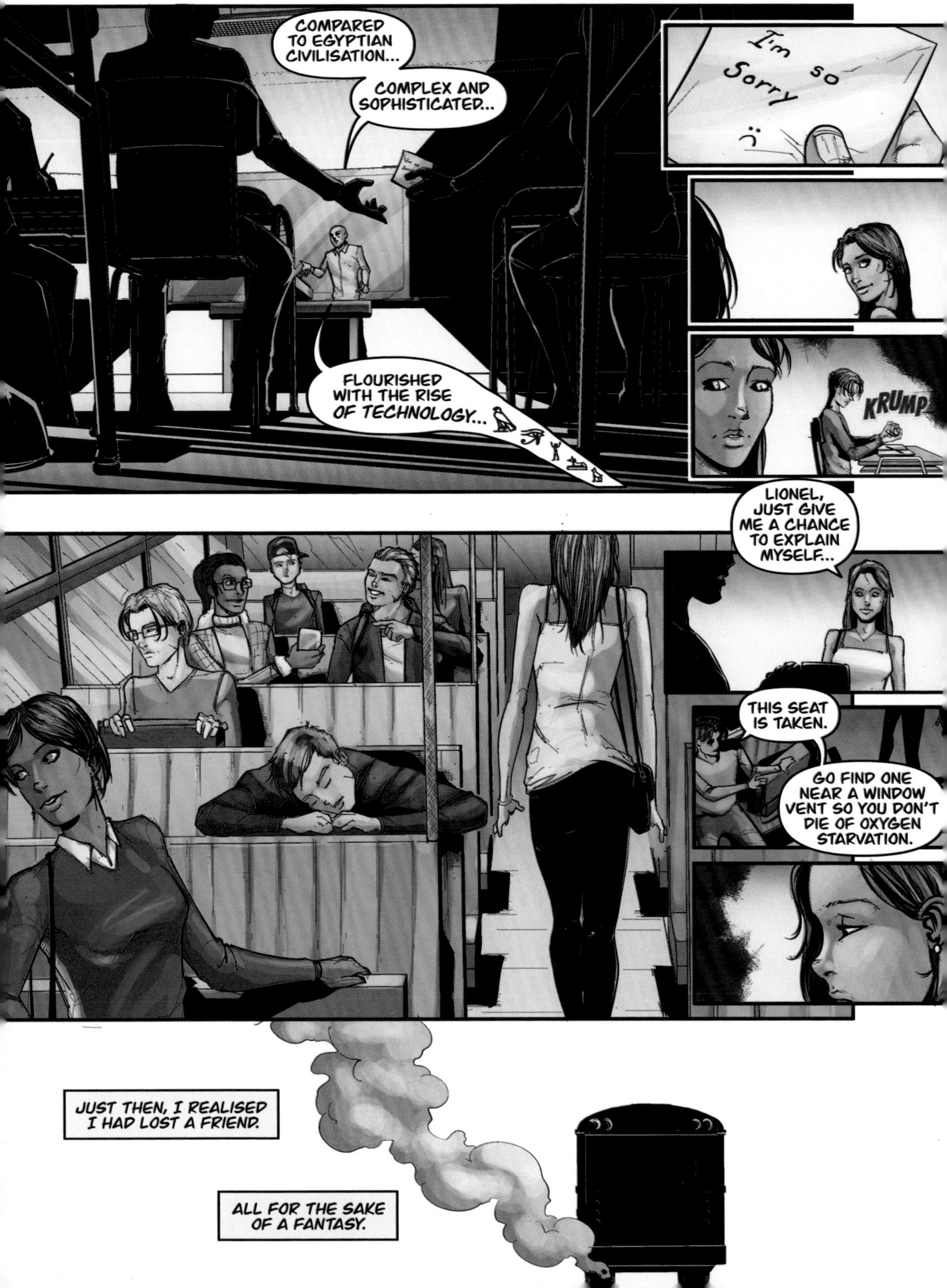

COMPARED TO EGYPTIAN CIVILISATION...
COMPLEX AND SOPHISTICATED...
FLOURISHED WITH THE RISE OF TECHNOLOGY...
I'm so Sorry :(
KRUMP
LIONEL, JUST GIVE ME A CHANCE TO EXPLAIN MYSELF...
THIS SEAT IS TAKEN.
GO FIND ONE NEAR A WINDOW VENT SO YOU DON'T DIE OF OXYGEN STARVATION.
JUST THEN, I REALISED I HAD LOST A FRIEND.
ALL FOR THE SAKE OF A FANTASY.

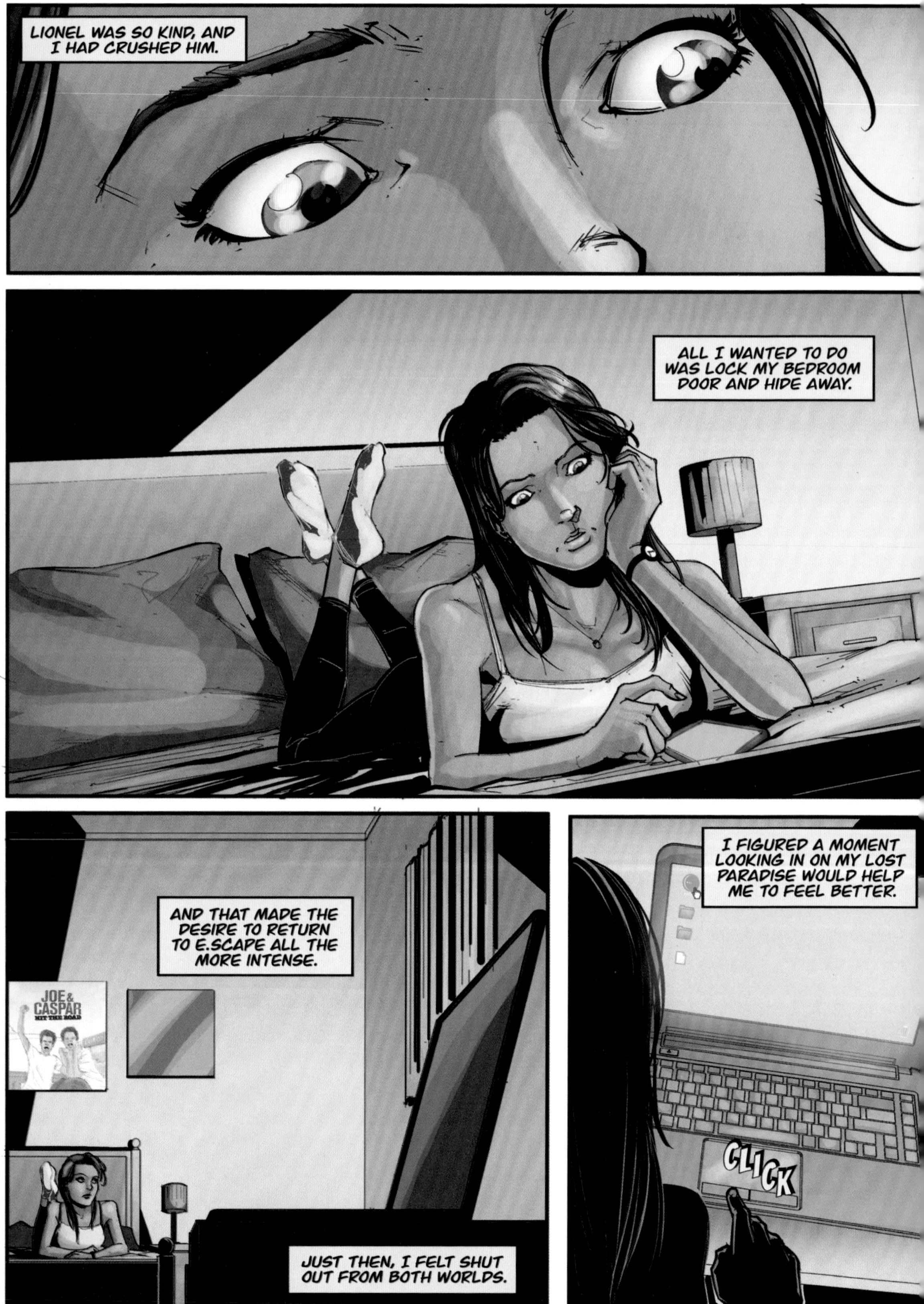
LIONEL WAS SO KIND, AND I HAD CRUSHED HIM.
ALL I WANTED TO DO WAS LOCK MY BEDROOM DOOR AND HIDE AWAY.
AND THAT MADE THE DESIRE TO RETURN TO E.SCAPE ALL THE MORE INTENSE.
JOE & CASPAR HIT THE ROAD
JUST THEN, I FELT SHUT OUT FROM BOTH WORLDS.
I FIGURED A MOMENT LOOKING IN ON MY LOST PARADISE WOULD HELP ME TO FEEL BETTER.
CLICK

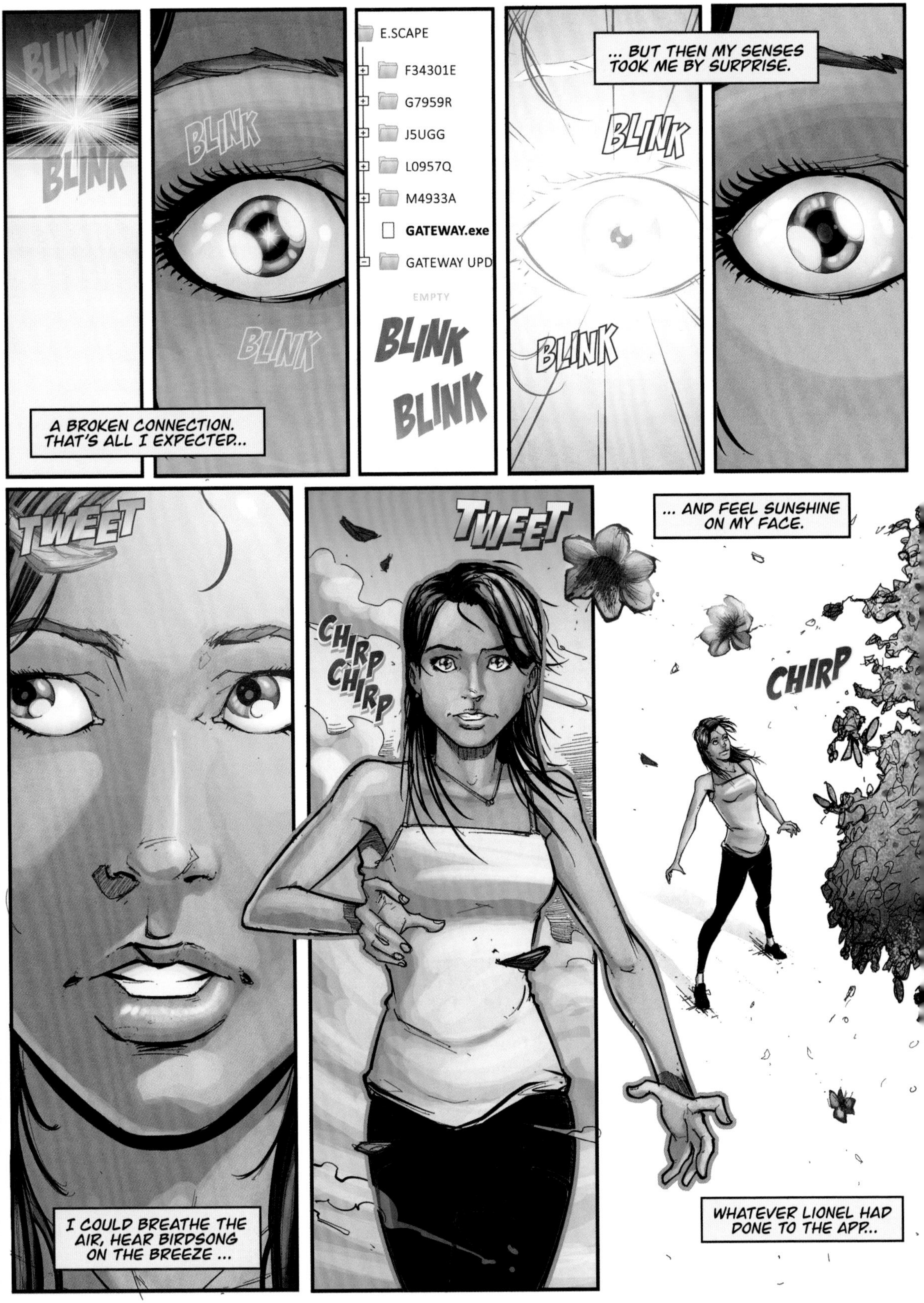
BLINK
BLINK
BLINK
BLINK
A BROKEN CONNECTION. THAT'S ALL I EXPECTED...
E.SCAPE
F34301E
G7959R
J5UGG
L0957Q
M4933A
GATEWAY.exe
GATEWAY UPD
EMPTY
BLINK
BLINK
... BUT THEN MY SENSES TOOK ME BY SURPRISE.
BLINK
BLINK
TWEET
I COULD BREATHE THE AIR, HEAR BIRDSONG ON THE BREEZE ...
TWEET
CHIRP
CHIRP
CHIRP
... AND FEEL SUNSHINE ON MY FACE.
CHIRP
WHATEVER LIONEL HAD DONE TO THE APP...

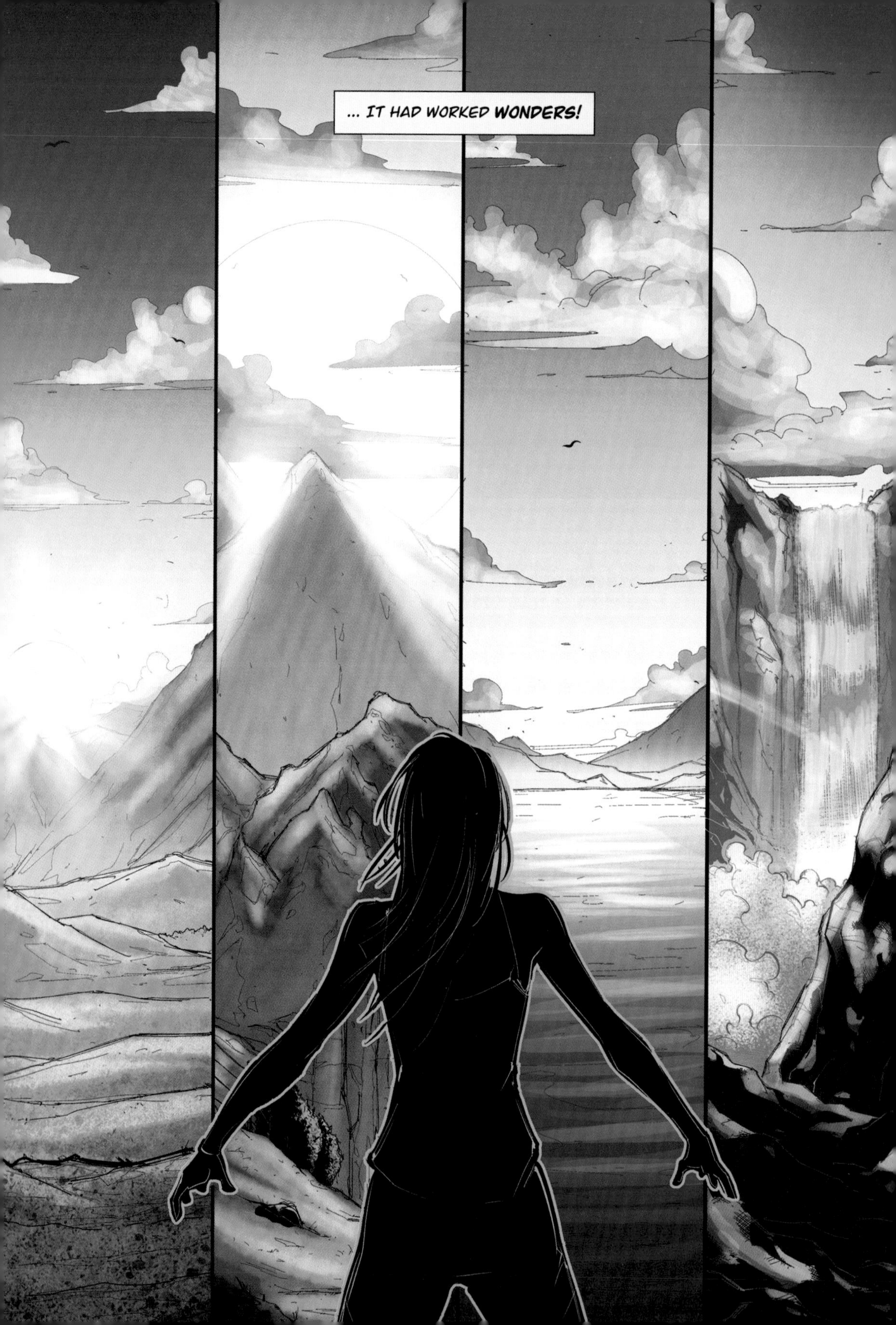
... IT HAD WORKED WONDERS!

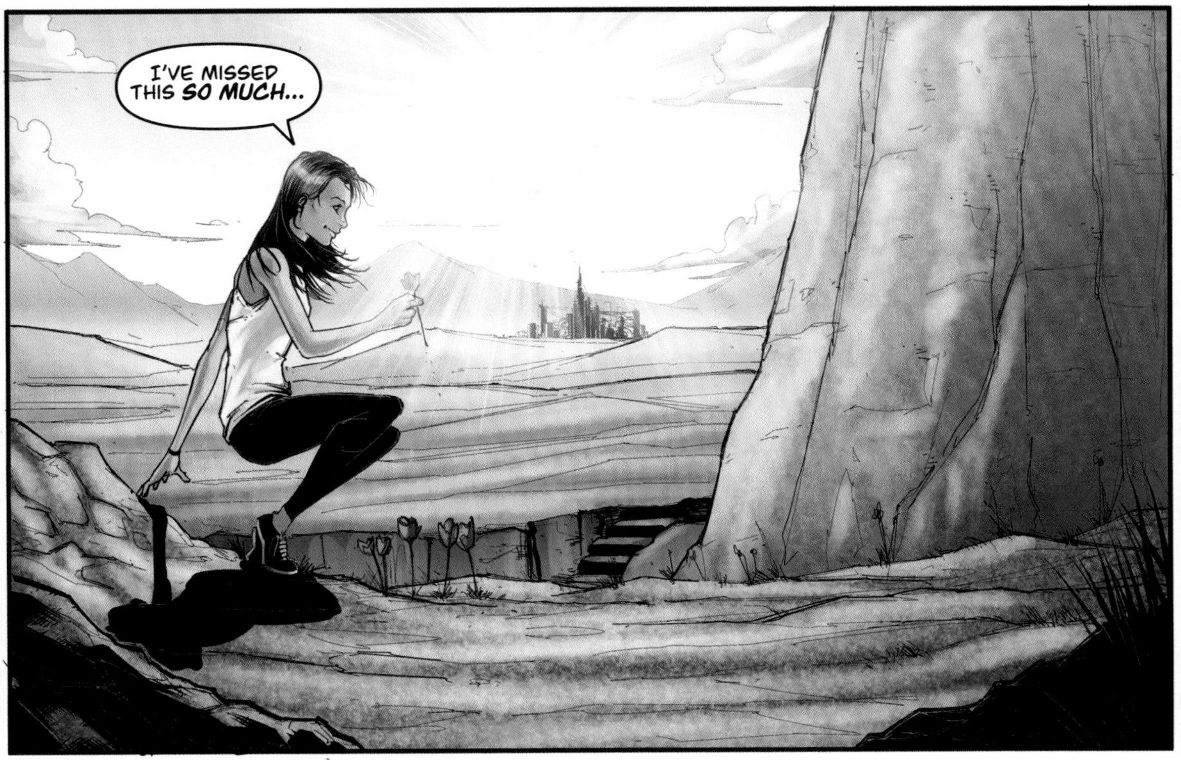
I'VE MISSED THIS SO MUCH...

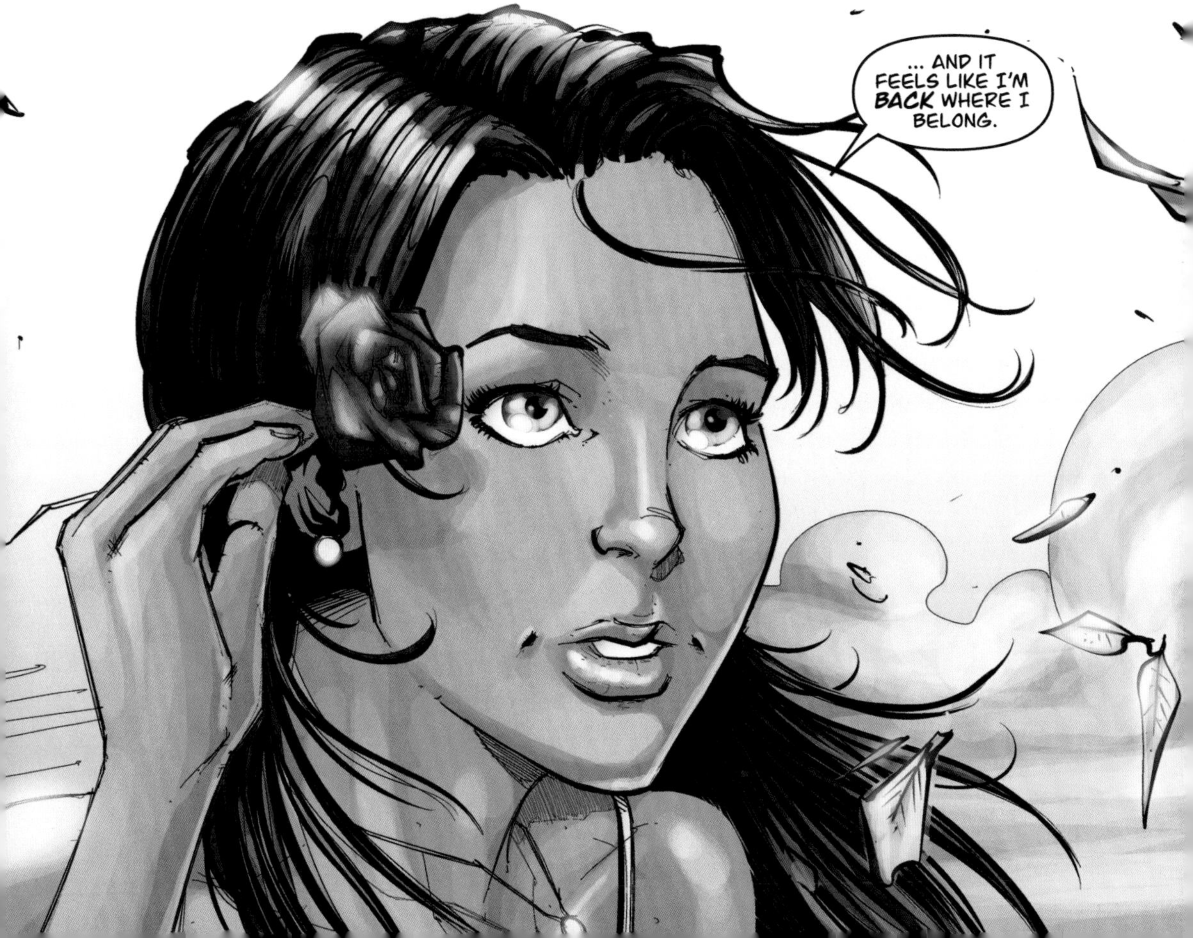
... AND IT FEELS LIKE I'M BACK WHERE I BELONG.

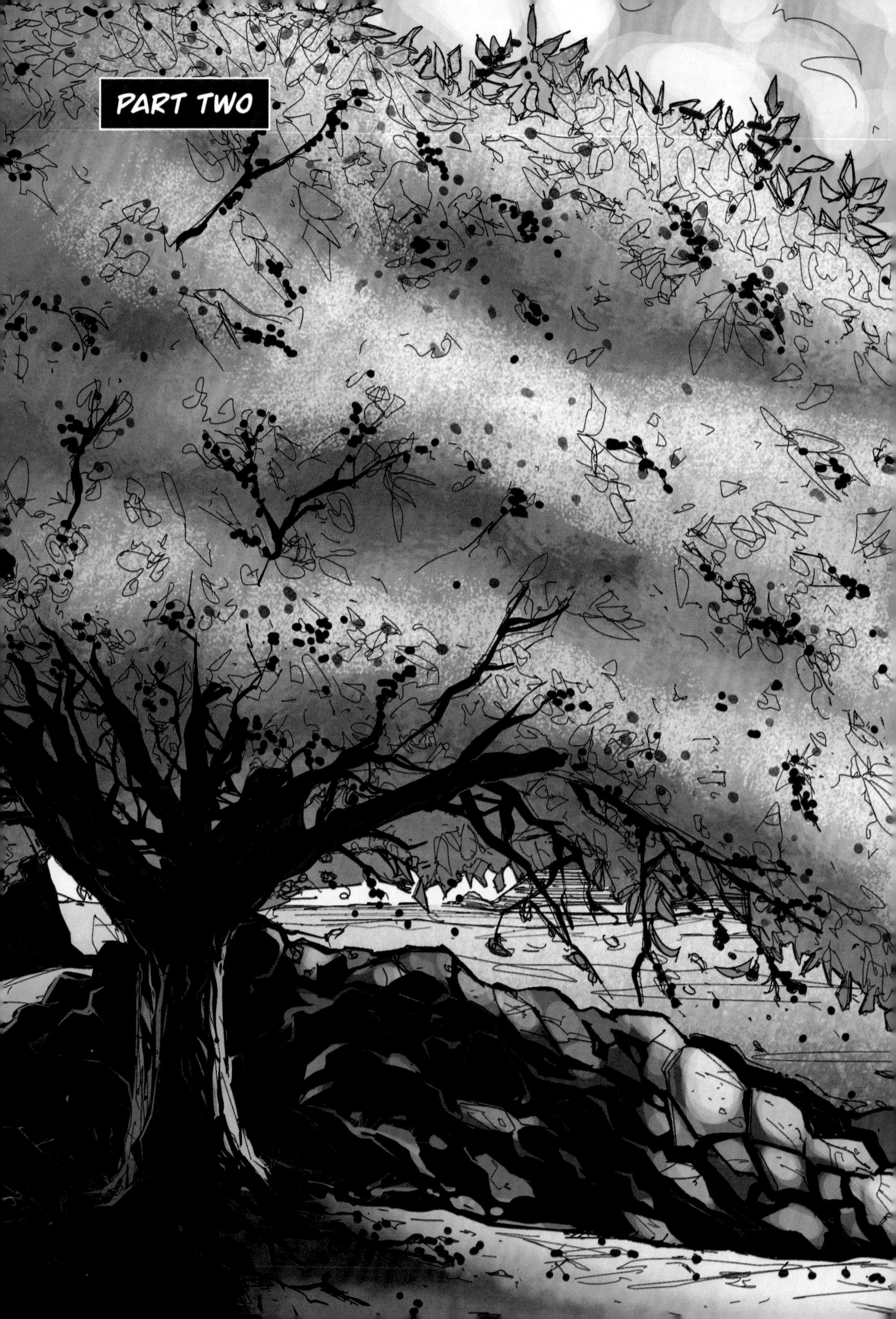
PART TWO

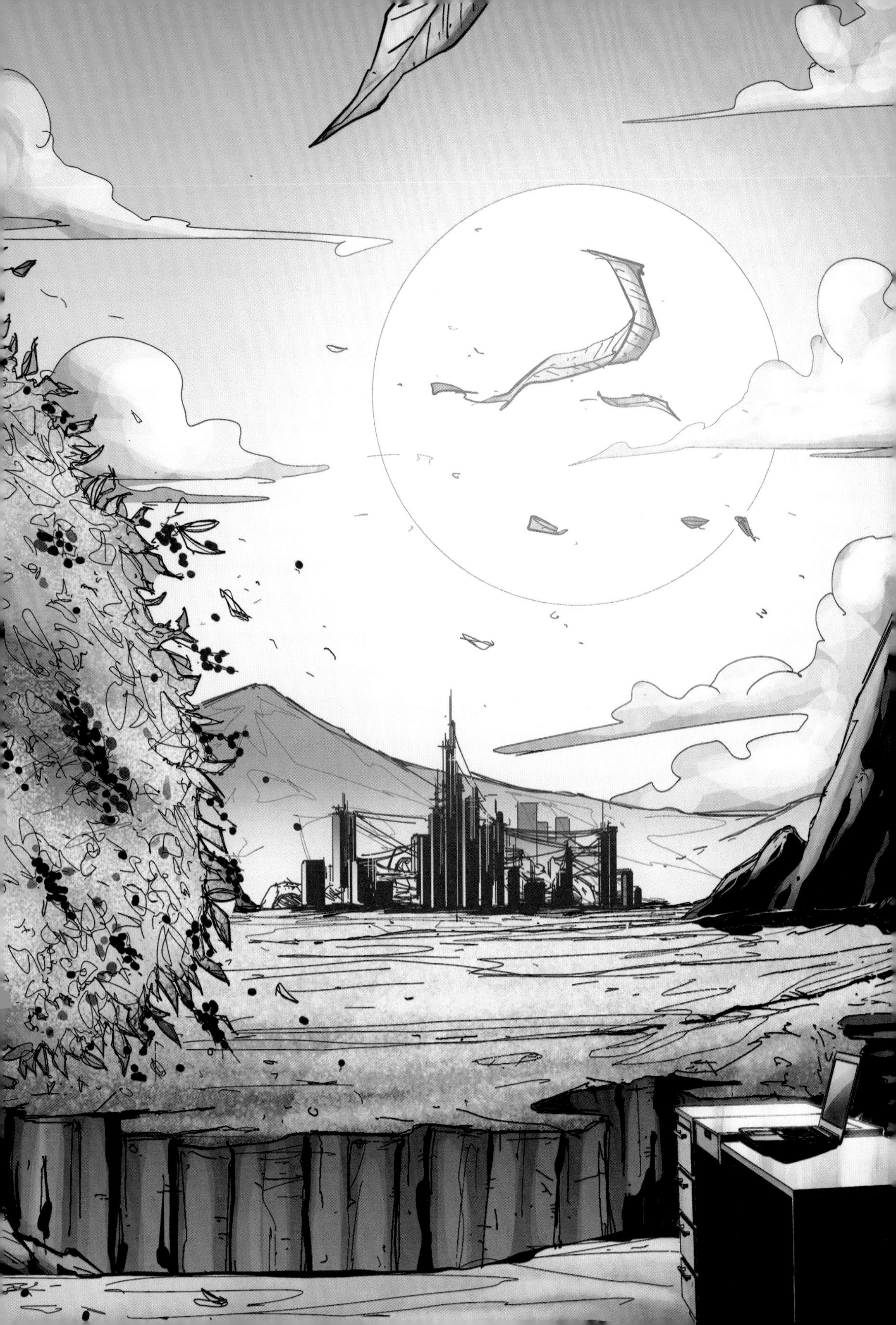

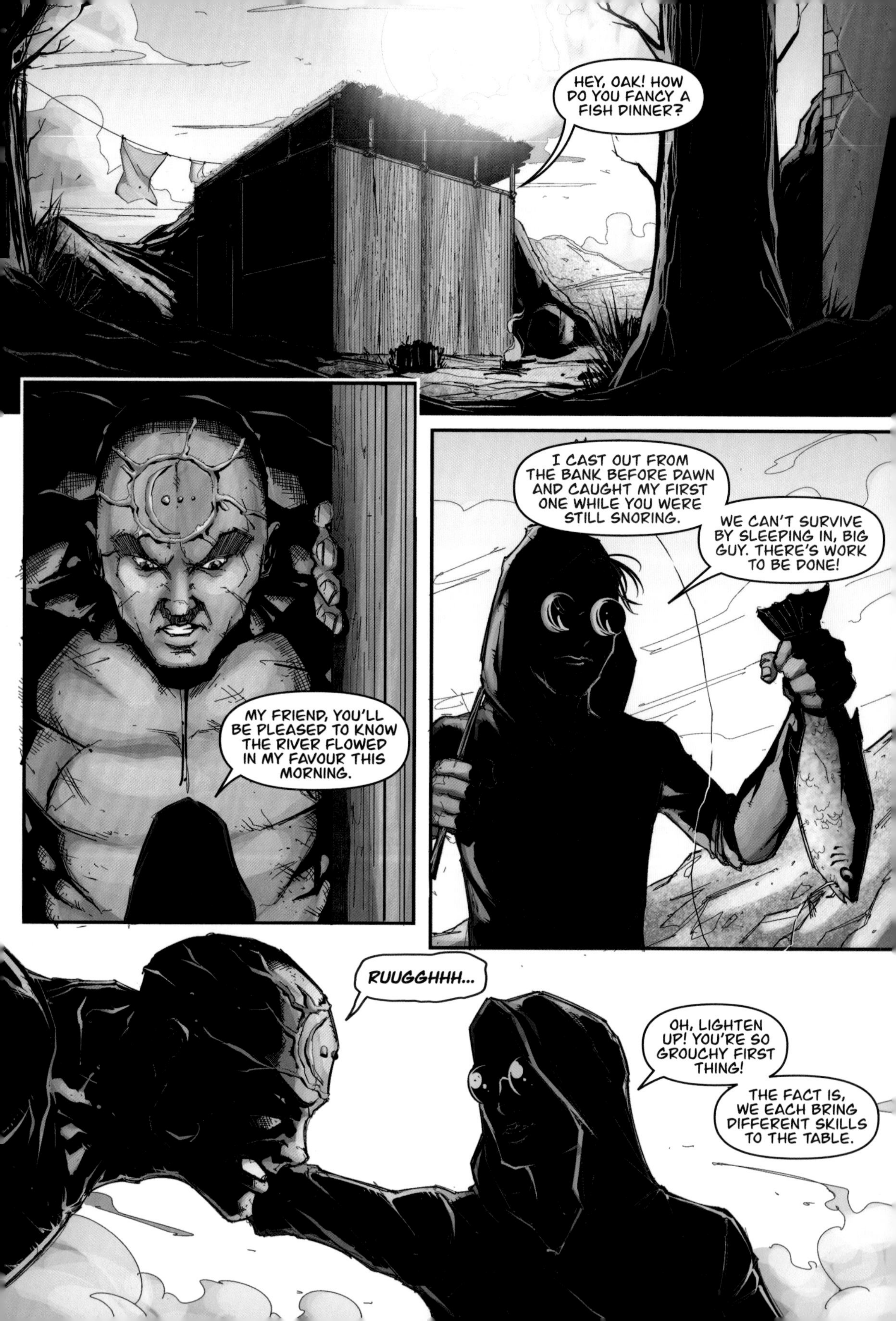
HEY, OAK! HOW DO YOU FANCY A FISH DINNER?
MY FRIEND, YOU'LL BE PLEASED TO KNOW THE RIVER FLOWED IN MY FAVOUR THIS MORNING.
I CAST OUT FROM THE BANK BEFORE DAWN AND CAUGHT MY FIRST ONE WHILE YOU WERE STILL SNORING.
WE CAN'T SURVIVE BY SLEEPING IN, BIG GUY. THERE'S WORK TO BE DONE!
RUUGGHHH...
OH, LIGHTEN UP! YOU'RE SO GROUCHY FIRST THING!
THE FACT IS, WE EACH BRING DIFFERENT SKILLS TO THE TABLE.

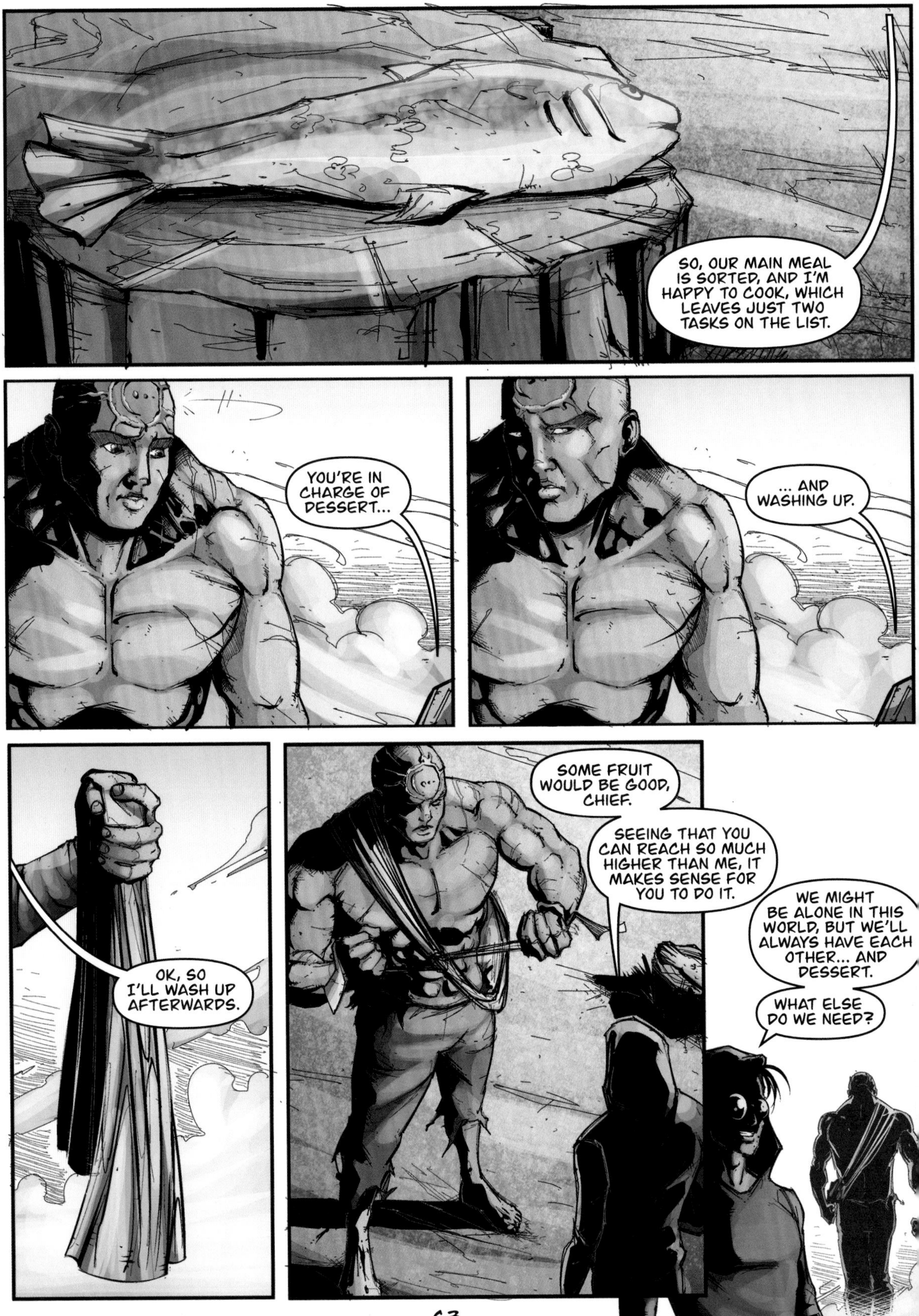
SO, OUR MAIN MEAL IS SORTED, AND I'M HAPPY TO COOK, WHICH LEAVES JUST TWO TASKS ON THE LIST.
YOU'RE IN CHARGE OF DESSERT...
... AND WASHING UP.
OK, SO I'LL WASH UP AFTERWARDS.
SOME FRUIT WOULD BE GOOD, CHIEF.
SEEING THAT YOU CAN REACH SO MUCH HIGHER THAN ME, IT MAKES SENSE FOR YOU TO DO IT.
WE MIGHT BE ALONE IN THIS WORLD, BUT WE'LL ALWAYS HAVE EACH OTHER... AND DESSERT.
WHAT ELSE DO WE NEED?

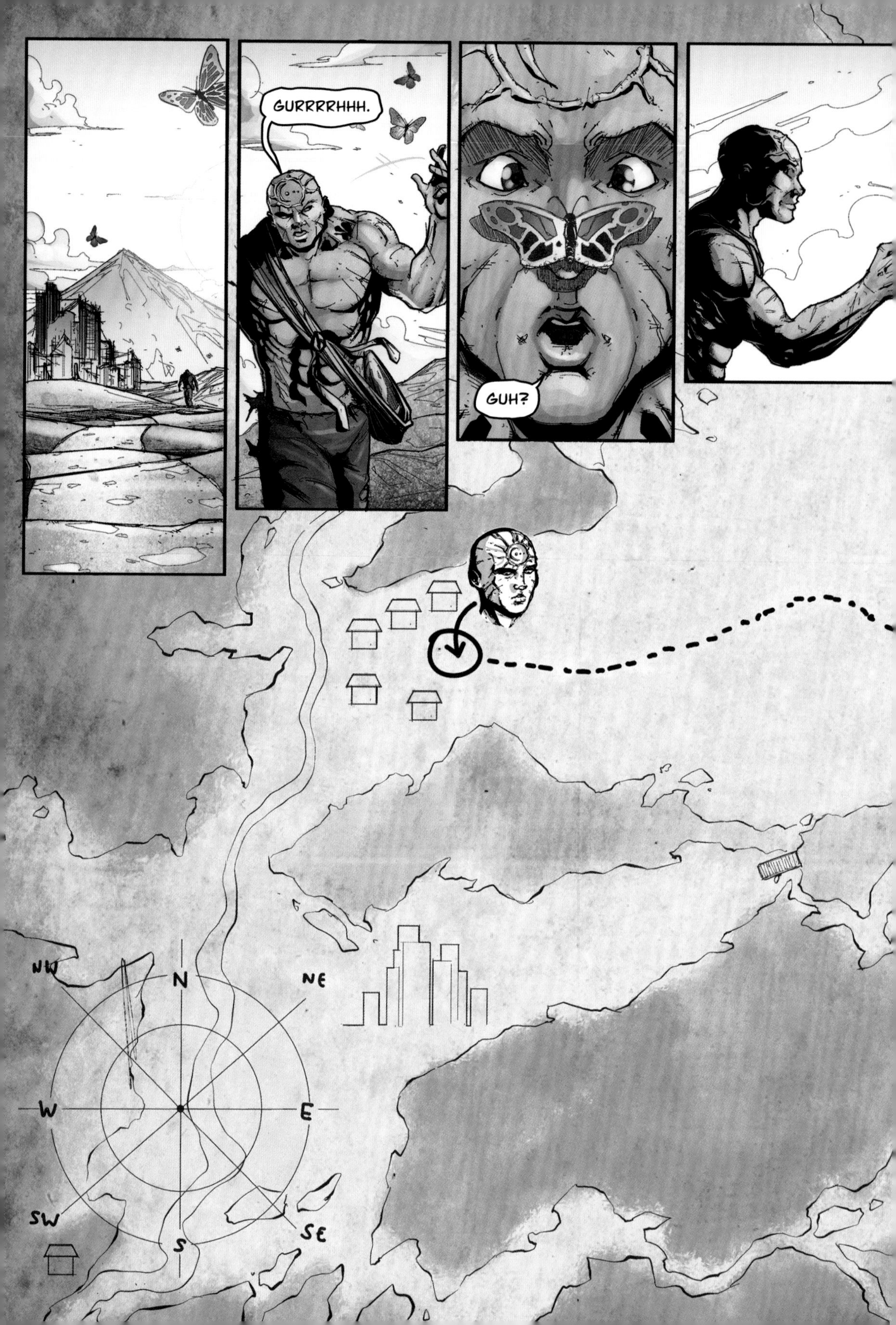
GURRRRHHH.
GUH?
N
NW
NE
W
E
SW
SE
S

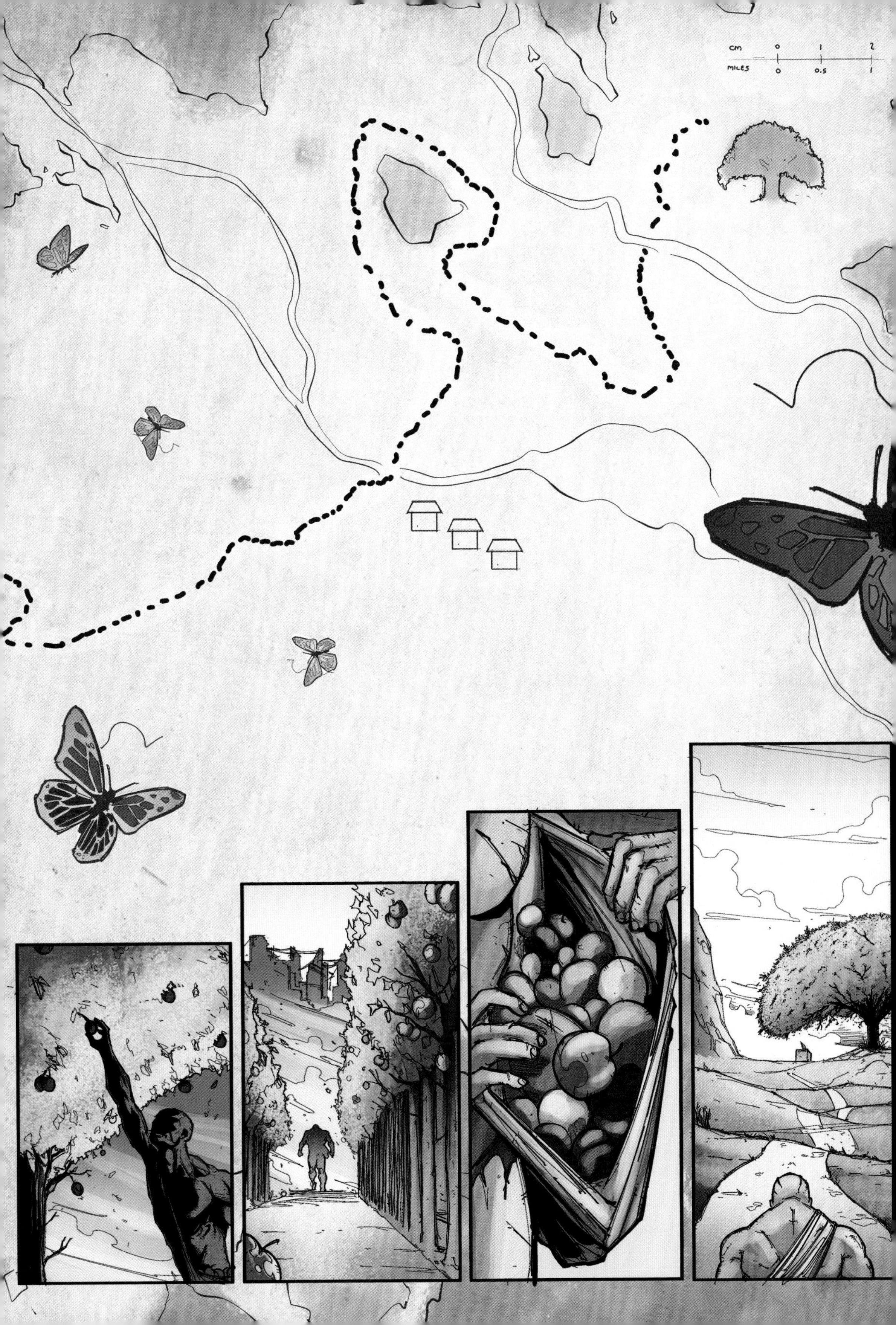
CM 0 1 2
MILES 0 0.5 1

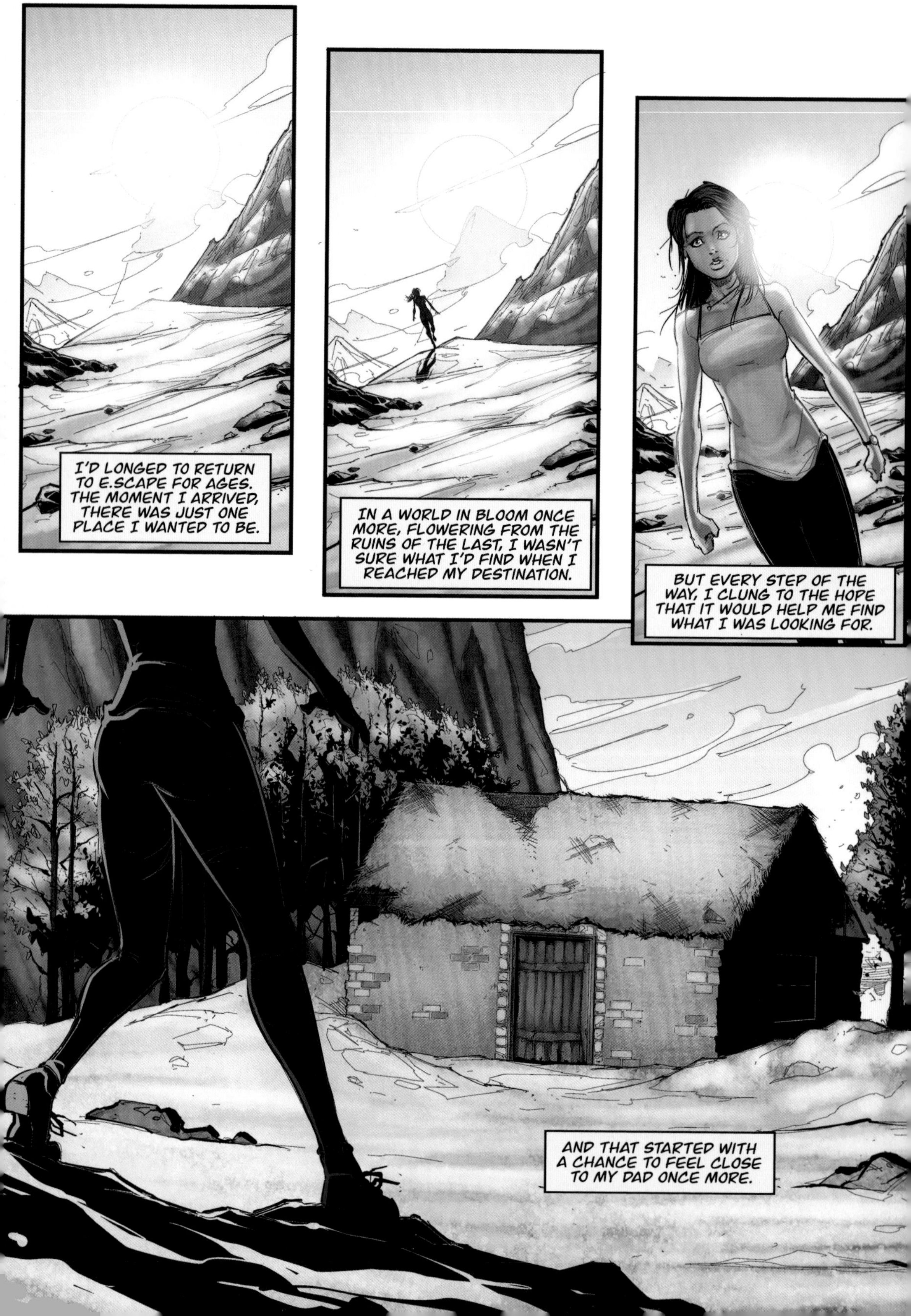
I'D LONGED TO RETURN TO E.SCAPE FOR AGES. THE MOMENT I ARRIVED, THERE WAS JUST ONE PLACE I WANTED TO BE.
IN A WORLD IN BLOOM ONCE MORE, FLOWERING FROM THE RUINS OF THE LAST, I WASN'T SURE WHAT I'D FIND WHEN I REACHED MY DESTINATION.
BUT EVERY STEP OF THE WAY, I CLUNG TO THE HOPE THAT IT WOULD HELP ME FIND WHAT I WAS LOOKING FOR.
AND THAT STARTED WITH A CHANCE TO FEEL CLOSE TO MY DAD ONCE MORE.

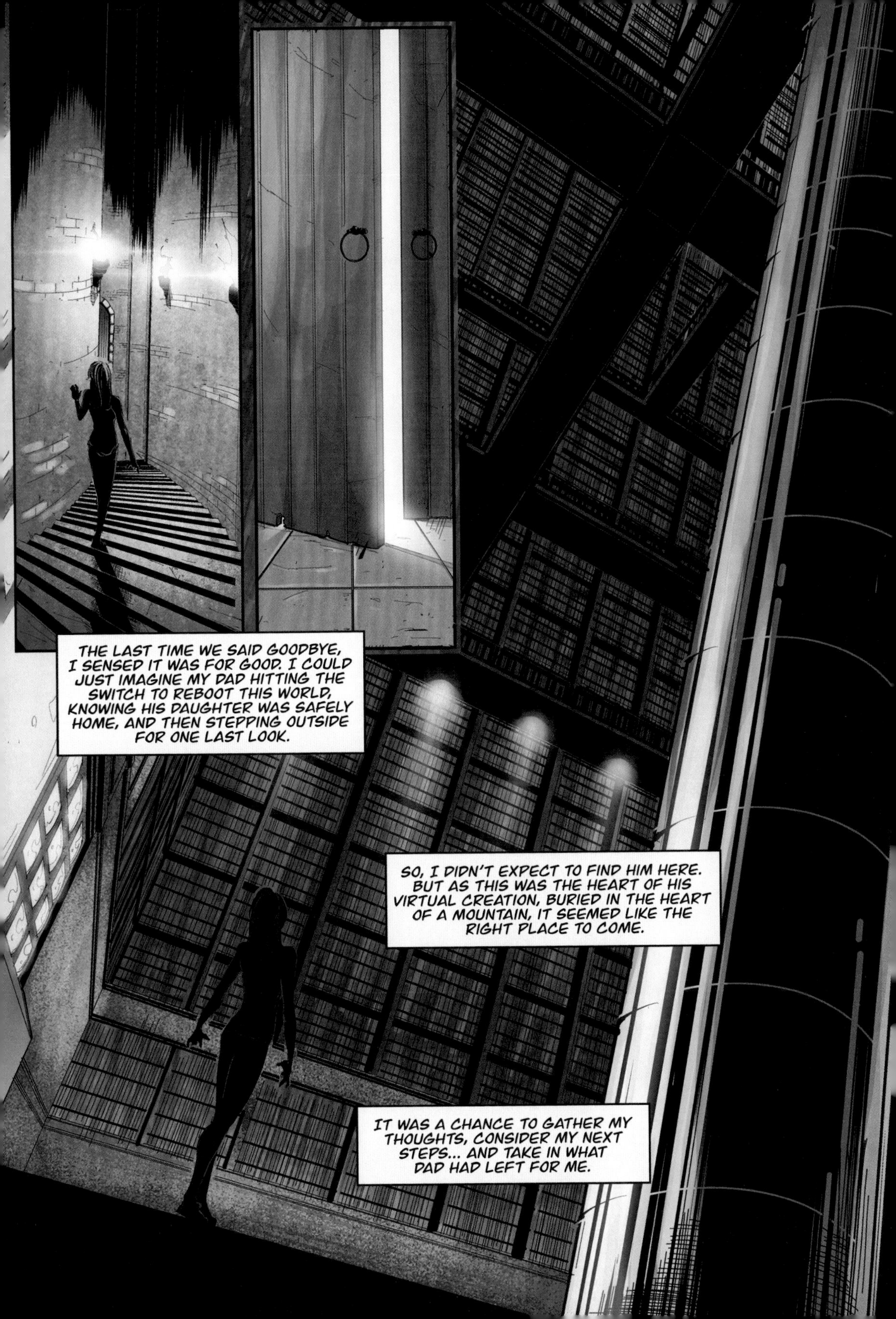
THE LAST TIME WE SAID GOODBYE, I SENSED IT WAS FOR GOOD. I COULD JUST IMAGINE MY DAD HITTING THE SWITCH TO REBOOT THIS WORLD, KNOWING HIS DAUGHTER WAS SAFELY HOME, AND THEN STEPPING OUTSIDE FOR ONE LAST LOOK.
SO, I DIDN'T EXPECT TO FIND HIM HERE. BUT AS THIS WAS THE HEART OF HIS VIRTUAL CREATION, BURIED IN THE HEART OF A MOUNTAIN, IT SEEMED LIKE THE RIGHT PLACE TO COME.
IT WAS A CHANCE TO GATHER MY THOUGHTS, CONSIDER MY NEXT STEPS... AND TAKE IN WHAT DAD HAD LEFT FOR ME.

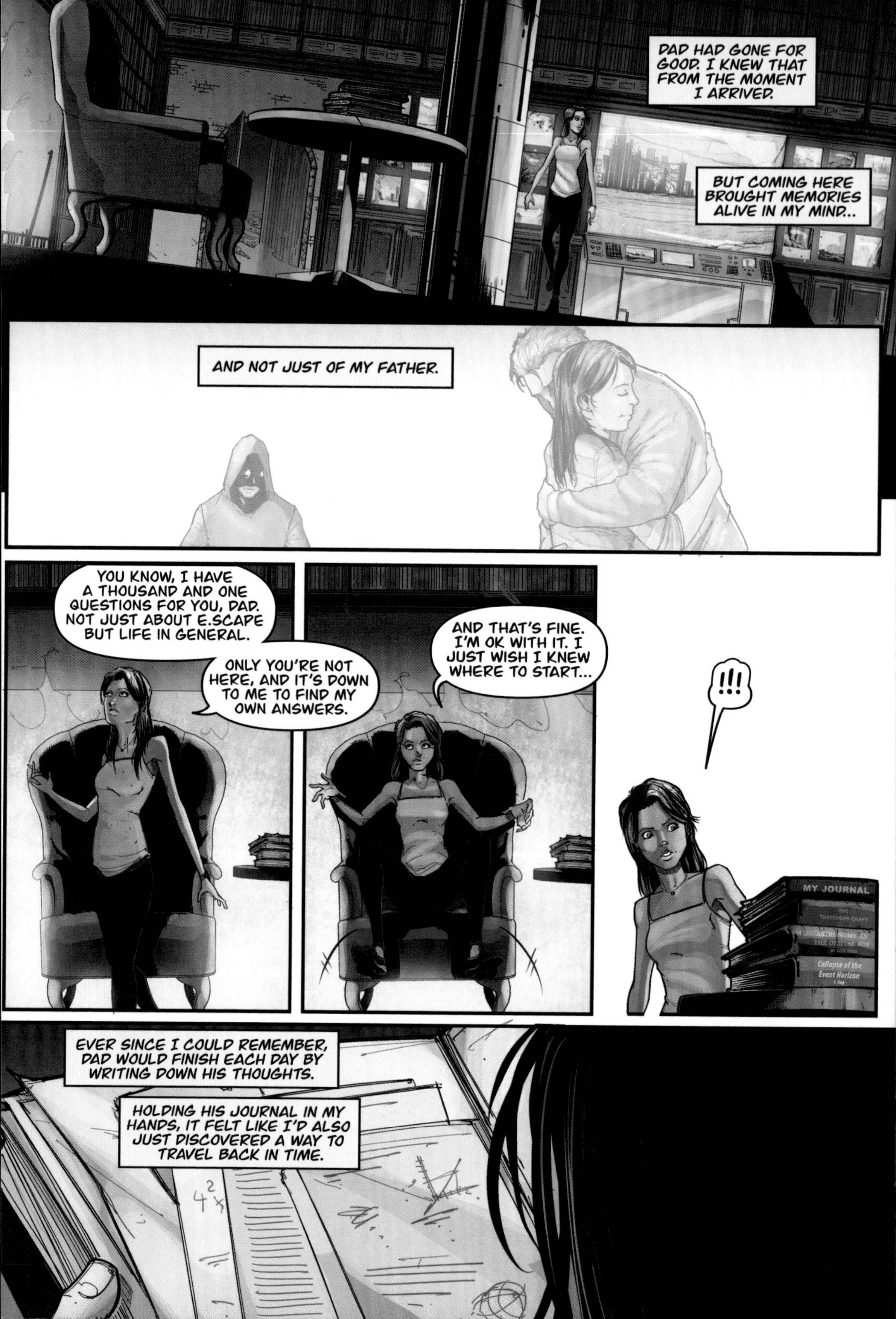
DAD HAD GONE FOR GOOD. I KNEW THAT FROM THE MOMENT I ARRIVED.
BUT COMING HERE BROUGHT MEMORIES ALIVE IN MY MIND...
AND NOT JUST OF MY FATHER.
YOU KNOW, I HAVE A THOUSAND AND ONE QUESTIONS FOR YOU, DAD. NOT JUST ABOUT E.SCAPE BUT LIFE IN GENERAL.
ONLY YOU'RE NOT HERE, AND IT'S DOWN TO ME TO FIND MY OWN ANSWERS.
AND THAT'S FINE. I'M OK WITH IT. I JUST WISH I KNEW WHERE TO START...
!!!
MY JOURNAL
THE THATCHERS CRAFT
ASTRONOMY IN THE DIGITAL AGE
Collapse of the Event Horizon
EVER SINCE I COULD REMEMBER, DAD WOULD FINISH EACH DAY BY WRITING DOWN HIS THOUGHTS.
HOLDING HIS JOURNAL IN MY HANDS, IT FELT LIKE I'D ALSO JUST DISCOVERED A WAY TO TRAVEL BACK IN TIME.

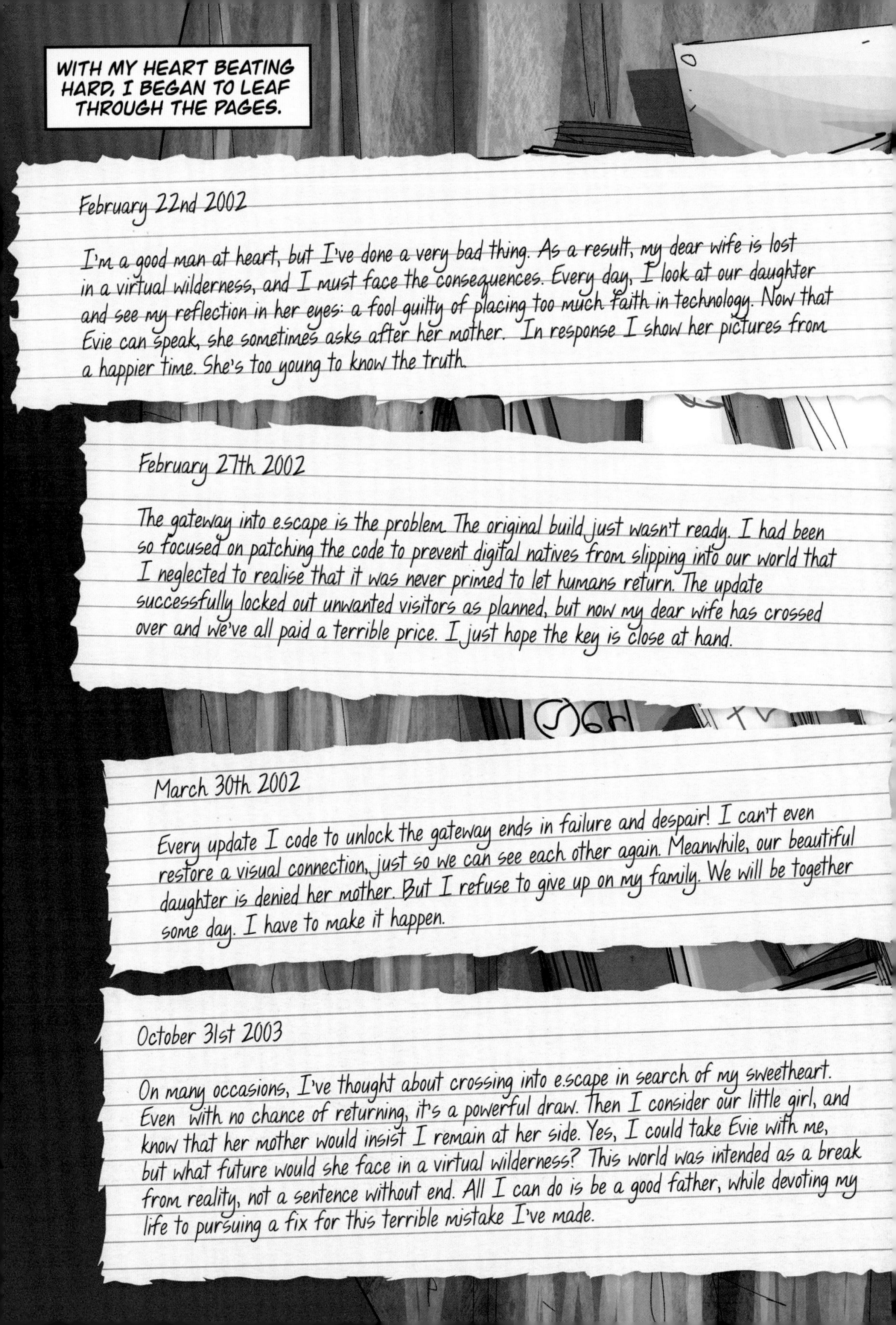
WITH MY HEART BEATING HARD, I BEGAN TO LEAF THROUGH THE PAGES.
February 22nd 2002
I'm a good man at heart, but I've done a very bad thing. As a result, my dear wife is lost in a virtual wilderness, and I must face the consequences. Every day, I look at our daughter and see my reflection in her eyes: a fool guilty of placing too much faith in technology. Now that Evie can speak, she sometimes asks after her mother. In response I show her pictures from a happier time. She's too young to know the truth.
February 27th 2002
The gateway into e.scape is the problem. The original build just wasn't ready. I had been so focused on patching the code to prevent digital natives from slipping into our world that I neglected to realise that it was never primed to let humans return. The update successfully locked out unwanted visitors as planned, but now my dear wife has crossed over and we've all paid a terrible price. I just hope the key is close at hand.
March 30th 2002
Every update I code to unlock the gateway ends in failure and despair! I can't even restore a visual connection, just so we can see each other again. Meanwhile, our beautiful daughter is denied her mother. But I refuse to give up on my family. We will be together some day. I have to make it happen.
October 31st 2003
On many occasions, I've thought about crossing into e.scape in search of my sweetheart. Even with no chance of returning, it's a powerful draw. Then I consider our little girl, and know that her mother would insist I remain at her side. Yes, I could take Evie with me, but what future would she face in a virtual wilderness? This world was intended as a break from reality, not a sentence without end. All I can do is be a good father, while devoting my life to pursuing a fix for this terrible mistake I've made.

December 24th 2003

The festive season is upon us once again. Unlike the last dark years, I'm hoping the surprise
I have in store will light up Evie's life. For I've created a chat interface that might just connect
us to her mum. It's a long shot, but I can only think that every day my wife must return to the
place where she arrived in e.scape - hoping to come home. The virtual laptop she'll find there won't
bring her back just yet. Even so, she can open up a message window on my screen so we can chat
- and take comfort in the fact that we're with her in spirit.

March 7th, 2004

Another year and this nightmare continues. The message window is permanently open on
my screen. I dream of the moment that letters and words appear as she types them from
her virtual keyboard. I am ready to reply, but the cursor just blinks and blinks - marking
every second of this seemingly endless sentence that keeps us apart.

September 13th 2005

Evie started school this week. I'm so proud of her (even if she did get on the wrong bus
on her first day) and know her mum would feel the same way. When I'm not working on
the gateway, I find myself blending photographs of how our daughter looks today with
images of me and her mother from our time together. Some are so good that for a moment
I'm convinced they're real. It comes as a comfort, until my attention returns to the
accursed code. I will crack this!

April 9th 2006

'Is she dead?' asked Evie yesterday, which took me completely by surprise.
I couldn't answer her for tears, which told her everything I would wish
her to know right now.

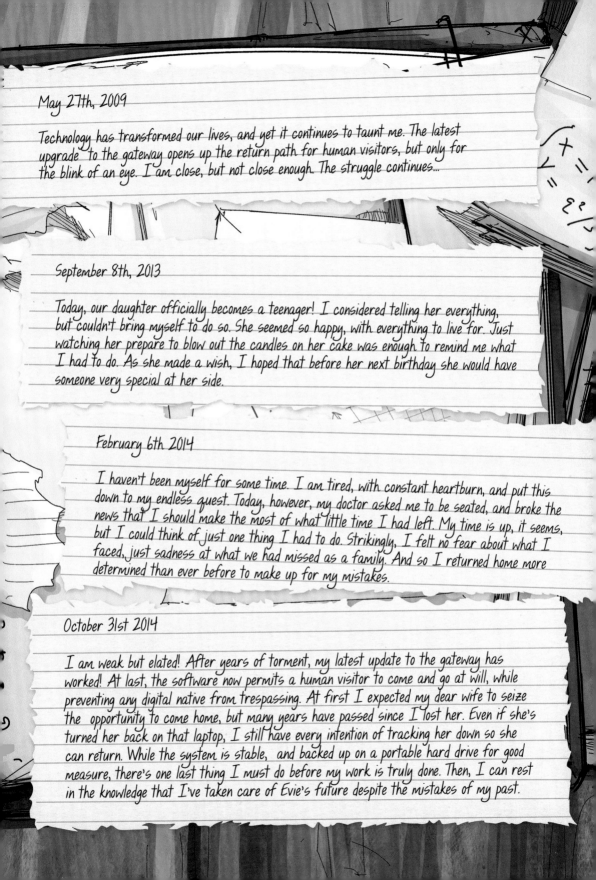

May 27th, 2009

Technology has transformed our lives, and yet it continues to taunt me. The latest upgrade to the gateway opens up the return path for human visitors, but only for the blink of an eye. I am close, but not close enough. The struggle continues...

September 8th, 2013

Today, our daughter officially becomes a teenager! I considered telling her everything, but couldn't bring myself to do so. She seemed so happy, with everything to live for. Just watching her prepare to blow out the candles on her cake was enough to remind me what I had to do. As she made a wish, I hoped that before her next birthday she would have someone very special at her side.

February 6th 2014

I haven't been myself for some time. I am tired, with constant heartburn, and put this down to my endless quest. Today, however, my doctor asked me to be seated, and broke the news that I should make the most of what little time I had left. My time is up, it seems, but I could think of just one thing I had to do. Strikingly, I felt no fear about what I faced, just sadness at what we had missed as a family. And so I returned home more determined than ever before to make up for my mistakes.

October 31st 2014

I am weak but elated! After years of torment, my latest update to the gateway has worked! At last, the software now permits a human visitor to come and go at will, while preventing any digital native from trespassing. At first I expected my dear wife to seize the opportunity to come home, but many years have passed since I lost her. Even if she's turned her back on that laptop, I still have every intention of tracking her down so she can return. While the system is stable, and backed up on a portable hard drive for good measure, there's one last thing I must do before my work is truly done. Then, I can rest in the knowledge that I've taken care of Evie's future despite the mistakes of my past.

June 17th, 2015

Evie knows I'm dying now. I can't hide that from her any more. Even so, she's determined that life at home goes on as normal, which is exactly as I wish it to be. I'll always be with her in spirit, just as I am with her mother. And soon I hope the time will come when Evie feels closer to us both. I have now recorded instructions that will guide her to e.scape when she's ready. There, in a realm programmed to reflect her personality, she will find a sanctuary. A place to rest and recharge so she might make the most of her life in the real world.

$$\int \frac{d^2}{d}$$

September 10th, 2015

Until now I've always kept this journal safely tucked away under the water tank in the loft. Evie will read it one day, no doubt, but that has to be in the right time and place. And so, having stashed the portable hard drive in my favourite hiding place (for I'm no longer a man who takes risks), I now find myself facing the webcam with the book in my lap. The undertaking has exhausted me, but I'm ready at last to make my final journey. I've left instructions for Evie, but I won't say goodbye. Why? Because we will see each other again.

I just hope that I can say the same thing about my poor, beloved wife. For she has to be out there somewhere - adrift in a virtual world - awaiting a connection.

Final update

Time moves differently here in e.scape. It feels like I have been here for an eternity, and yet I know the end is near. Evie has arrived, but a corrupting influence followed her. No doubt her cousin, Mallory, will change for the better on their return, but it leaves me to take drastic digital measures. We've said our goodbyes, and in a moment from now I must wipe all life from the surface of e.scape in order to reboot it. Even if it means letting go of those she found here, my final wish is that my daughter might come back one day - and find the sun shining again.

For with light, there is hope. And should you find yourself reading these last words of mine, Evie, maybe you will understand why I never gave in to darkness.

Dad X

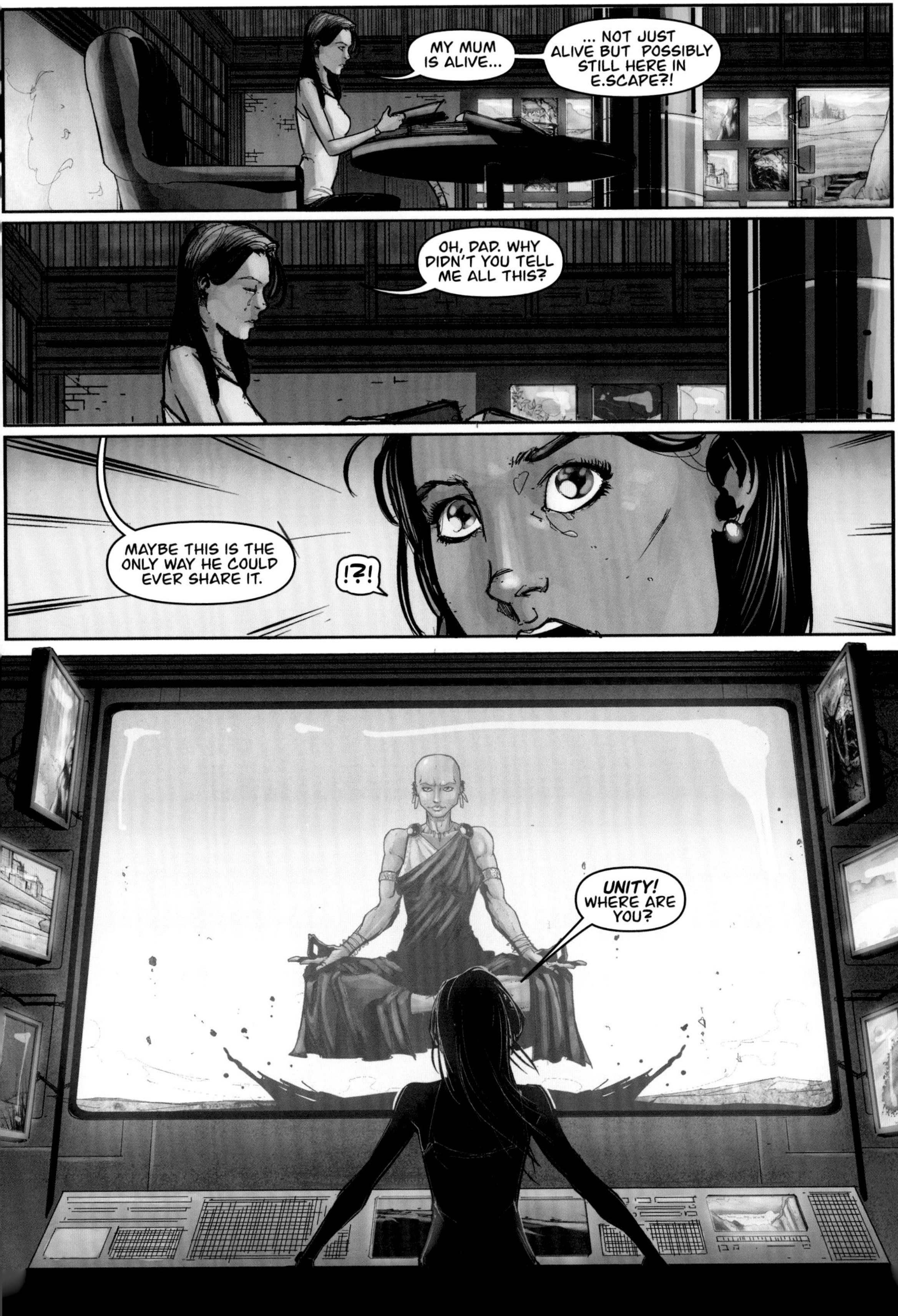
MY MUM IS ALIVE...
... NOT JUST ALIVE BUT POSSIBLY STILL HERE IN E.SCAPE?!
OH, DAD. WHY DIDN'T YOU TELL ME ALL THIS?
MAYBE THIS IS THE ONLY WAY HE COULD EVER SHARE IT.
!?!
UNITY! WHERE ARE YOU?

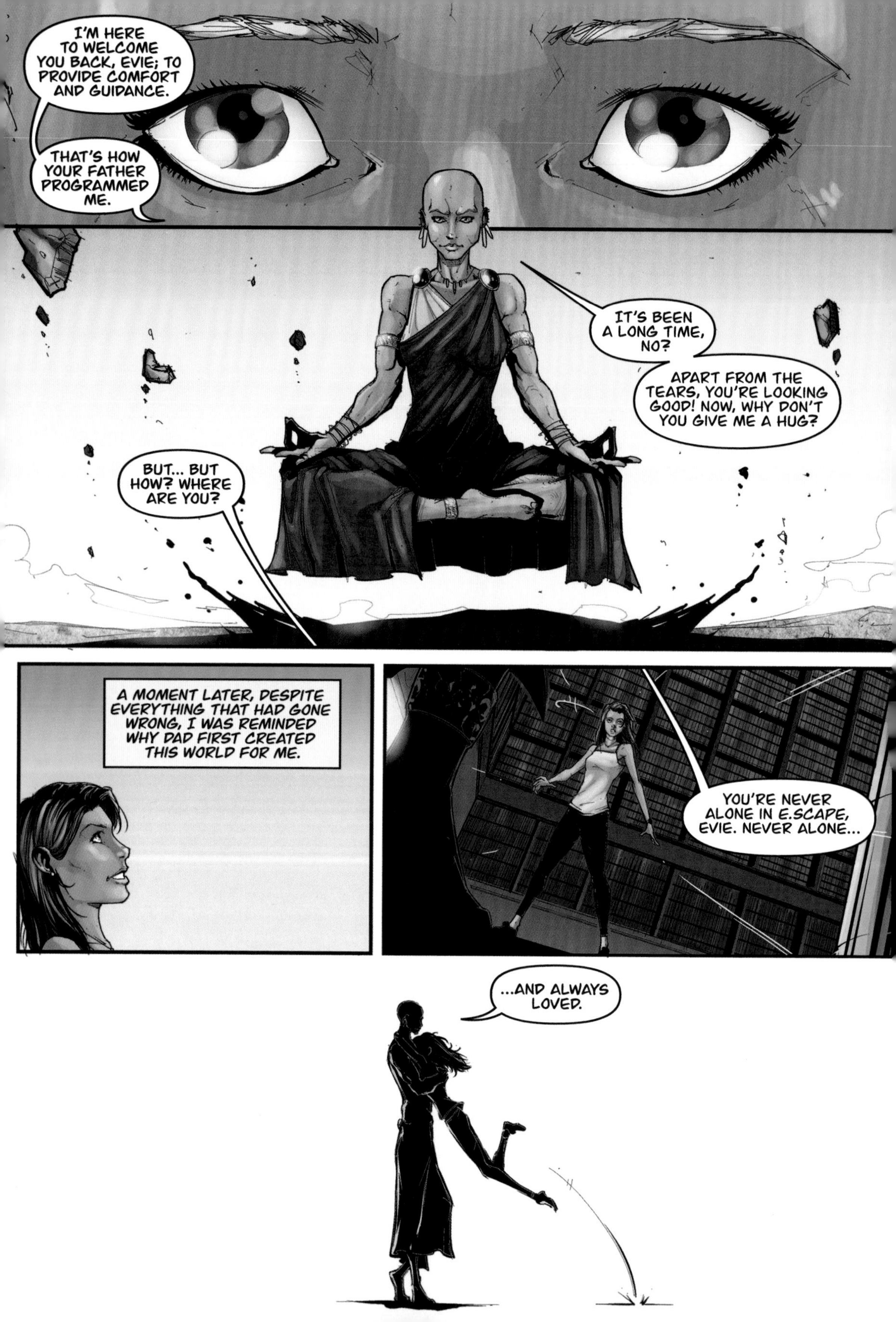
I'M HERE TO WELCOME YOU BACK, EVIE; TO PROVIDE COMFORT AND GUIDANCE.
THAT'S HOW YOUR FATHER PROGRAMMED ME.
IT'S BEEN A LONG TIME, NO?
APART FROM THE TEARS, YOU'RE LOOKING GOOD! NOW, WHY DON'T YOU GIVE ME A HUG?
BUT... BUT HOW? WHERE ARE YOU?
A MOMENT LATER, DESPITE EVERYTHING THAT HAD GONE WRONG, I WAS REMINDED WHY DAD FIRST CREATED THIS WORLD FOR ME.
YOU'RE NEVER ALONE IN E.SCAPE, EVIE. NEVER ALONE...
...AND ALWAYS LOVED.

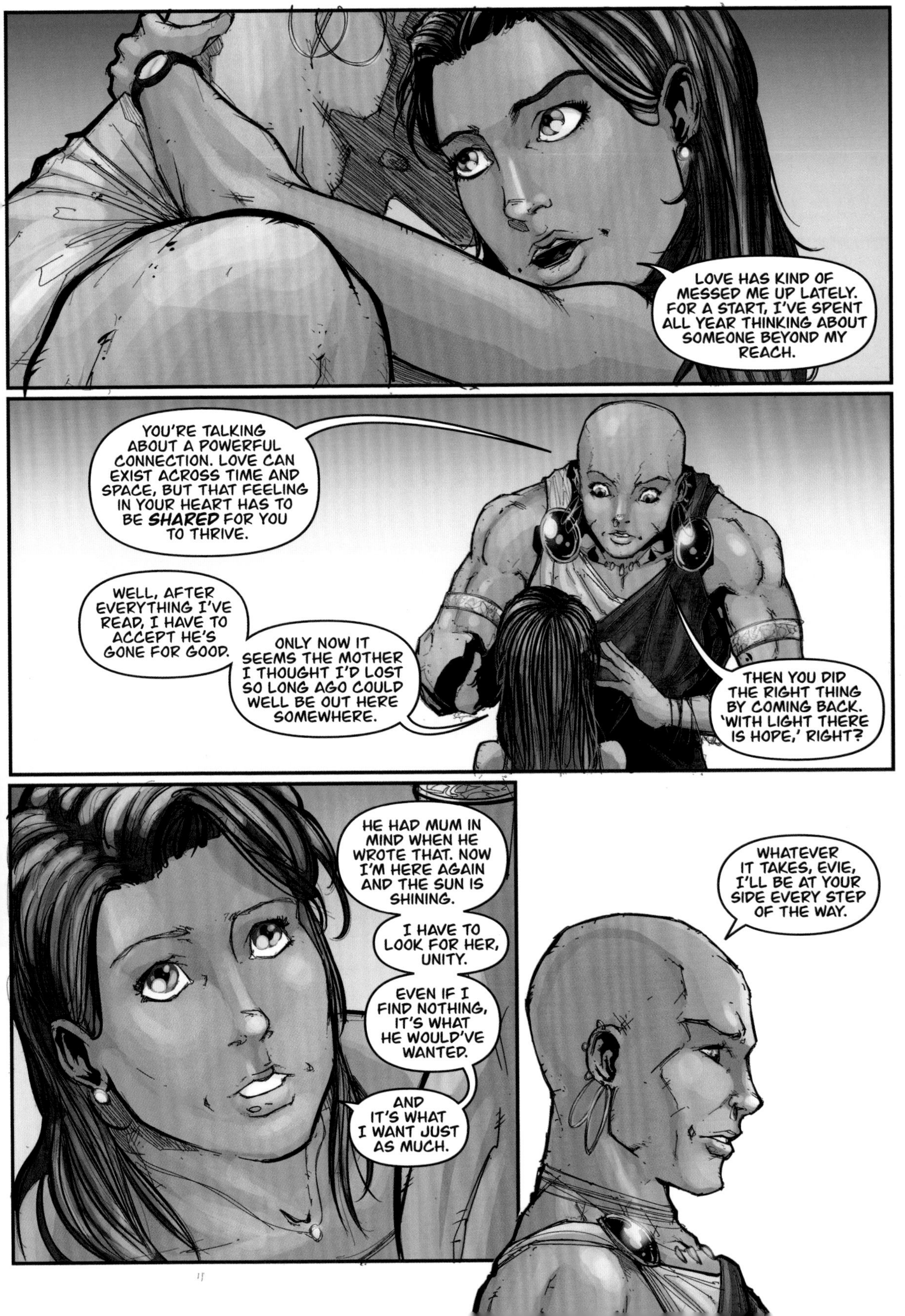
LOVE HAS KIND OF MESSED ME UP LATELY. FOR A START, I'VE SPENT ALL YEAR THINKING ABOUT SOMEONE BEYOND MY REACH.
YOU'RE TALKING ABOUT A POWERFUL CONNECTION. LOVE CAN EXIST ACROSS TIME AND SPACE, BUT THAT FEELING IN YOUR HEART HAS TO BE SHARED FOR YOU TO THRIVE.
WELL, AFTER EVERYTHING I'VE READ, I HAVE TO ACCEPT HE'S GONE FOR GOOD.
ONLY NOW IT SEEMS THE MOTHER I THOUGHT I'D LOST SO LONG AGO COULD WELL BE OUT HERE SOMEWHERE.
THEN YOU DID THE RIGHT THING BY COMING BACK. 'WITH LIGHT THERE IS HOPE,' RIGHT?
HE HAD MUM IN MIND WHEN HE WROTE THAT. NOW I'M HERE AGAIN AND THE SUN IS SHINING.
I HAVE TO LOOK FOR HER, UNITY.
EVEN IF I FIND NOTHING, IT'S WHAT HE WOULD'VE WANTED.
AND IT'S WHAT I WANT JUST AS MUCH.
WHATEVER IT TAKES, EVIE, I'LL BE AT YOUR SIDE EVERY STEP OF THE WAY.

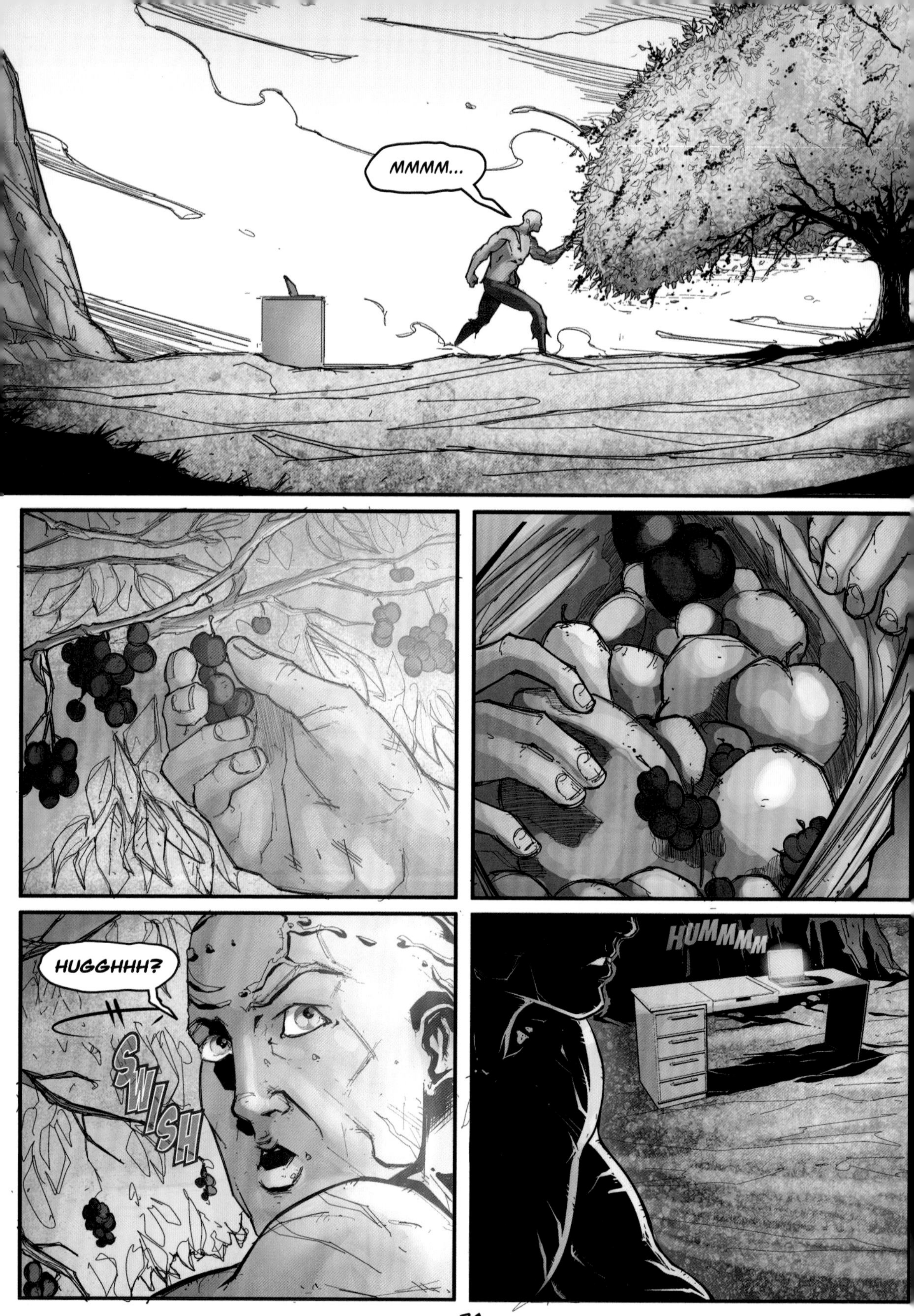
MMMM...
HUGGHHH?
SWISH
HUMMMM

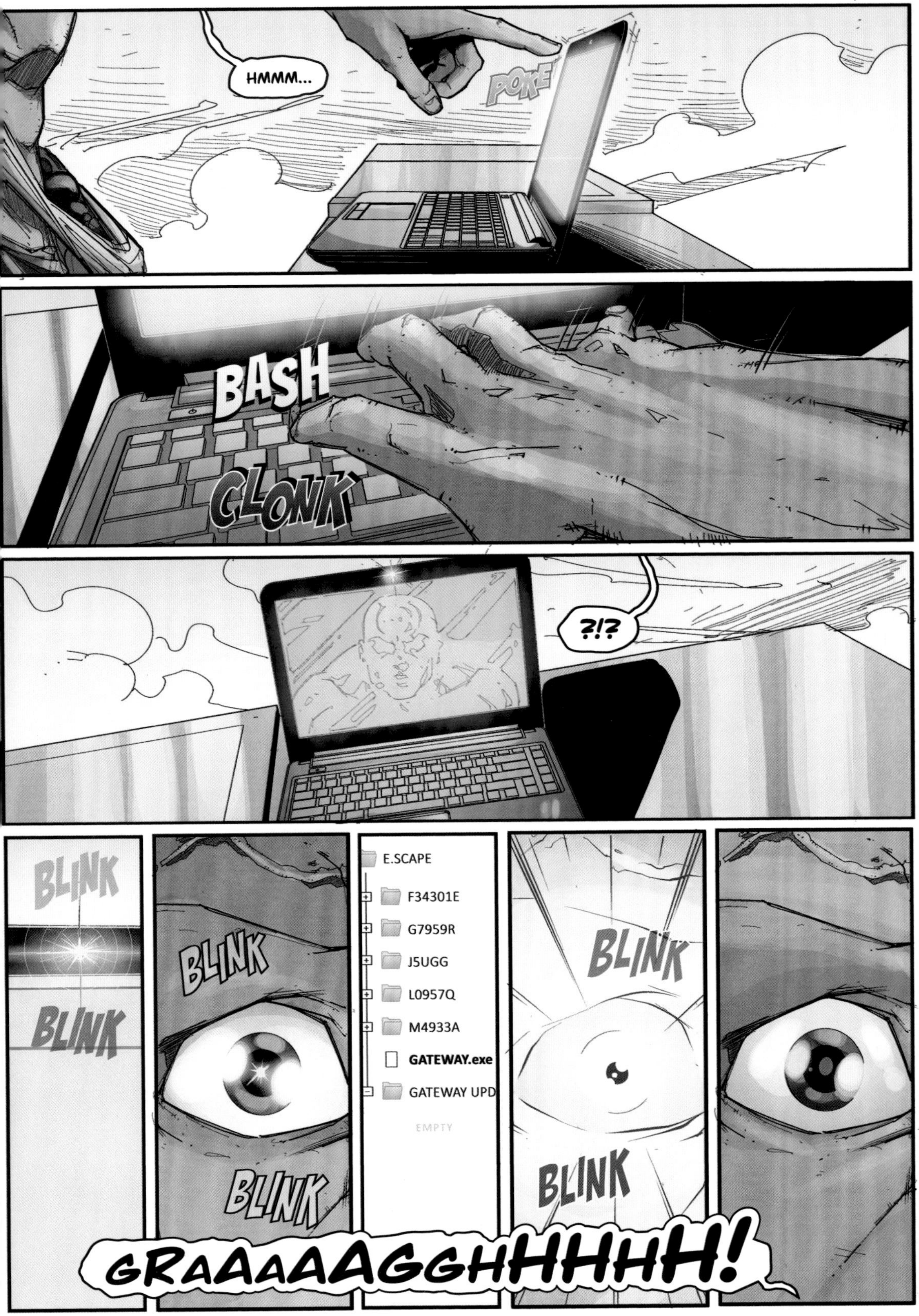
HMMM...
POKE
BASH
CLONK
?!?
BLINK
BLINK
BLINK
BLINK
E.SCAPE
F34301E
G7959R
J5UGG
L0957Q
M4933A
GATEWAY.exe
GATEWAY UPD
EMPTY
BLINK
BLINK
GRAAAAAGGHHHHHH!

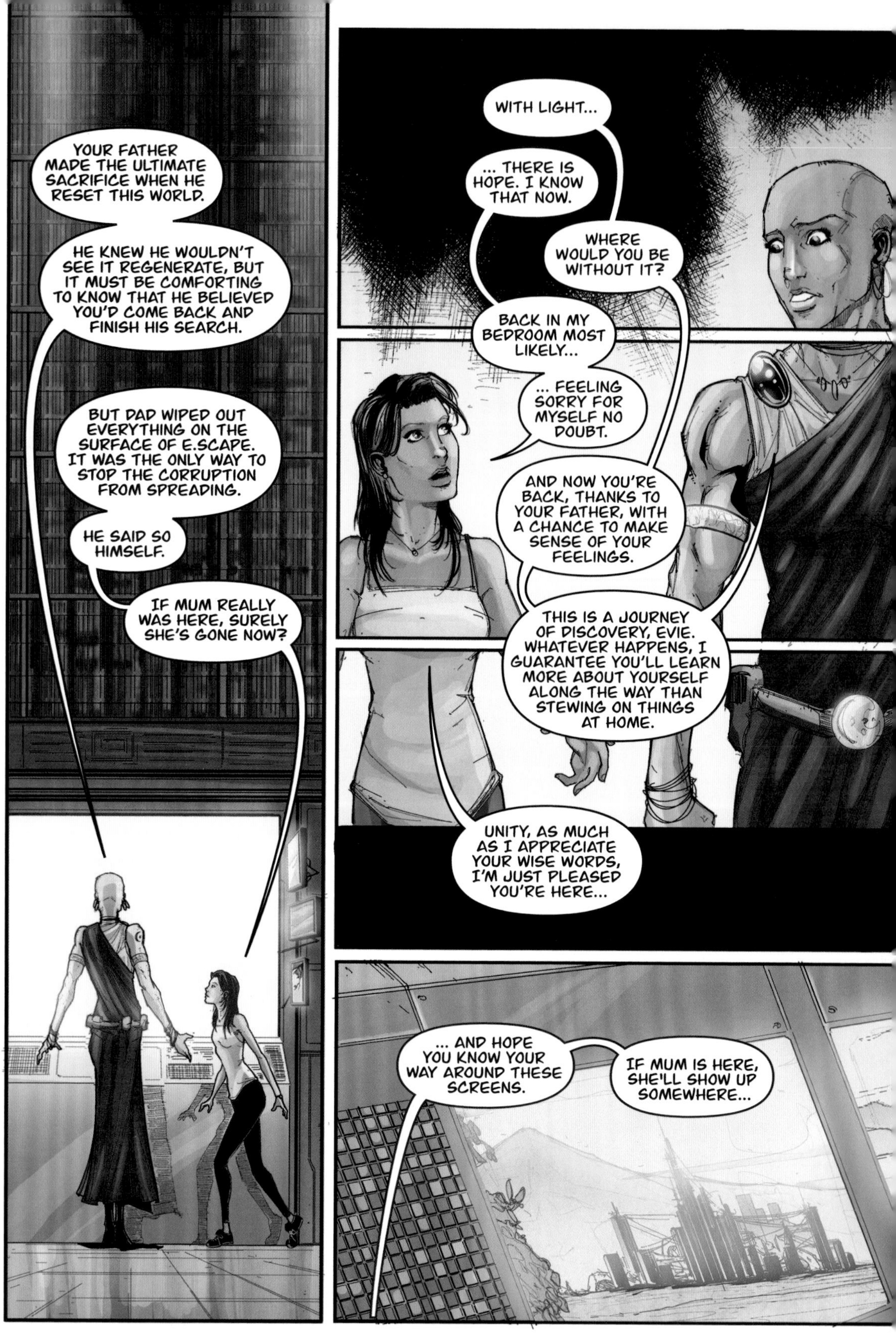
YOUR FATHER MADE THE ULTIMATE SACRIFICE WHEN HE RESET THIS WORLD.
HE KNEW HE WOULDN'T SEE IT REGENERATE, BUT IT MUST BE COMFORTING TO KNOW THAT HE BELIEVED YOU'D COME BACK AND FINISH HIS SEARCH.
BUT DAD WIPED OUT EVERYTHING ON THE SURFACE OF E.SCAPE. IT WAS THE ONLY WAY TO STOP THE CORRUPTION FROM SPREADING.
HE SAID SO HIMSELF.
IF MUM REALLY WAS HERE, SURELY SHE'S GONE NOW?
WITH LIGHT...
... THERE IS HOPE. I KNOW THAT NOW.
WHERE WOULD YOU BE WITHOUT IT?
BACK IN MY BEDROOM MOST LIKELY...
... FEELING SORRY FOR MYSELF NO DOUBT.
AND NOW YOU'RE BACK, THANKS TO YOUR FATHER, WITH A CHANCE TO MAKE SENSE OF YOUR FEELINGS.
THIS IS A JOURNEY OF DISCOVERY, EVIE. WHATEVER HAPPENS, I GUARANTEE YOU'LL LEARN MORE ABOUT YOURSELF ALONG THE WAY THAN STEWING ON THINGS AT HOME.
UNITY, AS MUCH AS I APPRECIATE YOUR WISE WORDS, I'M JUST PLEASED YOU'RE HERE...
... AND HOPE YOU KNOW YOUR WAY AROUND THESE SCREENS.
IF MUM IS HERE, SHE'LL SHOW UP SOMEWHERE...

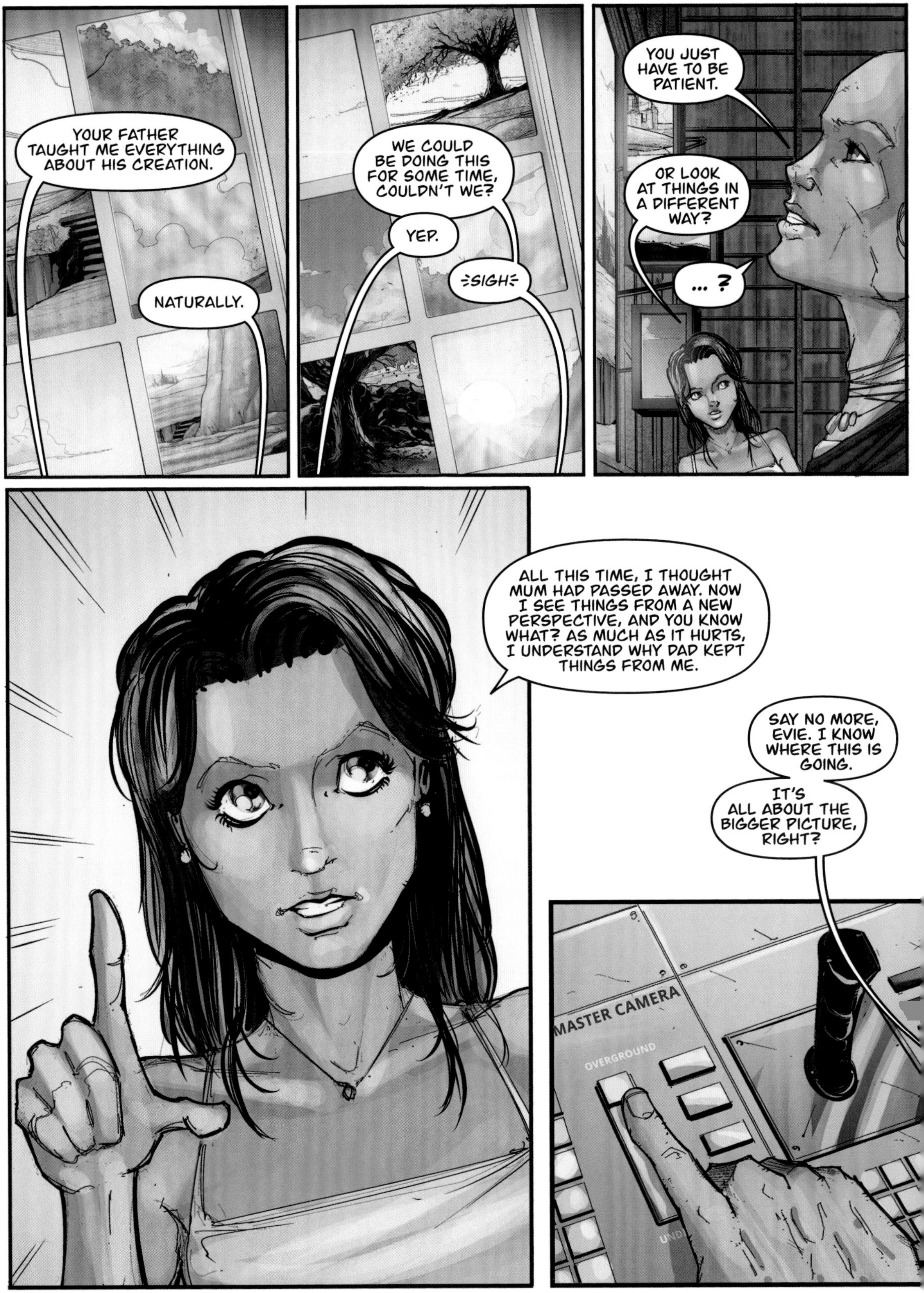
YOUR FATHER TAUGHT ME EVERYTHING ABOUT HIS CREATION.
NATURALLY.
WE COULD BE DOING THIS FOR SOME TIME, COULDN'T WE?
YEP.
SIGH
YOU JUST HAVE TO BE PATIENT.
OR LOOK AT THINGS IN A DIFFERENT WAY?
... ?
ALL THIS TIME, I THOUGHT MUM HAD PASSED AWAY. NOW I SEE THINGS FROM A NEW PERSPECTIVE, AND YOU KNOW WHAT? AS MUCH AS IT HURTS, I UNDERSTAND WHY DAD KEPT THINGS FROM ME.
SAY NO MORE, EVIE. I KNOW WHERE THIS IS GOING.
IT'S ALL ABOUT THE BIGGER PICTURE, RIGHT?
MASTER CAMERA
OVERGROUND

FOR ONCE, I HAD A CHANCE TO APPRECIATE MY DAD'S LIFE WORK.

I JUST COULDN'T IMAGINE THE TORMENT HE HAD PUT HIMSELF THROUGH, KNOWING THAT MUM WAS TRAPPED IN A MIRACLE OF HIS CREATION.

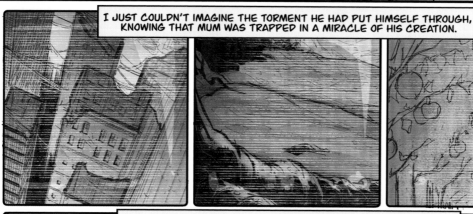

I COULD ONLY THINK HE'D SCOURED THIS LAND AS WE WERE NOW:

HOLDING OUT HOPE AGAINST ALL ODDS, BUT ENDING UP WITH NOTHING.

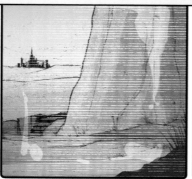

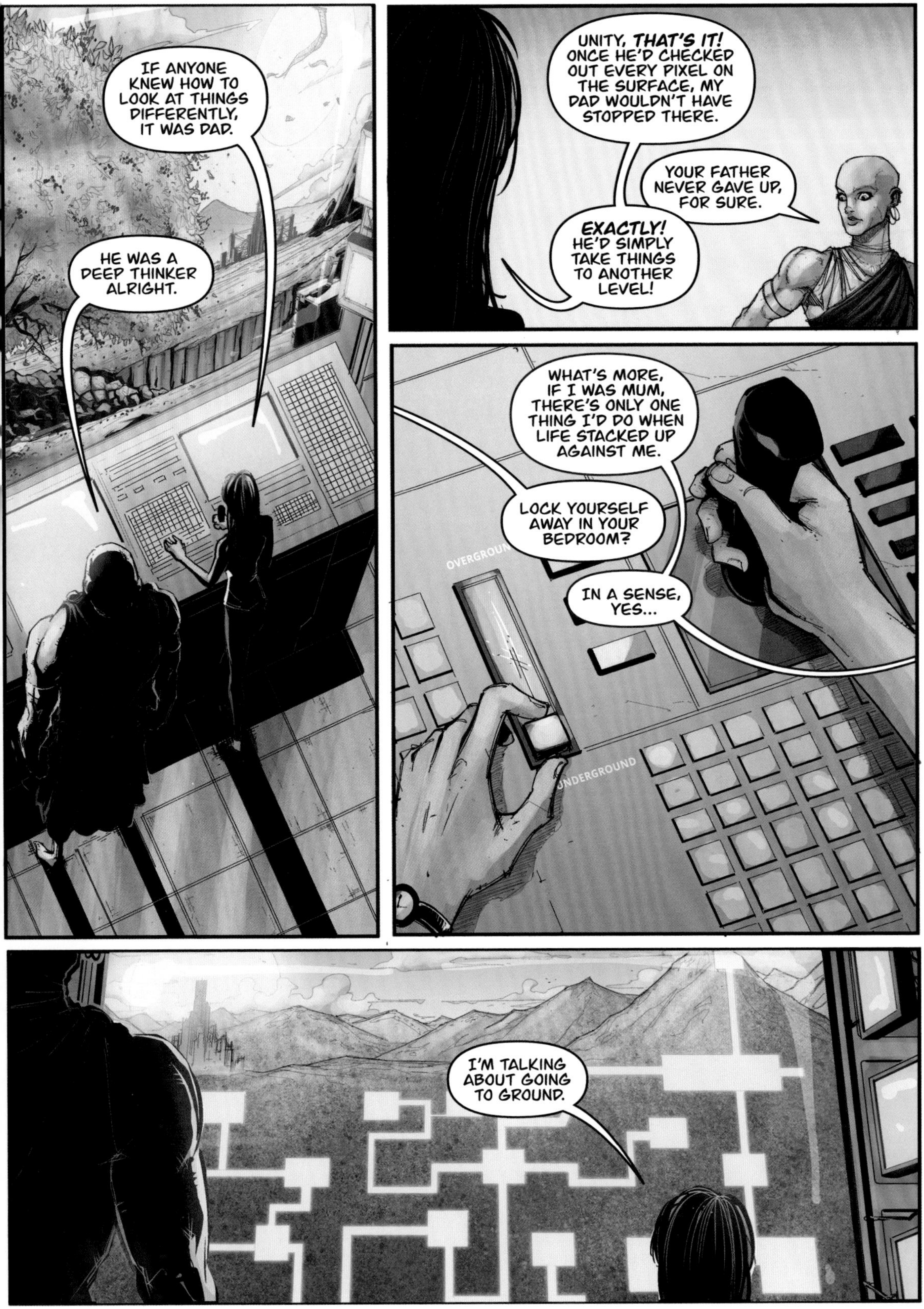
IF ANYONE KNEW HOW TO LOOK AT THINGS DIFFERENTLY, IT WAS DAD.
HE WAS A DEEP THINKER ALRIGHT.
UNITY, THAT'S IT! ONCE HE'D CHECKED OUT EVERY PIXEL ON THE SURFACE, MY DAD WOULDN'T HAVE STOPPED THERE.
YOUR FATHER NEVER GAVE UP, FOR SURE.
EXACTLY! HE'D SIMPLY TAKE THINGS TO ANOTHER LEVEL!
WHAT'S MORE, IF I WAS MUM, THERE'S ONLY ONE THING I'D DO WHEN LIFE STACKED UP AGAINST ME.
LOCK YOURSELF AWAY IN YOUR BEDROOM?
OVERGROUND
IN A SENSE, YES...
UNDERGROUND
I'M TALKING ABOUT GOING TO GROUND.

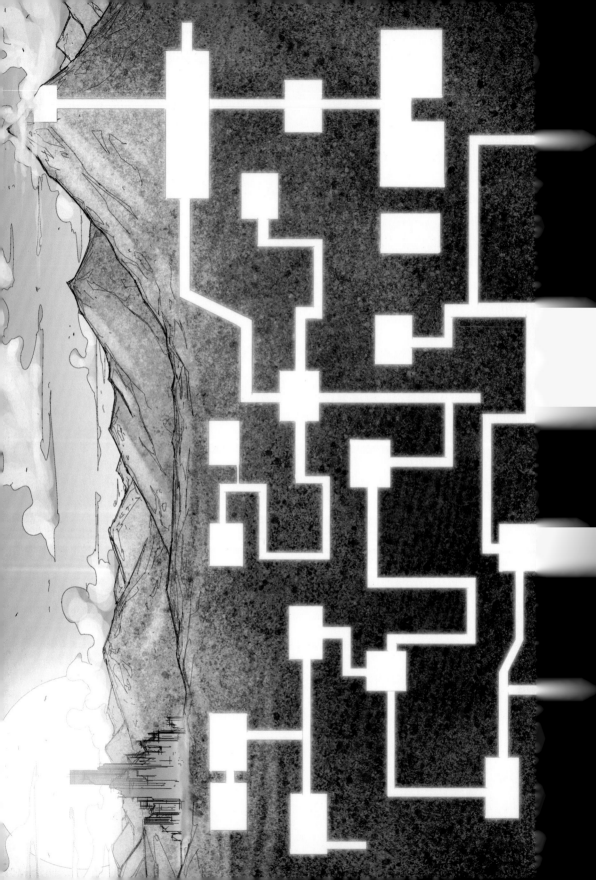

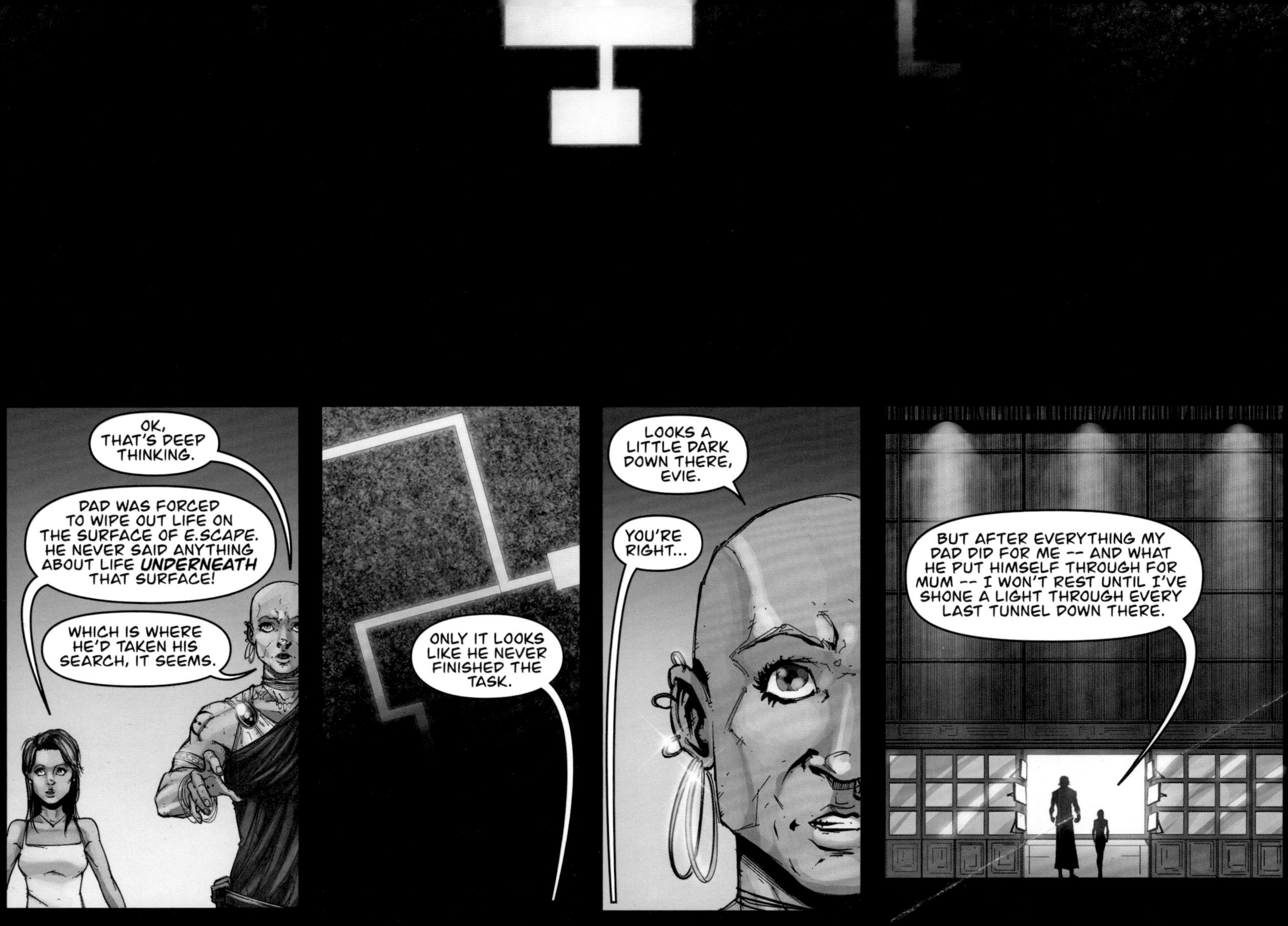
OK, THAT'S DEEP THINKING.
DAD WAS FORCED TO WIPE OUT LIFE ON THE SURFACE OF E.SCAPE. HE NEVER SAID ANYTHING ABOUT LIFE ***UNDERNEATH*** THAT SURFACE!
WHICH IS WHERE HE'D TAKEN HIS SEARCH, IT SEEMS.
ONLY IT LOOKS LIKE HE NEVER FINISHED THE TASK.
LOOKS A LITTLE DARK DOWN THERE, EVIE.
YOU'RE RIGHT...
BUT AFTER EVERYTHING MY DAD DID FOR ME -- AND WHAT HE PUT HIMSELF THROUGH FOR MUM -- I WON'T REST UNTIL I'VE SHONE A LIGHT THROUGH EVERY LAST TUNNEL DOWN THERE.

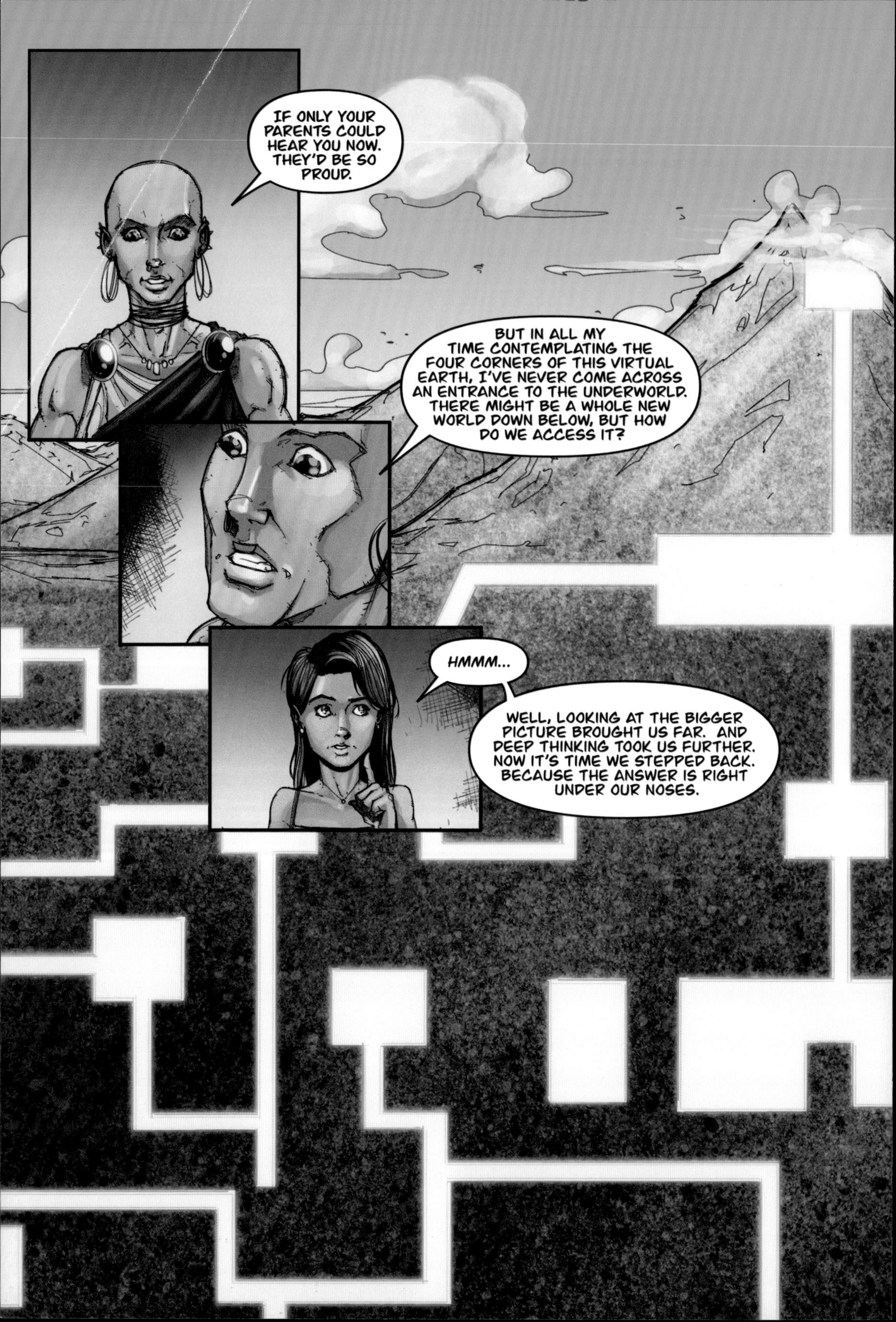
IF ONLY YOUR PARENTS COULD HEAR YOU NOW. THEY'D BE SO PROUD.
BUT IN ALL MY TIME CONTEMPLATING THE FOUR CORNERS OF THIS VIRTUAL EARTH, I'VE NEVER COME ACROSS AN ENTRANCE TO THE UNDERWORLD. THERE MIGHT BE A WHOLE NEW WORLD DOWN BELOW, BUT HOW DO WE ACCESS IT?
HMMM...
WELL, LOOKING AT THE BIGGER PICTURE BROUGHT US FAR. AND DEEP THINKING TOOK US FURTHER. NOW IT'S TIME WE STEPPED BACK. BECAUSE THE ANSWER IS RIGHT UNDER OUR NOSES.

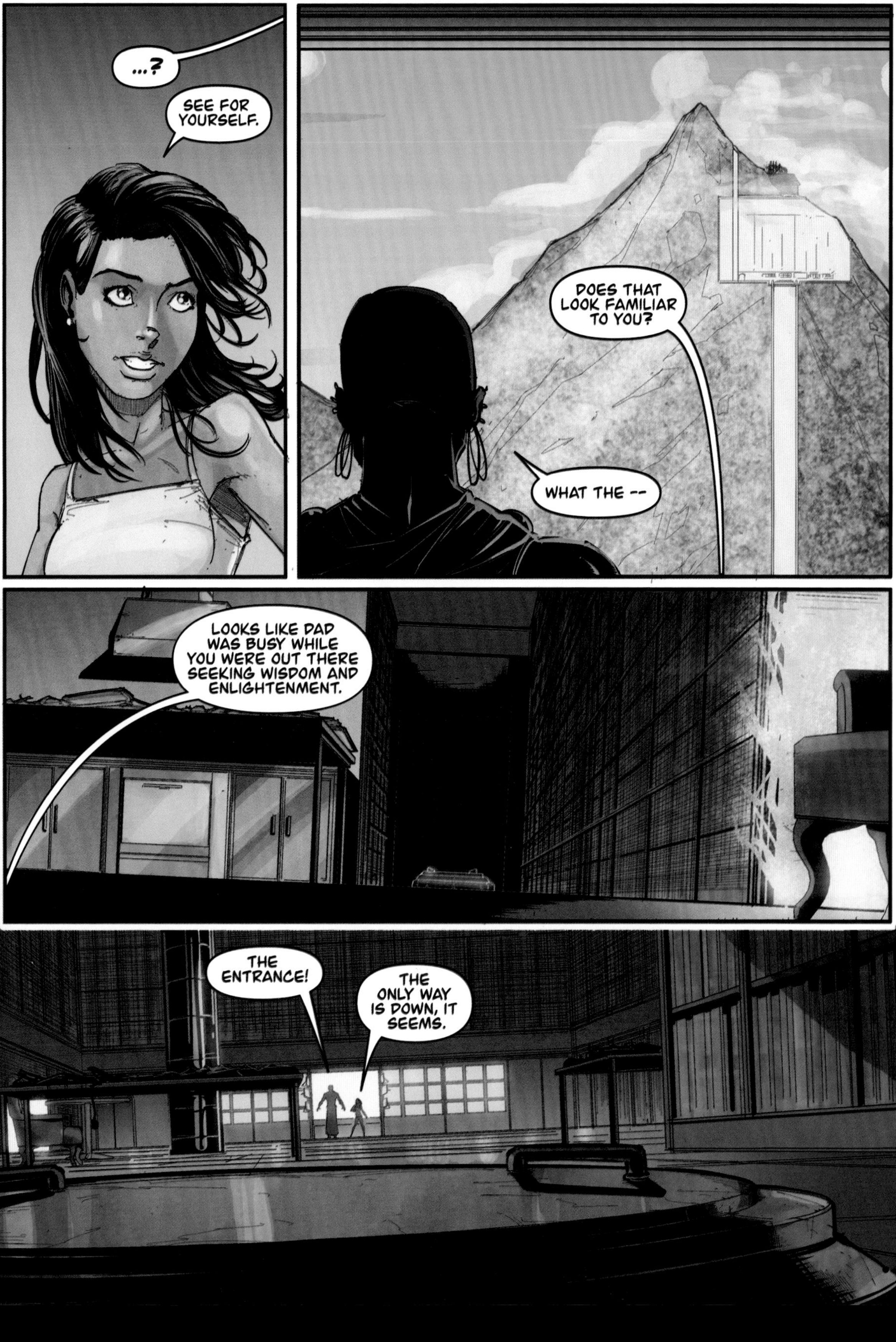
...?
SEE FOR YOURSELF.
DOES THAT LOOK FAMILIAR TO YOU?
WHAT THE --
LOOKS LIKE DAD WAS BUSY WHILE YOU WERE OUT THERE SEEKING WISDOM AND ENLIGHTENMENT.
THE ENTRANCE!
THE ONLY WAY IS DOWN, IT SEEMS.

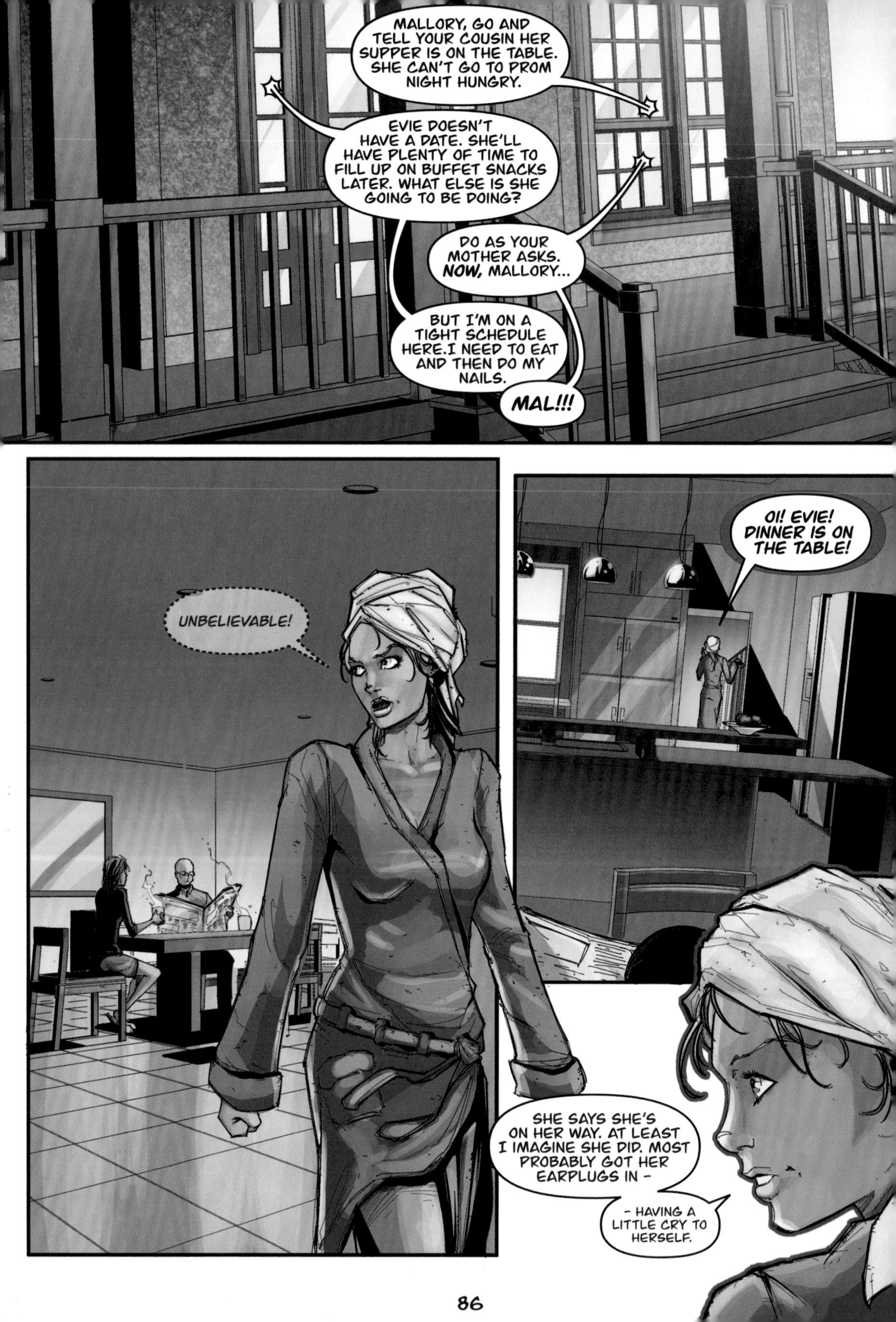
MALLORY, GO AND TELL YOUR COUSIN HER SUPPER IS ON THE TABLE. SHE CAN'T GO TO PROM NIGHT HUNGRY.
EVIE DOESN'T HAVE A DATE. SHE'LL HAVE PLENTY OF TIME TO FILL UP ON BUFFET SNACKS LATER. WHAT ELSE IS SHE GOING TO BE DOING?
DO AS YOUR MOTHER ASKS. NOW, MALLORY...
BUT I'M ON A TIGHT SCHEDULE HERE.I NEED TO EAT AND THEN DO MY NAILS.
MAL!!!
UNBELIEVABLE!
OI! EVIE! DINNER IS ON THE TABLE!
SHE SAYS SHE'S ON HER WAY. AT LEAST I IMAGINE SHE DID. MOST PROBABLY GOT HER EARPLUGS IN –
– HAVING A LITTLE CRY TO HERSELF.

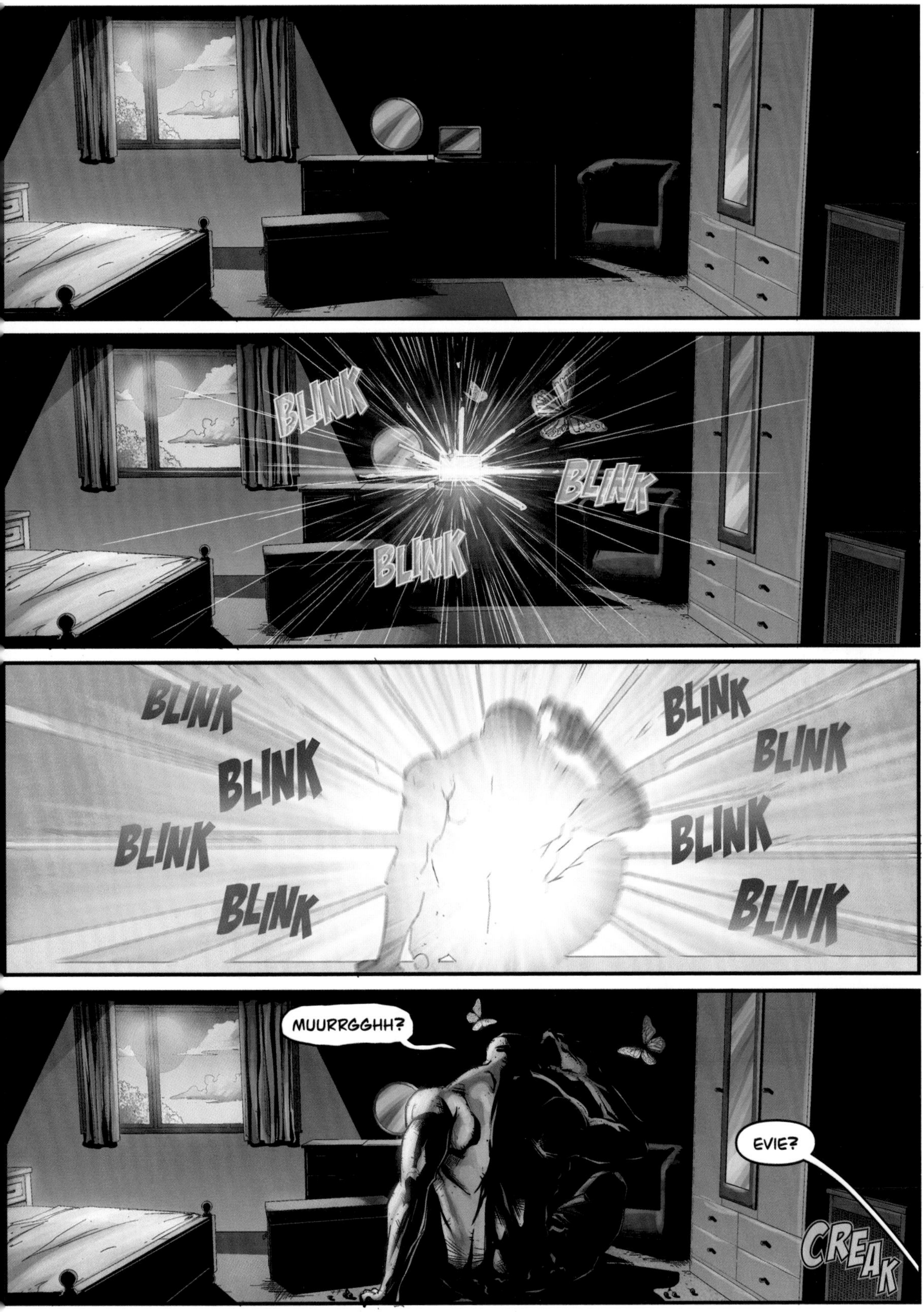
BLINK
BLINK
BLINK
BLINK
BLINK
BLINK
BLINK
BLINK
BLINK
BLINK
BLINK
MUURRGGHH?
EVIE?
CREAK

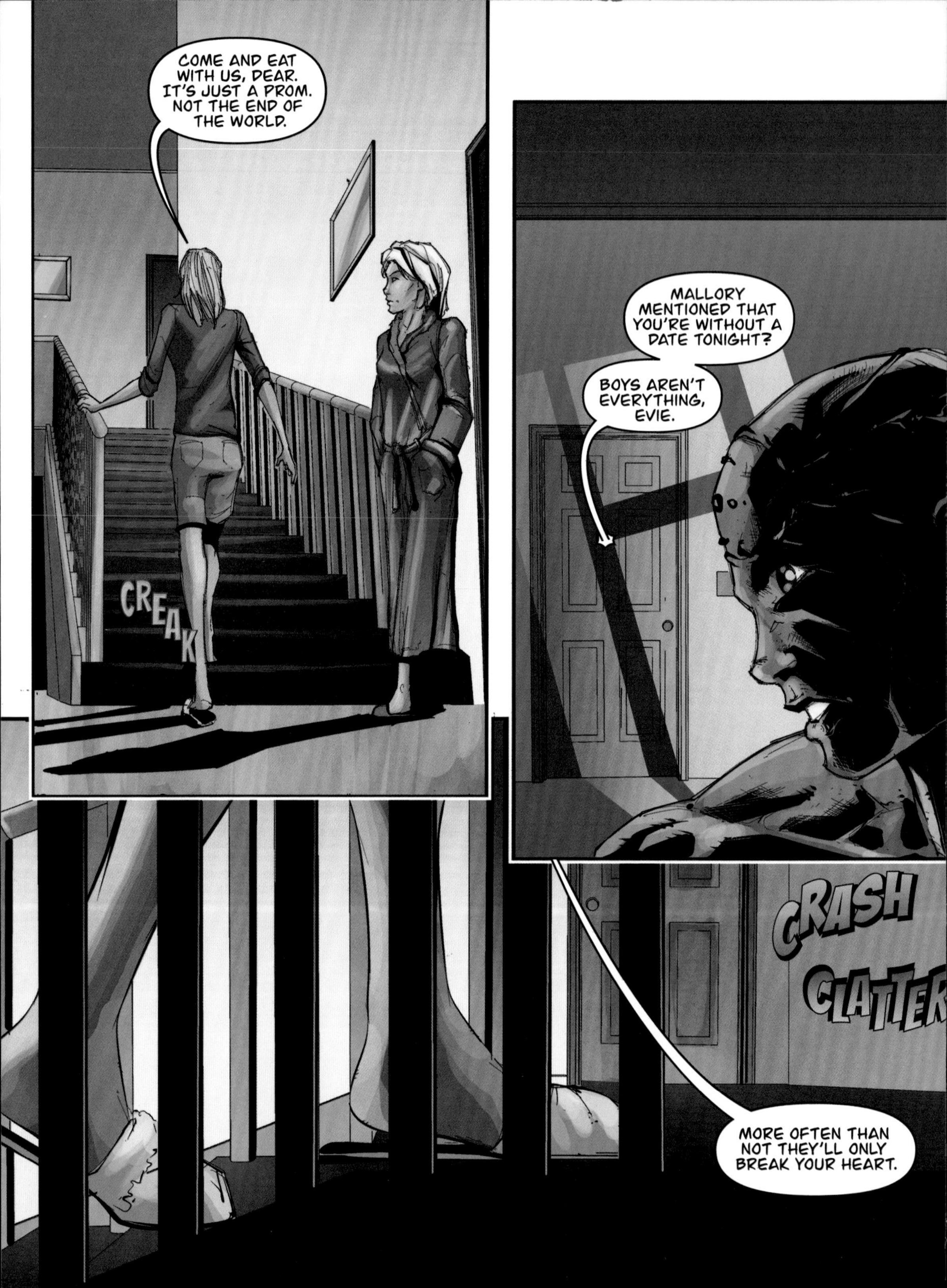
COME AND EAT WITH US, DEAR. IT'S JUST A PROM. NOT THE END OF THE WORLD.
CREAK
MALLORY MENTIONED THAT YOU'RE WITHOUT A DATE TONIGHT?
BOYS AREN'T EVERYTHING, EVIE.
CRASH
CLATTER
MORE OFTEN THAN NOT THEY'LL ONLY BREAK YOUR HEART.

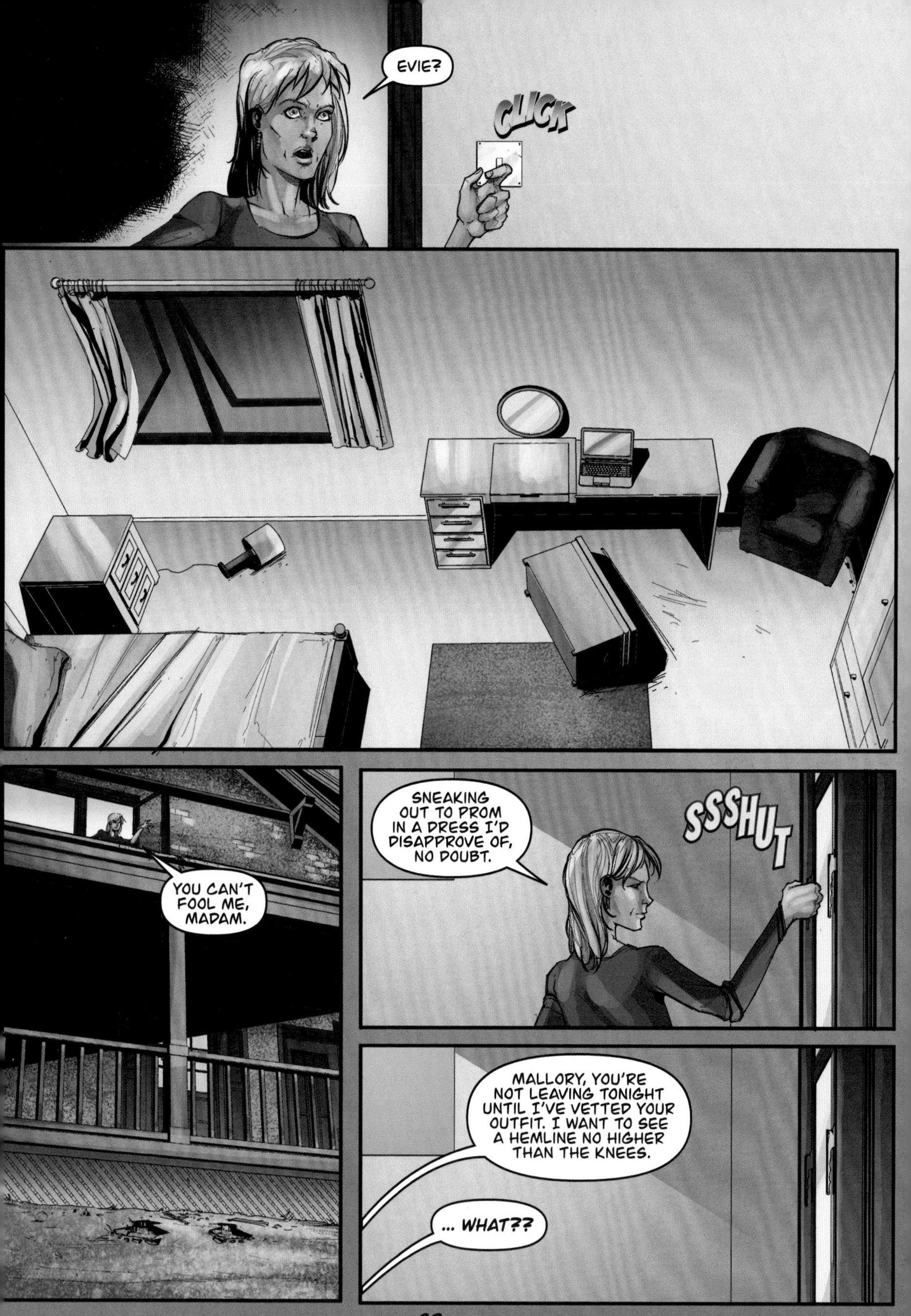
EVIE?
CLICK
SNEAKING OUT TO PROM IN A DRESS I'D DISAPPROVE OF, NO DOUBT.
SSSHUT
YOU CAN'T FOOL ME, MADAM.
MALLORY, YOU'RE NOT LEAVING TONIGHT UNTIL I'VE VETTED YOUR OUTFIT. I WANT TO SEE A HEMLINE NO HIGHER THAN THE KNEES.
... WHAT??

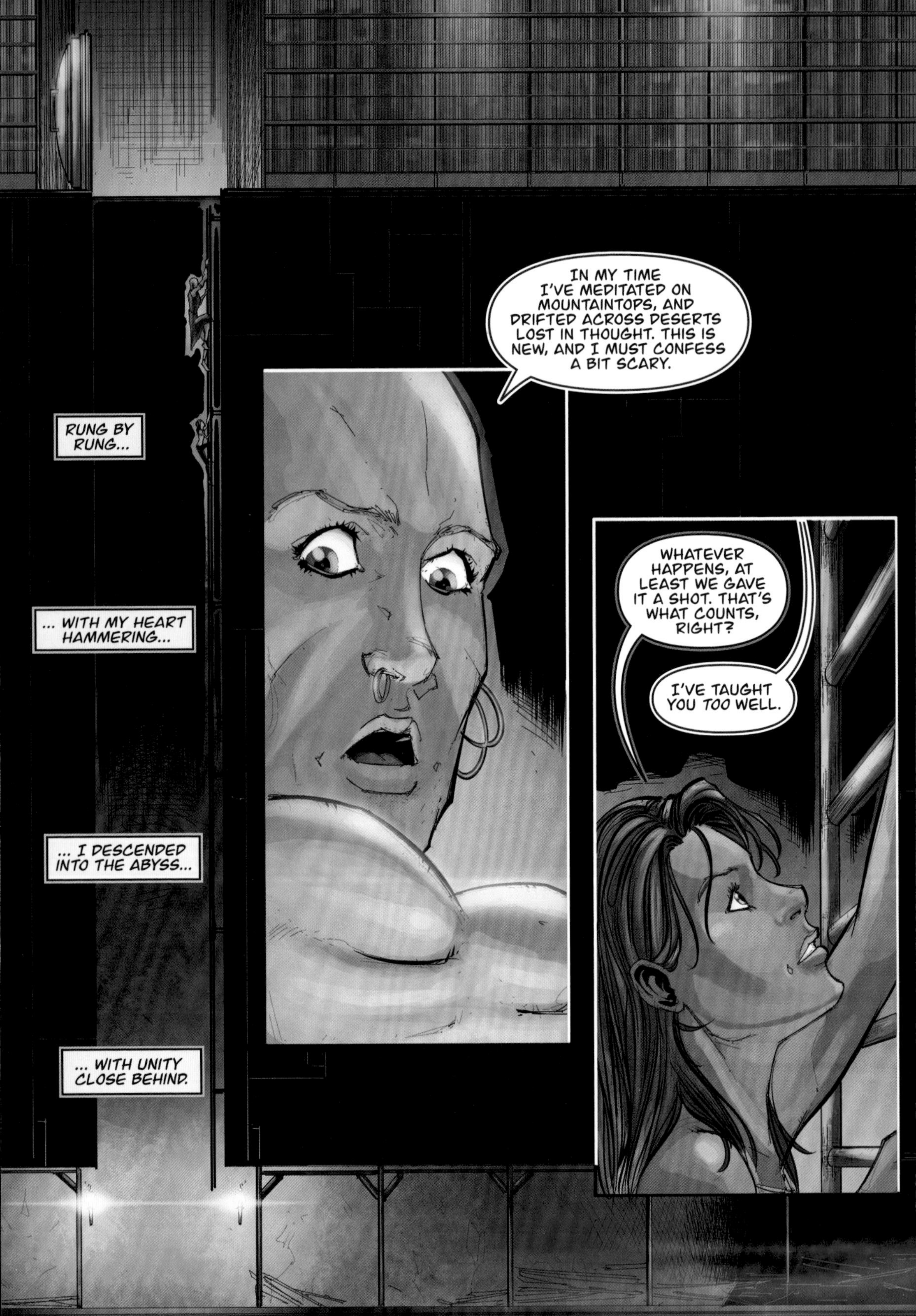
RUNG BY RUNG...
IN MY TIME I'VE MEDITATED ON MOUNTAINTOPS, AND DRIFTED ACROSS DESERTS LOST IN THOUGHT. THIS IS NEW, AND I MUST CONFESS A BIT SCARY.
... WITH MY HEART HAMMERING...
WHATEVER HAPPENS, AT LEAST WE GAVE IT A SHOT. THAT'S WHAT COUNTS, RIGHT?
I'VE TAUGHT YOU TOO WELL.
... I DESCENDED INTO THE ABYSS...
... WITH UNITY CLOSE BEHIND.

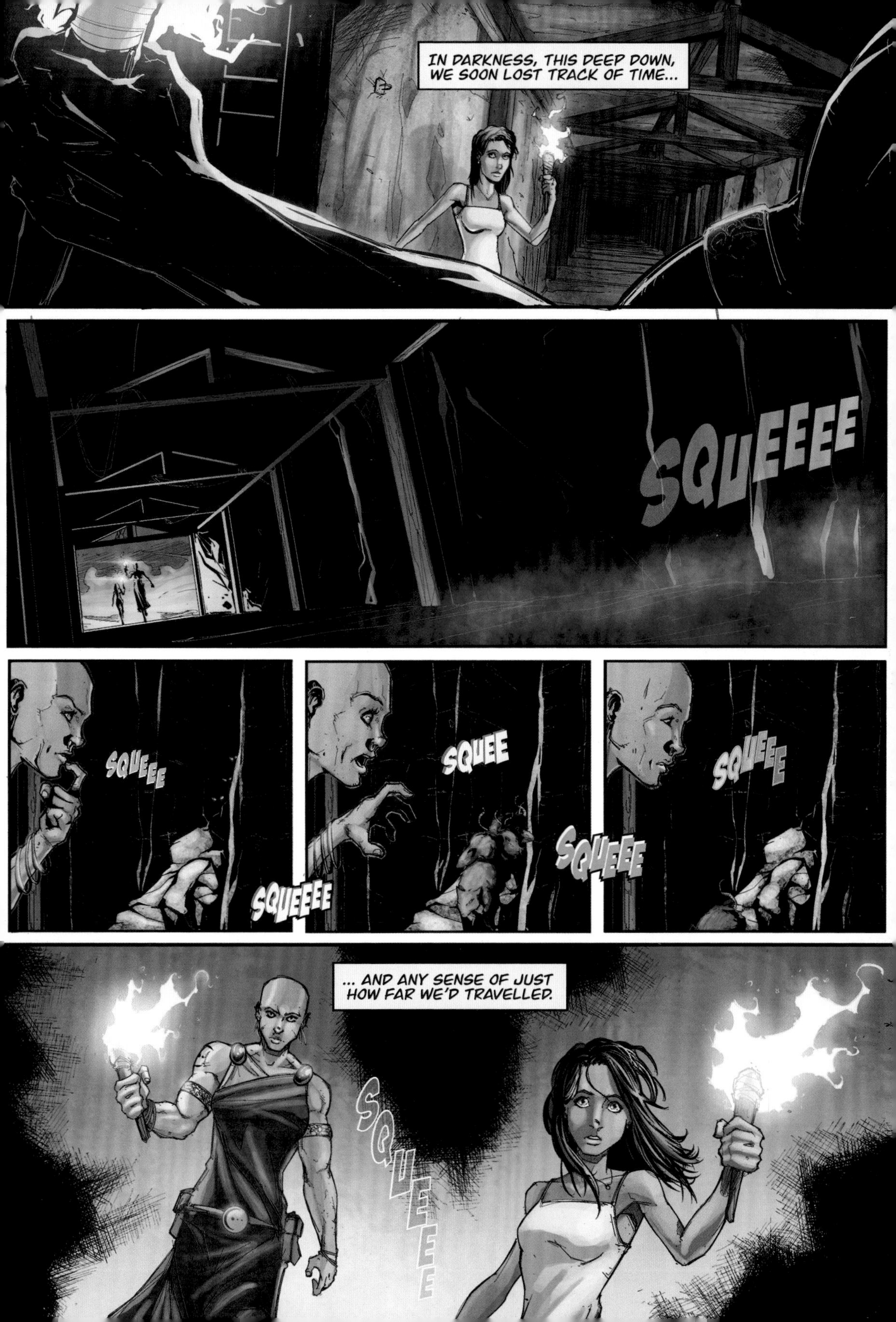

IN DARKNESS, THIS DEEP DOWN, WE SOON LOST TRACK OF TIME...
SQUEEEE
SQUEEE
SQUEEEE
SQUEE
SQUEEE
SQUEEE
... AND ANY SENSE OF JUST HOW FAR WE'D TRAVELLED.
SQUEEE

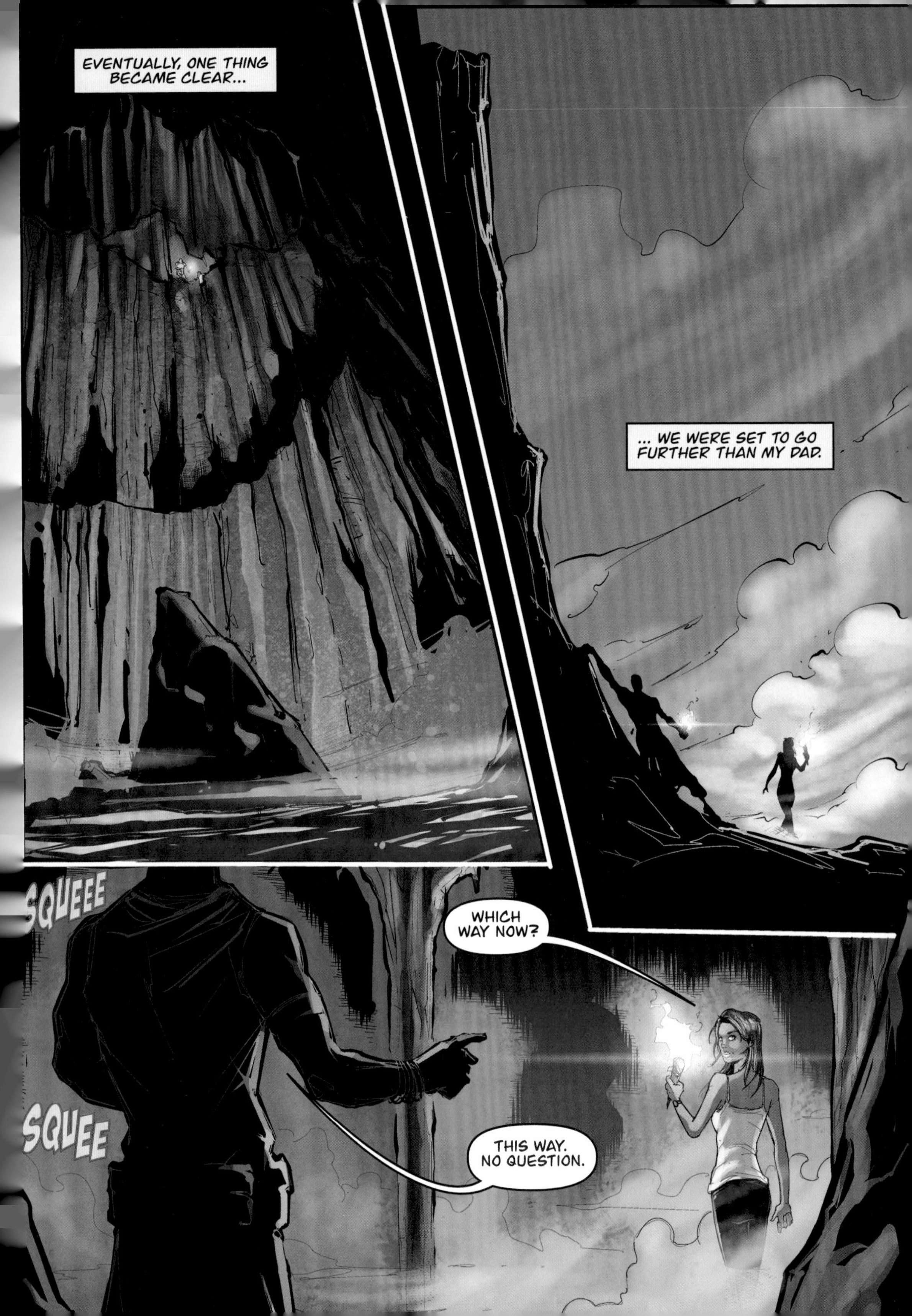
EVENTUALLY, ONE THING BECAME CLEAR...
... WE WERE SET TO GO FURTHER THAN MY DAD.
SQUEEE
WHICH WAY NOW?
SQUEE
THIS WAY. NO QUESTION.

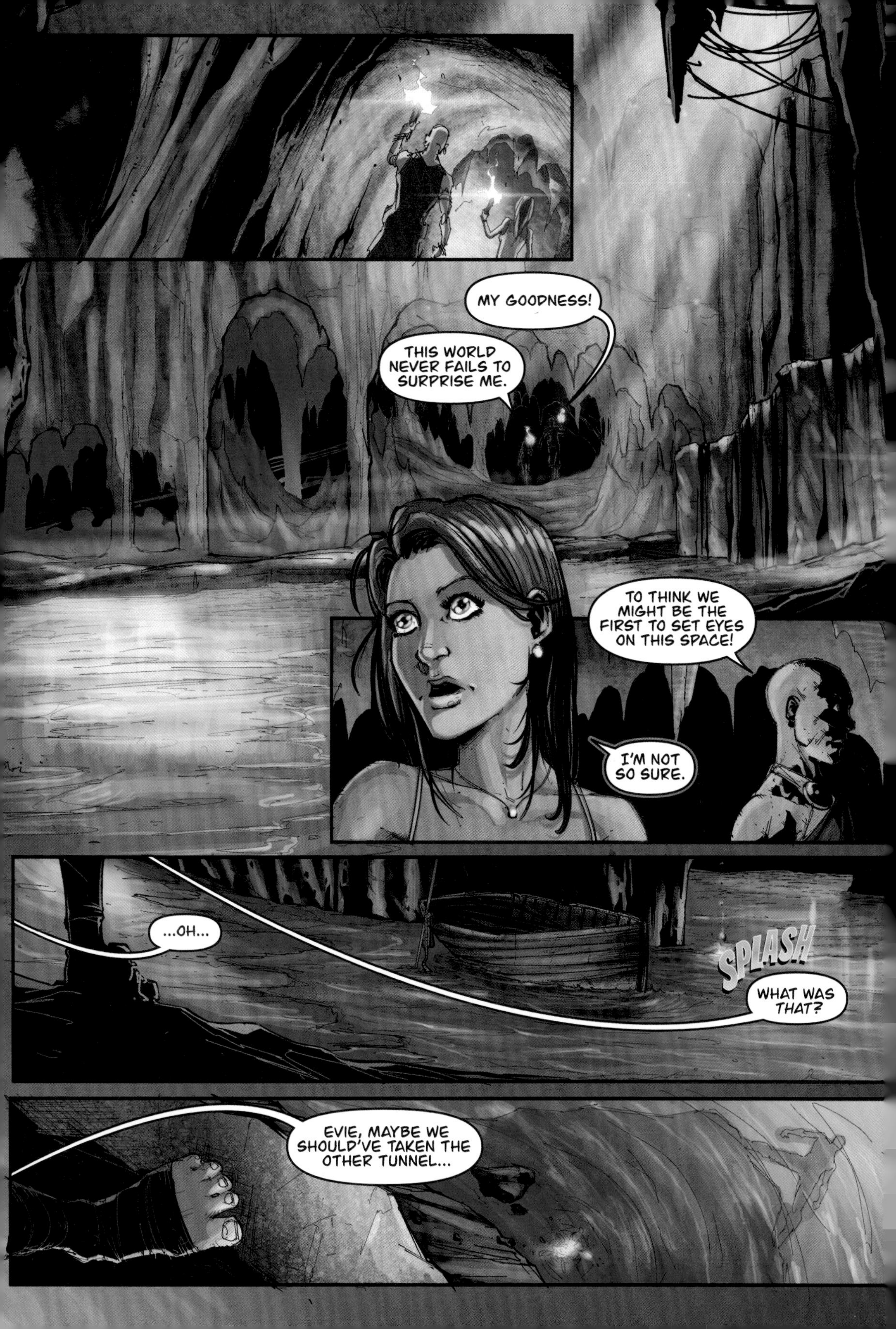
MY GOODNESS!
THIS WORLD NEVER FAILS TO SURPRISE ME.
TO THINK WE MIGHT BE THE FIRST TO SET EYES ON THIS SPACE!
I'M NOT SO SURE.
...OH...
SPLASH
WHAT WAS THAT?
EVIE, MAYBE WE SHOULD'VE TAKEN THE OTHER TUNNEL...

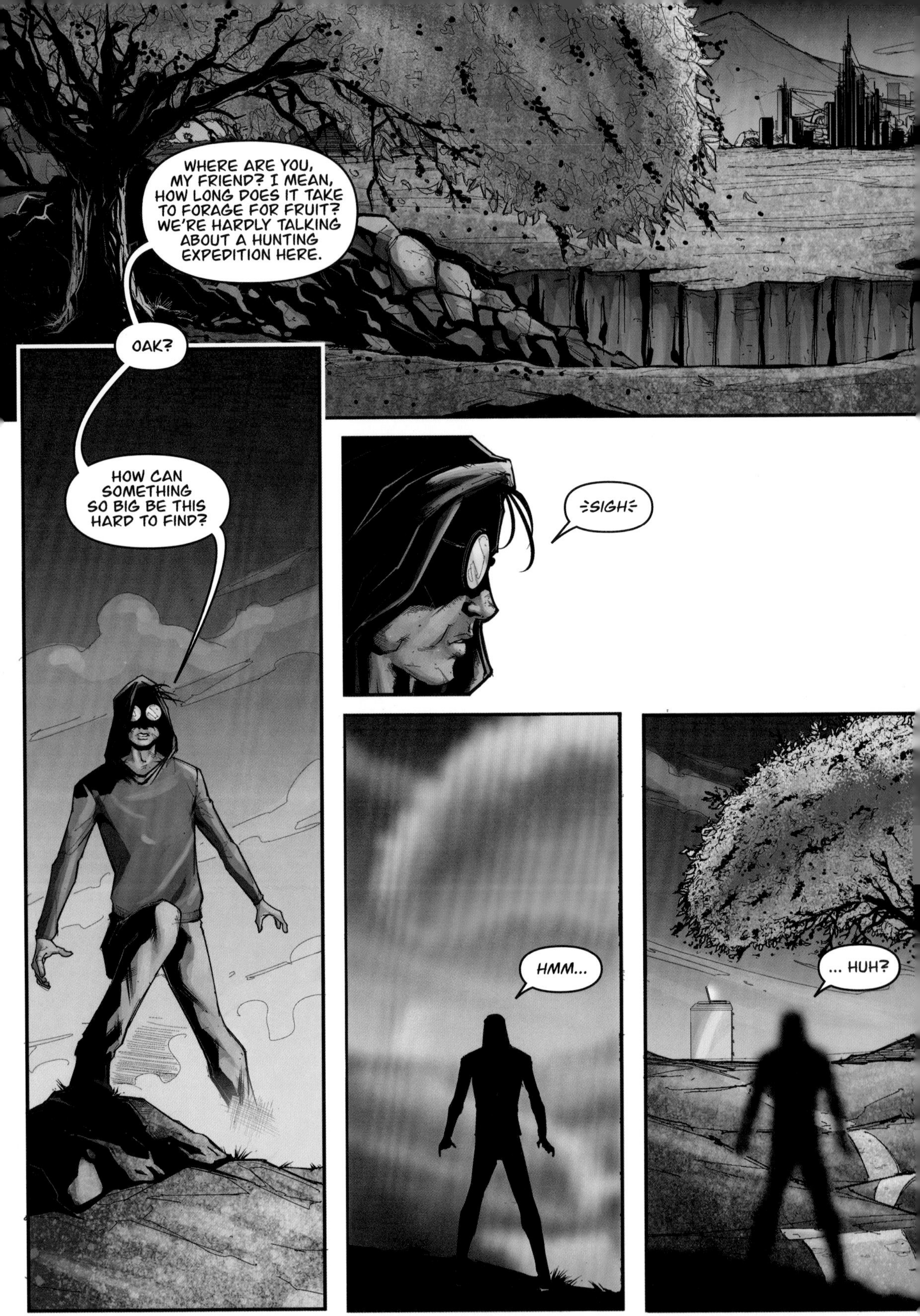
WHERE ARE YOU, MY FRIEND? I MEAN, HOW LONG DOES IT TAKE TO FORAGE FOR FRUIT? WE'RE HARDLY TALKING ABOUT A HUNTING EXPEDITION HERE.
OAK?
HOW CAN SOMETHING SO BIG BE THIS HARD TO FIND?
SIGH
HMM...
... HUH?

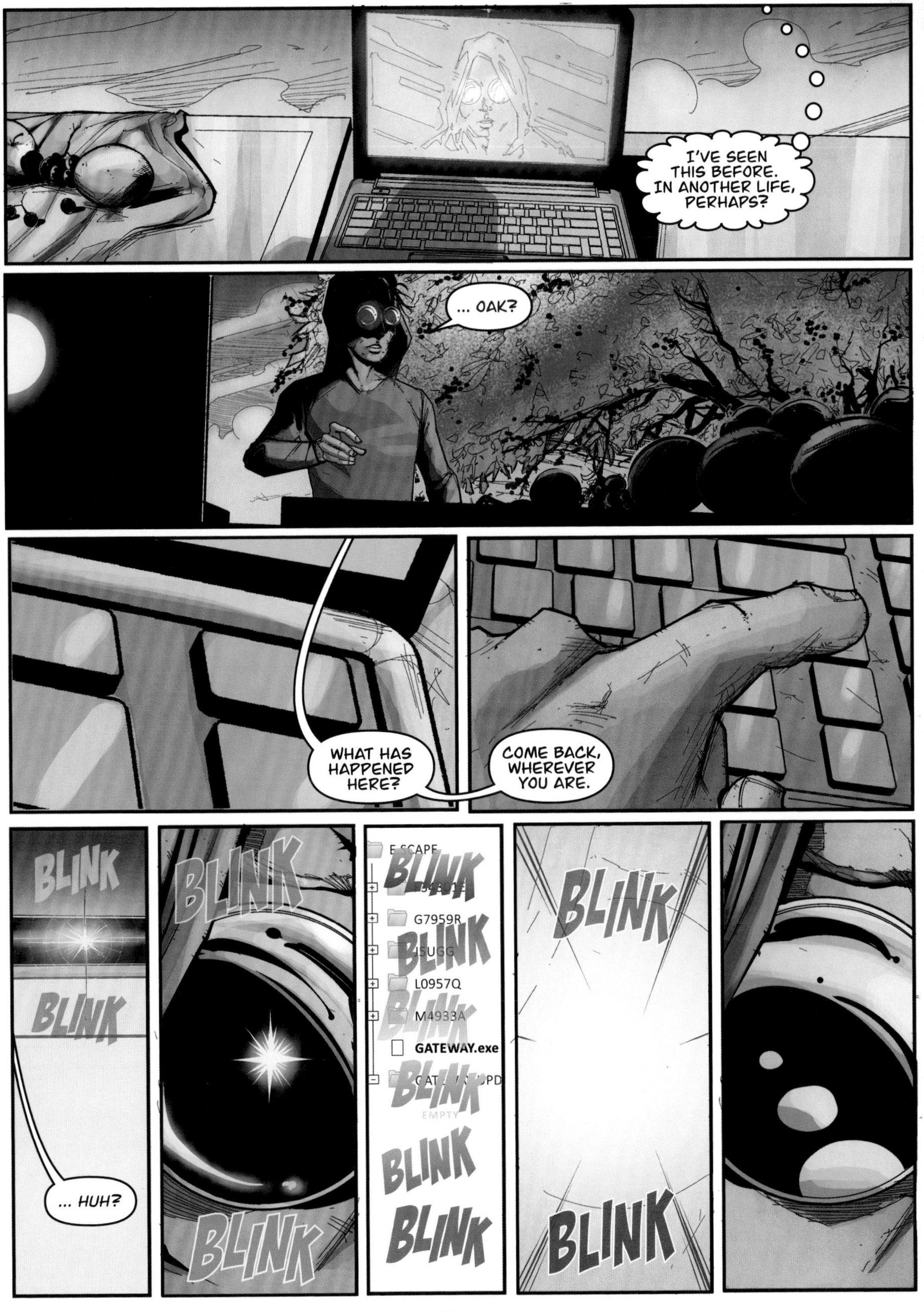
I'VE SEEN THIS BEFORE. IN ANOTHER LIFE, PERHAPS?
... OAK?
WHAT HAS HAPPENED HERE?
COME BACK, WHEREVER YOU ARE.
BLINK
BLINK
... HUH?
BLINK
BLINK
E-SCAPE
G7959R
L0957Q
M4933A
GATEWAY.exe
EMPTY
BLINK
BLINK
BLINK
BLINK
BLINK
BLINK
BLINK
BLINK

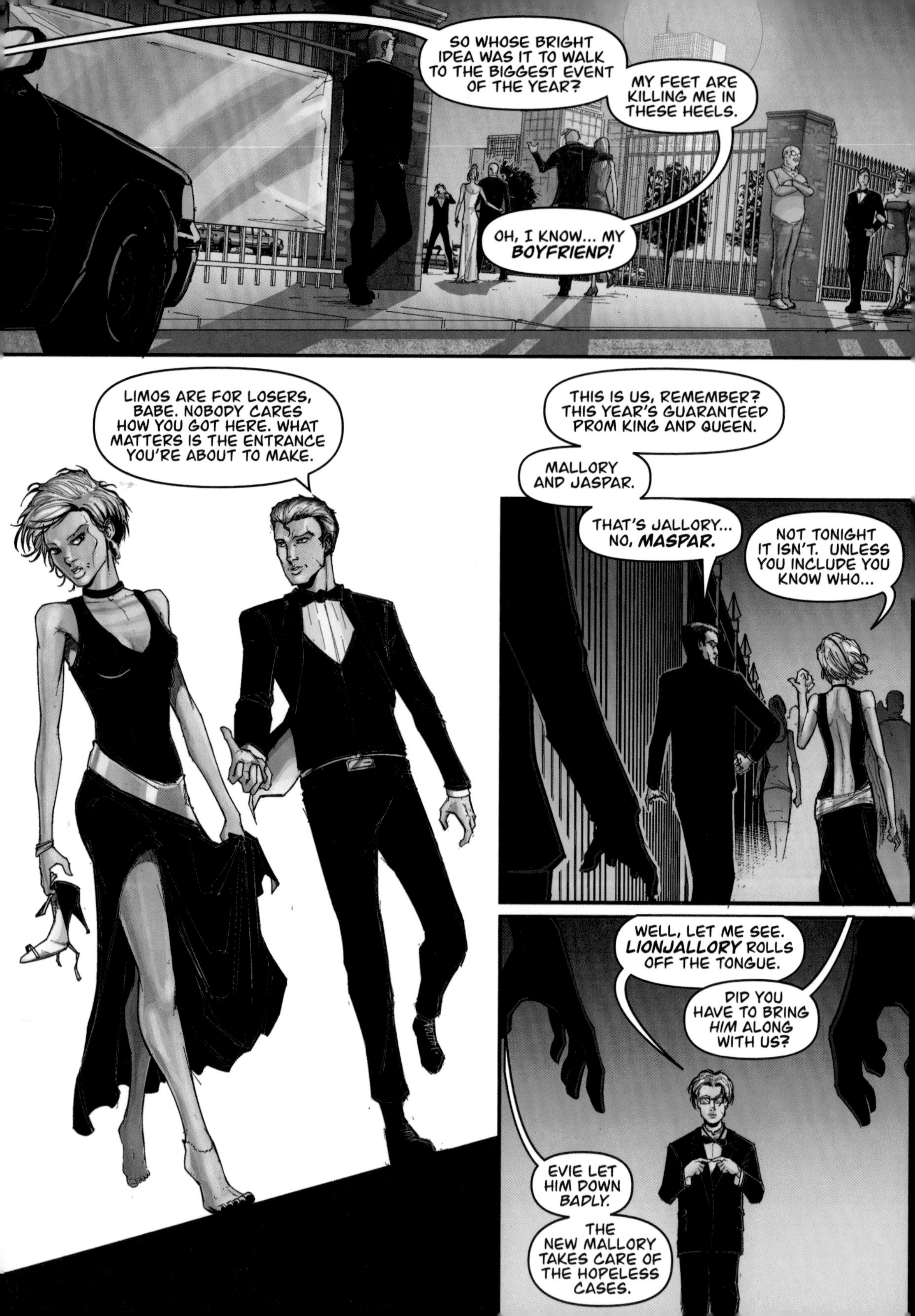
SO WHOSE BRIGHT IDEA WAS IT TO WALK TO THE BIGGEST EVENT OF THE YEAR?
MY FEET ARE KILLING ME IN THESE HEELS.
OH, I KNOW... MY *BOYFRIEND!*
LIMOS ARE FOR LOSERS, BABE. NOBODY CARES HOW YOU GOT HERE. WHAT MATTERS IS THE ENTRANCE YOU'RE ABOUT TO MAKE.
THIS IS US, REMEMBER? THIS YEAR'S GUARANTEED PROM KING AND QUEEN.
MALLORY AND JASPAR.
THAT'S JALLORY... NO, *MASPAR.*
NOT TONIGHT IT ISN'T. UNLESS YOU INCLUDE YOU KNOW WHO...
WELL, LET ME SEE. *LIONJALLORY* ROLLS OFF THE TONGUE.
DID YOU HAVE TO BRING *HIM* ALONG WITH US?
EVIE LET HIM DOWN BADLY.
THE NEW MALLORY TAKES CARE OF THE HOPELESS CASES.

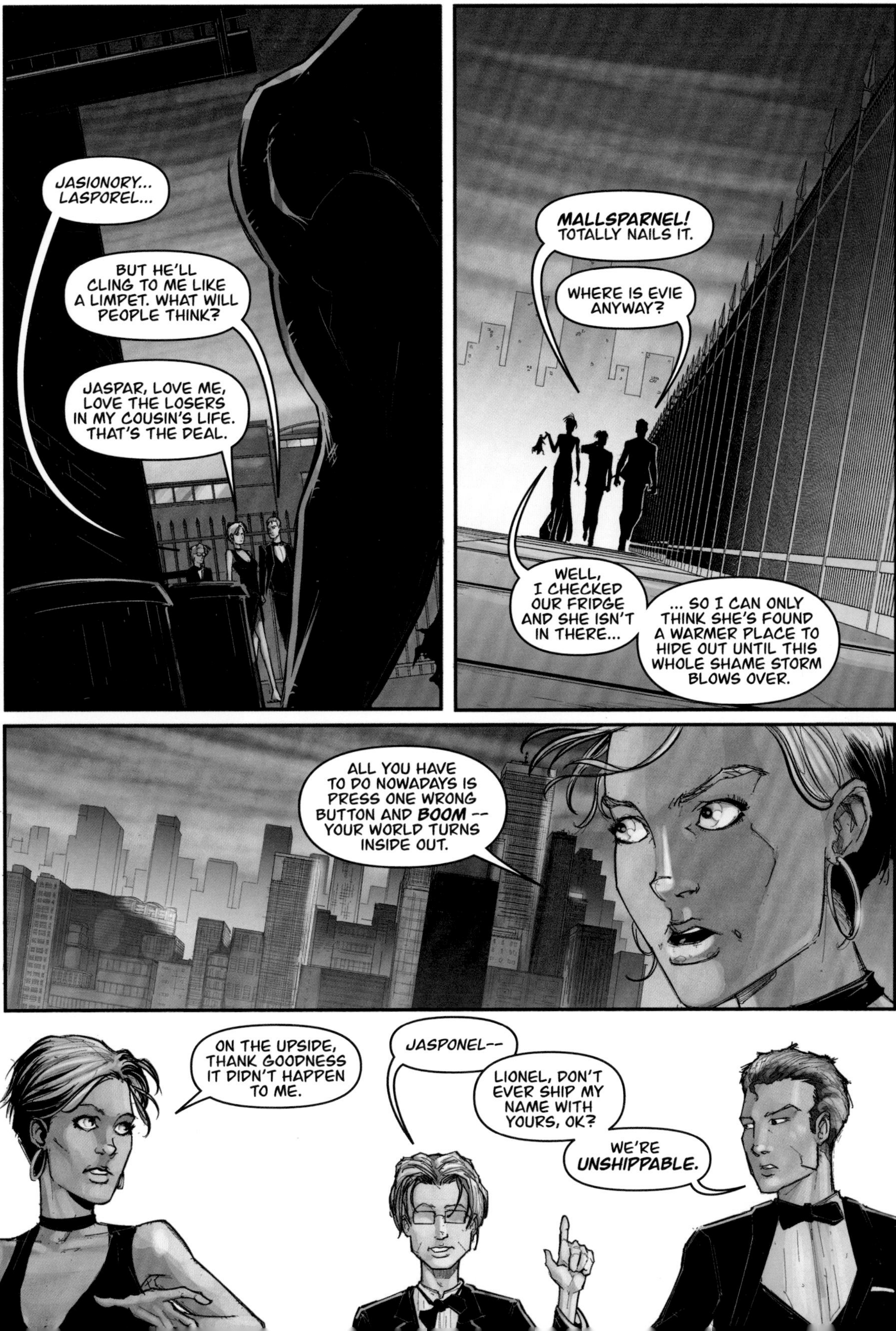
JASIONORY... LASPOREL...
BUT HE'LL CLING TO ME LIKE A LIMPET. WHAT WILL PEOPLE THINK?
JASPAR, LOVE ME, LOVE THE LOSERS IN MY COUSIN'S LIFE. THAT'S THE DEAL.
MALLSPARNEL! TOTALLY NAILS IT.
WHERE IS EVIE ANYWAY?
WELL, I CHECKED OUR FRIDGE AND SHE ISN'T IN THERE...
... SO I CAN ONLY THINK SHE'S FOUND A WARMER PLACE TO HIDE OUT UNTIL THIS WHOLE SHAME STORM BLOWS OVER.
ALL YOU HAVE TO DO NOWADAYS IS PRESS ONE WRONG BUTTON AND BOOM -- YOUR WORLD TURNS INSIDE OUT.
ON THE UPSIDE, THANK GOODNESS IT DIDN'T HAPPEN TO ME.
JASPONEL--
LIONEL, DON'T EVER SHIP MY NAME WITH YOURS, OK?
WE'RE UNSHIPPABLE.

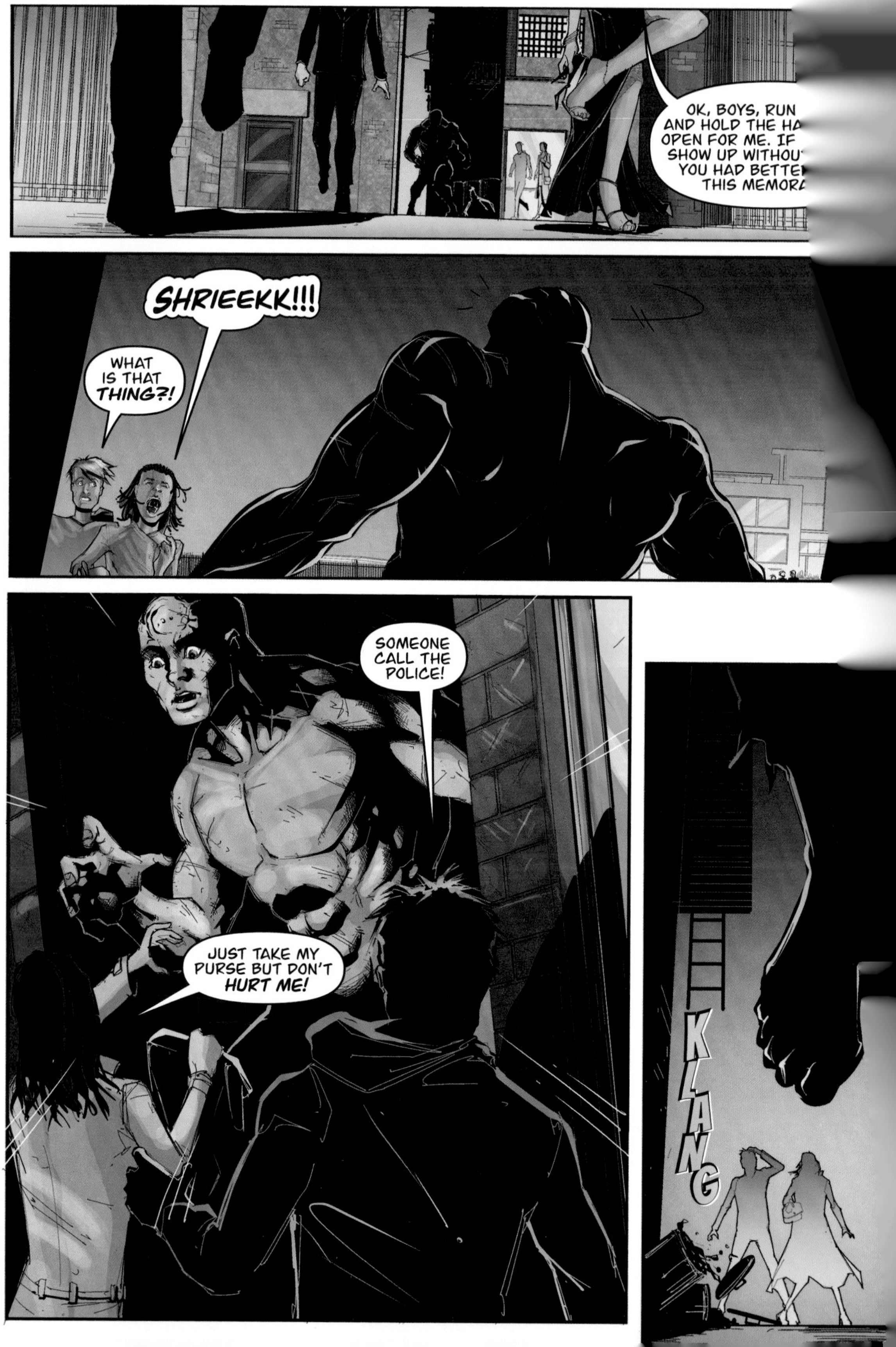
OK, BOYS, RUN AND HOLD THE HA OPEN FOR ME. IF SHOW UP WITHOUT YOU HAD BETTER THIS MEMORA
SHRIEEKK!!!
WHAT IS THAT THING?!
SOMEONE CALL THE POLICE!
JUST TAKE MY PURSE BUT DON'T HURT ME!
KLANG

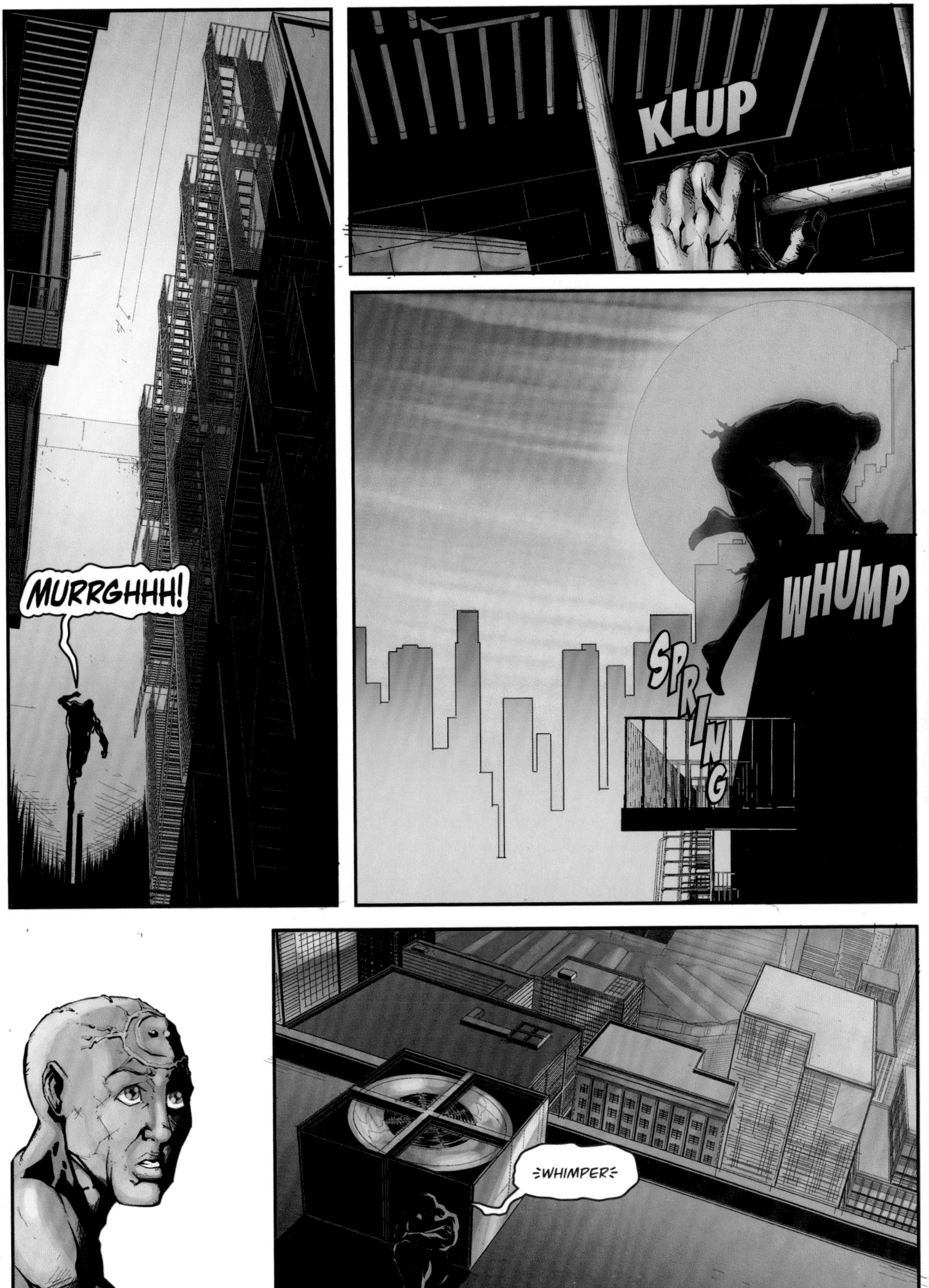
MURRGHHH!
KLUP
SPRING
WHUMP
WHIMPER

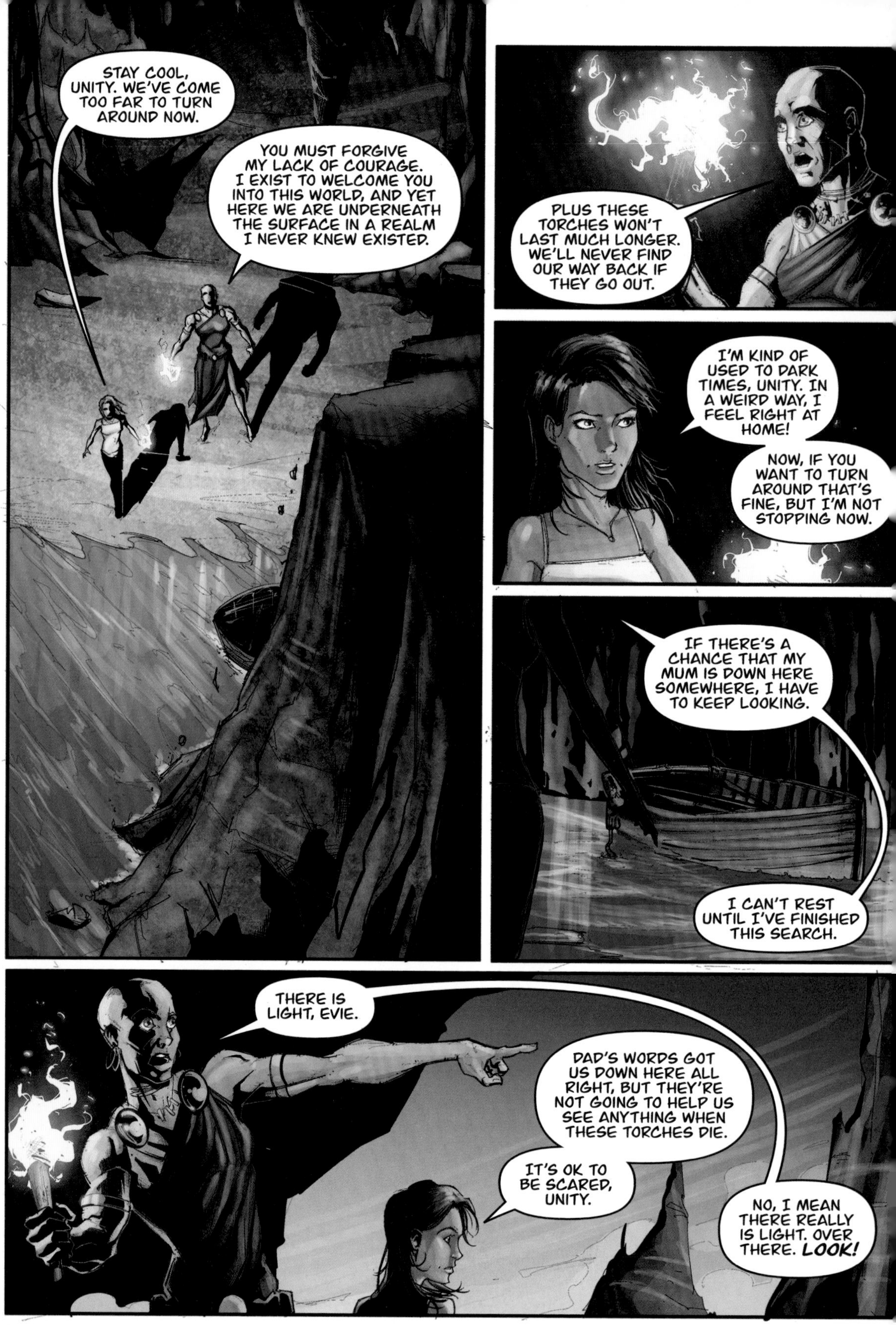
STAY COOL, UNITY. WE'VE COME TOO FAR TO TURN AROUND NOW.
YOU MUST FORGIVE MY LACK OF COURAGE. I EXIST TO WELCOME YOU INTO THIS WORLD, AND YET HERE WE ARE UNDERNEATH THE SURFACE IN A REALM I NEVER KNEW EXISTED.
PLUS THESE TORCHES WON'T LAST MUCH LONGER. WE'LL NEVER FIND OUR WAY BACK IF THEY GO OUT.
I'M KIND OF USED TO DARK TIMES, UNITY. IN A WEIRD WAY, I FEEL RIGHT AT HOME!
NOW, IF YOU WANT TO TURN AROUND THAT'S FINE, BUT I'M NOT STOPPING NOW.
IF THERE'S A CHANCE THAT MY MUM IS DOWN HERE SOMEWHERE, I HAVE TO KEEP LOOKING.
I CAN'T REST UNTIL I'VE FINISHED THIS SEARCH.
THERE IS LIGHT, EVIE.
DAD'S WORDS GOT US DOWN HERE ALL RIGHT, BUT THEY'RE NOT GOING TO HELP US SEE ANYTHING WHEN THESE TORCHES DIE.
IT'S OK TO BE SCARED, UNITY.
NO, I MEAN THERE REALLY IS LIGHT. OVER THERE. LOOK!

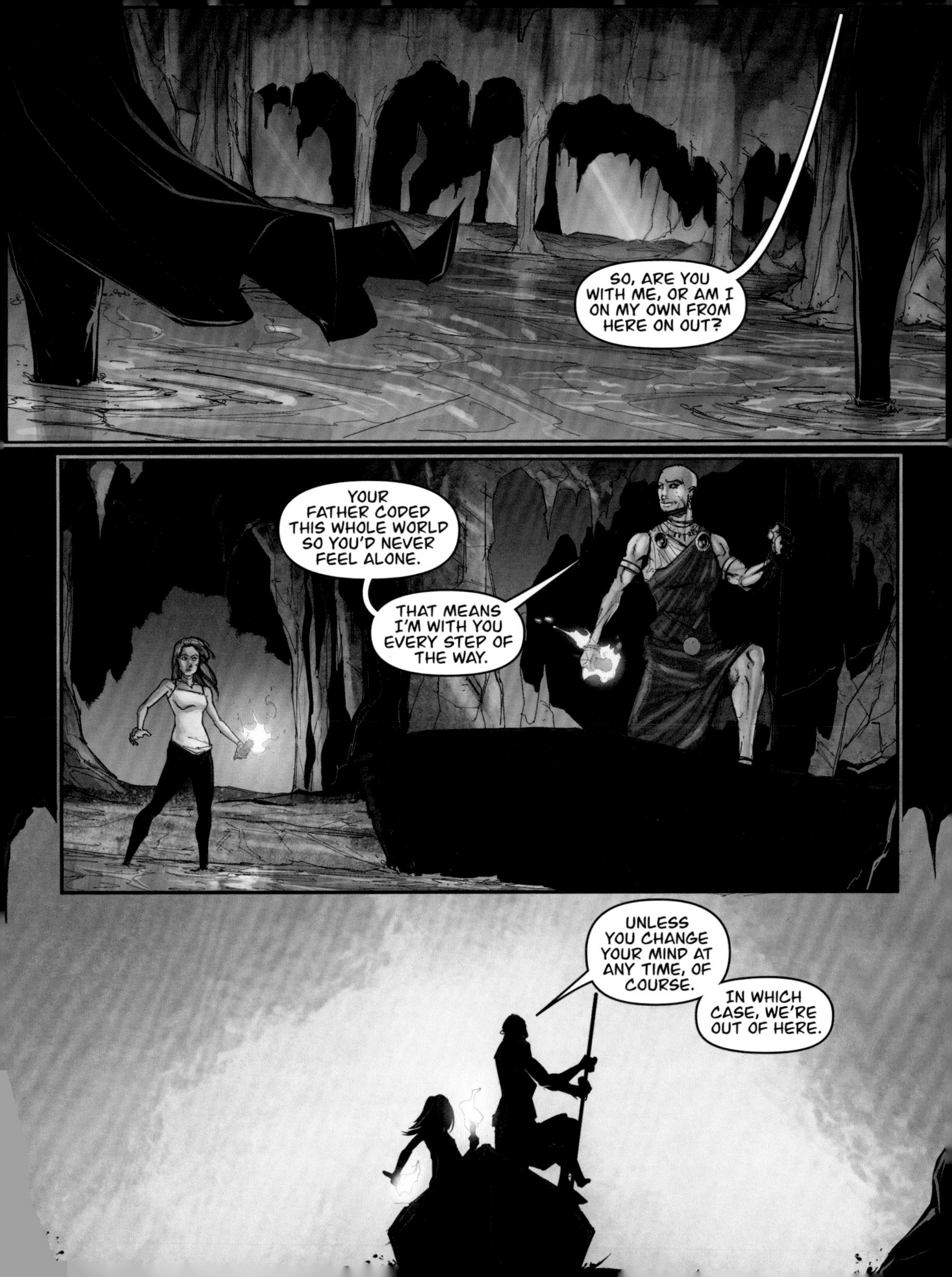

SO, ARE YOU WITH ME, OR AM I ON MY OWN FROM HERE ON OUT?
YOUR FATHER CODED THIS WHOLE WORLD SO YOU'D NEVER FEEL ALONE.
THAT MEANS I'M WITH YOU EVERY STEP OF THE WAY.
UNLESS YOU CHANGE YOUR MIND AT ANY TIME, OF COURSE.
IN WHICH CASE, WE'RE OUT OF HERE.

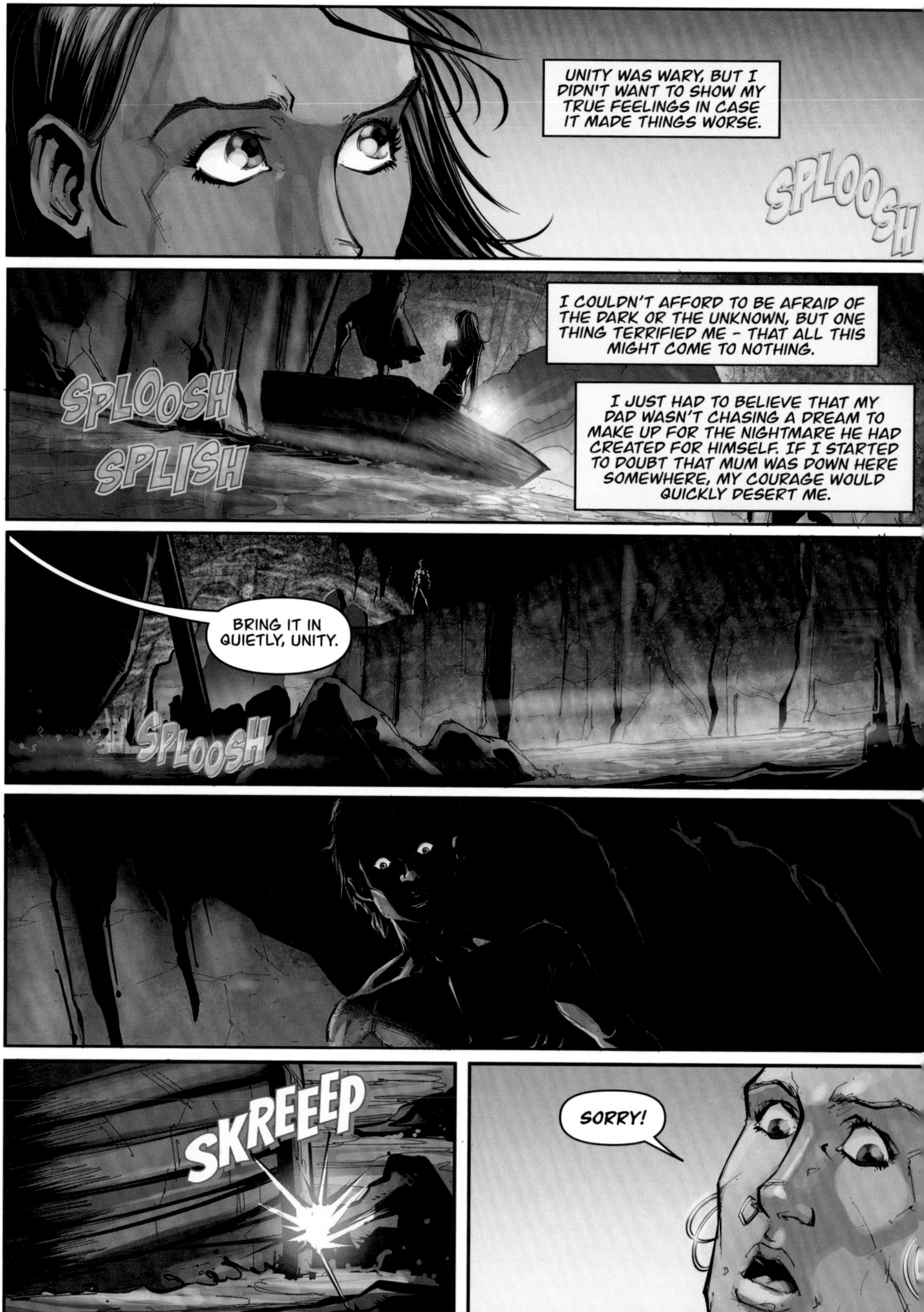
UNITY WAS WARY, BUT I DIDN'T WANT TO SHOW MY TRUE FEELINGS IN CASE IT MADE THINGS WORSE.
SPLOOSH
I COULDN'T AFFORD TO BE AFRAID OF THE DARK OR THE UNKNOWN, BUT ONE THING TERRIFIED ME - THAT ALL THIS MIGHT COME TO NOTHING.
I JUST HAD TO BELIEVE THAT MY DAD WASN'T CHASING A DREAM TO MAKE UP FOR THE NIGHTMARE HE HAD CREATED FOR HIMSELF. IF I STARTED TO DOUBT THAT MUM WAS DOWN HERE SOMEWHERE, MY COURAGE WOULD QUICKLY DESERT ME.
SPLOOSH
SPLISH
BRING IT IN QUIETLY, UNITY.
SPLOOSH
SKREEEP
SORRY!

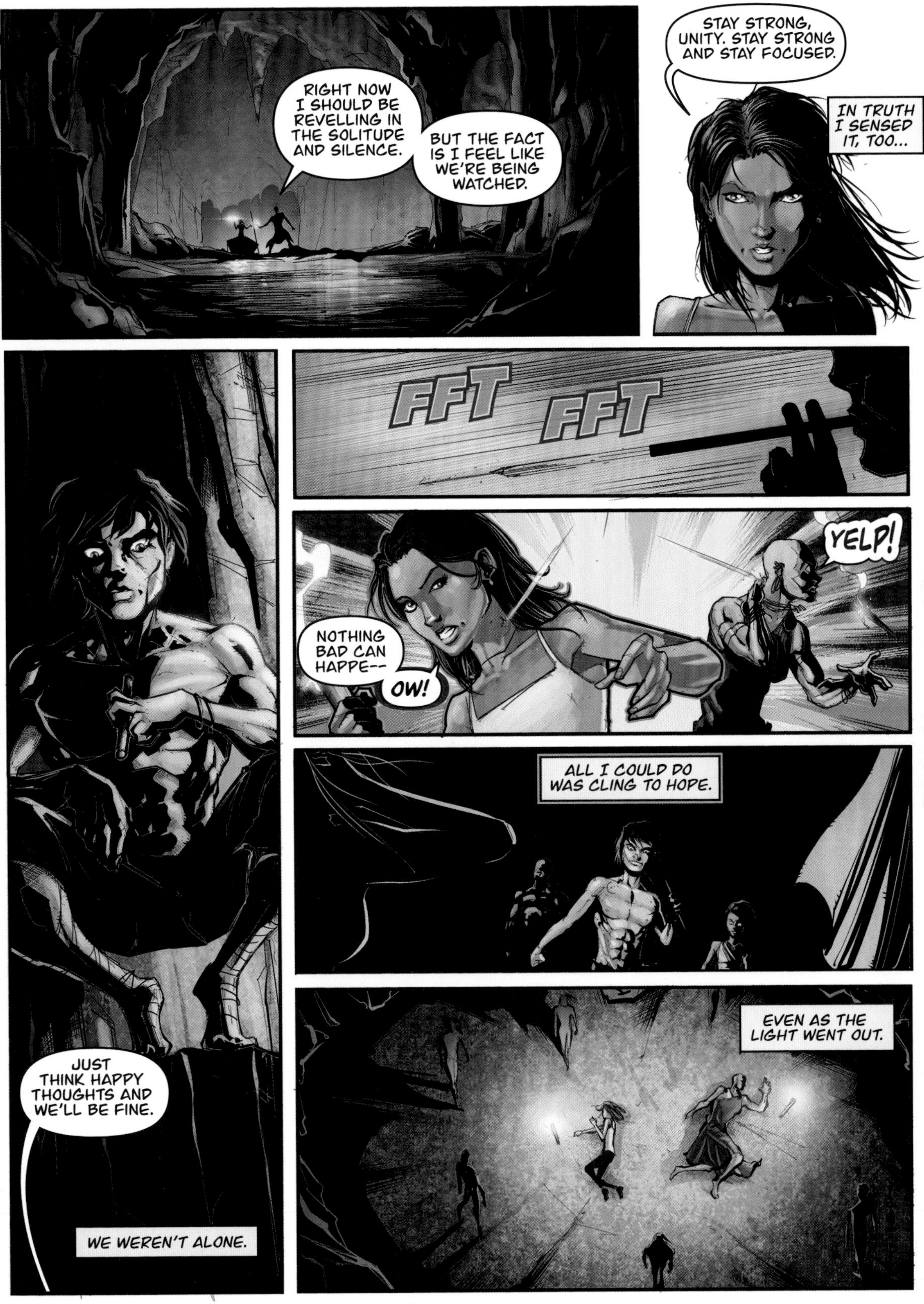
RIGHT NOW I SHOULD BE REVELLING IN THE SOLITUDE AND SILENCE.
BUT THE FACT IS I FEEL LIKE WE'RE BEING WATCHED.
STAY STRONG, UNITY. STAY STRONG AND STAY FOCUSED.
IN TRUTH I SENSED IT, TOO...
JUST THINK HAPPY THOUGHTS AND WE'LL BE FINE.
WE WEREN'T ALONE.
FFT FFT
NOTHING BAD CAN HAPPE--
OW!
YELP!
ALL I COULD DO WAS CLING TO HOPE.
EVEN AS THE LIGHT WENT OUT.

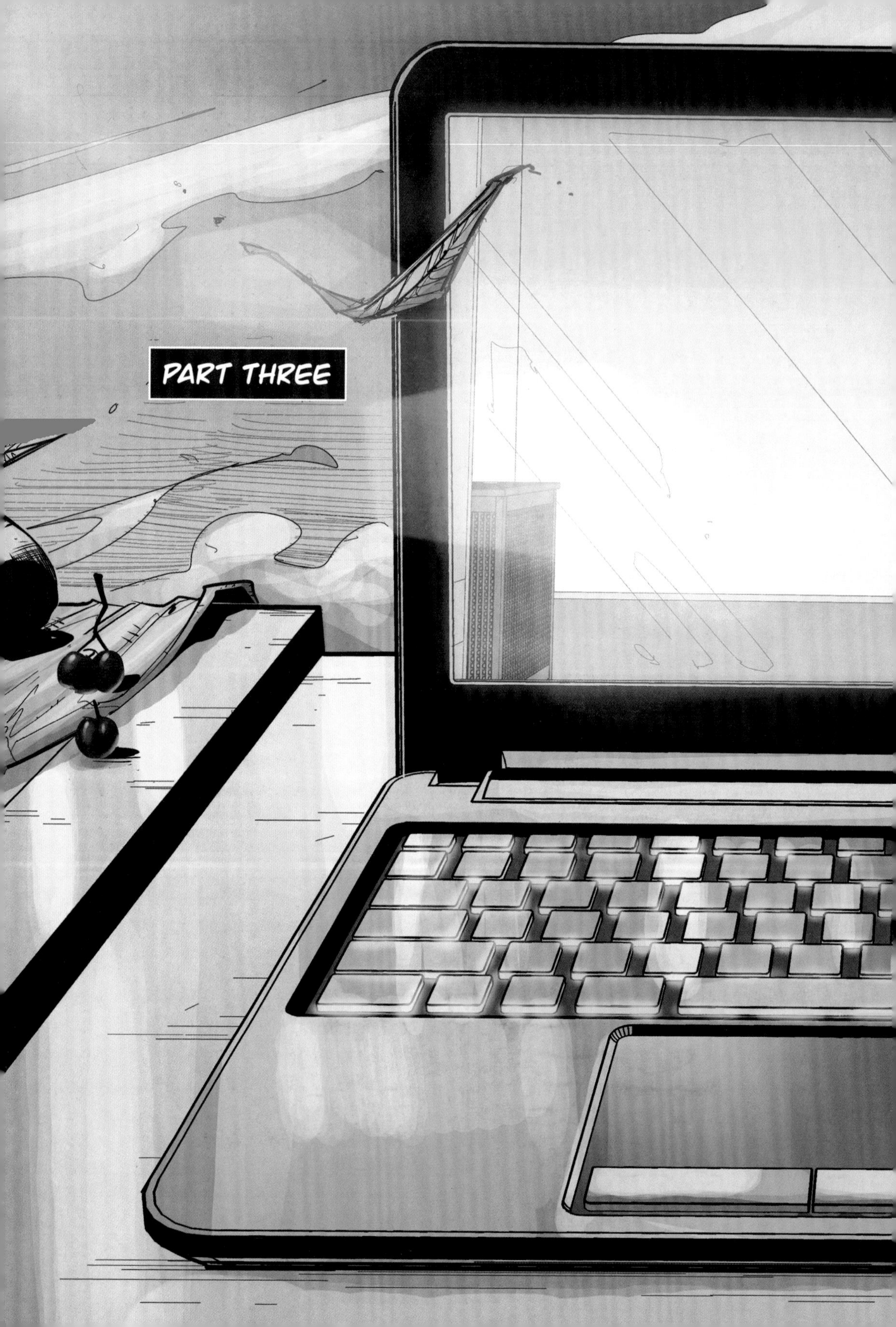
PART THREE

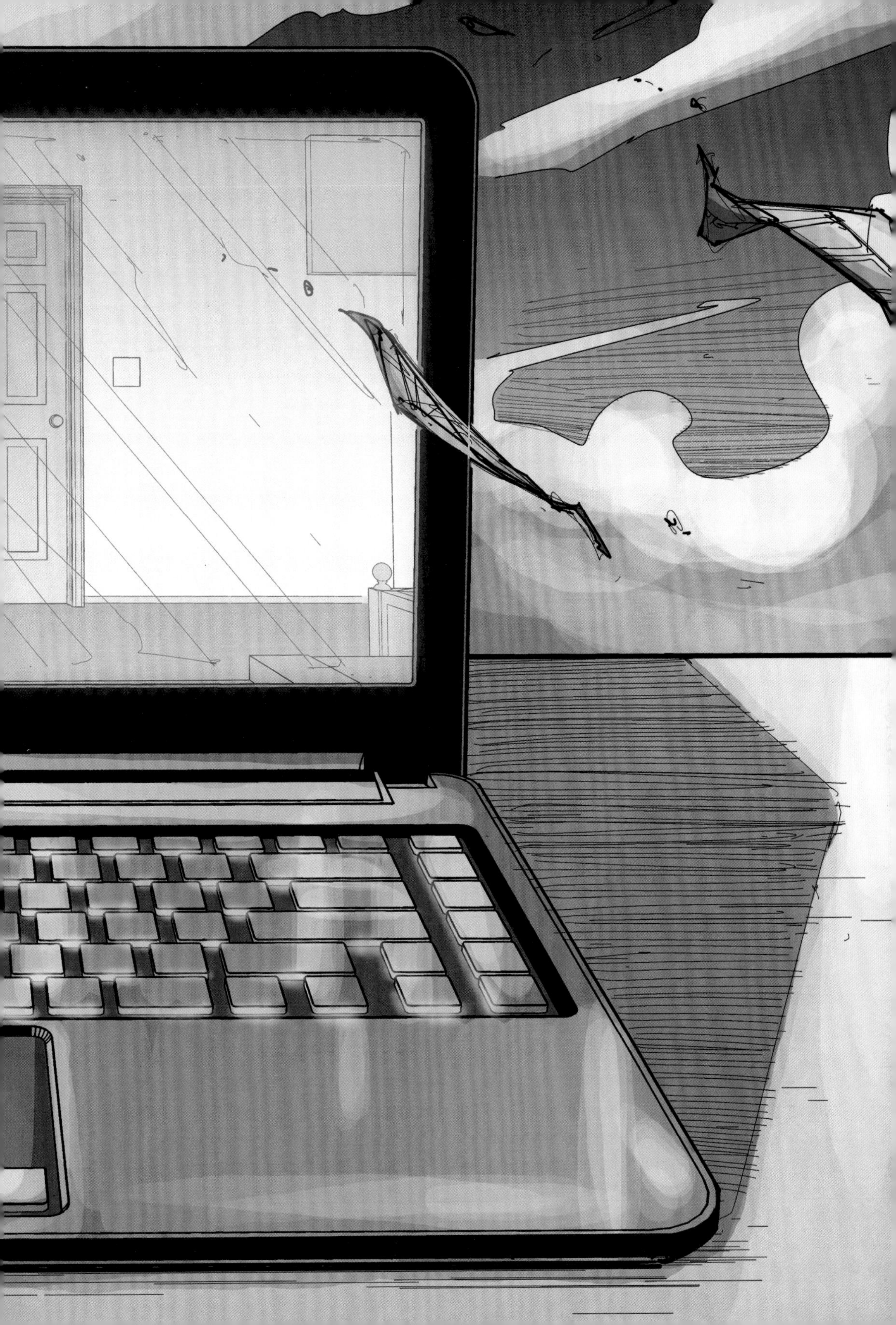

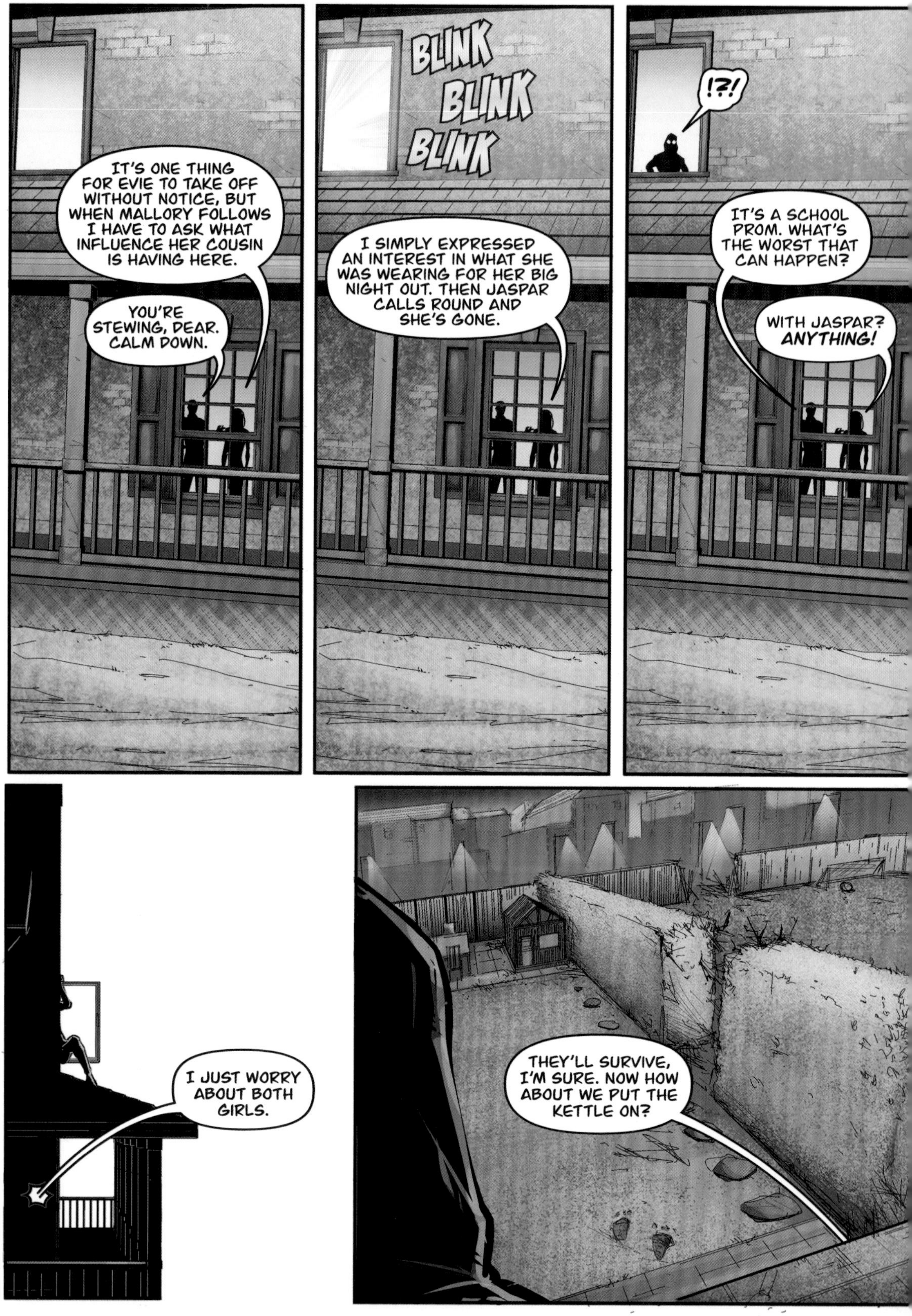
IT'S ONE THING FOR EVIE TO TAKE OFF WITHOUT NOTICE, BUT WHEN MALLORY FOLLOWS I HAVE TO ASK WHAT INFLUENCE HER COUSIN IS HAVING HERE.
YOU'RE STEWING, DEAR. CALM DOWN.
BLINK
BLINK
BLINK
I SIMPLY EXPRESSED AN INTEREST IN WHAT SHE WAS WEARING FOR HER BIG NIGHT OUT. THEN JASPAR CALLS ROUND AND SHE'S GONE.
!?!
IT'S A SCHOOL PROM. WHAT'S THE WORST THAT CAN HAPPEN?
WITH JASPAR? ANYTHING!
I JUST WORRY ABOUT BOTH GIRLS.
THEY'LL SURVIVE, I'M SURE. NOW HOW ABOUT WE PUT THE KETTLE ON?

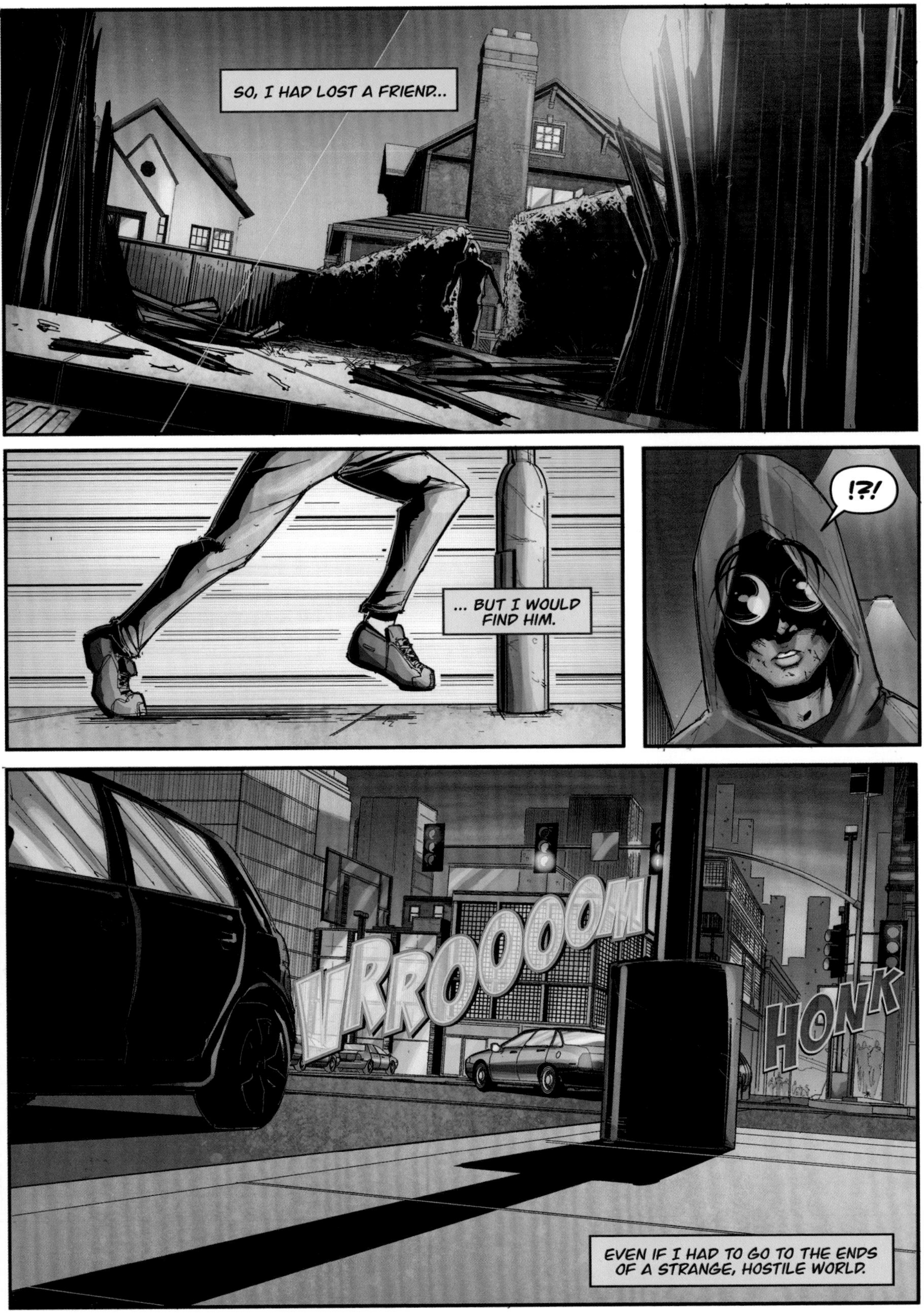

SO, I HAD LOST A FRIEND...
... BUT I WOULD FIND HIM.
!?!
VRROOOOOM
HONK
EVEN IF I HAD TO GO TO THE ENDS OF A STRANGE, HOSTILE WORLD.

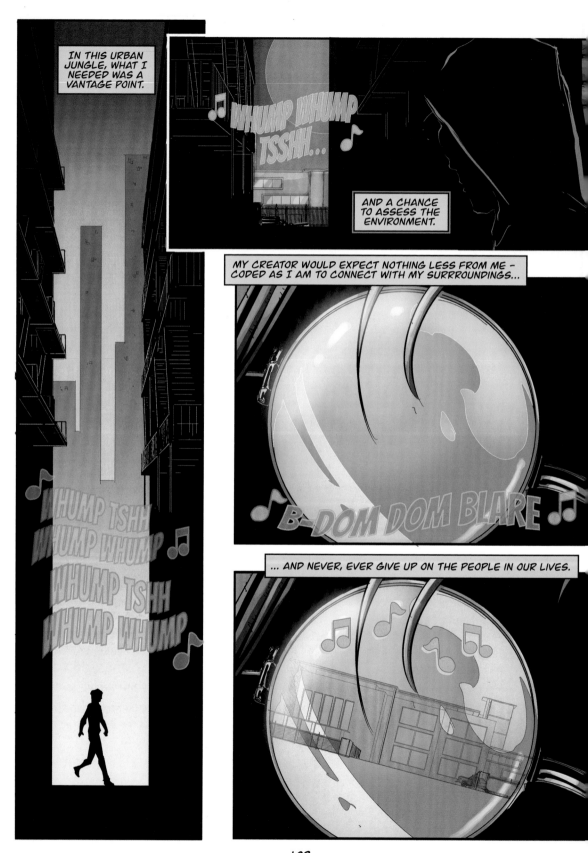

IN THIS URBAN JUNGLE, WHAT I NEEDED WAS A VANTAGE POINT.

♪ WHUMP WHUMP TSSHH... ♪

AND A CHANCE TO ASSESS THE ENVIRONMENT.

MY CREATOR WOULD EXPECT NOTHING LESS FROM ME – CODED AS I AM TO CONNECT WITH MY SURROUNDINGS...

♪ B-DOM DOM BLARE ♪

... AND NEVER, EVER GIVE UP ON THE PEOPLE IN OUR LIVES.

♪ WHUMP TSHH WHUMP WHUMP ♪ WHUMP TSHH WHUMP WHUMP ♪

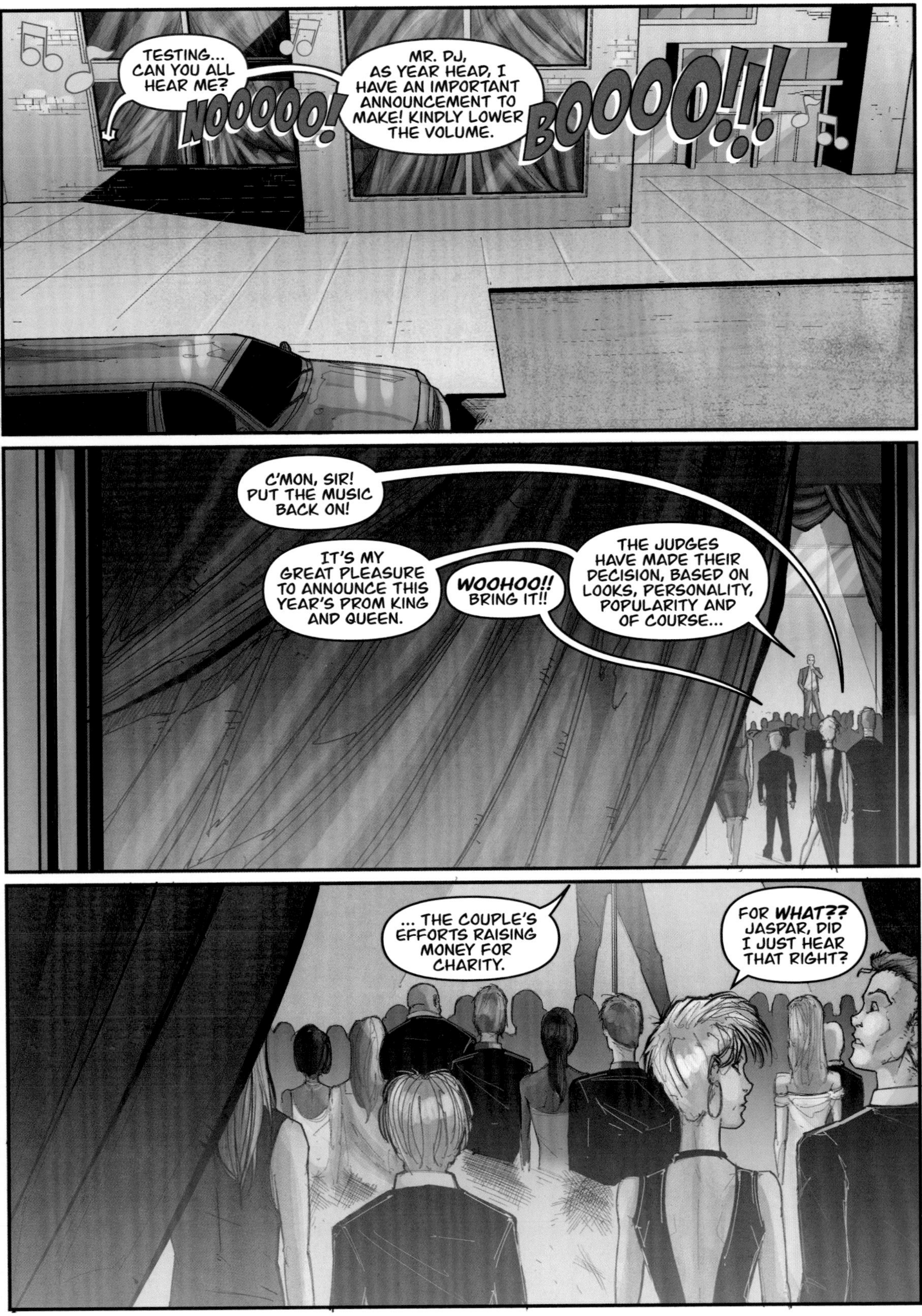
TESTING... CAN YOU ALL HEAR ME?
NOOOOO!
MR. DJ, AS YEAR HEAD, I HAVE AN IMPORTANT ANNOUNCEMENT TO MAKE! KINDLY LOWER THE VOLUME.
BOOOOO!!!
C'MON, SIR! PUT THE MUSIC BACK ON!
IT'S MY GREAT PLEASURE TO ANNOUNCE THIS YEAR'S PROM KING AND QUEEN.
WOOHOO!! BRING IT!!
THE JUDGES HAVE MADE THEIR DECISION, BASED ON LOOKS, PERSONALITY, POPULARITY AND OF COURSE...
... THE COUPLE'S EFFORTS RAISING MONEY FOR CHARITY.
FOR WHAT?? JASPAR, DID I JUST HEAR THAT RIGHT?

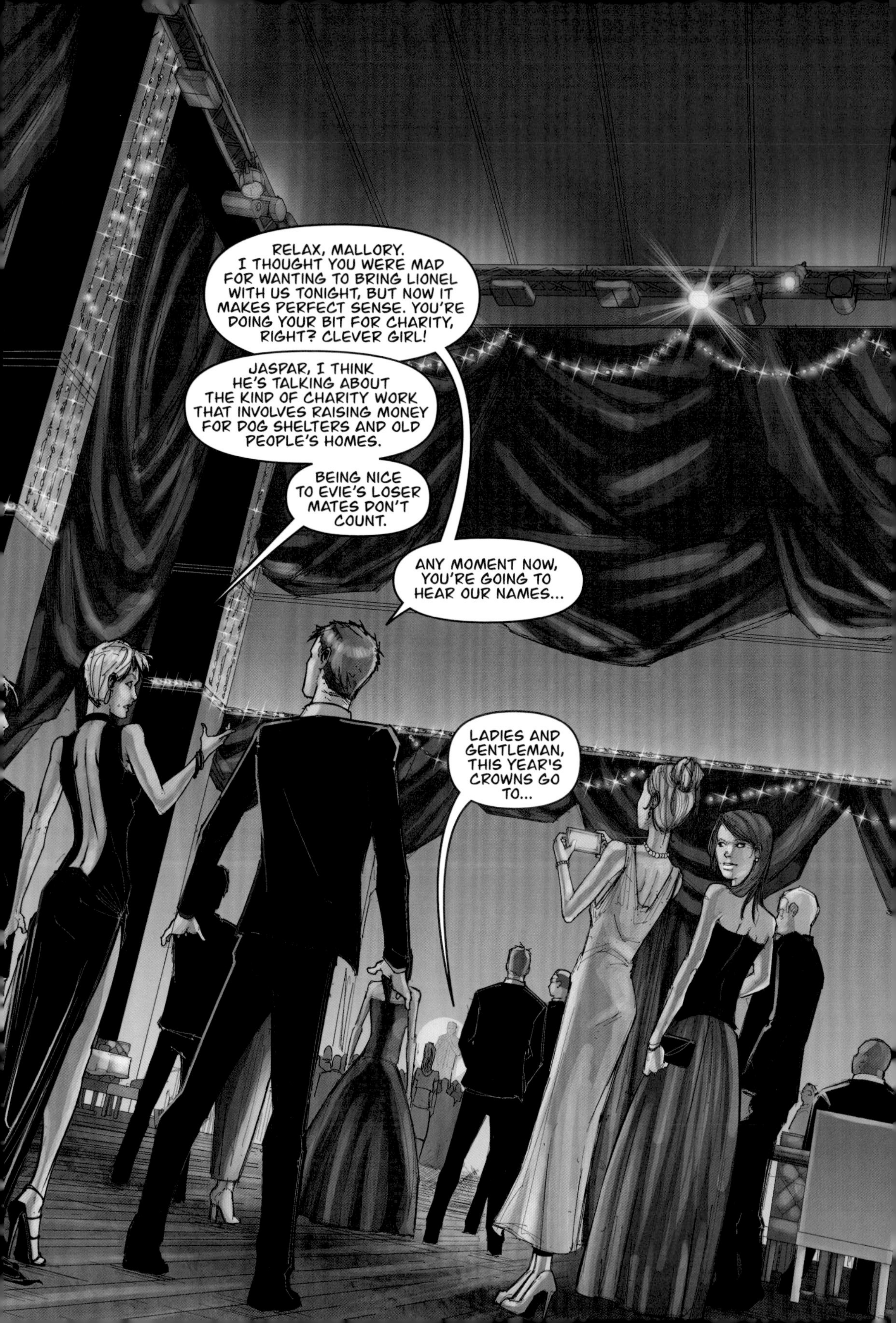
RELAX, MALLORY. I THOUGHT YOU WERE MAD FOR WANTING TO BRING LIONEL WITH US TONIGHT, BUT NOW IT MAKES PERFECT SENSE. YOU'RE DOING YOUR BIT FOR CHARITY, RIGHT? CLEVER GIRL!
JASPAR, I THINK HE'S TALKING ABOUT THE KIND OF CHARITY WORK THAT INVOLVES RAISING MONEY FOR DOG SHELTERS AND OLD PEOPLE'S HOMES.
BEING NICE TO EVIE'S LOSER MATES DON'T COUNT.
ANY MOMENT NOW, YOU'RE GOING TO HEAR OUR NAMES...
LADIES AND GENTLEMAN, THIS YEAR'S CROWNS GO TO...

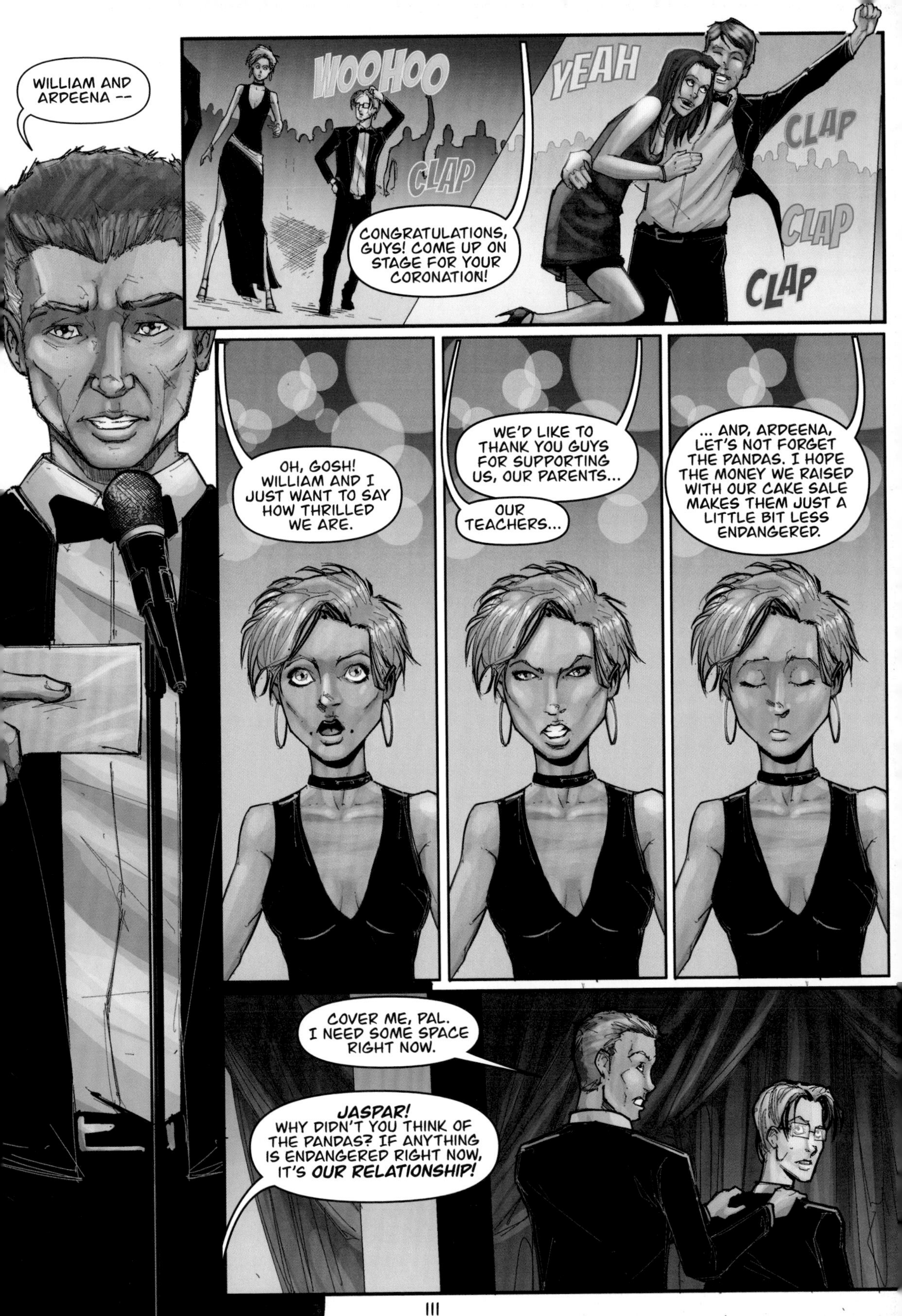
WILLIAM AND ARDEENA --
WOOHOO
CLAP
CONGRATULATIONS, GUYS! COME UP ON STAGE FOR YOUR CORONATION!
YEAH
CLAP
CLAP
CLAP
OH, GOSH! WILLIAM AND I JUST WANT TO SAY HOW THRILLED WE ARE.
WE'D LIKE TO THANK YOU GUYS FOR SUPPORTING US, OUR PARENTS...
OUR TEACHERS...
... AND, ARDEENA, LET'S NOT FORGET THE PANDAS. I HOPE THE MONEY WE RAISED WITH OUR CAKE SALE MAKES THEM JUST A LITTLE BIT LESS ENDANGERED.
COVER ME, PAL. I NEED SOME SPACE RIGHT NOW.
JASPAR! WHY DIDN'T YOU THINK OF THE PANDAS? IF ANYTHING IS ENDANGERED RIGHT NOW, IT'S ***OUR RELATIONSHIP!***

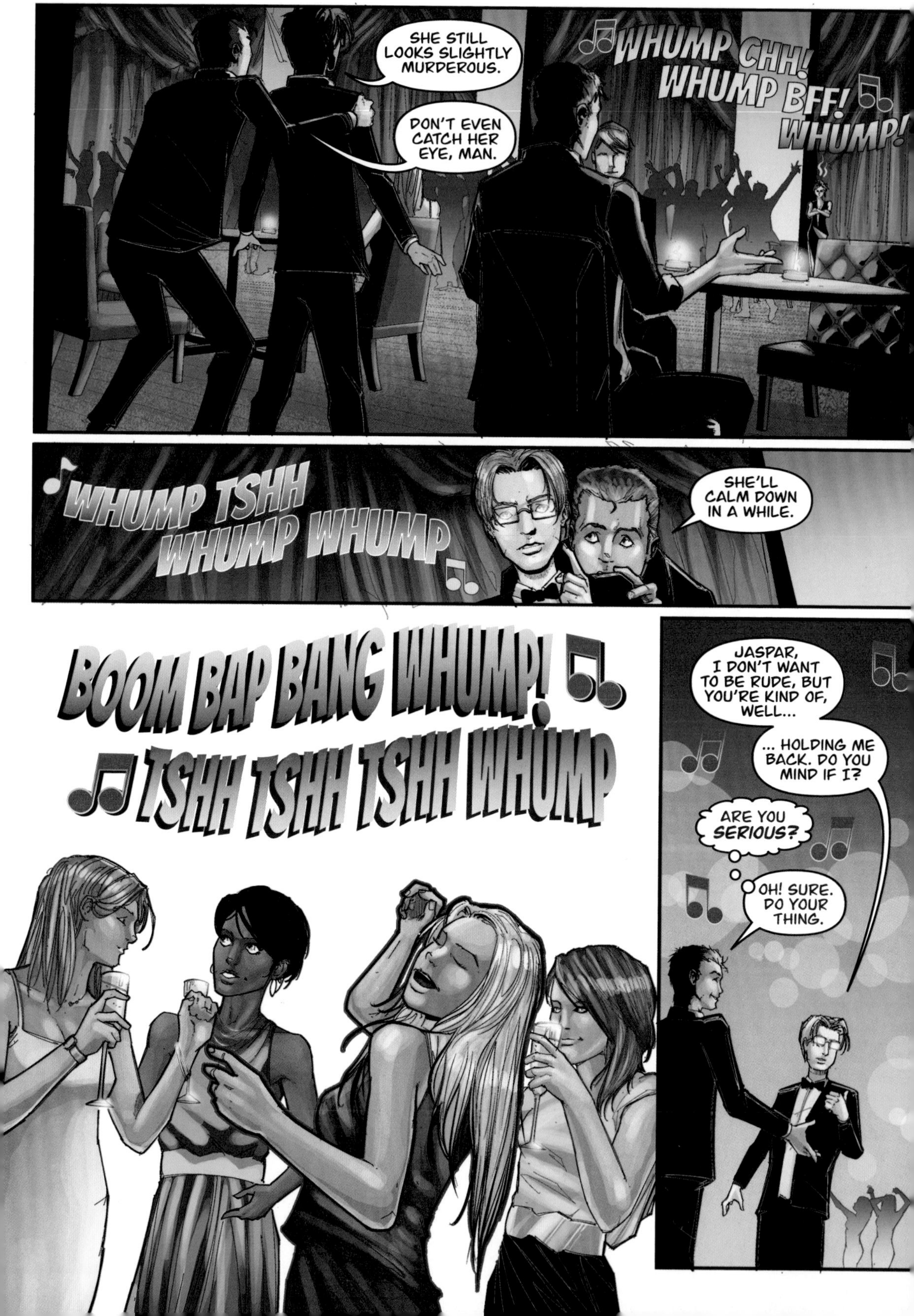
SHE STILL LOOKS SLIGHTLY MURDEROUS.
DON'T EVEN CATCH HER EYE, MAN.
WHUMP CHH! WHUMP BFF! WHUMP!
WHUMP TSHH WHUMP WHUMP
SHE'LL CALM DOWN IN A WHILE.
BOOM BAP BANG WHUMP!
TSHH TSHH TSHH WHUMP
JASPAR, I DON'T WANT TO BE RUDE, BUT YOU'RE KIND OF, WELL...
... HOLDING ME BACK. DO YOU MIND IF I?
ARE YOU SERIOUS?
OH! SURE. DO YOUR THING.

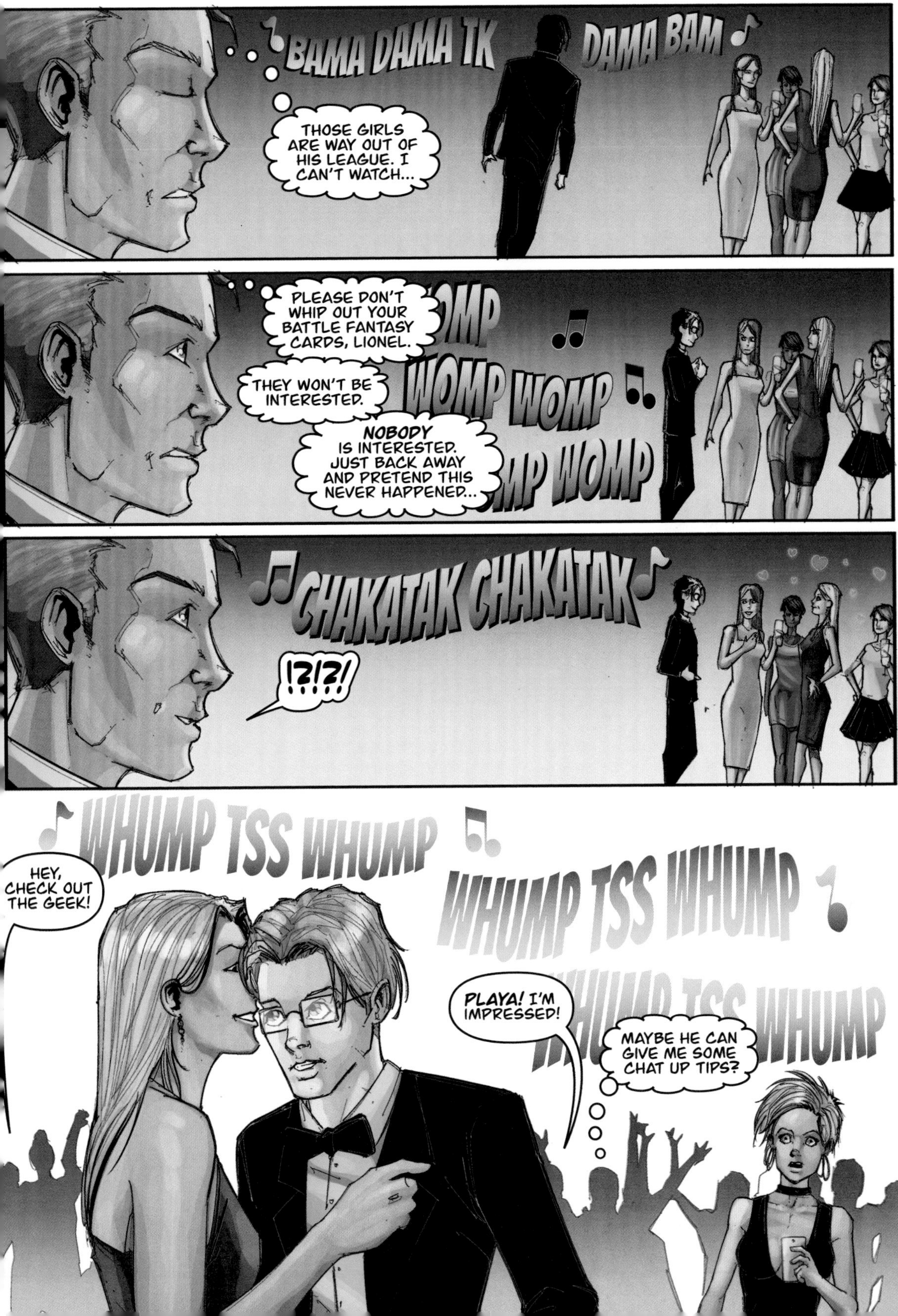
BAMA DAMA TK
DAMA BAM
THOSE GIRLS ARE WAY OUT OF HIS LEAGUE. I CAN'T WATCH...
PLEASE DON'T WHIP OUT YOUR BATTLE FANTASY CARDS, LIONEL.
THEY WON'T BE INTERESTED.
WOMP WOMP
NOBODY IS INTERESTED. JUST BACK AWAY AND PRETEND THIS NEVER HAPPENED...
CHAKATAK CHAKATAK
!?!?!
WHUMP TSS WHUMP
HEY, CHECK OUT THE GEEK!
WHUMP TSS WHUMP
PLAYA! I'M IMPRESSED!
MAYBE HE CAN GIVE ME SOME CHAT UP TIPS?

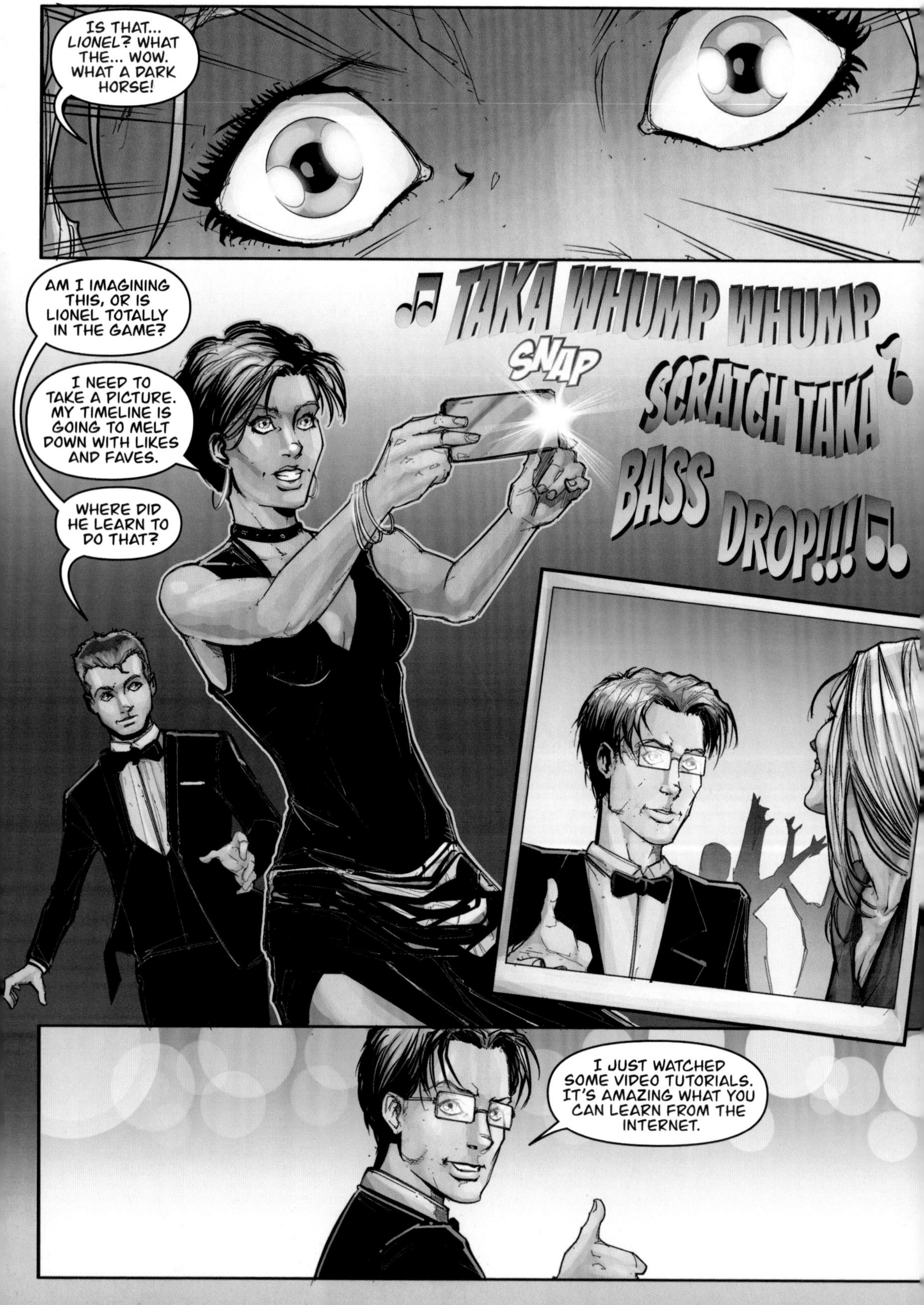
IS THAT... LIONEL? WHAT THE... WOW. WHAT A DARK HORSE!
AM I IMAGINING THIS, OR IS LIONEL TOTALLY IN THE GAME?
I NEED TO TAKE A PICTURE. MY TIMELINE IS GOING TO MELT DOWN WITH LIKES AND FAVES.
WHERE DID HE LEARN TO DO THAT?
TAKA WHUMP WHUMP
SNAP
SCRATCH TAKA
BASS DROP!!!
I JUST WATCHED SOME VIDEO TUTORIALS. IT'S AMAZING WHAT YOU CAN LEARN FROM THE INTERNET.

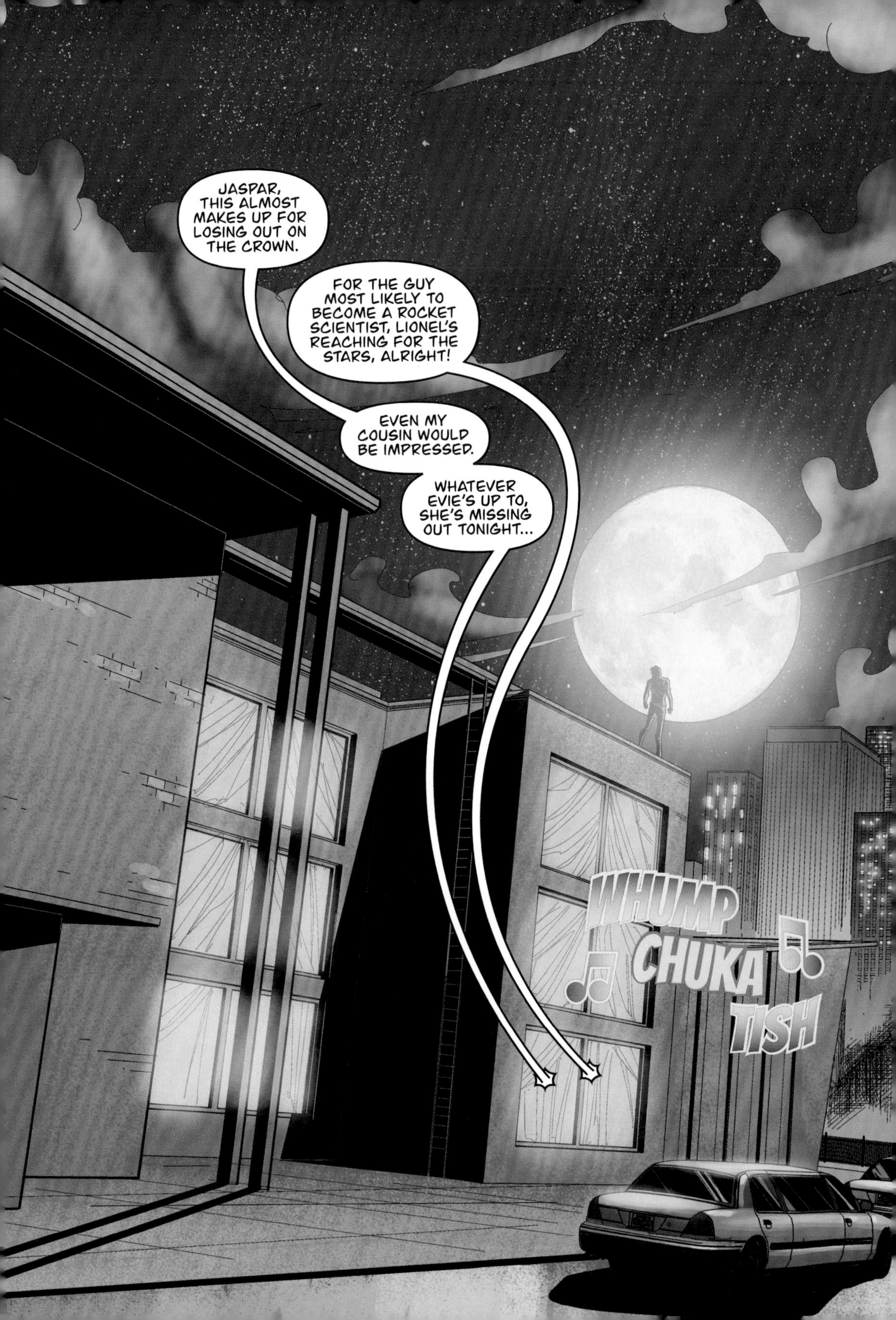
JASPAR, THIS ALMOST MAKES UP FOR LOSING OUT ON THE CROWN.
FOR THE GUY MOST LIKELY TO BECOME A ROCKET SCIENTIST, LIONEL'S REACHING FOR THE STARS, ALRIGHT!
EVEN MY COUSIN WOULD BE IMPRESSED.
WHATEVER EVIE'S UP TO, SHE'S MISSING OUT TONIGHT...
WHUMP
CHUKA
TISH

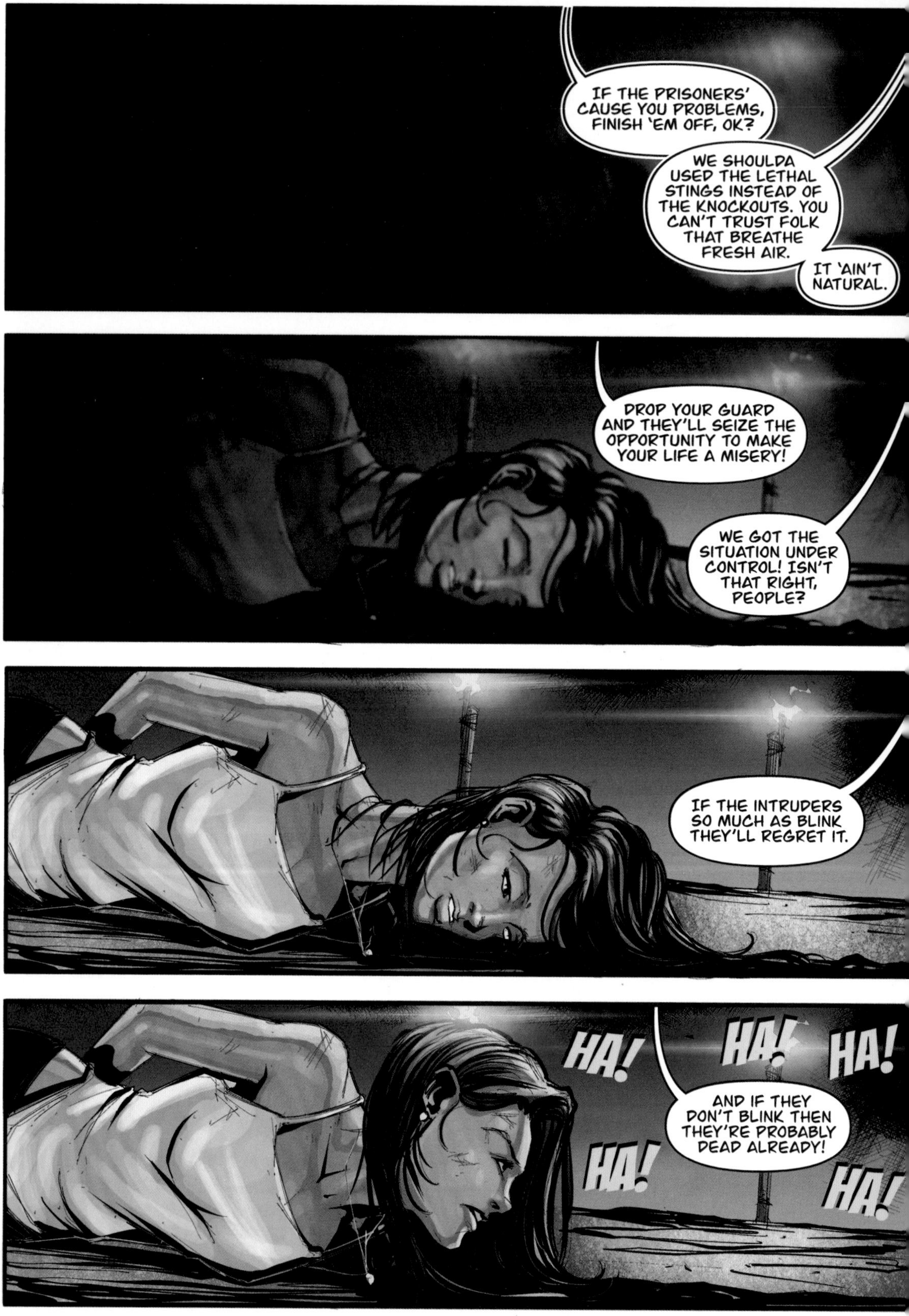
IF THE PRISONERS' CAUSE YOU PROBLEMS, FINISH 'EM OFF, OK?
WE SHOULDA USED THE LETHAL STINGS INSTEAD OF THE KNOCKOUTS. YOU CAN'T TRUST FOLK THAT BREATHE FRESH AIR.
IT 'AIN'T NATURAL.
DROP YOUR GUARD AND THEY'LL SEIZE THE OPPORTUNITY TO MAKE YOUR LIFE A MISERY!
WE GOT THE SITUATION UNDER CONTROL! ISN'T THAT RIGHT, PEOPLE?
IF THE INTRUDERS SO MUCH AS BLINK THEY'LL REGRET IT.
HA!
HA!
HA!
AND IF THEY DON'T BLINK THEN THEY'RE PROBABLY DEAD ALREADY!
HA!
HA!

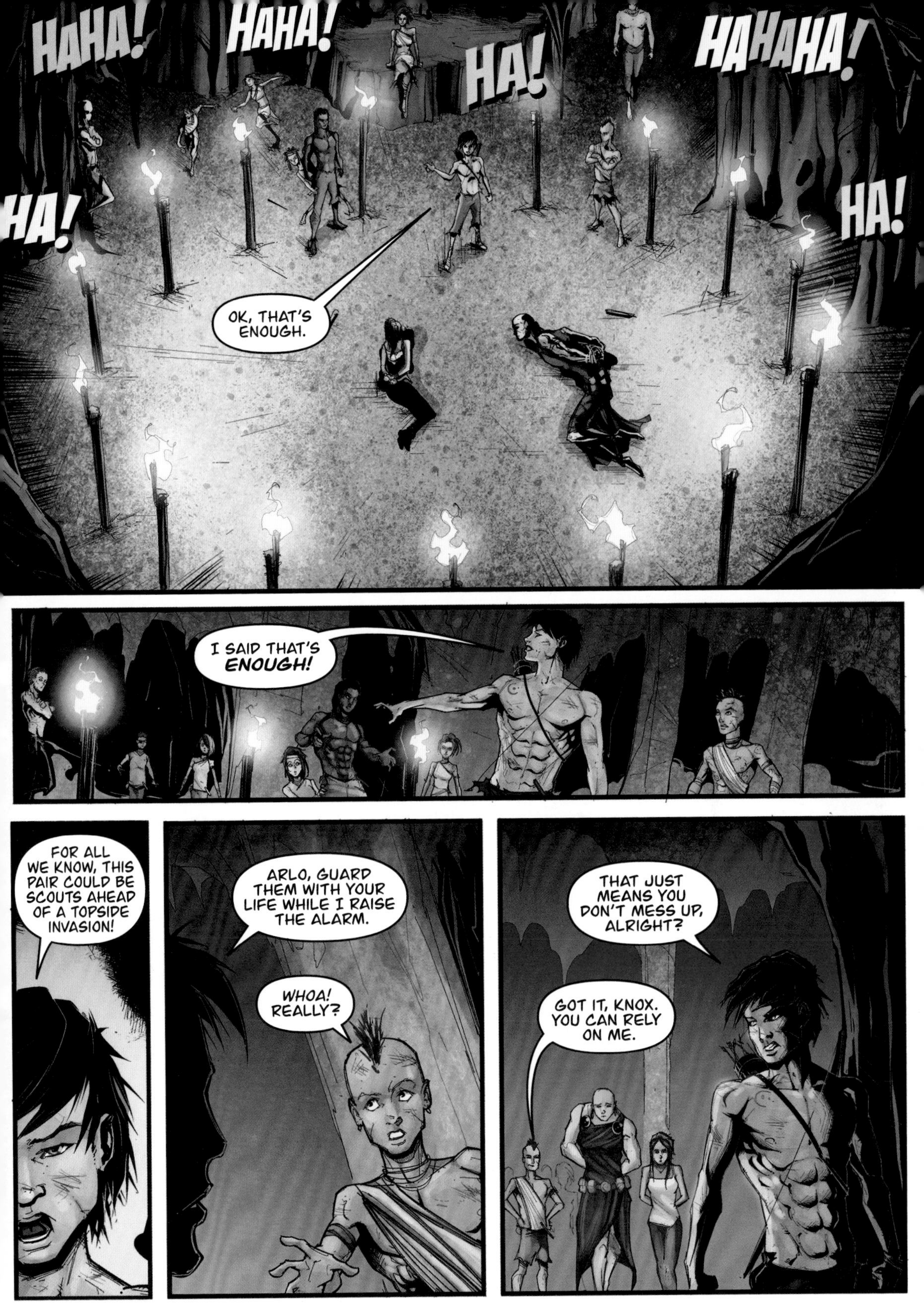
HAHA!
HAHA!
HA!
HAHAHA!
HA!
HA!
OK, THAT'S ENOUGH.
I SAID THAT'S ENOUGH!
FOR ALL WE KNOW, THIS PAIR COULD BE SCOUTS AHEAD OF A TOPSIDE INVASION!
ARLO, GUARD THEM WITH YOUR LIFE WHILE I RAISE THE ALARM.
WHOA! REALLY?
THAT JUST MEANS YOU DON'T MESS UP, ALRIGHT?
GOT IT, KNOX. YOU CAN RELY ON ME.

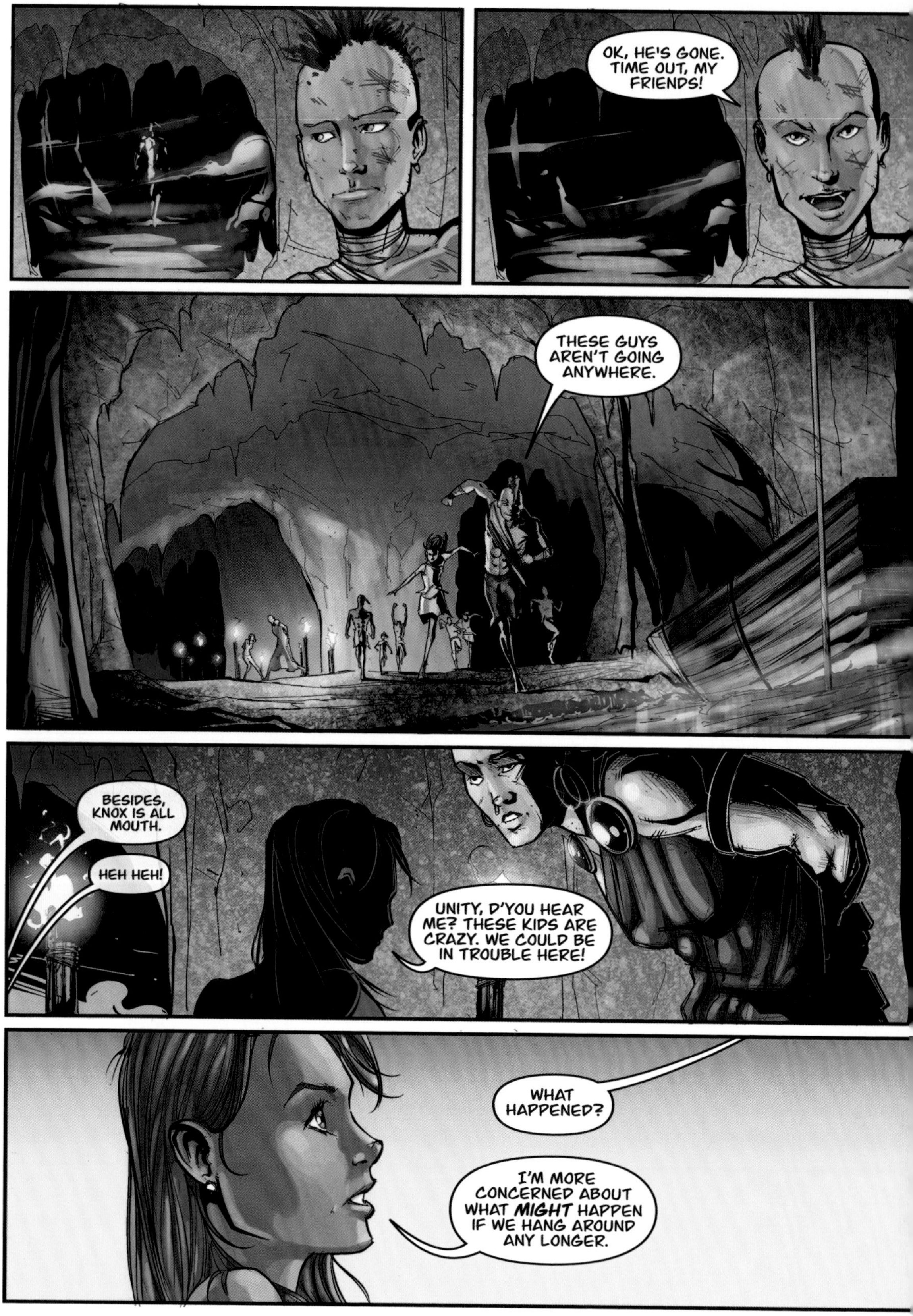

OK, HE'S GONE. TIME OUT, MY FRIENDS!
THESE GUYS AREN'T GOING ANYWHERE.
BESIDES, KNOX IS ALL MOUTH.
HEH HEH!
UNITY, D'YOU HEAR ME? THESE KIDS ARE CRAZY. WE COULD BE IN TROUBLE HERE!
WHAT HAPPENED?
I'M MORE CONCERNED ABOUT WHAT ***MIGHT*** HAPPEN IF WE HANG AROUND ANY LONGER.

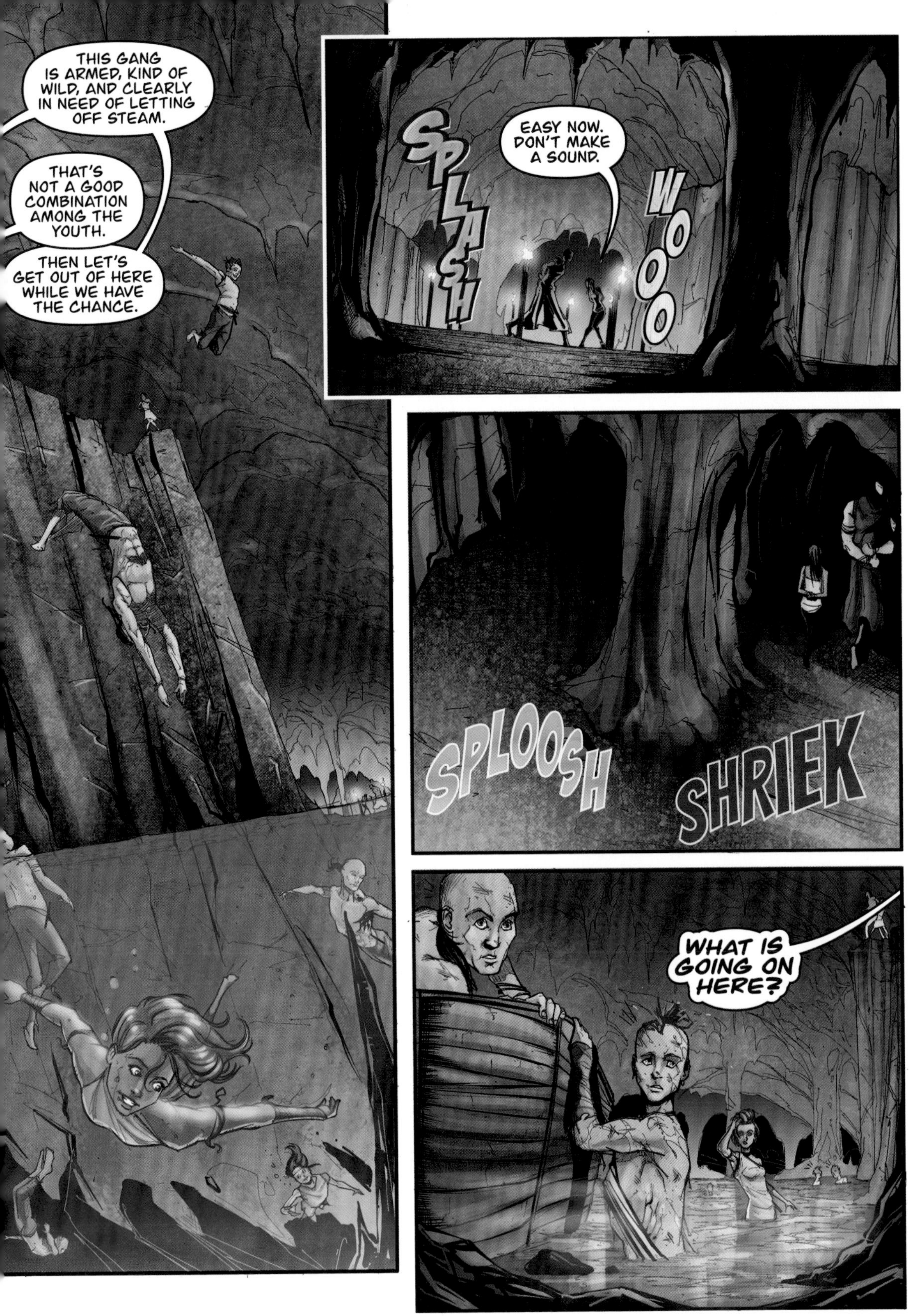
THIS GANG IS ARMED, KIND OF WILD, AND CLEARLY IN NEED OF LETTING OFF STEAM.
THAT'S NOT A GOOD COMBINATION AMONG THE YOUTH.
THEN LET'S GET OUT OF HERE WHILE WE HAVE THE CHANCE.
SPLASH
EASY NOW. DON'T MAKE A SOUND.
WOOO
SPLOOSH
SHRIEK
WHAT IS GOING ON HERE?

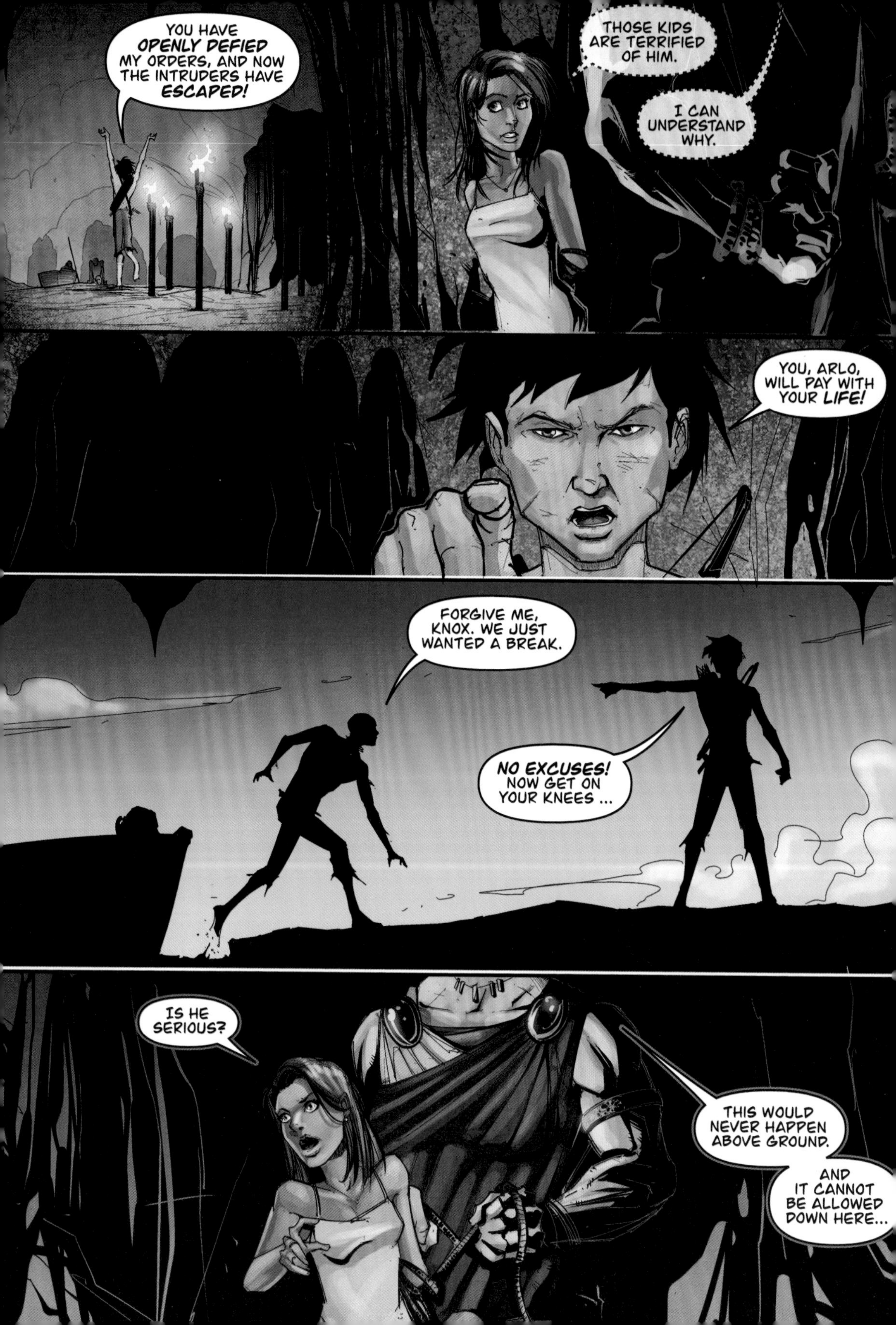
YOU HAVE OPENLY DEFIED MY ORDERS, AND NOW THE INTRUDERS HAVE ESCAPED!
THOSE KIDS ARE TERRIFIED OF HIM.
I CAN UNDERSTAND WHY.
YOU, ARLO, WILL PAY WITH YOUR LIFE!
FORGIVE ME, KNOX. WE JUST WANTED A BREAK.
NO EXCUSES! NOW GET ON YOUR KNEES ...
IS HE SERIOUS?
THIS WOULD NEVER HAPPEN ABOVE GROUND.
AND IT CANNOT BE ALLOWED DOWN HERE...

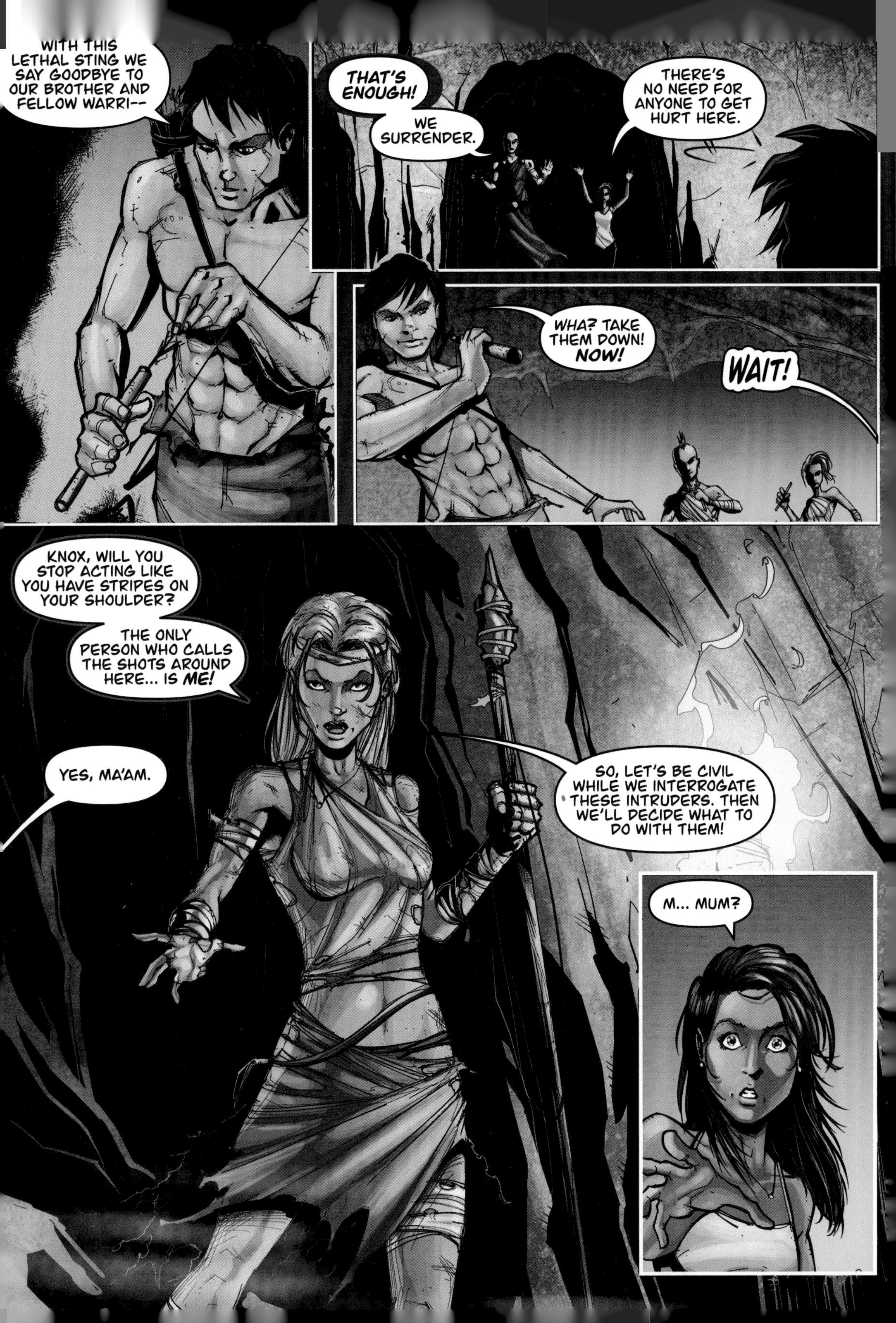
WITH THIS LETHAL STING WE SAY GOODBYE TO OUR BROTHER AND FELLOW WARRI--
THAT'S ENOUGH!
WE SURRENDER.
THERE'S NO NEED FOR ANYONE TO GET HURT HERE.
WHA? TAKE THEM DOWN! NOW!
WAIT!
KNOX, WILL YOU STOP ACTING LIKE YOU HAVE STRIPES ON YOUR SHOULDER?
THE ONLY PERSON WHO CALLS THE SHOTS AROUND HERE... IS ME!
YES, MA'AM.
SO, LET'S BE CIVIL WHILE WE INTERROGATE THESE INTRUDERS. THEN WE'LL DECIDE WHAT TO DO WITH THEM!
M... MUM?

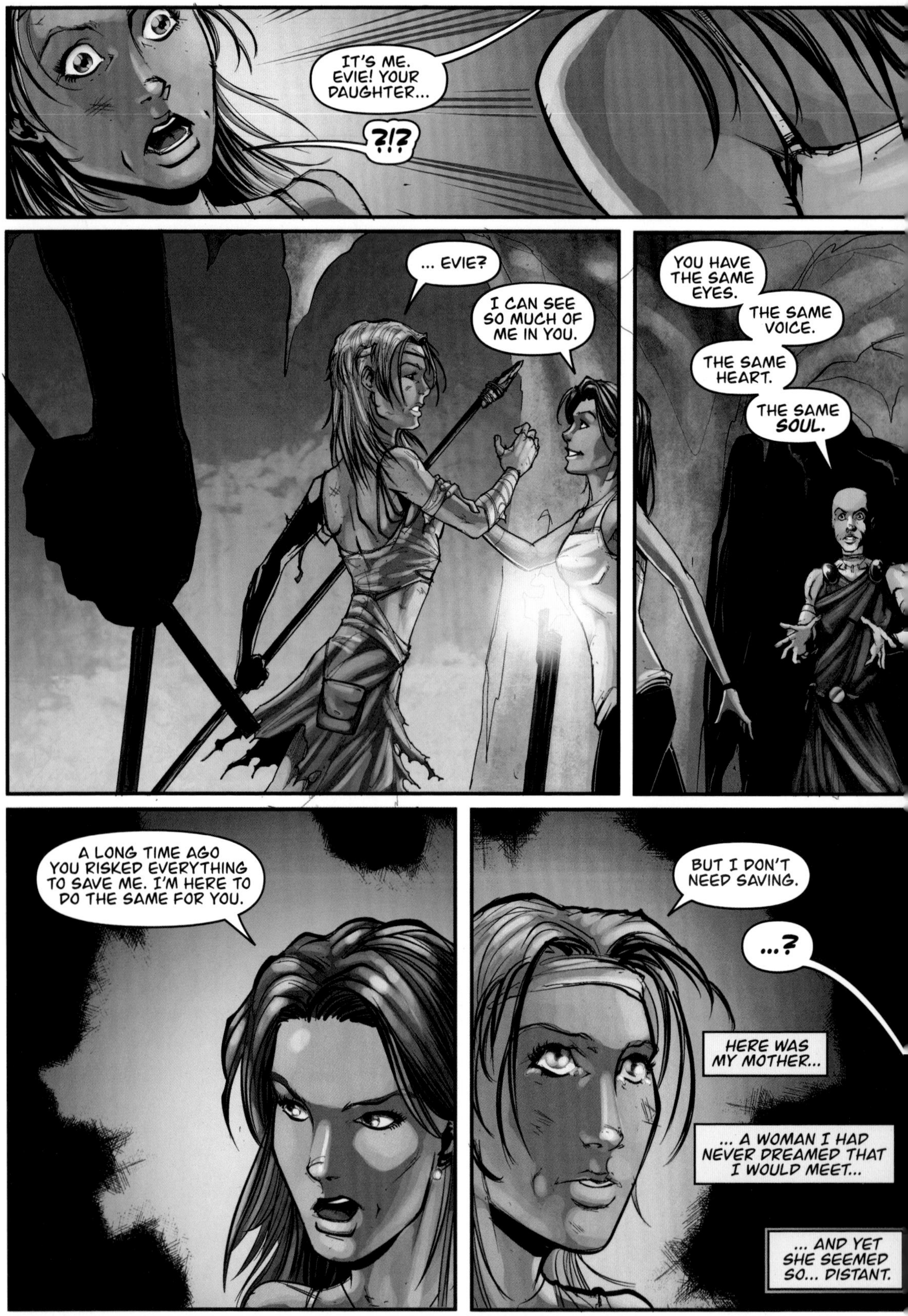
IT'S ME. EVIE! YOUR DAUGHTER...
?!?
... EVIE?
I CAN SEE SO MUCH OF ME IN YOU.
YOU HAVE THE SAME EYES.
THE SAME VOICE.
THE SAME HEART.
THE SAME SOUL.
A LONG TIME AGO YOU RISKED EVERYTHING TO SAVE ME. I'M HERE TO DO THE SAME FOR YOU.
BUT I DON'T NEED SAVING.
...?
HERE WAS MY MOTHER...
... A WOMAN I HAD NEVER DREAMED THAT I WOULD MEET...
... AND YET SHE SEEMED SO... DISTANT.

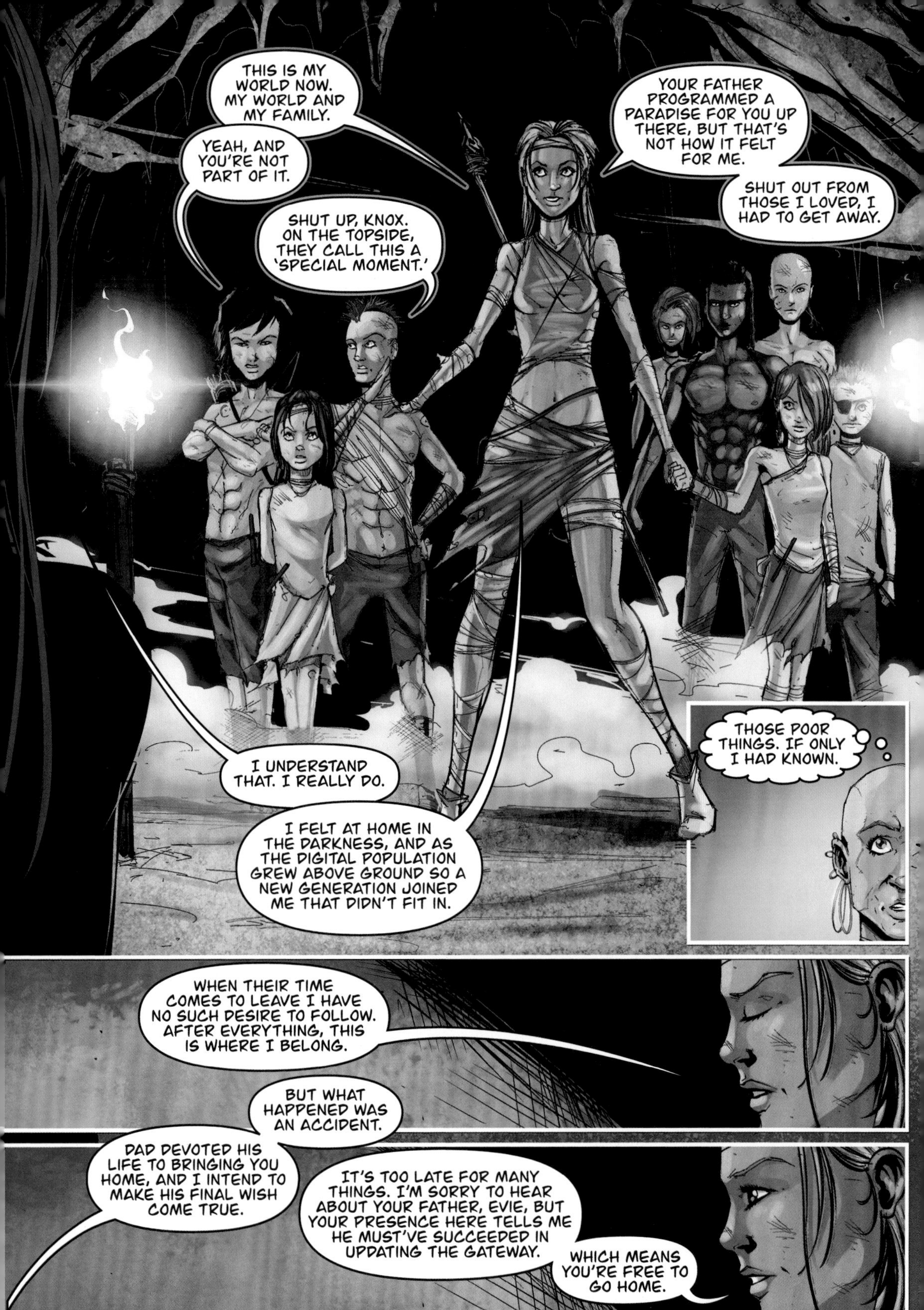
THIS IS MY WORLD NOW. MY WORLD AND MY FAMILY.
YEAH, AND YOU'RE NOT PART OF IT.
SHUT UP, KNOX. ON THE TOPSIDE, THEY CALL THIS A 'SPECIAL MOMENT.'
YOUR FATHER PROGRAMMED A PARADISE FOR YOU UP THERE, BUT THAT'S NOT HOW IT FELT FOR ME.
SHUT OUT FROM THOSE I LOVED, I HAD TO GET AWAY.
I UNDERSTAND THAT. I REALLY DO.
I FELT AT HOME IN THE DARKNESS, AND AS THE DIGITAL POPULATION GREW ABOVE GROUND SO A NEW GENERATION JOINED ME THAT DIDN'T FIT IN.
THOSE POOR THINGS. IF ONLY I HAD KNOWN.
WHEN THEIR TIME COMES TO LEAVE I HAVE NO SUCH DESIRE TO FOLLOW. AFTER EVERYTHING, THIS IS WHERE I BELONG.
BUT WHAT HAPPENED WAS AN ACCIDENT.
DAD DEVOTED HIS LIFE TO BRINGING YOU HOME, AND I INTEND TO MAKE HIS FINAL WISH COME TRUE.
IT'S TOO LATE FOR MANY THINGS. I'M SORRY TO HEAR ABOUT YOUR FATHER, EVIE, BUT YOUR PRESENCE HERE TELLS ME HE MUST'VE SUCCEEDED IN UPDATING THE GATEWAY.
WHICH MEANS YOU'RE FREE TO GO HOME.

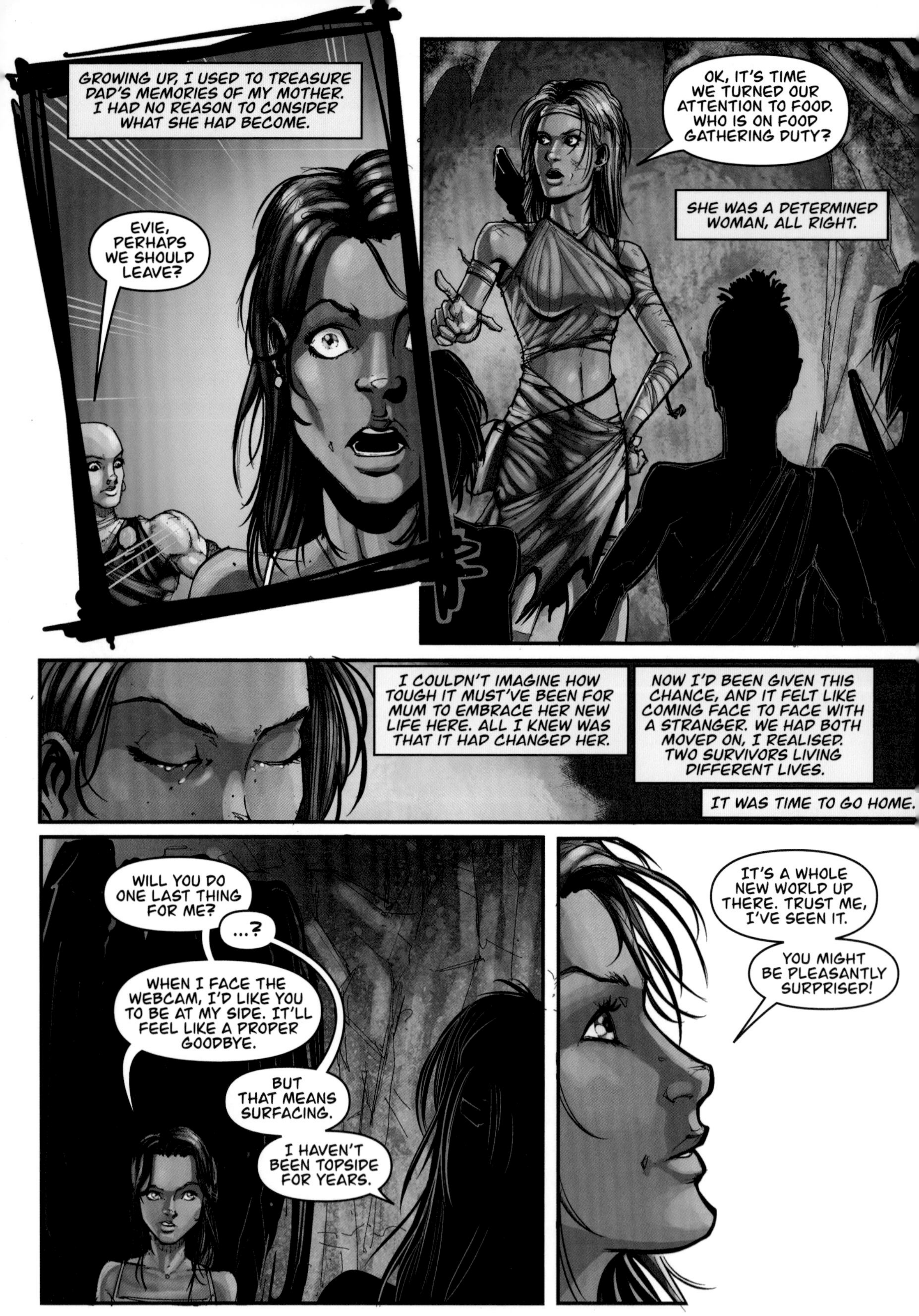

GROWING UP, I USED TO TREASURE DAD'S MEMORIES OF MY MOTHER. I HAD NO REASON TO CONSIDER WHAT SHE HAD BECOME.
EVIE, PERHAPS WE SHOULD LEAVE?
OK, IT'S TIME WE TURNED OUR ATTENTION TO FOOD. WHO IS ON FOOD GATHERING DUTY?
SHE WAS A DETERMINED WOMAN, ALL RIGHT.
I COULDN'T IMAGINE HOW TOUGH IT MUST'VE BEEN FOR MUM TO EMBRACE HER NEW LIFE HERE. ALL I KNEW WAS THAT IT HAD CHANGED HER.
NOW I'D BEEN GIVEN THIS CHANCE, AND IT FELT LIKE COMING FACE TO FACE WITH A STRANGER. WE HAD BOTH MOVED ON, I REALISED. TWO SURVIVORS LIVING DIFFERENT LIVES.
IT WAS TIME TO GO HOME.
WILL YOU DO ONE LAST THING FOR ME?
...?
WHEN I FACE THE WEBCAM, I'D LIKE YOU TO BE AT MY SIDE. IT'LL FEEL LIKE A PROPER GOODBYE.
BUT THAT MEANS SURFACING.
I HAVEN'T BEEN TOPSIDE FOR YEARS.
IT'S A WHOLE NEW WORLD UP THERE. TRUST ME, I'VE SEEN IT.
YOU MIGHT BE PLEASANTLY SURPRISED!

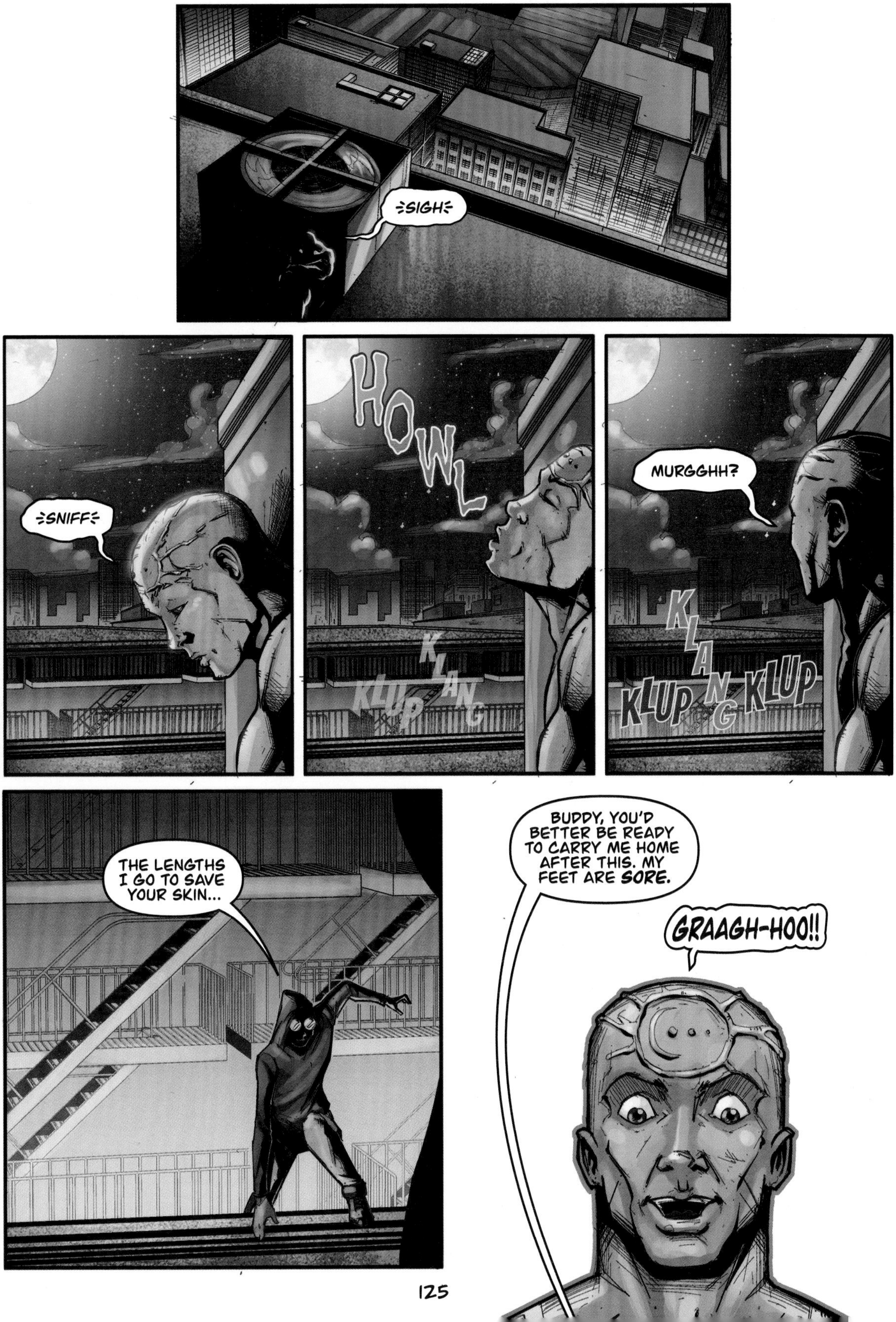
SIGH
SNIFF
HOWL
KLUP
KLANG
MURGGHH?
KLUP KLANG KLUP
THE LENGTHS I GO TO SAVE YOUR SKIN...
BUDDY, YOU'D BETTER BE READY TO CARRY ME HOME AFTER THIS. MY FEET ARE SORE.
GRAAGH-HOO!!

WELL, THAT WASN'T THERE WHEN I ARRIVED!

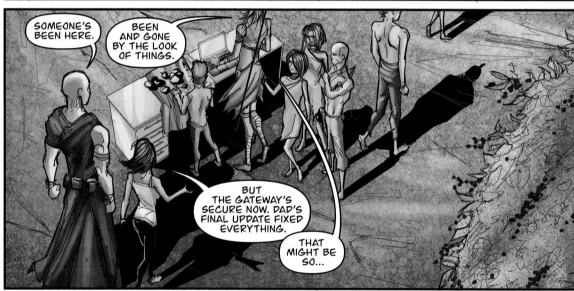

SOMEONE'S BEEN HERE.

BEEN AND GONE BY THE LOOK OF THINGS.

BUT THE GATEWAY'S SECURE NOW. DAD'S FINAL UPDATE FIXED EVERYTHING.

THAT MIGHT BE SO...

E.SCAPE

F34301E

C70F0B

BUT THE PROGRAM CONTAINS NO UPDATES. EVEN THE FIRST ONE THAT TRAPPED ME HERE IS MISSING. THIS IS THE ORIGINAL GATEWAY, EVIE...

!!

GATEWAY.exe

GATEWAY UPDATES

EMPTY

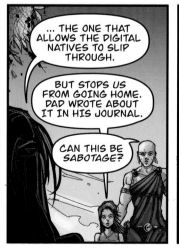

... THE ONE THAT ALLOWS THE DIGITAL NATIVES TO SLIP THROUGH.

BUT STOPS US FROM GOING HOME. DAD WROTE ABOUT IT IN HIS JOURNAL.

CAN THIS BE SABOTAGE?

ONLY ONE PERSON HAD ACCESS TO THE CODE, BUT HE'D NEVER DO SUCH A THING. NOT DELIBERATELY. I'M NOT EVEN SURE HE KNEW WHAT HE WAS DOING WHEN HE TRIED TO FIX IT, WHICH MEANS...

... OH.

OK, SO NOBODY SABOTAGED THE SOFTWARE... BUT SOMEONE MIGHT'VE MESSED UP.

BOSS, OVER HERE...

WHATEVER WENT THROUGH IS MASSIVE.

IT'S A BRUTE, MA'AM. MAKE NO MISTAKE.

THOSE AVATARS ARE PROGRAMMED TO PACK A PUNCH.

LET ME TAKE CARE OF THIS. I CAN BRING IT BACK.

OUT OF THE QUESTION.

?!?

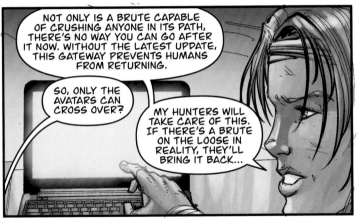

NOT ONLY IS A BRUTE CAPABLE OF CRUSHING ANYONE IN ITS PATH, THERE'S NO WAY YOU CAN GO AFTER IT NOW. WITHOUT THE LATEST UPDATE, THIS GATEWAY PREVENTS HUMANS FROM RETURNING.

SO, ONLY THE AVATARS CAN CROSS OVER?

MY HUNTERS WILL TAKE CARE OF THIS. IF THERE'S A BRUTE ON THE LOOSE IN REALITY, THEY'LL BRING IT BACK...

... DEAD OR ALIVE.

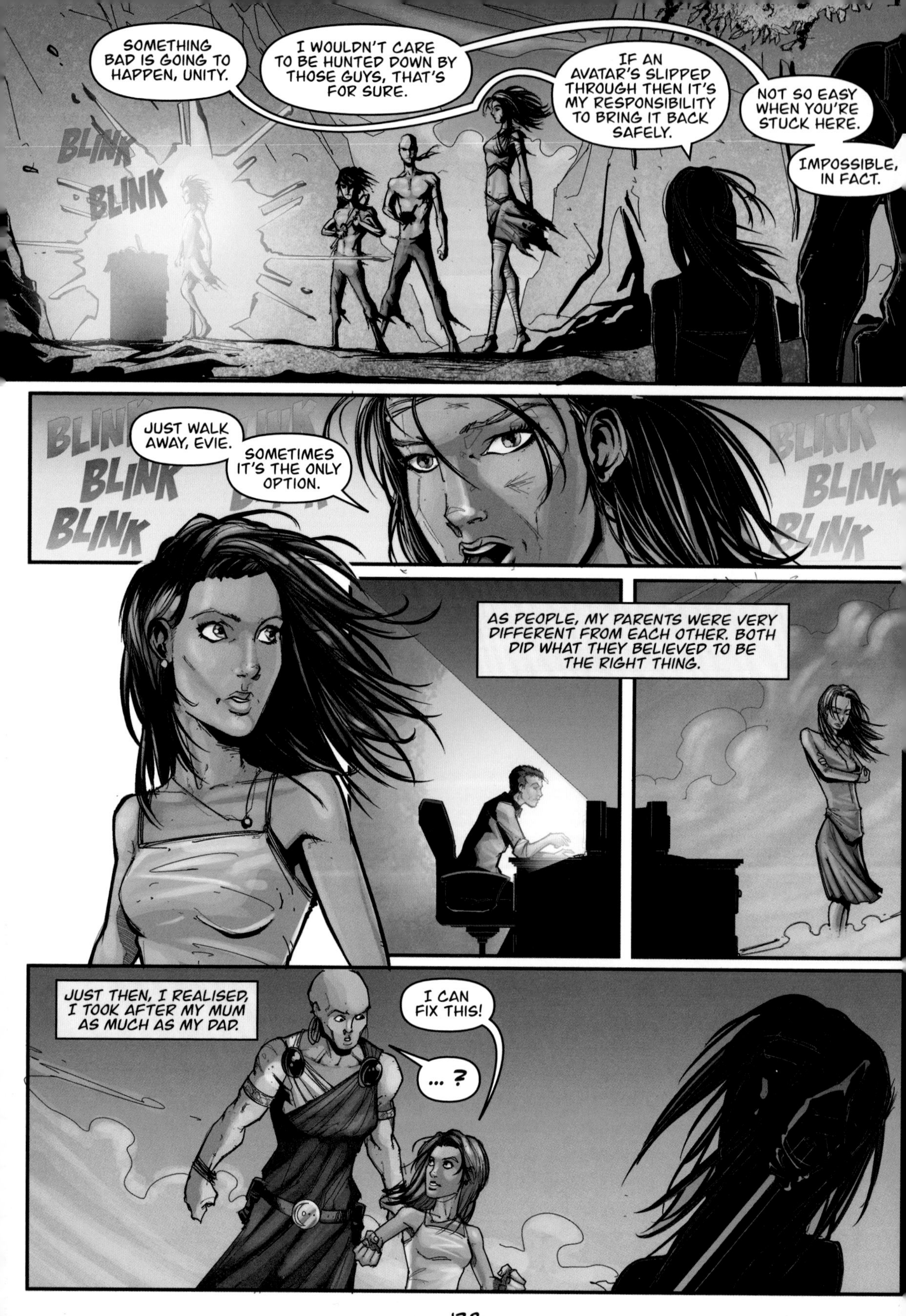
SOMETHING BAD IS GOING TO HAPPEN, UNITY.
I WOULDN'T CARE TO BE HUNTED DOWN BY THOSE GUYS, THAT'S FOR SURE.
IF AN AVATAR'S SLIPPED THROUGH THEN IT'S MY RESPONSIBILITY TO BRING IT BACK SAFELY.
NOT SO EASY WHEN YOU'RE STUCK HERE.
IMPOSSIBLE, IN FACT.
BLINK
BLINK
BLINK
BLINK
BLINK
JUST WALK AWAY, EVIE.
SOMETIMES IT'S THE ONLY OPTION.
BLINK
BLINK
BLINK
AS PEOPLE, MY PARENTS WERE VERY DIFFERENT FROM EACH OTHER. BOTH DID WHAT THEY BELIEVED TO BE THE RIGHT THING.
JUST THEN, I REALISED, I TOOK AFTER MY MUM AS MUCH AS MY DAD.
I CAN FIX THIS!
... ?

A LONG TIME AGO, **DAD** OPENED UP A WAY FOR **MUM** TO COMMUNICATE WITH HIM.

WHAT GOOD WOULD THAT HAVE DONE? APART FROM MAKE ME REALISE HOW MUCH I MISSED YOU ALL?

RIGHT NOW, IT COULD JUST BE THE LIFELINE WE NEED.

CONSIDER THIS TO BE AN **SOS**.

TO YOUR LAPTOP BACK HOME?

AND... WE HAVE **CONTACT!**

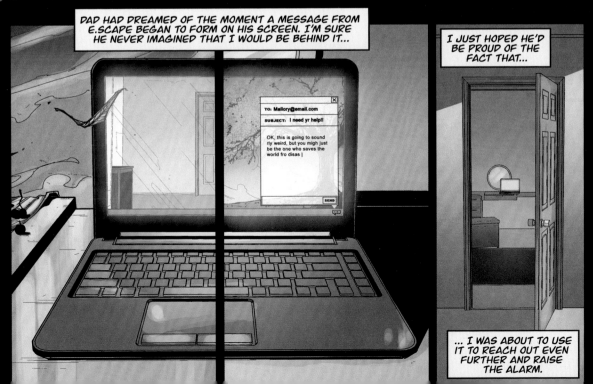

DAD HAD DREAMED OF THE MOMENT A MESSAGE FROM E.SCAPE BEGAN TO FORM ON HIS SCREEN. I'M SURE HE NEVER IMAGINED THAT I WOULD BE BEHIND IT...

I JUST HOPED HE'D BE PROUD OF THE FACT THAT...

TO: Mallory@email.com

SUBJECT: I need yr help!!

OK, this is going to sound rly weird, but you migh just be the one who saves the world fro disas |

SEND

... I WAS ABOUT TO USE IT TO REACH OUT EVEN FURTHER AND RAISE THE ALARM.

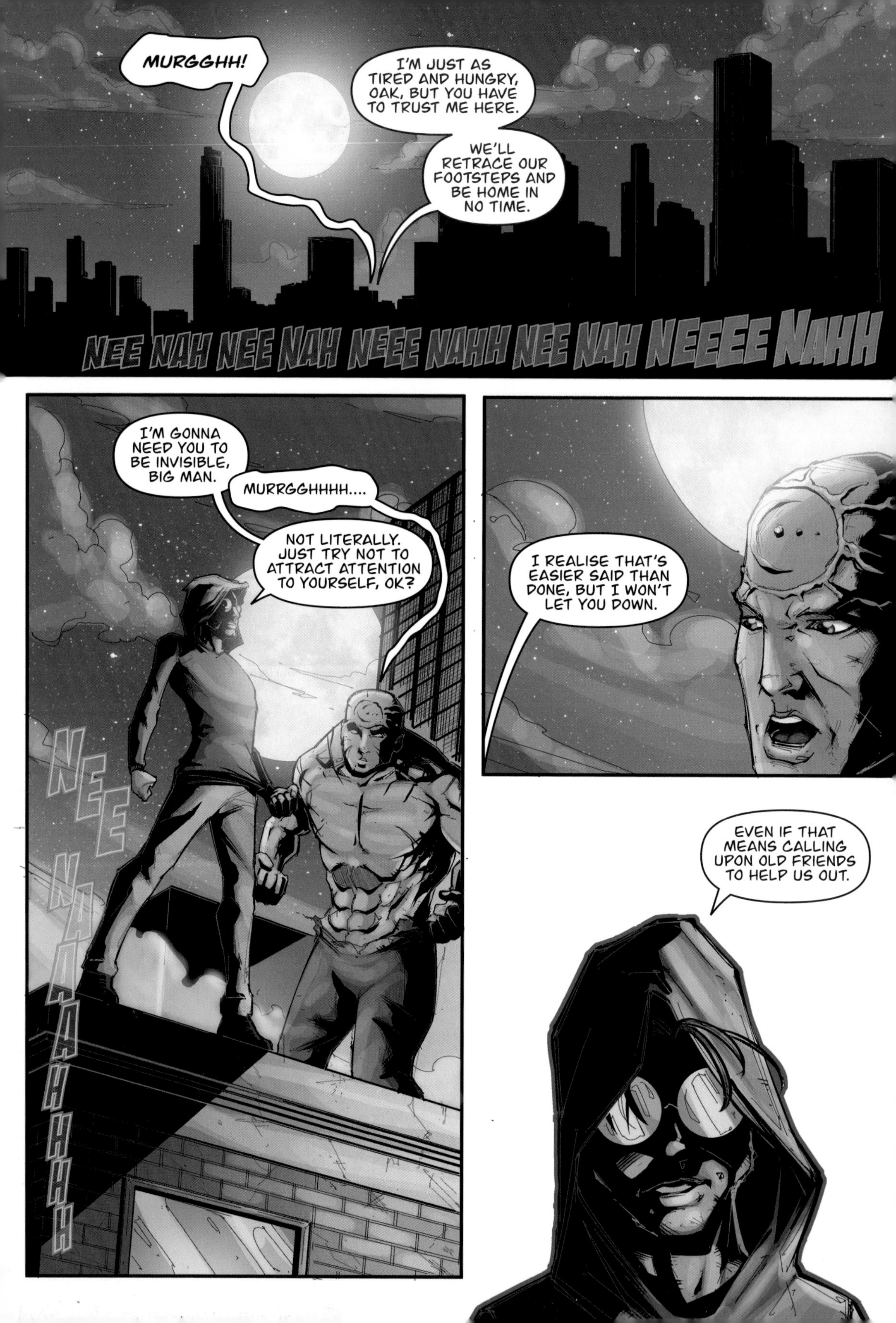
MURGGHH!
I'M JUST AS TIRED AND HUNGRY, OAK, BUT YOU HAVE TO TRUST ME HERE.
WE'LL RETRACE OUR FOOTSTEPS AND BE HOME IN NO TIME.
NEE NAH NEE NAH NEEE NAHH NEE NAH NEEEE NAHH
I'M GONNA NEED YOU TO BE INVISIBLE, BIG MAN.
MURRGGHHHH....
NOT LITERALLY. JUST TRY NOT TO ATTRACT ATTENTION TO YOURSELF, OK?
NEE NAAAAAHHHHH
I REALISE THAT'S EASIER SAID THAN DONE, BUT I WON'T LET YOU DOWN.
EVEN IF THAT MEANS CALLING UPON OLD FRIENDS TO HELP US OUT.

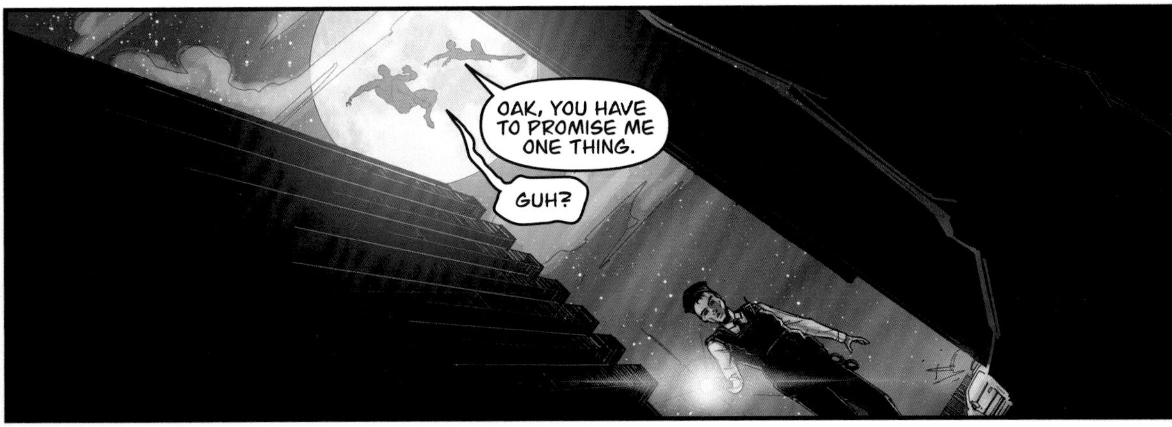
OAK, YOU HAVE TO PROMISE ME ONE THING.
GUH?

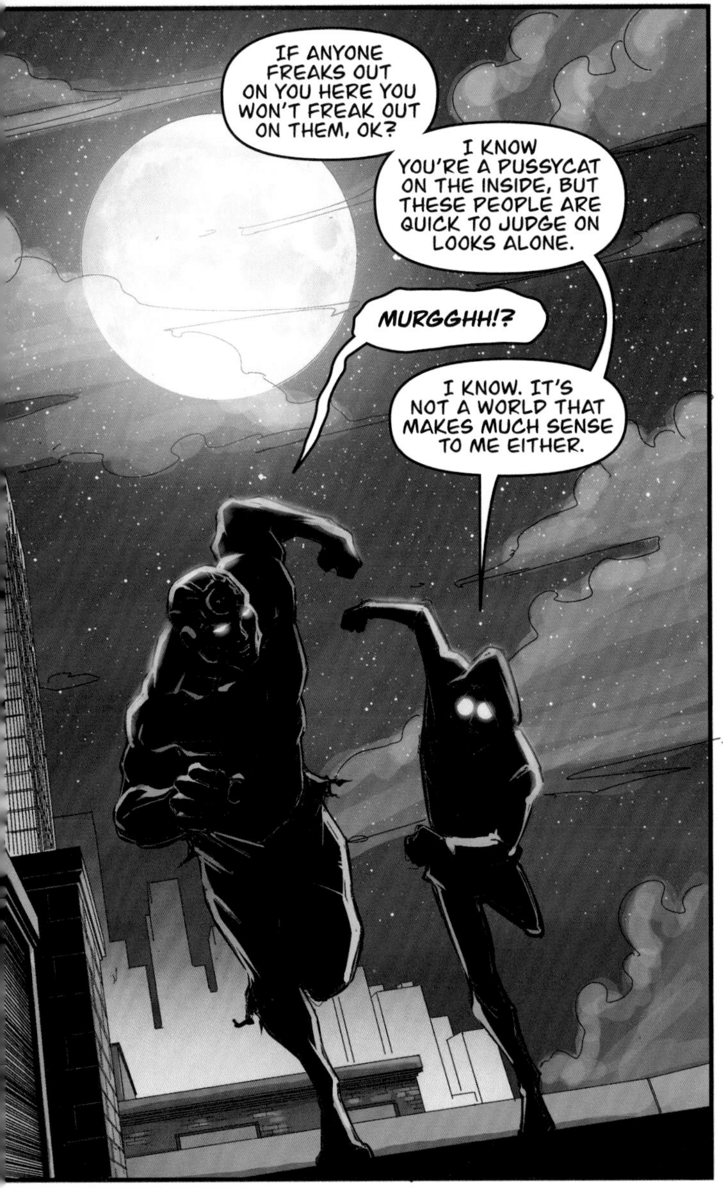
IF ANYONE FREAKS OUT ON YOU HERE YOU WON'T FREAK OUT ON THEM, OK?
I KNOW YOU'RE A PUSSYCAT ON THE INSIDE, BUT THESE PEOPLE ARE QUICK TO JUDGE ON LOOKS ALONE.
MURGGHH!?
I KNOW. IT'S NOT A WORLD THAT MAKES MUCH SENSE TO ME EITHER.

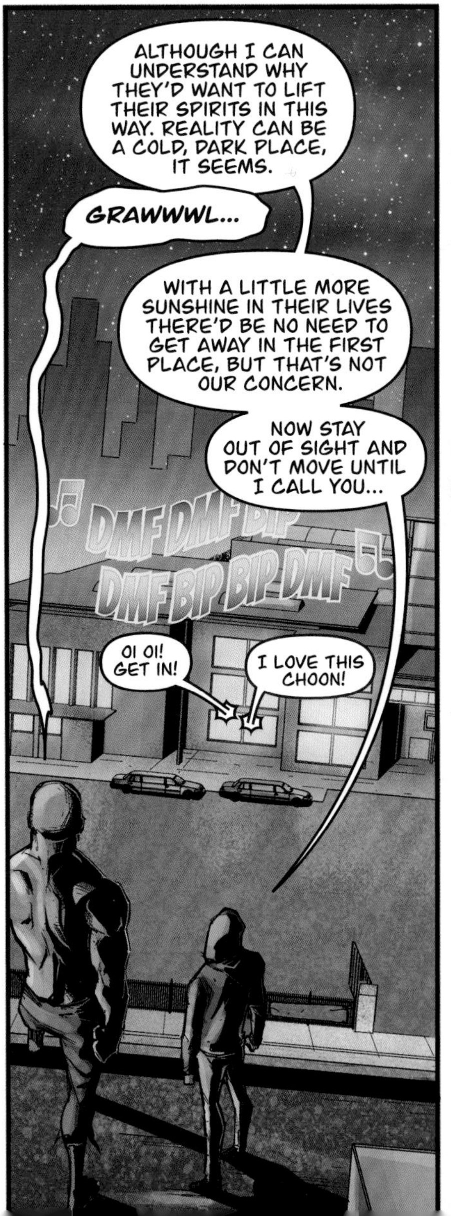
ALTHOUGH I CAN UNDERSTAND WHY THEY'D WANT TO LIFT THEIR SPIRITS IN THIS WAY. REALITY CAN BE A COLD, DARK PLACE, IT SEEMS.
GRAWWWL...
WITH A LITTLE MORE SUNSHINE IN THEIR LIVES THERE'D BE NO NEED TO GET AWAY IN THE FIRST PLACE, BUT THAT'S NOT OUR CONCERN.
NOW STAY OUT OF SIGHT AND DON'T MOVE UNTIL I CALL YOU...
DMF DMF BIP
DMF BIP BIP DMF
OI OI! GET IN!
I LOVE THIS CHOON!

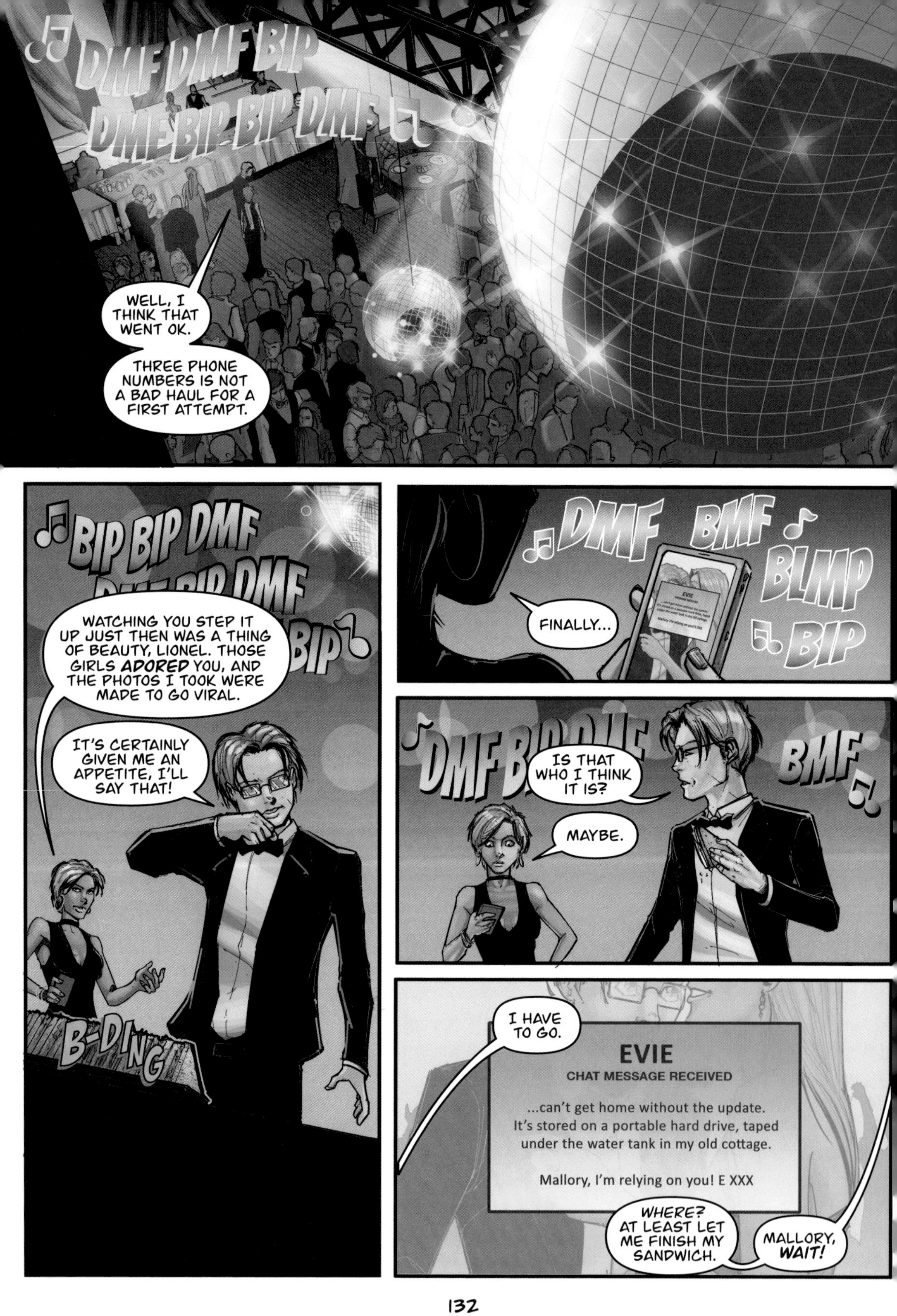
DMF DMF BIP
DMF BIP BIP DMF
WELL, I THINK THAT WENT OK.
THREE PHONE NUMBERS IS NOT A BAD HAUL FOR A FIRST ATTEMPT.
BIP BIP DMF
BIP DMF
BIP
WATCHING YOU STEP IT UP JUST THEN WAS A THING OF BEAUTY, LIONEL. THOSE GIRLS **ADORED** YOU, AND THE PHOTOS I TOOK WERE MADE TO GO VIRAL.
IT'S CERTAINLY GIVEN ME AN APPETITE, I'LL SAY THAT!
B-DING
DMF BMF
BLMP
BIP
FINALLY...
DMF
BMF
IS THAT WHO I THINK IT IS?
MAYBE.
I HAVE TO GO.
EVIE
CHAT MESSAGE RECEIVED
...can't get home without the update. It's stored on a portable hard drive, taped under the water tank in my old cottage.
Mallory, I'm relying on you! E XXX
WHERE? AT LEAST LET ME FINISH MY SANDWICH.
MALLORY, **WAIT!**

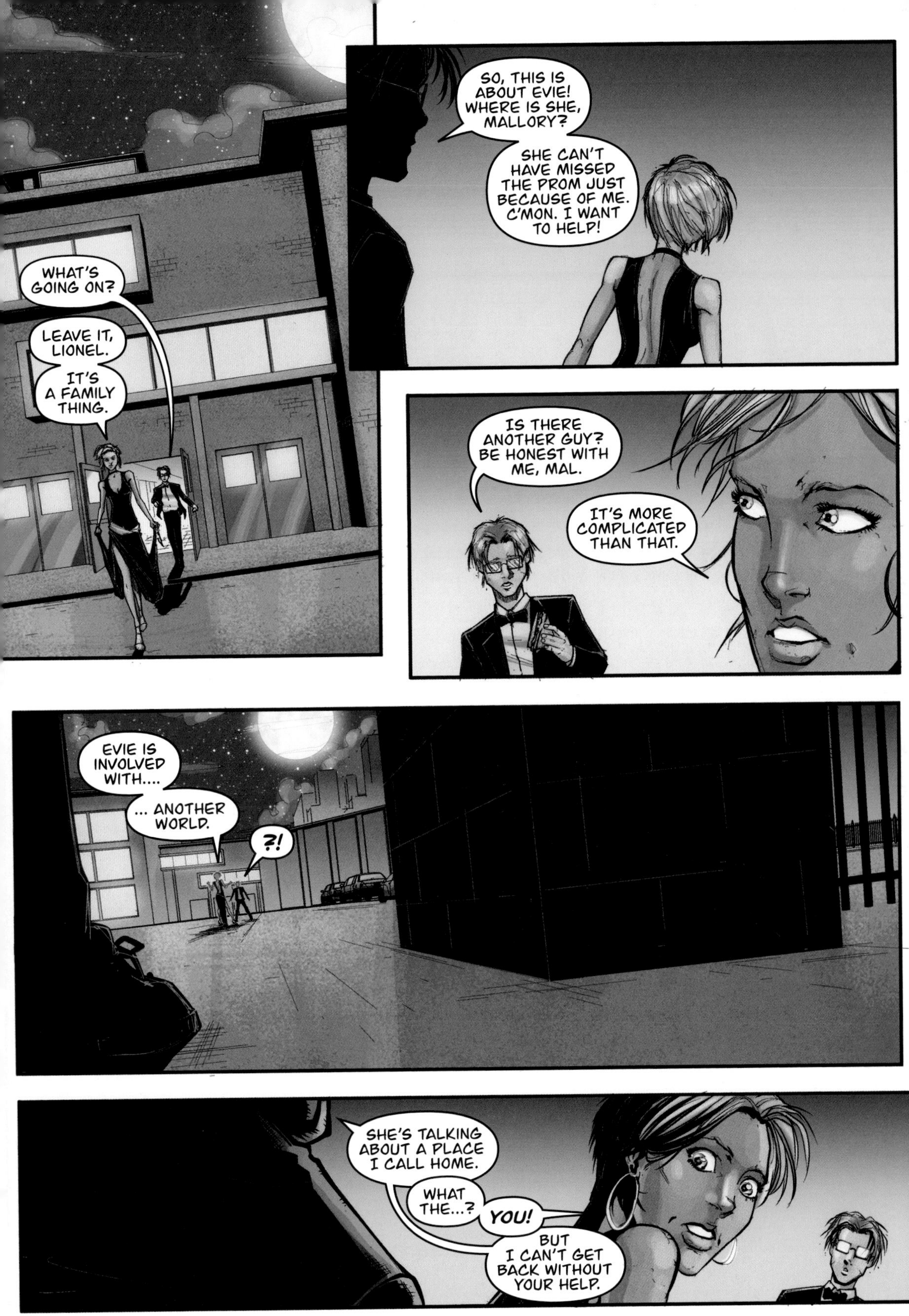

WHAT'S GOING ON?
LEAVE IT, LIONEL.
IT'S A FAMILY THING.
SO, THIS IS ABOUT EVIE! WHERE IS SHE, MALLORY?
SHE CAN'T HAVE MISSED THE PROM JUST BECAUSE OF ME. C'MON. I WANT TO HELP!
IS THERE ANOTHER GUY? BE HONEST WITH ME, MAL.
IT'S MORE COMPLICATED THAN THAT.
EVIE IS INVOLVED WITH....
... ANOTHER WORLD.
?!
SHE'S TALKING ABOUT A PLACE I CALL HOME.
WHAT THE...?
YOU!
BUT I CAN'T GET BACK WITHOUT YOUR HELP.

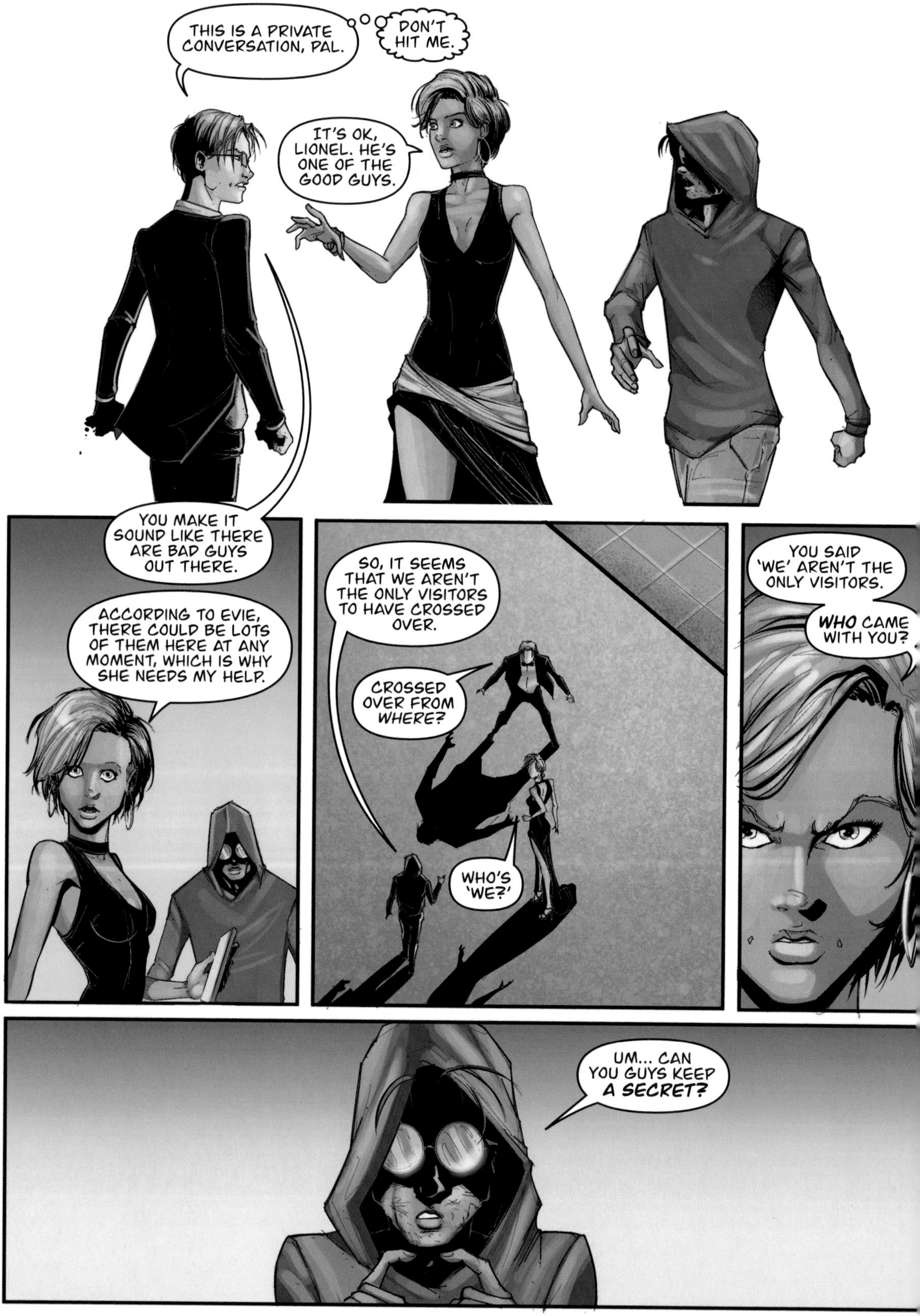
THIS IS A PRIVATE CONVERSATION, PAL.
DON'T HIT ME.
IT'S OK, LIONEL. HE'S ONE OF THE GOOD GUYS.
YOU MAKE IT SOUND LIKE THERE ARE BAD GUYS OUT THERE.
ACCORDING TO EVIE, THERE COULD BE LOTS OF THEM HERE AT ANY MOMENT, WHICH IS WHY SHE NEEDS MY HELP.
SO, IT SEEMS THAT WE AREN'T THE ONLY VISITORS TO HAVE CROSSED OVER.
CROSSED OVER FROM WHERE?
WHO'S 'WE?'
YOU SAID 'WE' AREN'T THE ONLY VISITORS.
WHO CAME WITH YOU?
UM... CAN YOU GUYS KEEP A SECRET?

OAK? IT'S ALRIGHT, BUDDY. YOU CAN SHOW YOURSELF.

SO, WHAT ARE WE LOOKING FOR HERE? A KITTEN?

OMG!

OK, NOT A KITTEN.

THE LAST TIME EVIE AND I SAW ONE OF THOSE, IT WAS KINDA FURIOUS.

THIS IS OAK. YOU HAVE MY WORD THAT HE'S HARMLESS.

AND HARD TO HIDE, RIGHT?

ALL I WANT TO DO IS GET HIM HOME.

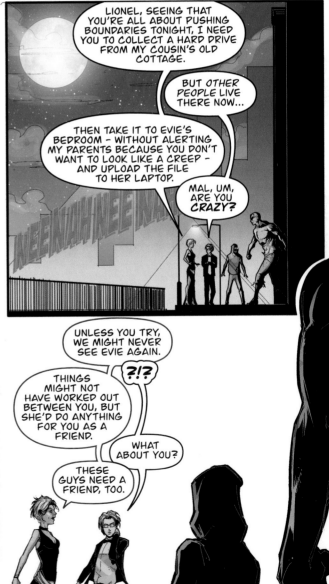

LIONEL, SEEING THAT YOU'RE ALL ABOUT PUSHING BOUNDARIES TONIGHT, I NEED YOU TO COLLECT A HARD DRIVE FROM MY COUSIN'S OLD COTTAGE.

BUT OTHER PEOPLE LIVE THERE NOW...

THEN TAKE IT TO EVIE'S BEDROOM – WITHOUT ALERTING MY PARENTS BECAUSE YOU DON'T WANT TO LOOK LIKE A CREEP – AND UPLOAD THE FILE TO HER LAPTOP.

MAL, UM, ARE YOU CRAZY?

NEENAH NEE NA

UNLESS YOU TRY, WE MIGHT NEVER SEE EVIE AGAIN.

?!?

THINGS MIGHT NOT HAVE WORKED OUT BETWEEN YOU, BUT SHE'D DO ANYTHING FOR YOU AS A FRIEND.

WHAT ABOUT YOU?

THESE GUYS NEED A FRIEND, TOO.

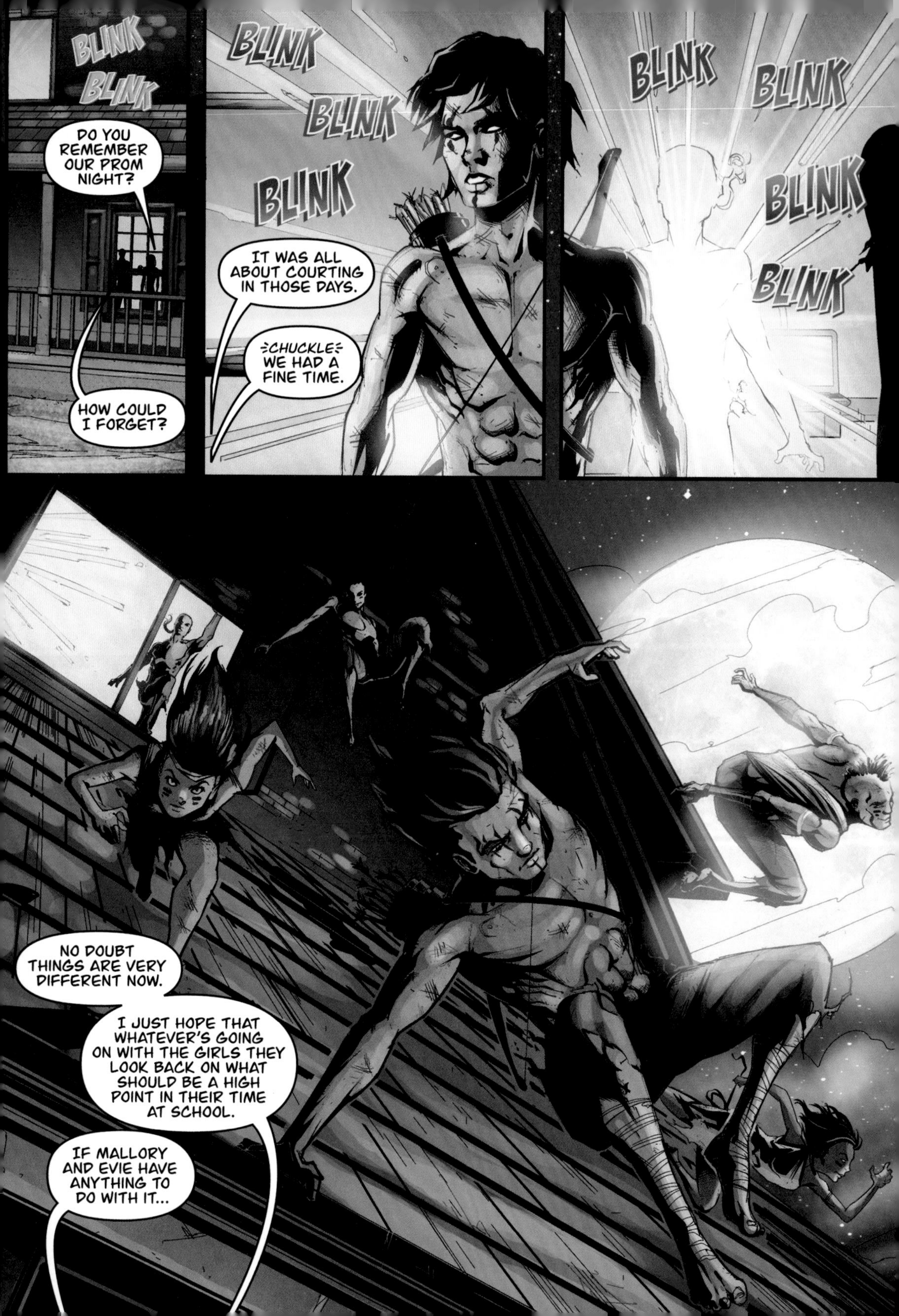
BLINK
BLINK
DO YOU REMEMBER OUR PROM NIGHT?
HOW COULD I FORGET?
BLINK
BLINK
BLINK
IT WAS ALL ABOUT COURTING IN THOSE DAYS.
CHUCKLE WE HAD A FINE TIME.
BLINK
BLINK
BLINK
BLINK
NO DOUBT THINGS ARE VERY DIFFERENT NOW.
I JUST HOPE THAT WHATEVER'S GOING ON WITH THE GIRLS THEY LOOK BACK ON WHAT SHOULD BE A HIGH POINT IN THEIR TIME AT SCHOOL.
IF MALLORY AND EVIE HAVE ANYTHING TO DO WITH IT...

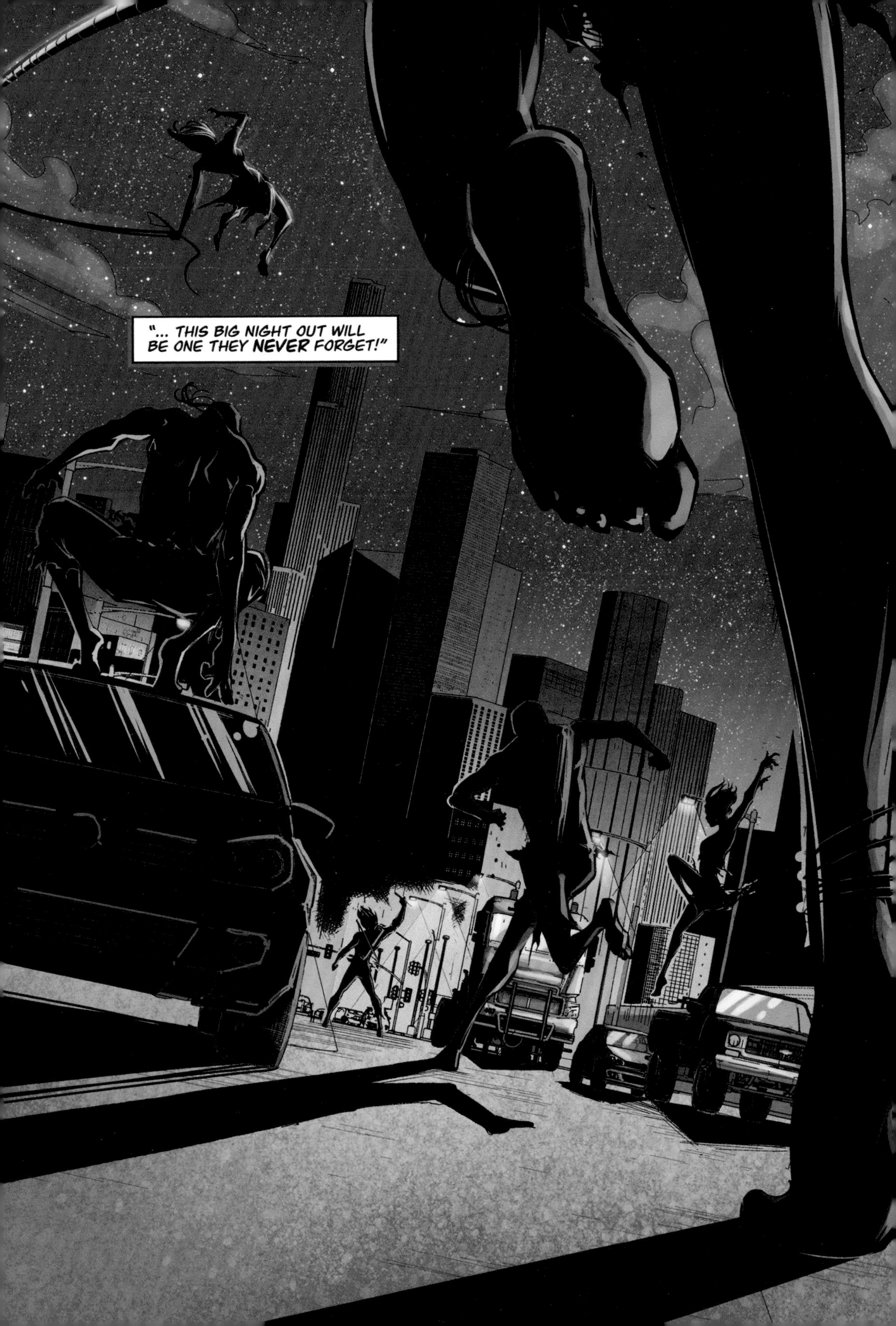
"... THIS BIG NIGHT OUT WILL BE ONE THEY NEVER FORGET!"

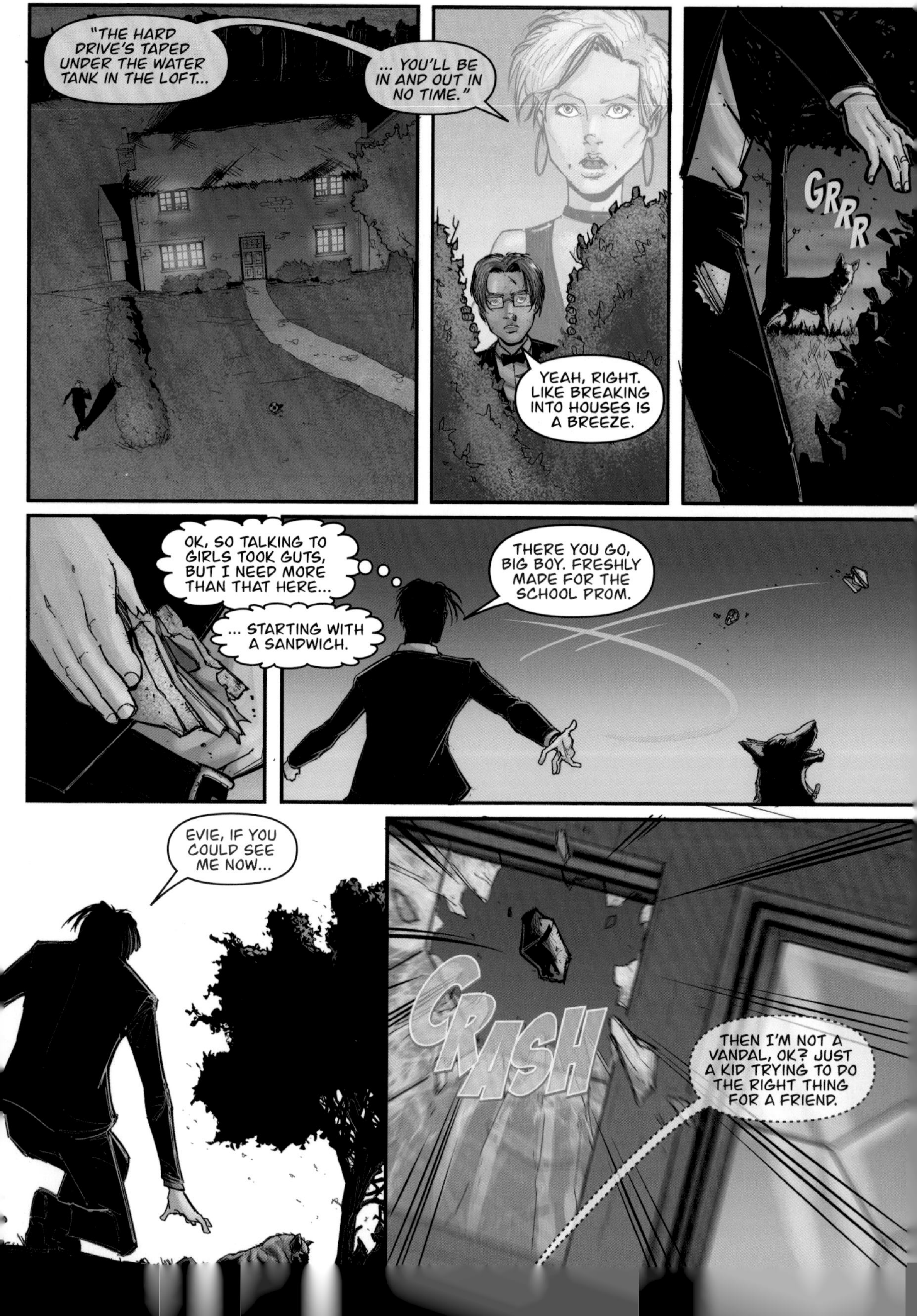
"THE HARD DRIVE'S TAPED UNDER THE WATER TANK IN THE LOFT...
... YOU'LL BE IN AND OUT IN NO TIME."
YEAH, RIGHT. LIKE BREAKING INTO HOUSES IS A BREEZE.
GRRR
OK, SO TALKING TO GIRLS TOOK GUTS, BUT I NEED MORE THAN THAT HERE...
... STARTING WITH A SANDWICH.
THERE YOU GO, BIG BOY. FRESHLY MADE FOR THE SCHOOL PROM.
EVIE, IF YOU COULD SEE ME NOW...
CRASH
THEN I'M NOT A VANDAL, OK? JUST A KID TRYING TO DO THE RIGHT THING FOR A FRIEND.

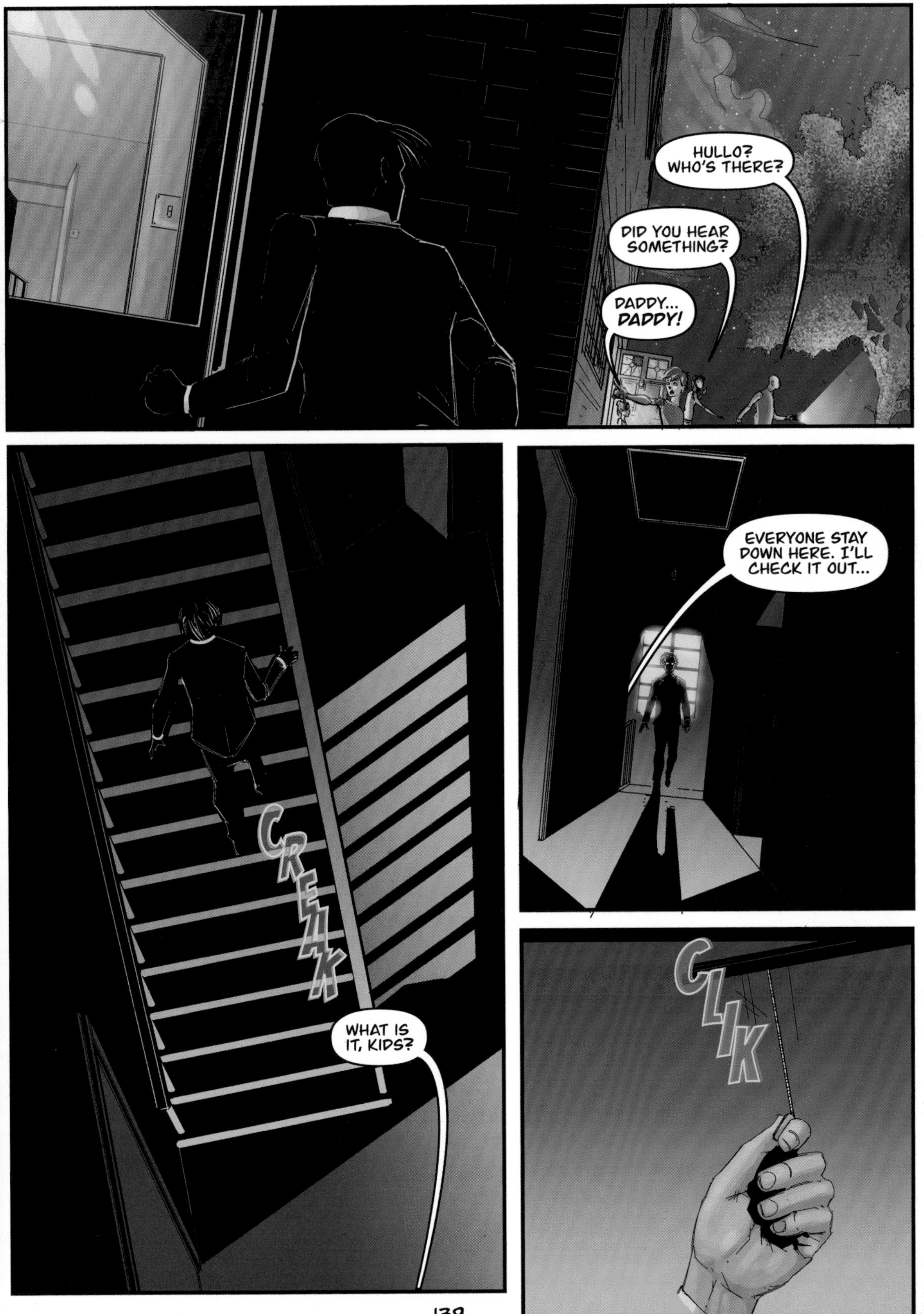
HULLO? WHO'S THERE?
DID YOU HEAR SOMETHING?
DADDY... **DADDY!**
CREAK
WHAT IS IT, KIDS?
EVERYONE STAY DOWN HERE. I'LL CHECK IT OUT...
CLIK

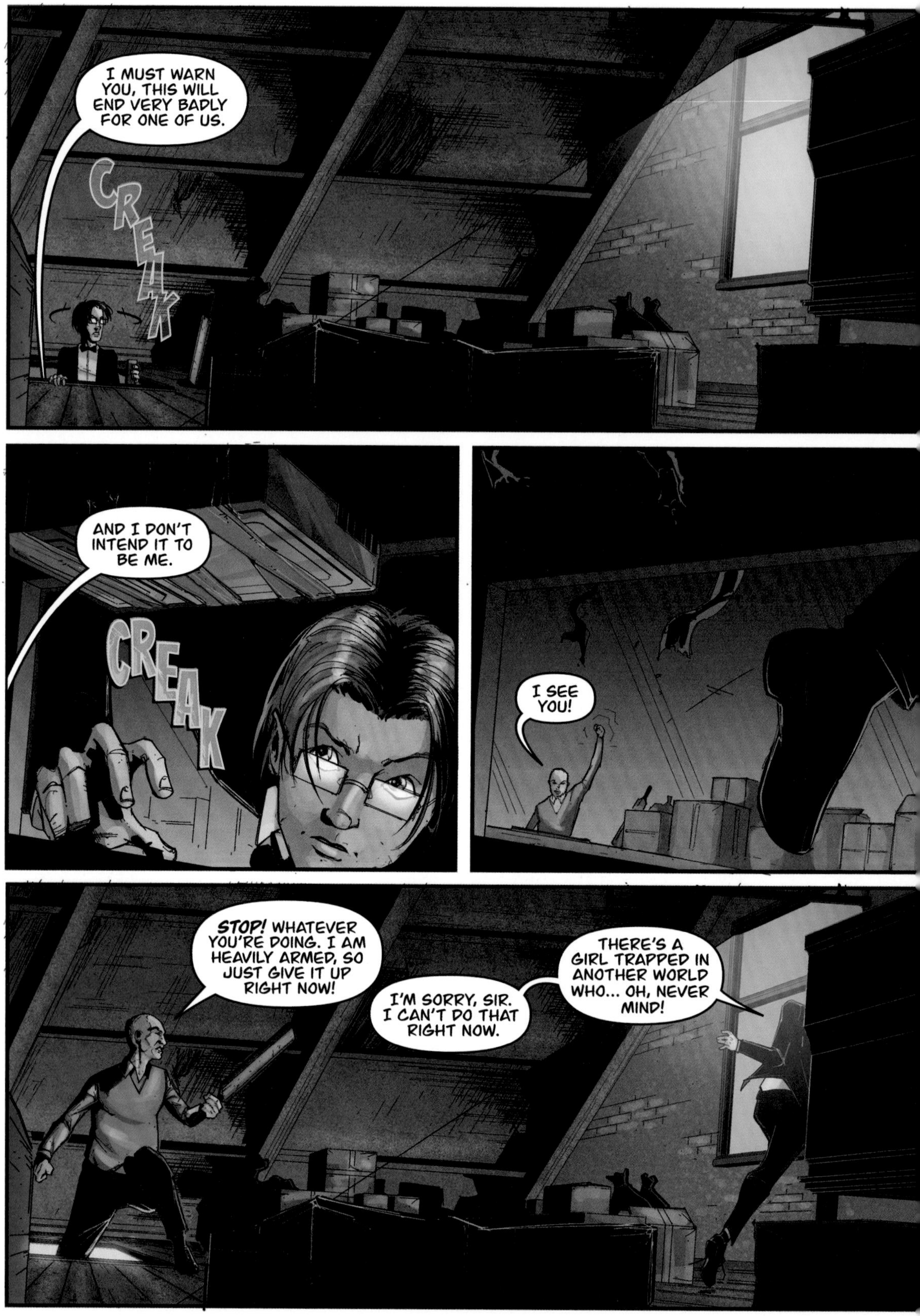
I MUST WARN YOU, THIS WILL END VERY BADLY FOR ONE OF US.
CREAK
AND I DON'T INTEND IT TO BE ME.
CREAK
I SEE YOU!
STOP! WHATEVER YOU'RE DOING. I AM HEAVILY ARMED, SO JUST GIVE IT UP RIGHT NOW!
I'M SORRY, SIR. I CAN'T DO THAT RIGHT NOW.
THERE'S A GIRL TRAPPED IN ANOTHER WORLD WHO... OH, NEVER MIND!

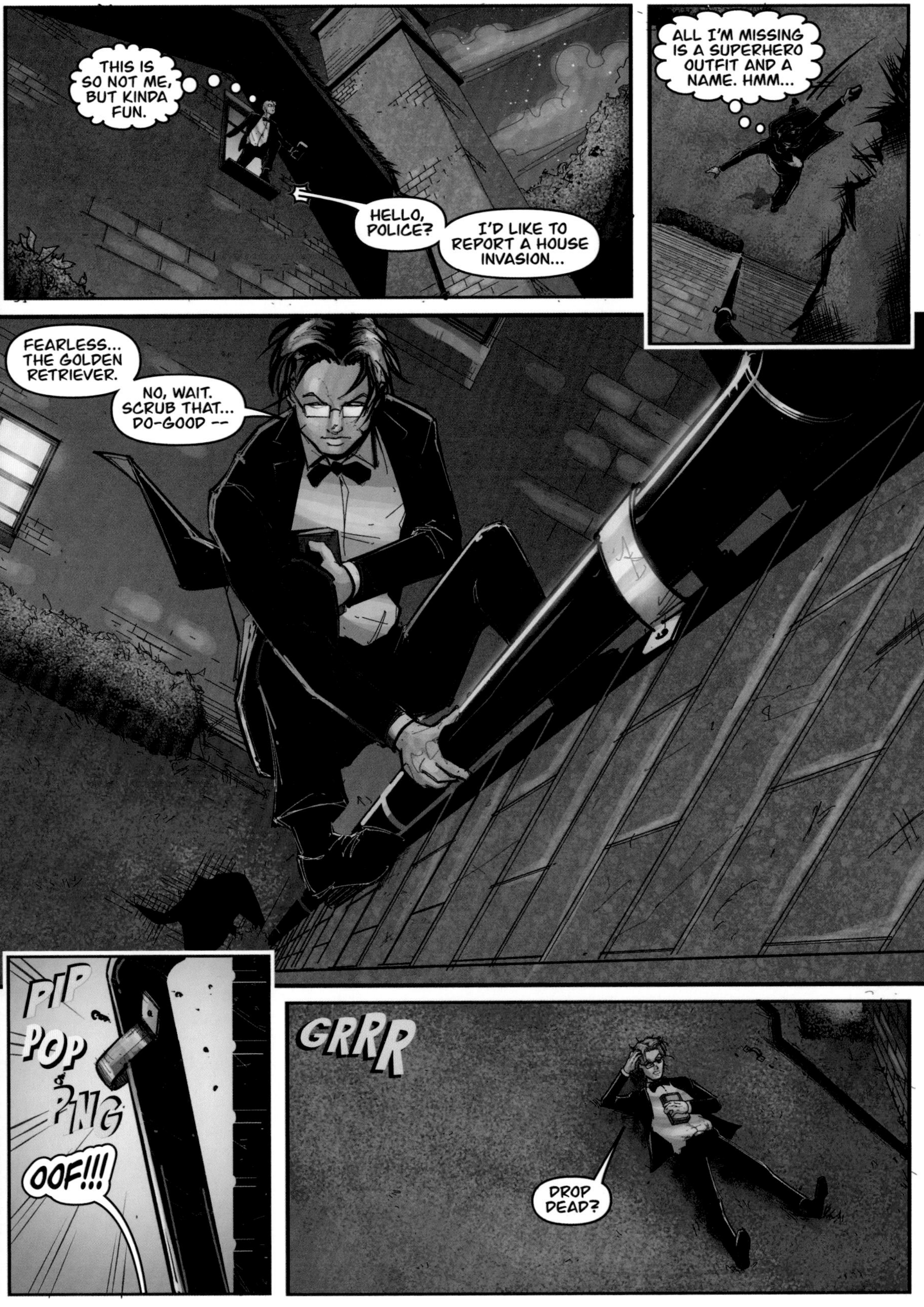
THIS IS SO NOT ME, BUT KINDA FUN.
HELLO, POLICE?
I'D LIKE TO REPORT A HOUSE INVASION...
ALL I'M MISSING IS A SUPERHERO OUTFIT AND A NAME. HMM...
FEARLESS... THE GOLDEN RETRIEVER.
NO, WAIT. SCRUB THAT... DO-GOOD --
PIP
POP
PING
OOF!!!
GRRR
DROP DEAD?

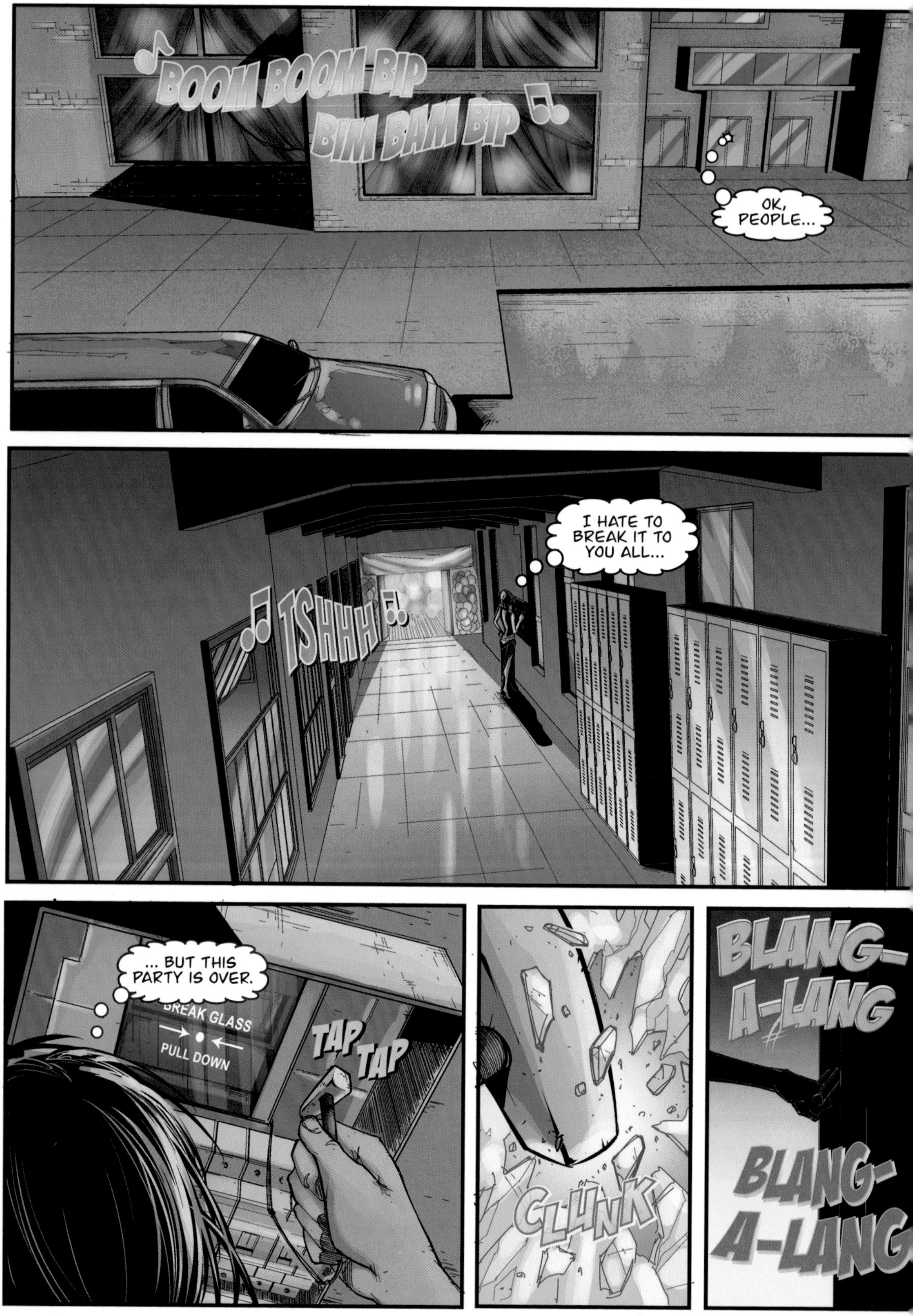
BOOM BOOM BIP
BIM BAM BIP
OK, PEOPLE...
I HATE TO BREAK IT TO YOU ALL...
TSHHH
... BUT THIS PARTY IS OVER.
BREAK GLASS
PULL DOWN
TAP TAP
CLUNK
BLANG-A-LANG
BLANG-A-LANG

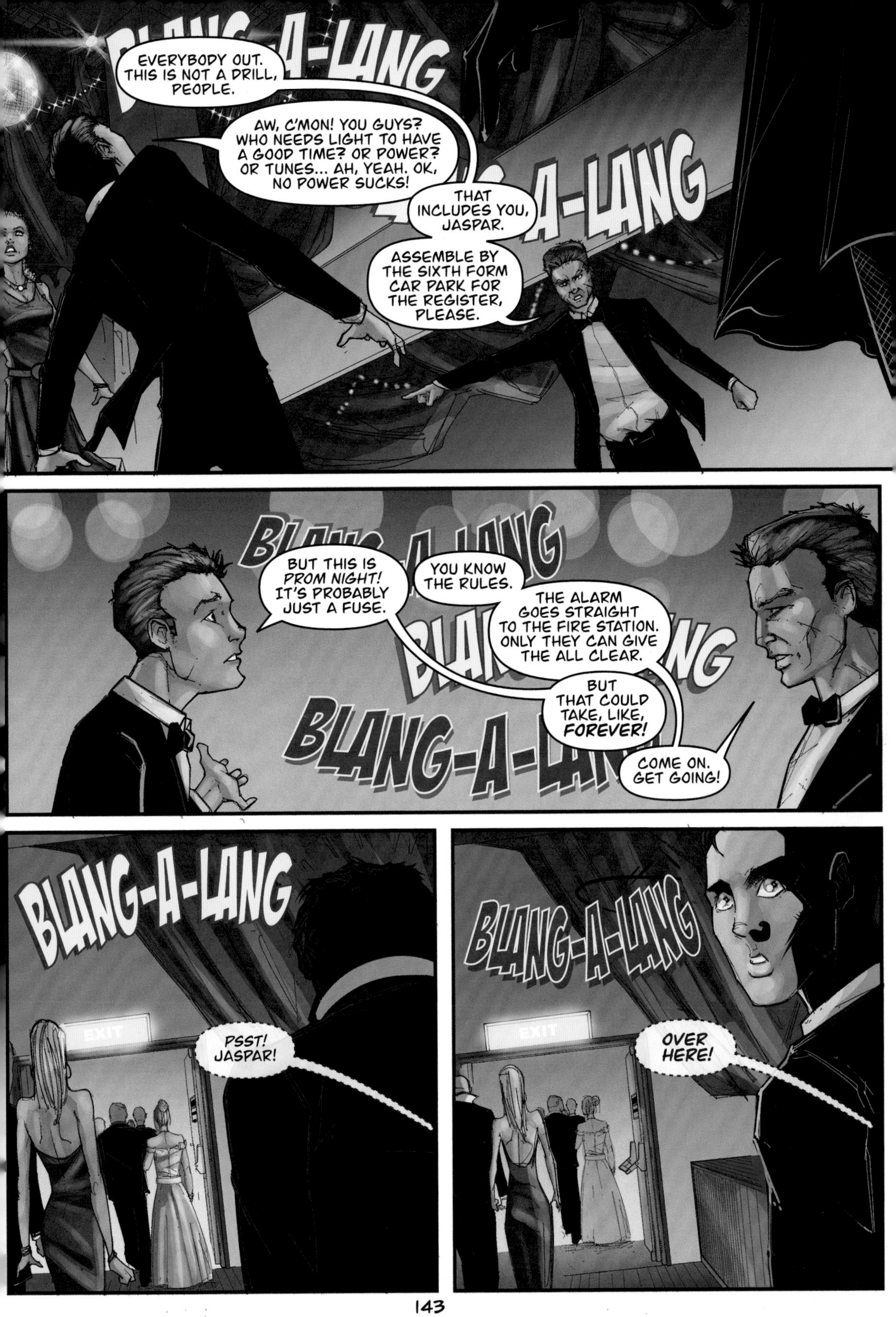
BLANG-A-LANG
EVERYBODY OUT. THIS IS NOT A DRILL, PEOPLE.
AW, C'MON! YOU GUYS? WHO NEEDS LIGHT TO HAVE A GOOD TIME? OR POWER? OR TUNES... AH, YEAH. OK, NO POWER SUCKS!
BLANG-A-LANG
THAT INCLUDES YOU, JASPAR.
ASSEMBLE BY THE SIXTH FORM CAR PARK FOR THE REGISTER, PLEASE.
BLANG-A-LANG
BUT THIS IS *PROM NIGHT!* IT'S PROBABLY JUST A FUSE.
YOU KNOW THE RULES.
THE ALARM GOES STRAIGHT TO THE FIRE STATION. ONLY THEY CAN GIVE THE ALL CLEAR.
BUT THAT COULD TAKE, LIKE, ***FOREVER!***
COME ON. GET GOING!
BLANG-A-LANG
PSST! JASPAR!
EXIT
BLANG-A-LANG
OVER HERE!
EXIT

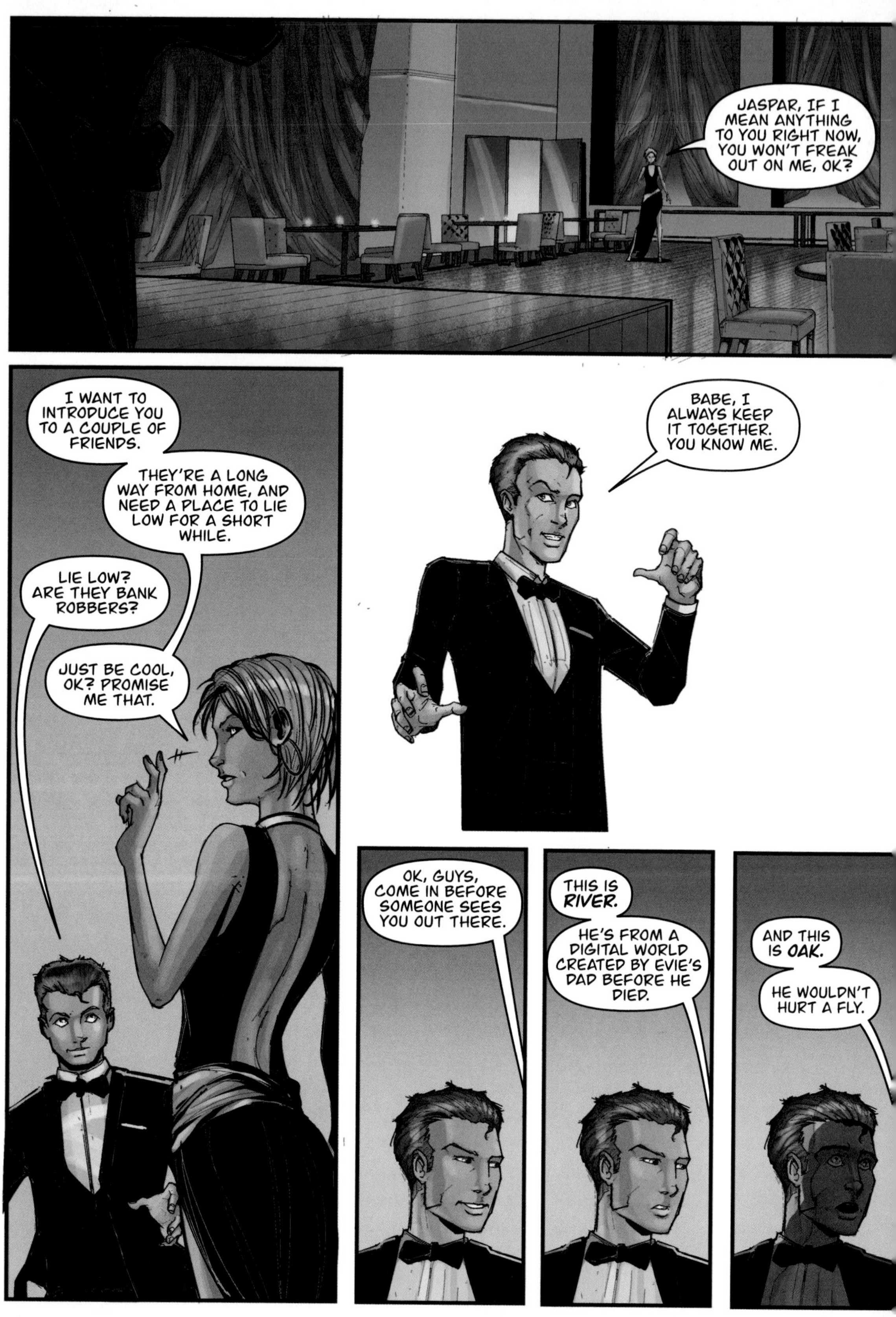
JASPAR, IF I MEAN ANYTHING TO YOU RIGHT NOW, YOU WON'T FREAK OUT ON ME, OK?
I WANT TO INTRODUCE YOU TO A COUPLE OF FRIENDS.
THEY'RE A LONG WAY FROM HOME, AND NEED A PLACE TO LIE LOW FOR A SHORT WHILE.
LIE LOW? ARE THEY BANK ROBBERS?
JUST BE COOL, OK? PROMISE ME THAT.
BABE, I ALWAYS KEEP IT TOGETHER. YOU KNOW ME.
OK, GUYS, COME IN BEFORE SOMEONE SEES YOU OUT THERE.
THIS IS RIVER.
HE'S FROM A DIGITAL WORLD CREATED BY EVIE'S DAD BEFORE HE DIED.
AND THIS IS OAK.
HE WOULDN'T HURT A FLY.

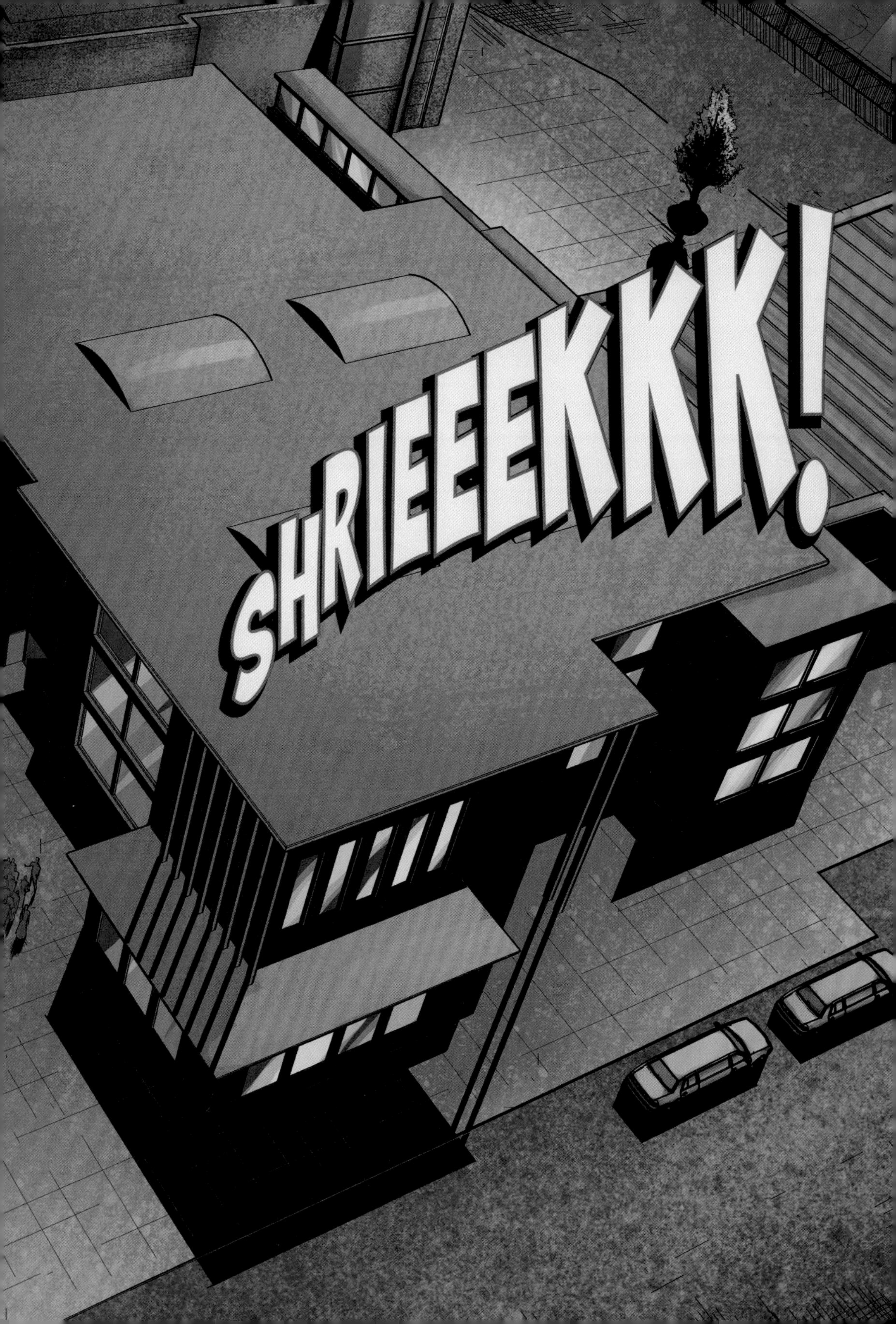
SHRIEEEKKK!

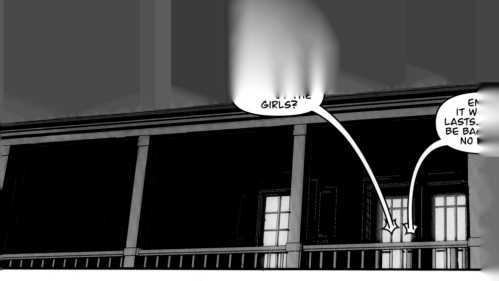

GIRLS?

EM
IT W
LASTS.
BE BAC
NO

DRAINPIPE, DON'T BE THE ≠PUFF≠ SECOND ONE TO ≠GRUNT≠ LET ME DOWN TONIGHT...

HNGHH!!

KLUP

EVIE, WHEREVER YOU ARE...

...WHATEVER'S GOING ON IN YOUR LIFE...

...AT THIS MOMENT IN TIME...

...I'M HERE FOR YOU.

JUST ABOUT...

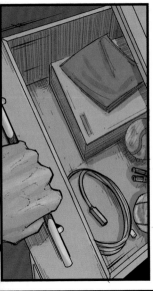

SO, THESE WOULD BE THE GATEWAY UPDATES I TRASHED. WHOOPS! WELL...

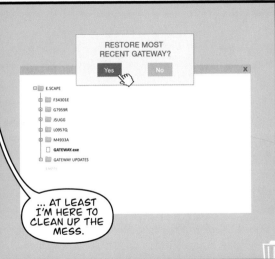

RESTORE MOST RECENT GATEWAY?

Yes   No

E.SCAPE
F34301E
G7959R
J5UGG
L0957Q
M4933A
GATEWAY.exe
GATEWAY UPDATES

... AT LEAST I'M HERE TO CLEAN UP THE MESS.

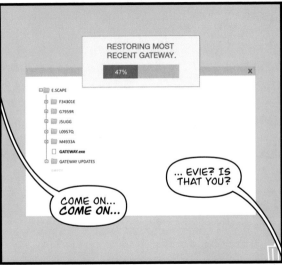

RESTORING MOST RECENT GATEWAY.

47%

E.SCAPE
F34301E
G7959R
J5UGG
L0957Q
M4933A
GATEWAY.exe
GATEWAY UPDATES

COME ON... COME ON...

... EVIE? IS THAT YOU?

EVIE? ARE YOU HOME? WE DIDN'T HEAR YOU COME IN.

!!!

COME ON DOWN, SWEETIE.

JUST ONCE THIS EVENING, I'D LIKE TO LEAVE A HOUSE THROUGH THE FRONT DOOR.

147

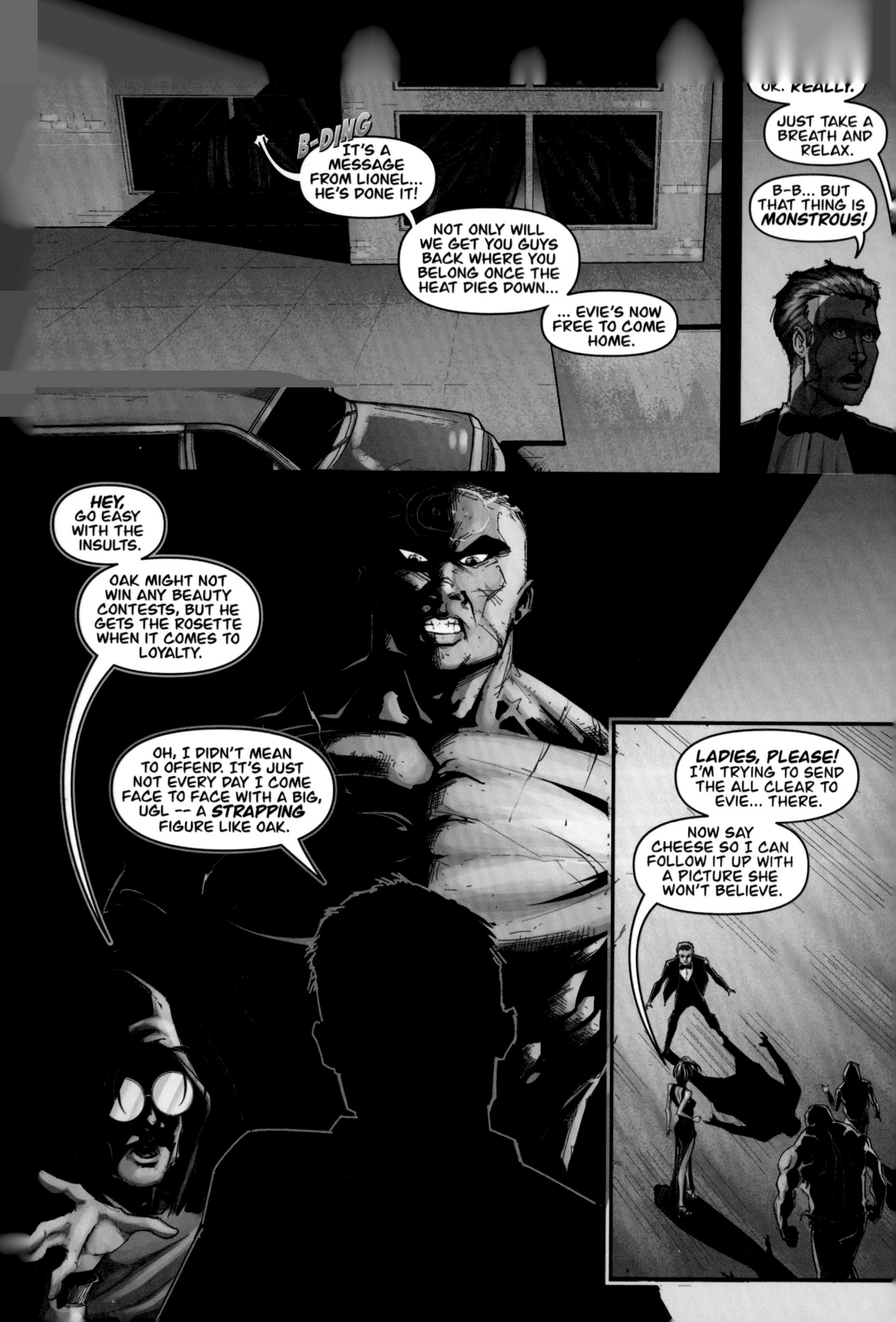
B-DING
IT'S A MESSAGE FROM LIONEL... HE'S DONE IT!
NOT ONLY WILL WE GET YOU GUYS BACK WHERE YOU BELONG ONCE THE HEAT DIES DOWN...
... EVIE'S NOW FREE TO COME HOME.
OK. REALLY.
JUST TAKE A BREATH AND RELAX.
B-B... BUT THAT THING IS MONSTROUS!
HEY, GO EASY WITH THE INSULTS.
OAK MIGHT NOT WIN ANY BEAUTY CONTESTS, BUT HE GETS THE ROSETTE WHEN IT COMES TO LOYALTY.
OH, I DIDN'T MEAN TO OFFEND. IT'S JUST NOT EVERY DAY I COME FACE TO FACE WITH A BIG, UGL -- A STRAPPING FIGURE LIKE OAK.
LADIES, PLEASE! I'M TRYING TO SEND THE ALL CLEAR TO EVIE... THERE.
NOW SAY CHEESE SO I CAN FOLLOW IT UP WITH A PICTURE SHE WON'T BELIEVE.

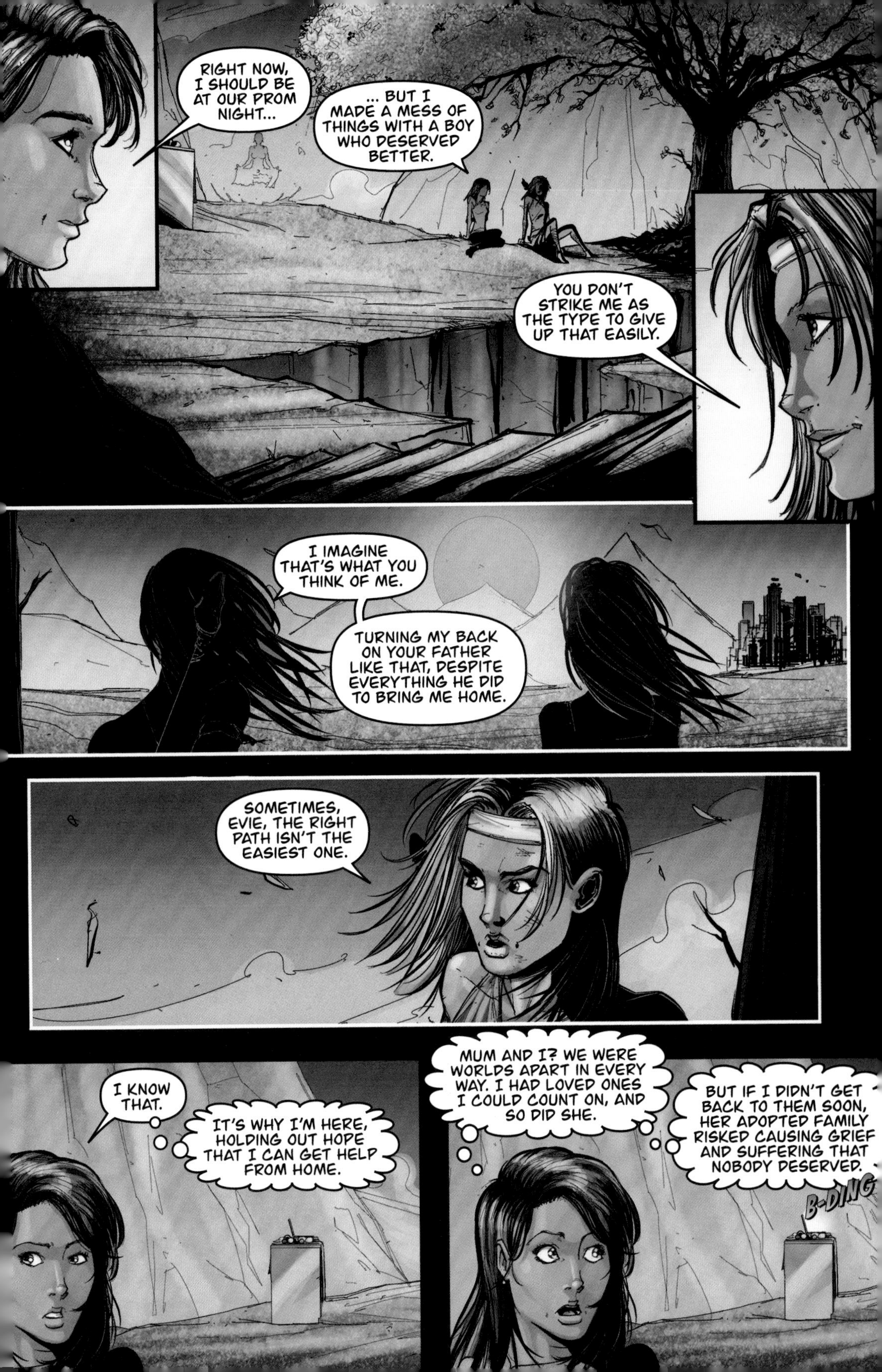
RIGHT NOW, I SHOULD BE AT OUR PROM NIGHT...
... BUT I MADE A MESS OF THINGS WITH A BOY WHO DESERVED BETTER.
YOU DON'T STRIKE ME AS THE TYPE TO GIVE UP THAT EASILY.
I IMAGINE THAT'S WHAT YOU THINK OF ME.
TURNING MY BACK ON YOUR FATHER LIKE THAT, DESPITE EVERYTHING HE DID TO BRING ME HOME.
SOMETIMES, EVIE, THE RIGHT PATH ISN'T THE EASIEST ONE.
I KNOW THAT.
IT'S WHY I'M HERE, HOLDING OUT HOPE THAT I CAN GET HELP FROM HOME.
MUM AND I? WE WERE WORLDS APART IN EVERY WAY. I HAD LOVED ONES I COULD COUNT ON, AND SO DID SHE.
BUT IF I DIDN'T GET BACK TO THEM SOON, HER ADOPTED FAMILY RISKED CAUSING GRIEF AND SUFFERING THAT NOBODY DESERVED.
B-DING

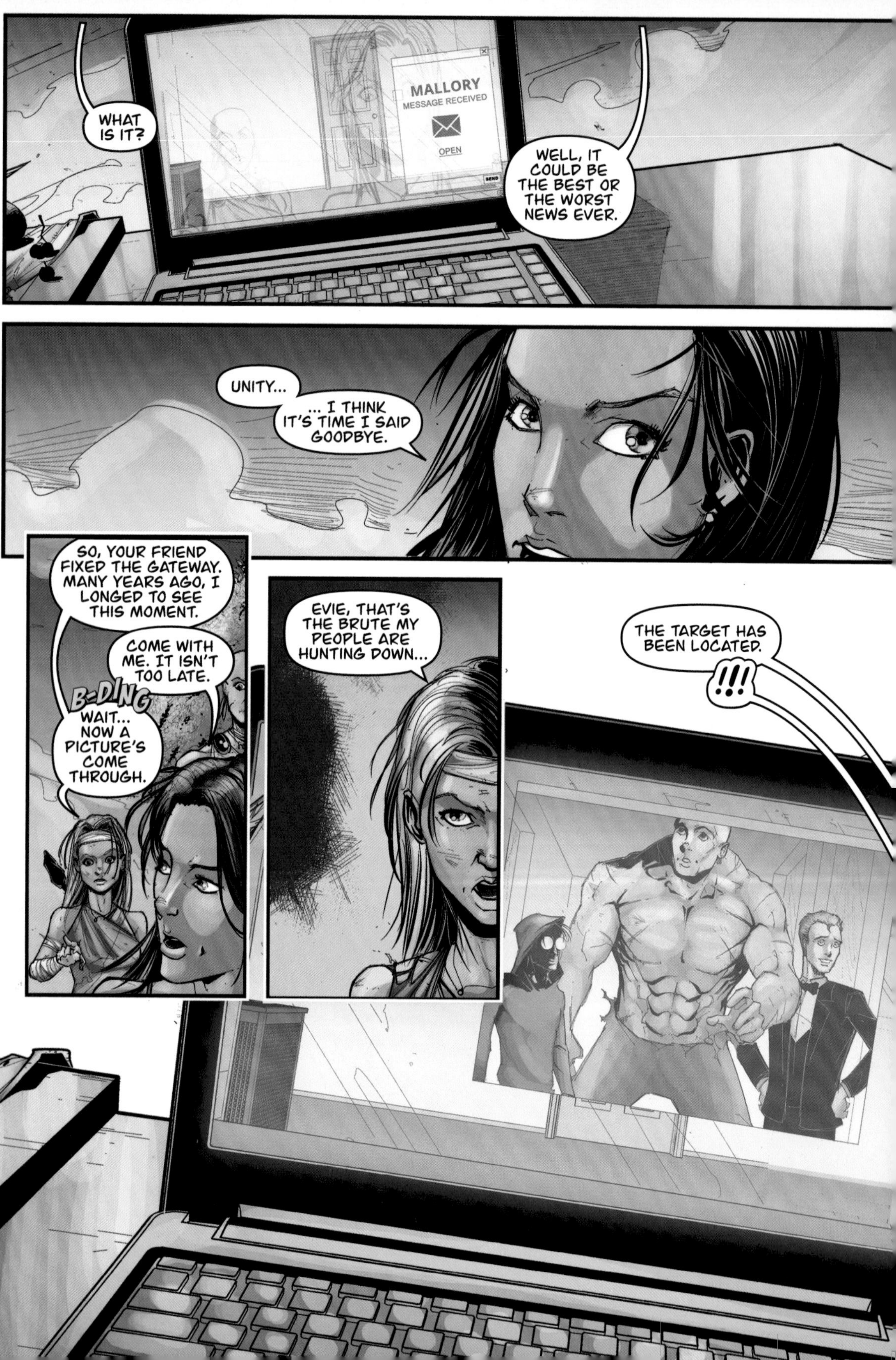
MALLORY
MESSAGE RECEIVED
OPEN
SEND
WHAT IS IT?
WELL, IT COULD BE THE BEST OR THE WORST NEWS EVER.
UNITY...
... I THINK IT'S TIME I SAID GOODBYE.
SO, YOUR FRIEND FIXED THE GATEWAY. MANY YEARS AGO, I LONGED TO SEE THIS MOMENT.
COME WITH ME. IT ISN'T TOO LATE.
B-DING
WAIT... NOW A PICTURE'S COME THROUGH.
EVIE, THAT'S THE BRUTE MY PEOPLE ARE HUNTING DOWN...
THE TARGET HAS BEEN LOCATED.
!!!

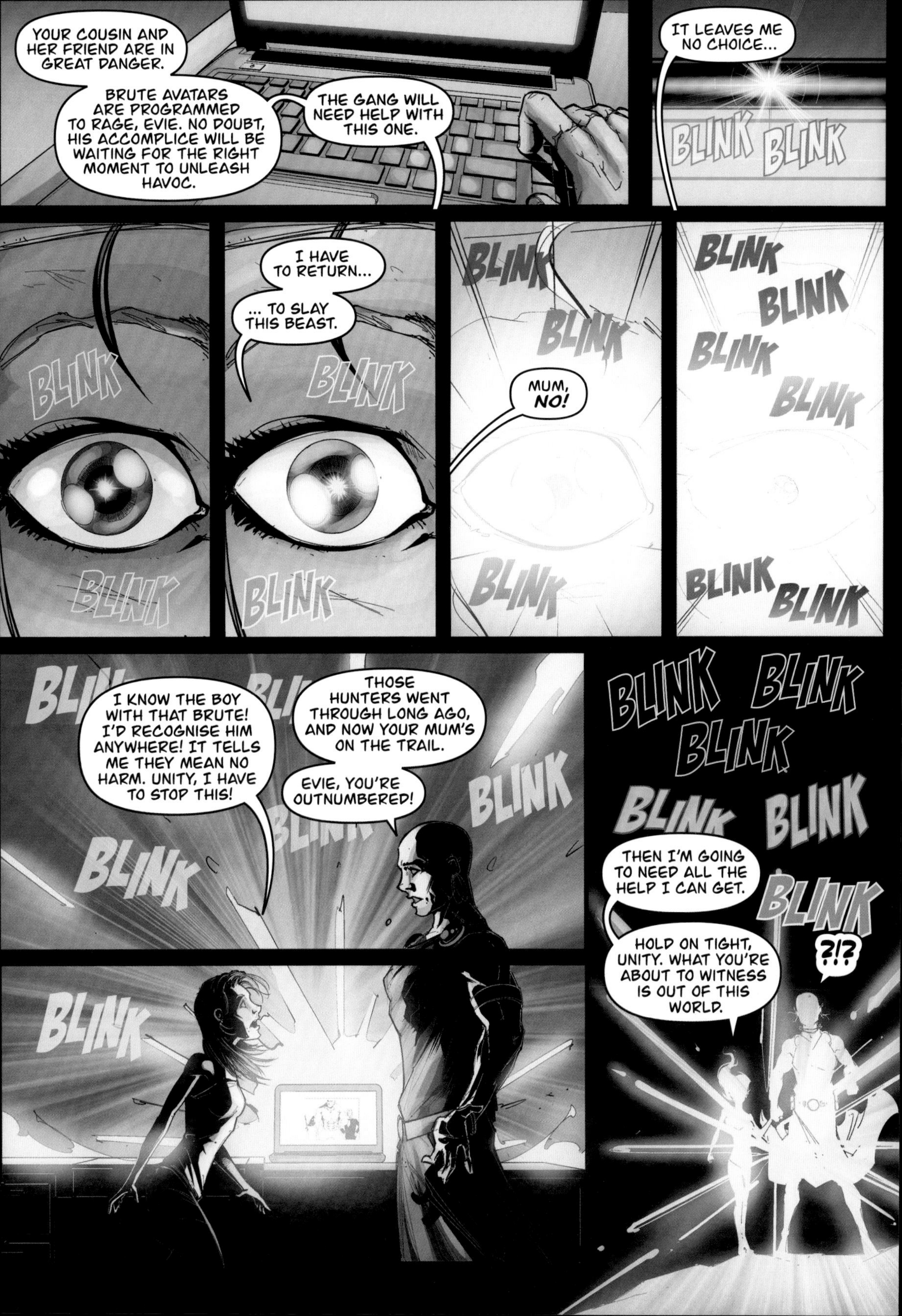
YOUR COUSIN AND HER FRIEND ARE IN GREAT DANGER.
BRUTE AVATARS ARE PROGRAMMED TO RAGE, EVIE. NO DOUBT, HIS ACCOMPLICE WILL BE WAITING FOR THE RIGHT MOMENT TO UNLEASH HAVOC.
THE GANG WILL NEED HELP WITH THIS ONE.
IT LEAVES ME NO CHOICE...
BLINK BLINK
BLINK
BLINK
I HAVE TO RETURN...
... TO SLAY THIS BEAST.
BLINK
BLINK
BLINK
BLINK
MUM, NO!
BLINK
BLINK
BLINK
BLINK
BLINK
BLINK
BLINK
BLINK
I KNOW THE BOY WITH THAT BRUTE! I'D RECOGNISE HIM ANYWHERE! IT TELLS ME THEY MEAN NO HARM. UNITY, I HAVE TO STOP THIS!
THOSE HUNTERS WENT THROUGH LONG AGO, AND NOW YOUR MUM'S ON THE TRAIL.
EVIE, YOU'RE OUTNUMBERED!
BLINK
BLINK
BLINK
BLINK BLINK
BLINK
BLINK BLINK
THEN I'M GOING TO NEED ALL THE HELP I CAN GET.
BLINK
?!?
HOLD ON TIGHT, UNITY. WHAT YOU'RE ABOUT TO WITNESS IS OUT OF THIS WORLD.

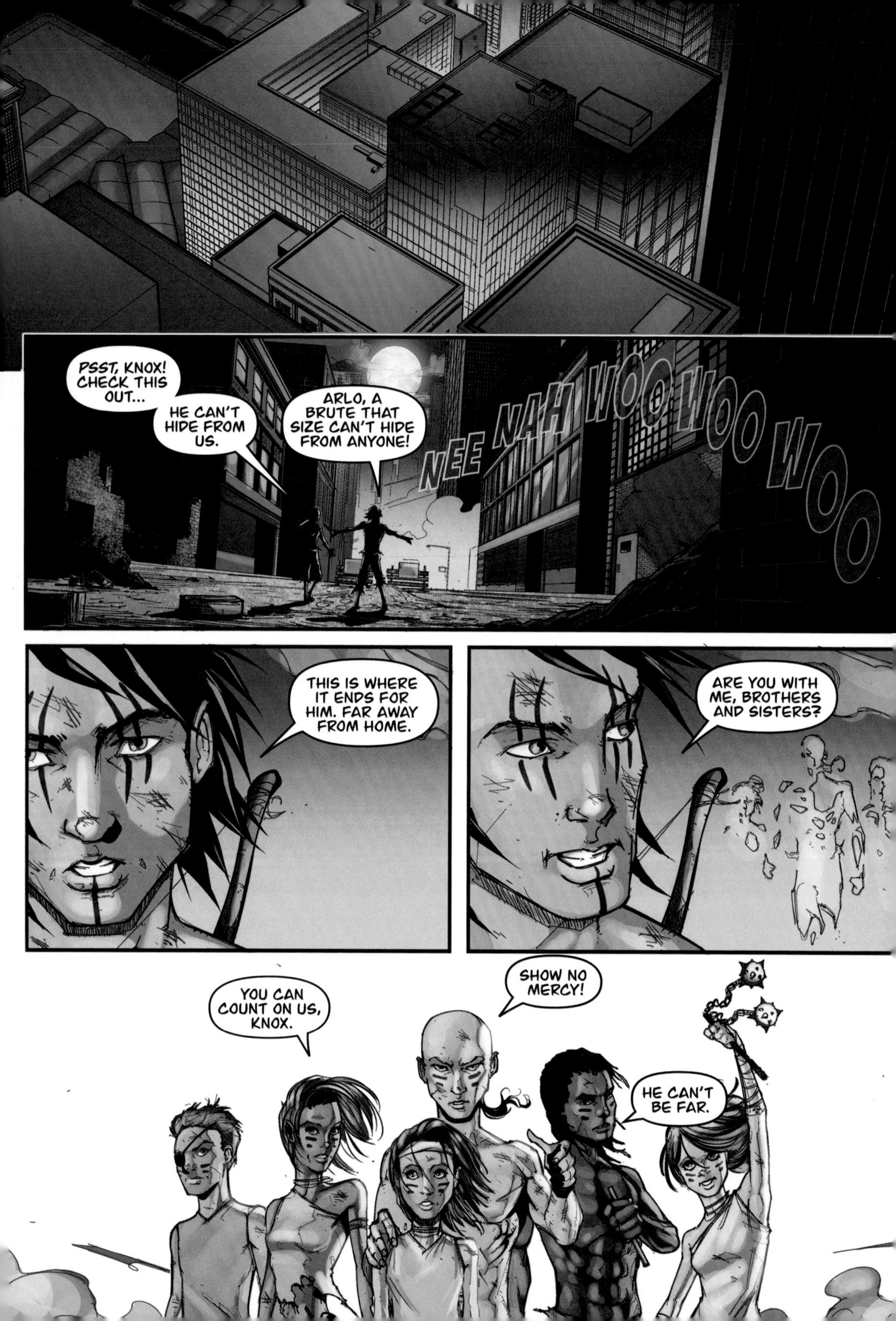
PSST, KNOX! CHECK THIS OUT...
HE CAN'T HIDE FROM US.
ARLO, A BRUTE THAT SIZE CAN'T HIDE FROM ANYONE!
NEE NAH WOO WOO WOO WOO
THIS IS WHERE IT ENDS FOR HIM. FAR AWAY FROM HOME.
ARE YOU WITH ME, BROTHERS AND SISTERS?
YOU CAN COUNT ON US, KNOX.
SHOW NO MERCY!
HE CAN'T BE FAR.

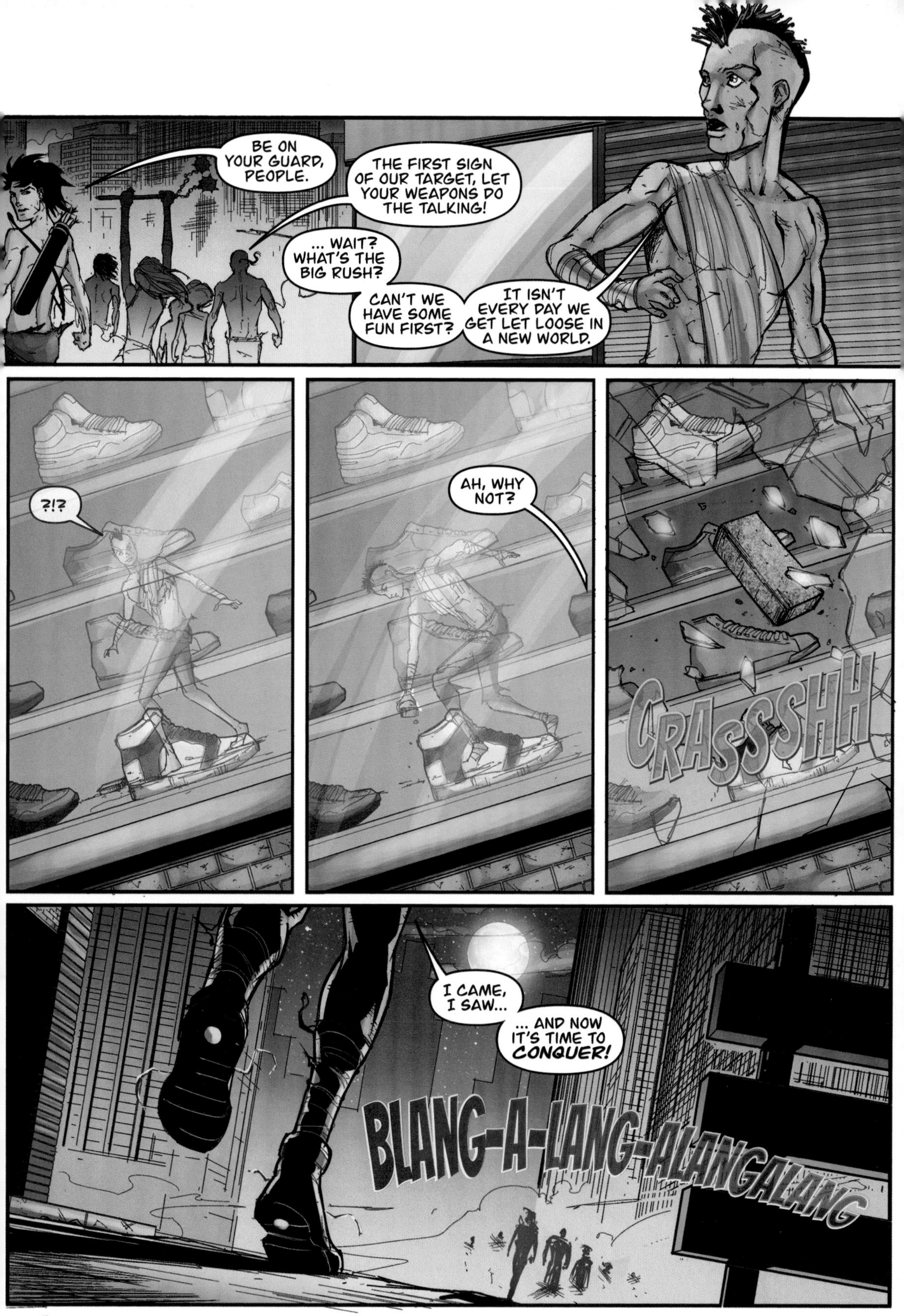

BE ON YOUR GUARD, PEOPLE.
THE FIRST SIGN OF OUR TARGET, LET YOUR WEAPONS DO THE TALKING!
... WAIT? WHAT'S THE BIG RUSH?
CAN'T WE HAVE SOME FUN FIRST?
IT ISN'T EVERY DAY WE GET LET LOOSE IN A NEW WORLD.
?!?
AH, WHY NOT?
CRASSSHH
I CAME, I SAW...
... AND NOW IT'S TIME TO CONQUER!
BLANG-A-LANG-ALANGALANG

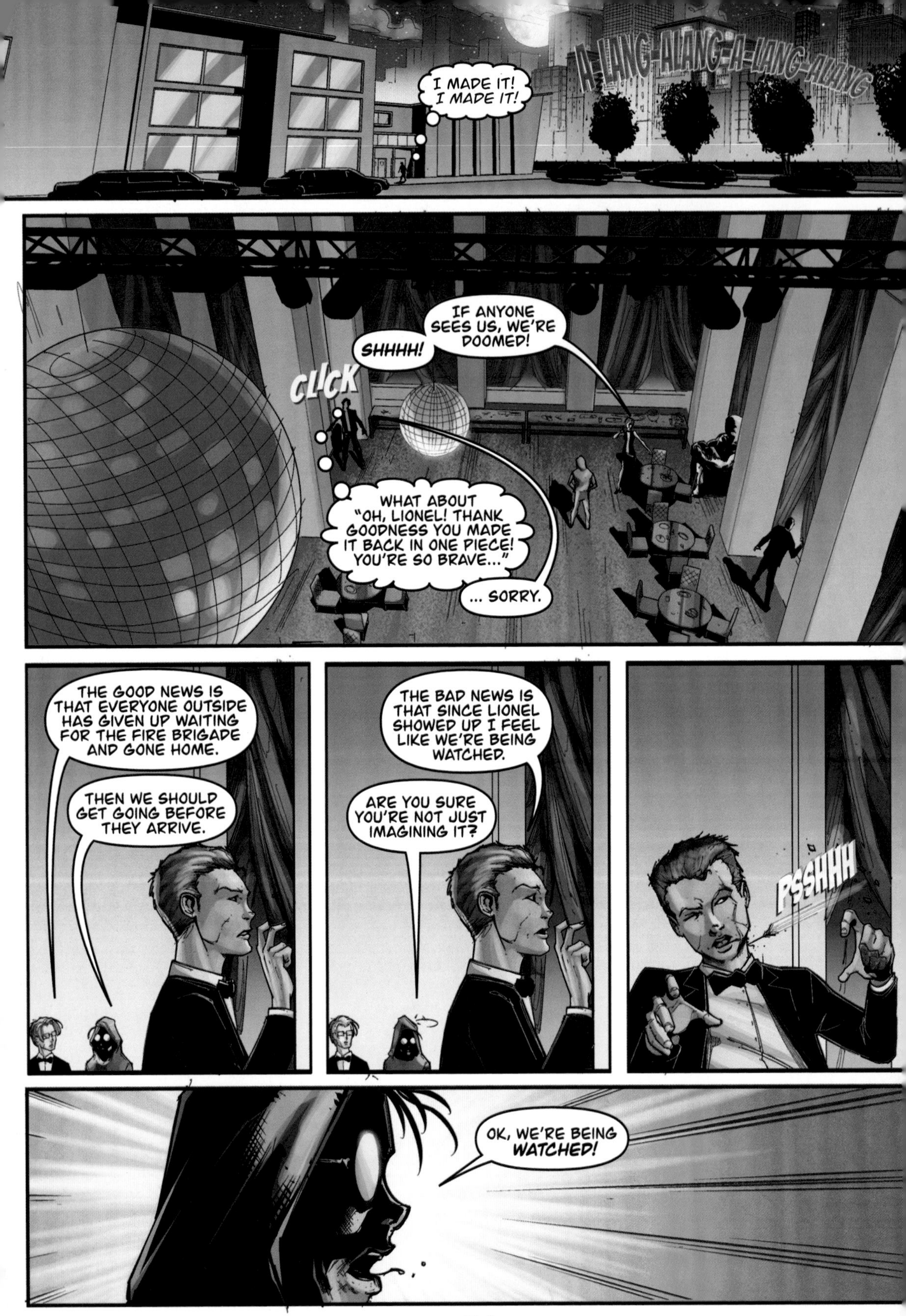
A-LANG-ALANG-A-LANG-ALANG
I MADE IT! I MADE IT!
CLICK
SHHHH!
IF ANYONE SEES US, WE'RE DOOMED!
WHAT ABOUT "OH, LIONEL! THANK GOODNESS YOU MADE IT BACK IN ONE PIECE! YOU'RE SO BRAVE..."
... SORRY.
THE GOOD NEWS IS THAT EVERYONE OUTSIDE HAS GIVEN UP WAITING FOR THE FIRE BRIGADE AND GONE HOME.
THEN WE SHOULD GET GOING BEFORE THEY ARRIVE.
THE BAD NEWS IS THAT SINCE LIONEL SHOWED UP I FEEL LIKE WE'RE BEING WATCHED.
ARE YOU SURE YOU'RE NOT JUST IMAGINING IT?
PSSHHH
OK, WE'RE BEING WATCHED!

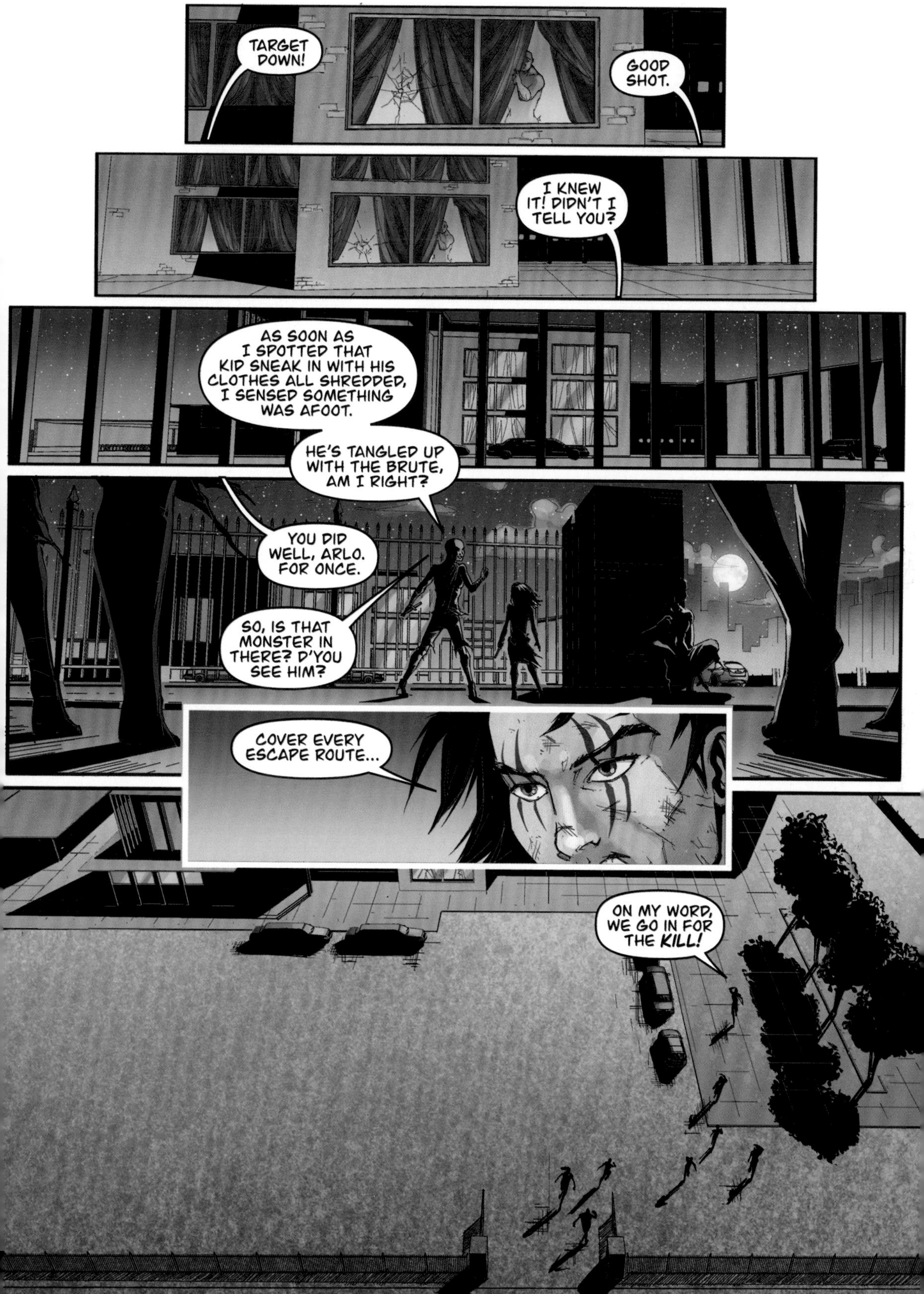
TARGET DOWN!
GOOD SHOT.
I KNEW IT! DIDN'T I TELL YOU?
AS SOON AS I SPOTTED THAT KID SNEAK IN WITH HIS CLOTHES ALL SHREDDED, I SENSED SOMETHING WAS AFOOT.
HE'S TANGLED UP WITH THE BRUTE, AM I RIGHT?
YOU DID WELL, ARLO. FOR ONCE.
SO, IS THAT MONSTER IN THERE? D'YOU SEE HIM?
COVER EVERY ESCAPE ROUTE...
ON MY WORD, WE GO IN FOR THE **KILL!**

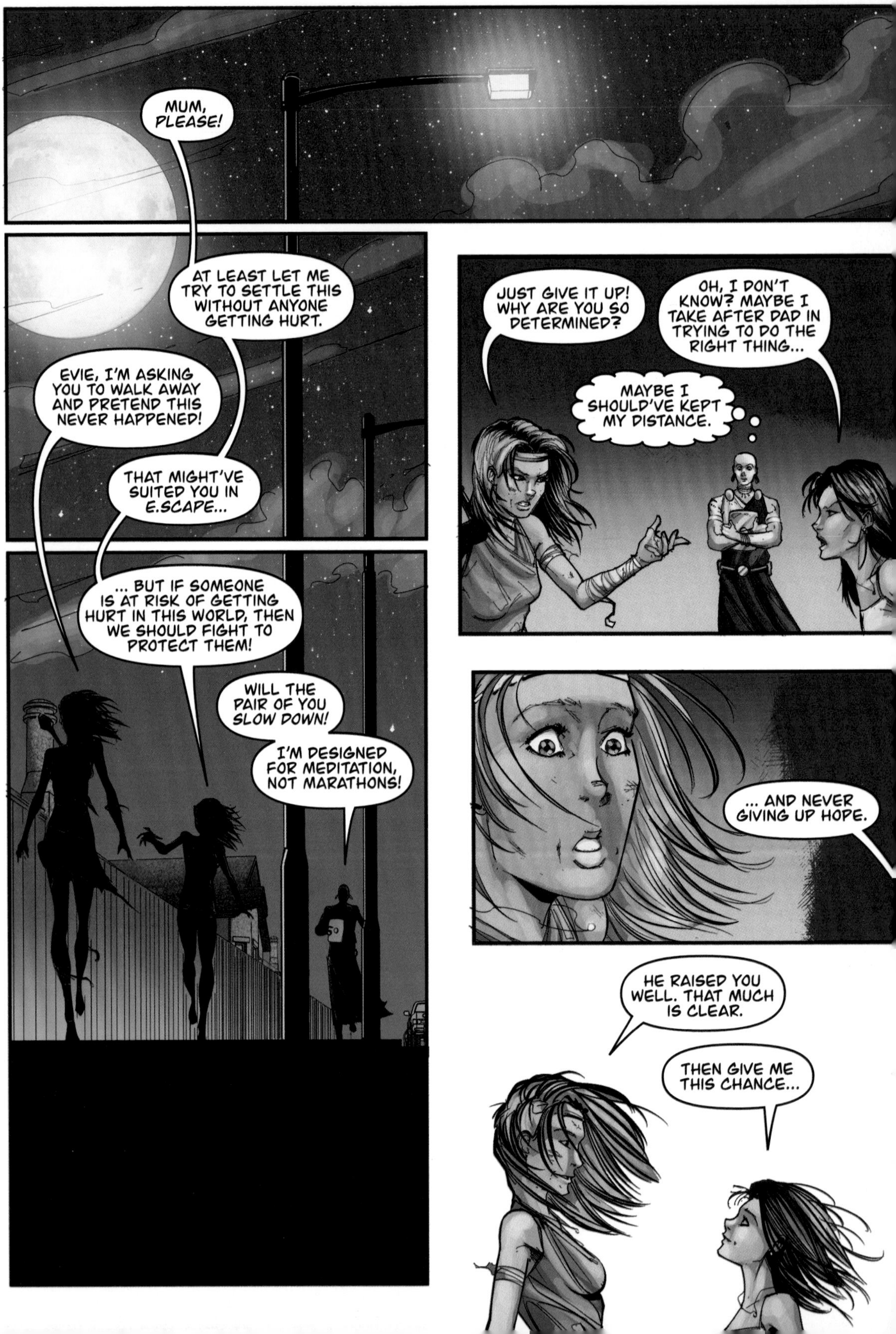
MUM, PLEASE!
AT LEAST LET ME TRY TO SETTLE THIS WITHOUT ANYONE GETTING HURT.
EVIE, I'M ASKING YOU TO WALK AWAY AND PRETEND THIS NEVER HAPPENED!
THAT MIGHT'VE SUITED YOU IN E.SCAPE...
... BUT IF SOMEONE IS AT RISK OF GETTING HURT IN THIS WORLD, THEN WE SHOULD FIGHT TO PROTECT THEM!
WILL THE PAIR OF YOU SLOW DOWN!
I'M DESIGNED FOR MEDITATION, NOT MARATHONS!
JUST GIVE IT UP! WHY ARE YOU SO DETERMINED?
OH, I DON'T KNOW? MAYBE I TAKE AFTER DAD IN TRYING TO DO THE RIGHT THING...
MAYBE I SHOULD'VE KEPT MY DISTANCE.
... AND NEVER GIVING UP HOPE.
HE RAISED YOU WELL. THAT MUCH IS CLEAR.
THEN GIVE ME THIS CHANCE...

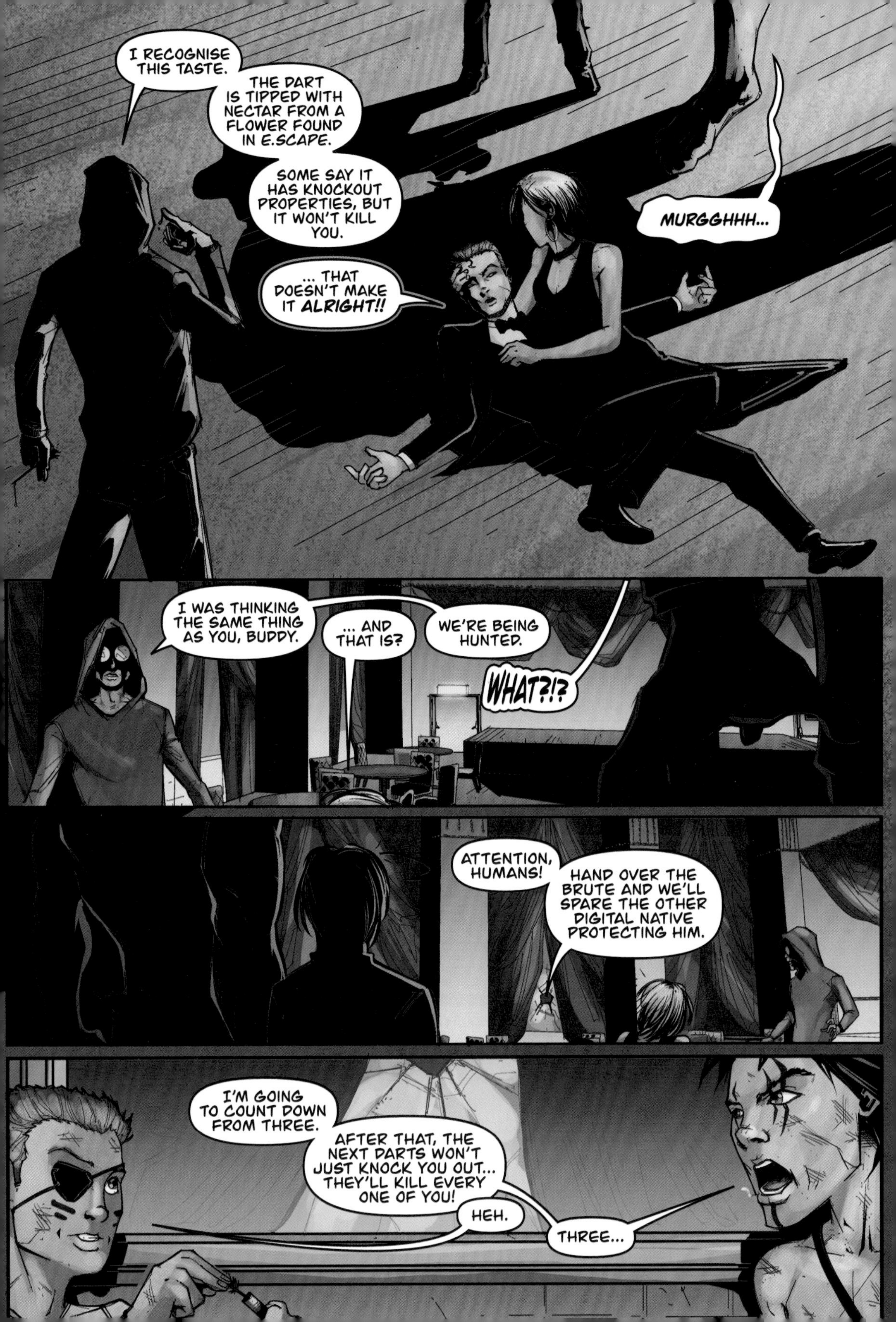
I RECOGNISE THIS TASTE.
THE DART IS TIPPED WITH NECTAR FROM A FLOWER FOUND IN E.SCAPE.
SOME SAY IT HAS KNOCKOUT PROPERTIES, BUT IT WON'T KILL YOU.
MURGGHHH...
... THAT DOESN'T MAKE IT ALRIGHT!!
I WAS THINKING THE SAME THING AS YOU, BUDDY.
... AND THAT IS?
WE'RE BEING HUNTED.
WHAT?!?
ATTENTION, HUMANS!
HAND OVER THE BRUTE AND WE'LL SPARE THE OTHER DIGITAL NATIVE PROTECTING HIM.
I'M GOING TO COUNT DOWN FROM THREE.
AFTER THAT, THE NEXT DARTS WON'T JUST KNOCK YOU OUT... THEY'LL KILL EVERY ONE OF YOU!
HEH.
THREE...

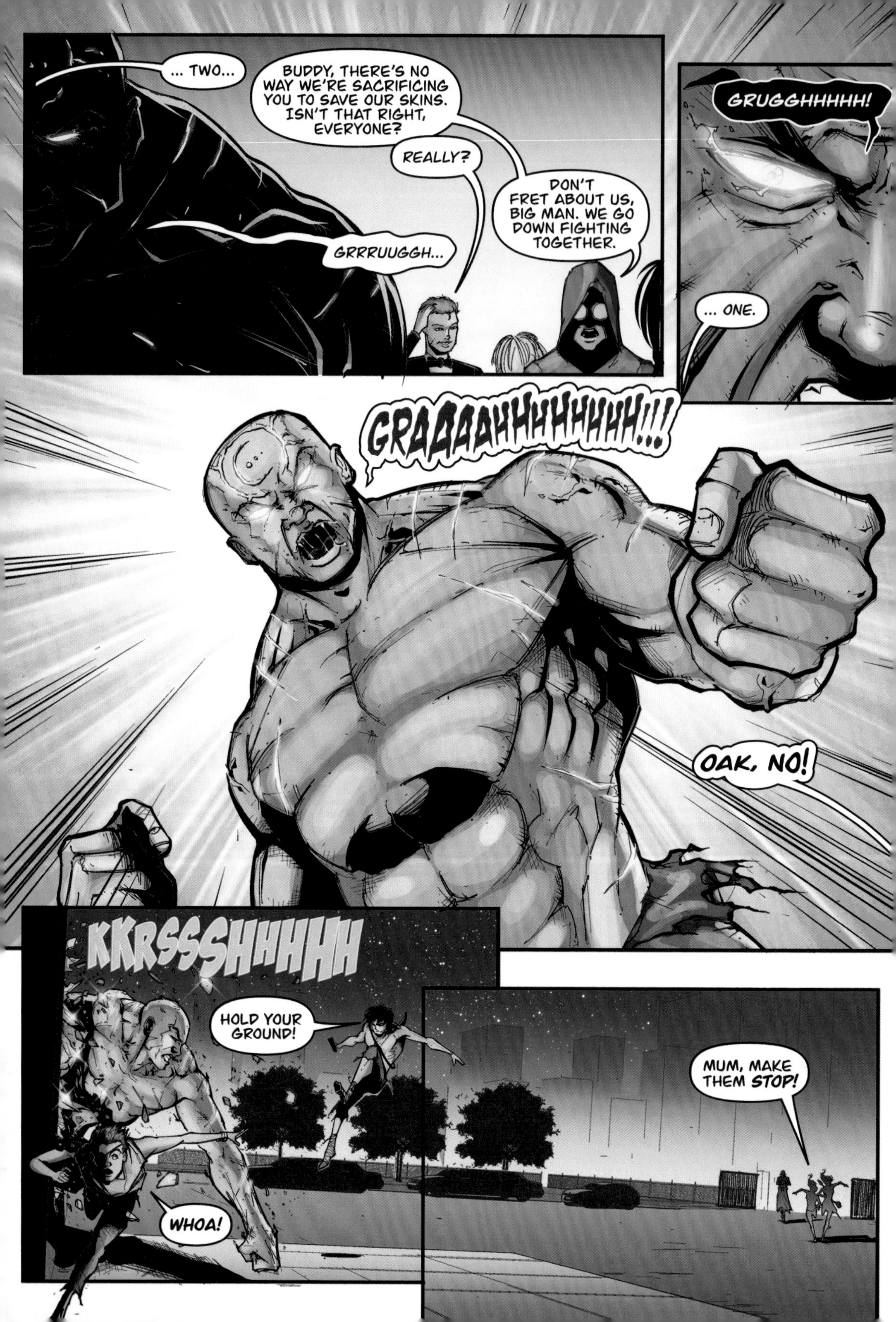
... TWO...
BUDDY, THERE'S NO WAY WE'RE SACRIFICING YOU TO SAVE OUR SKINS. ISN'T THAT RIGHT, EVERYONE?
REALLY?
DON'T FRET ABOUT US, BIG MAN. WE GO DOWN FIGHTING TOGETHER.
GRRRUUGGH...
GRUGGHHHHH!
... ONE.
GRAAAAHHHHHHH!!!
OAK, NO!
KKRSSSHHHHH
HOLD YOUR GROUND!
WHOA!
MUM, MAKE THEM STOP!

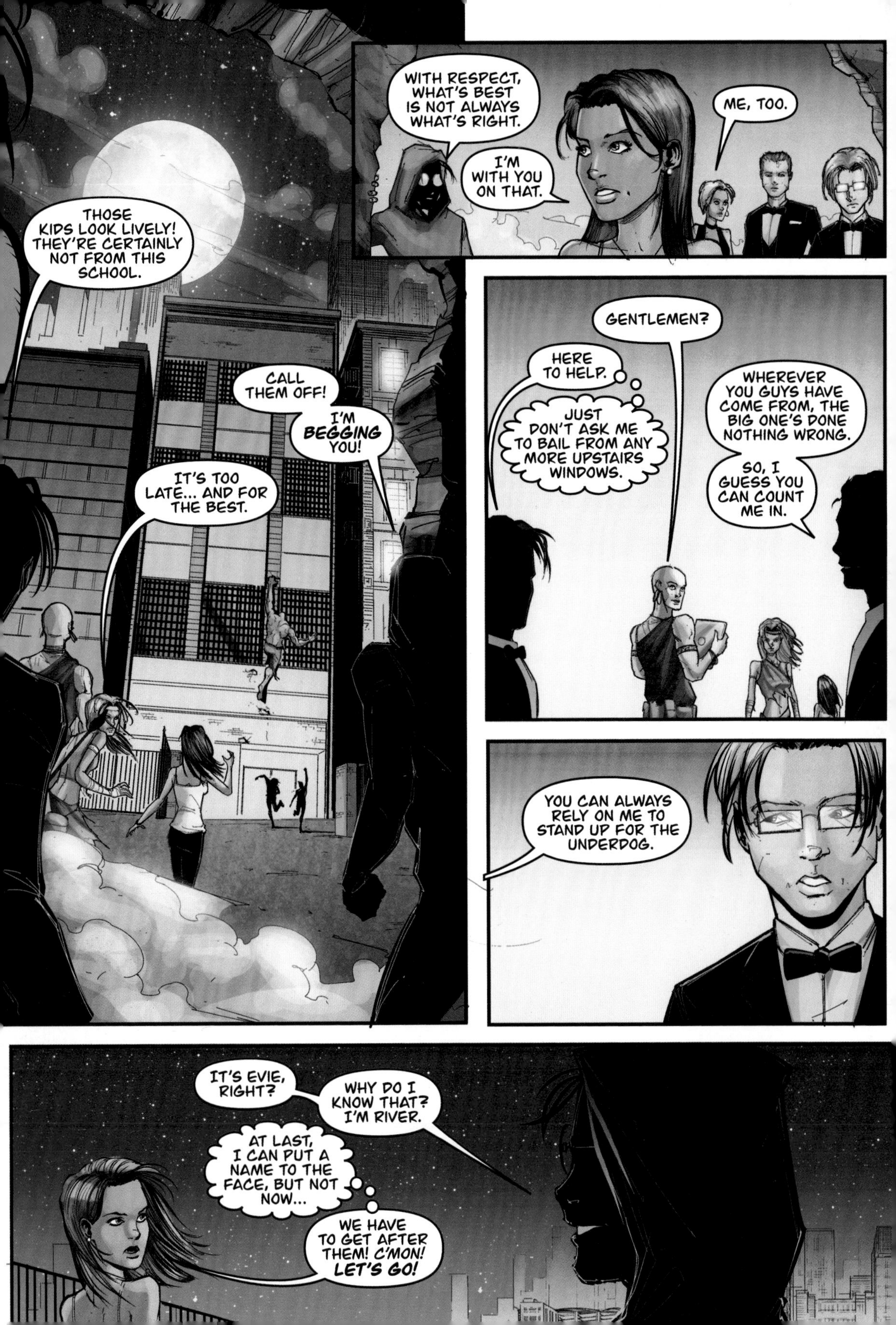
WITH RESPECT, WHAT'S BEST IS NOT ALWAYS WHAT'S RIGHT.
I'M WITH YOU ON THAT.
ME, TOO.
THOSE KIDS LOOK LIVELY! THEY'RE CERTAINLY NOT FROM THIS SCHOOL.
CALL THEM OFF!
I'M **BEGGING** YOU!
IT'S TOO LATE... AND FOR THE BEST.
GENTLEMEN?
HERE TO HELP.
JUST DON'T ASK ME TO BAIL FROM ANY MORE UPSTAIRS WINDOWS.
WHEREVER YOU GUYS HAVE COME FROM, THE BIG ONE'S DONE NOTHING WRONG.
SO, I GUESS YOU CAN COUNT ME IN.
YOU CAN ALWAYS RELY ON ME TO STAND UP FOR THE UNDERDOG.
IT'S EVIE, RIGHT?
WHY DO I KNOW THAT? I'M RIVER.
AT LAST, I CAN PUT A NAME TO THE FACE, BUT NOT NOW...
WE HAVE TO GET AFTER THEM! C'MON! **LET'S GO!**

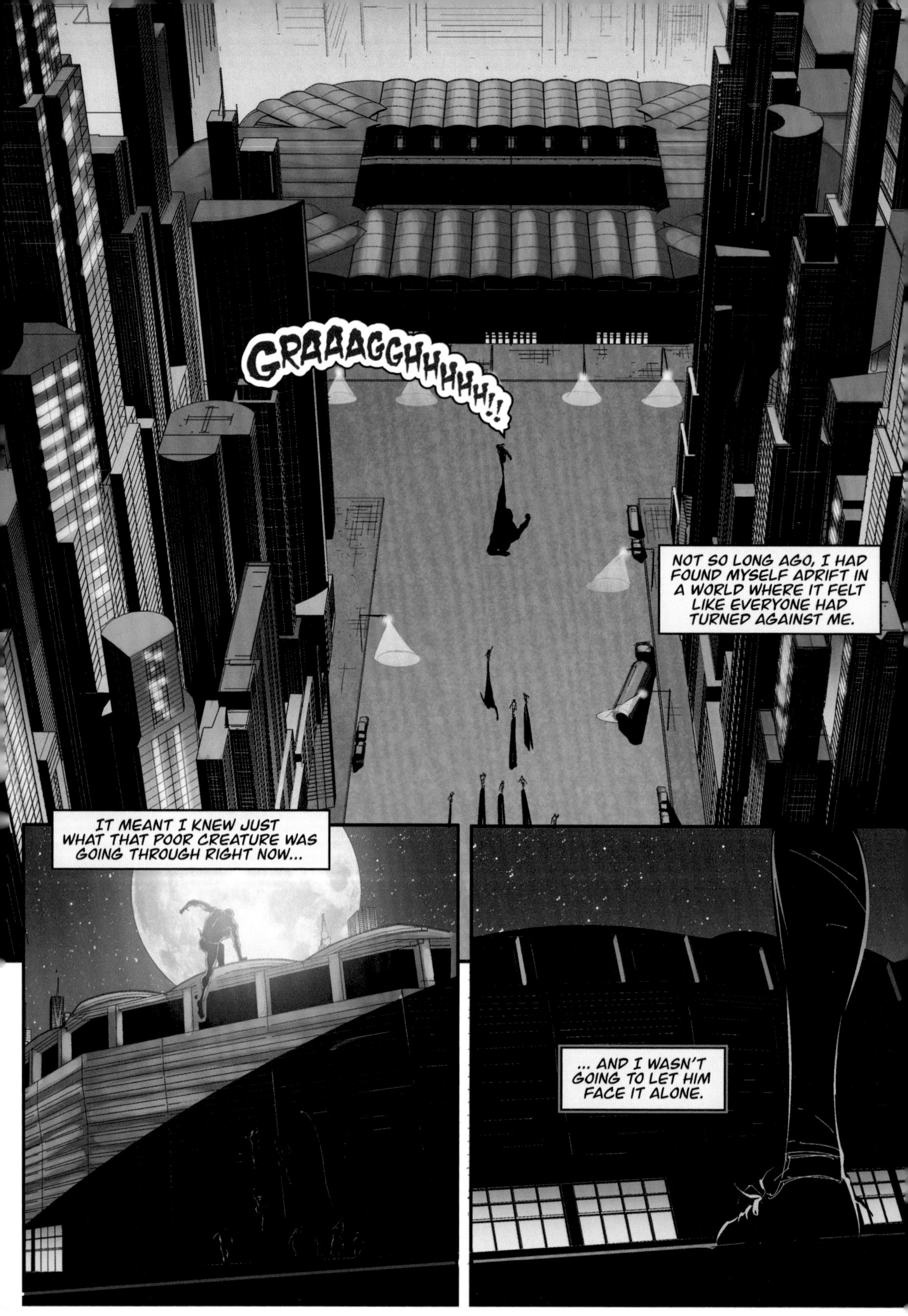
GRAAAGGHHHHH!!
NOT SO LONG AGO, I HAD FOUND MYSELF ADRIFT IN A WORLD WHERE IT FELT LIKE EVERYONE HAD TURNED AGAINST ME.
IT MEANT I KNEW JUST WHAT THAT POOR CREATURE WAS GOING THROUGH RIGHT NOW...
... AND I WASN'T GOING TO LET HIM FACE IT ALONE.

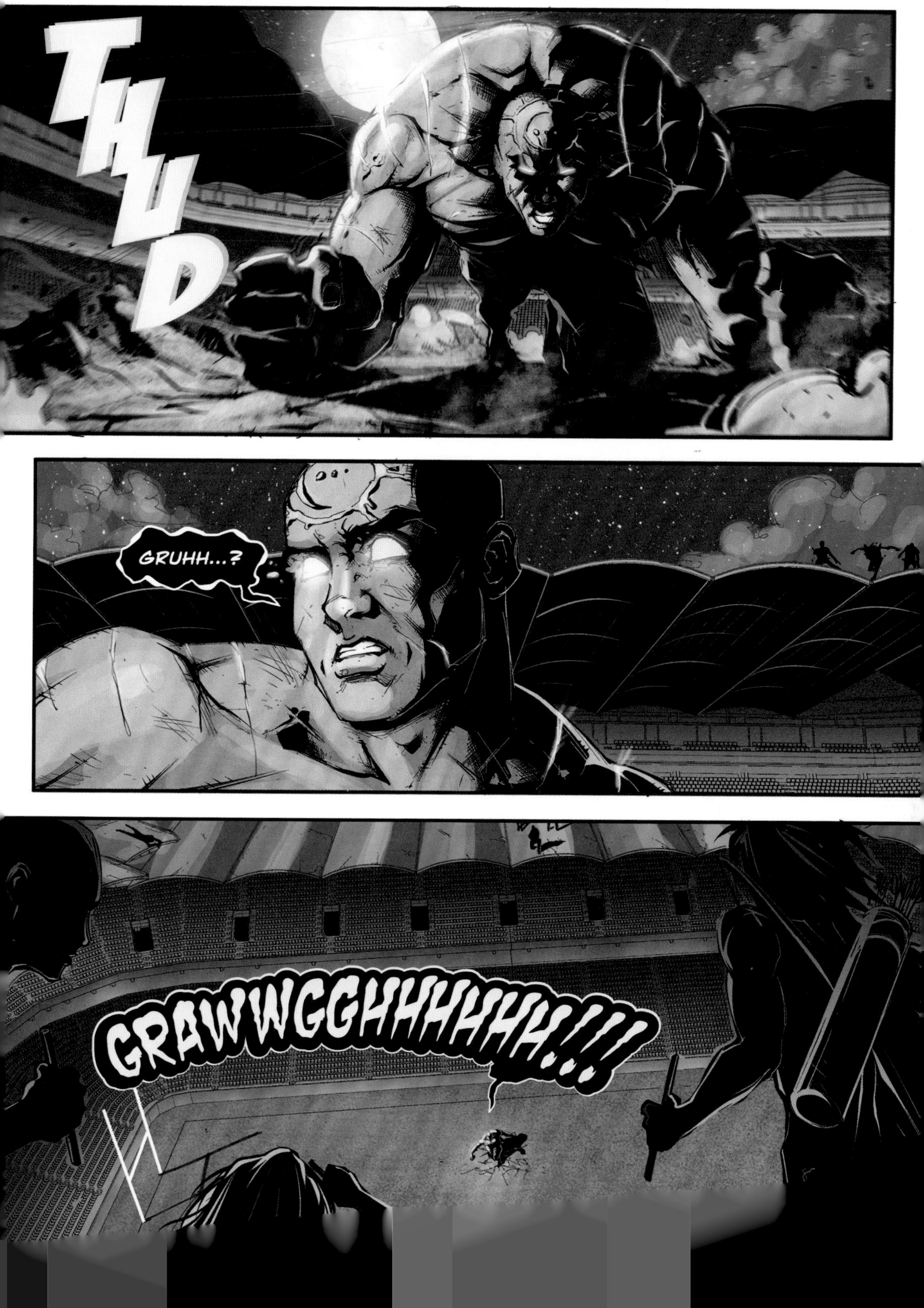
THUD
GRUHH...?
GRAWWGGHHHHHHH!!!

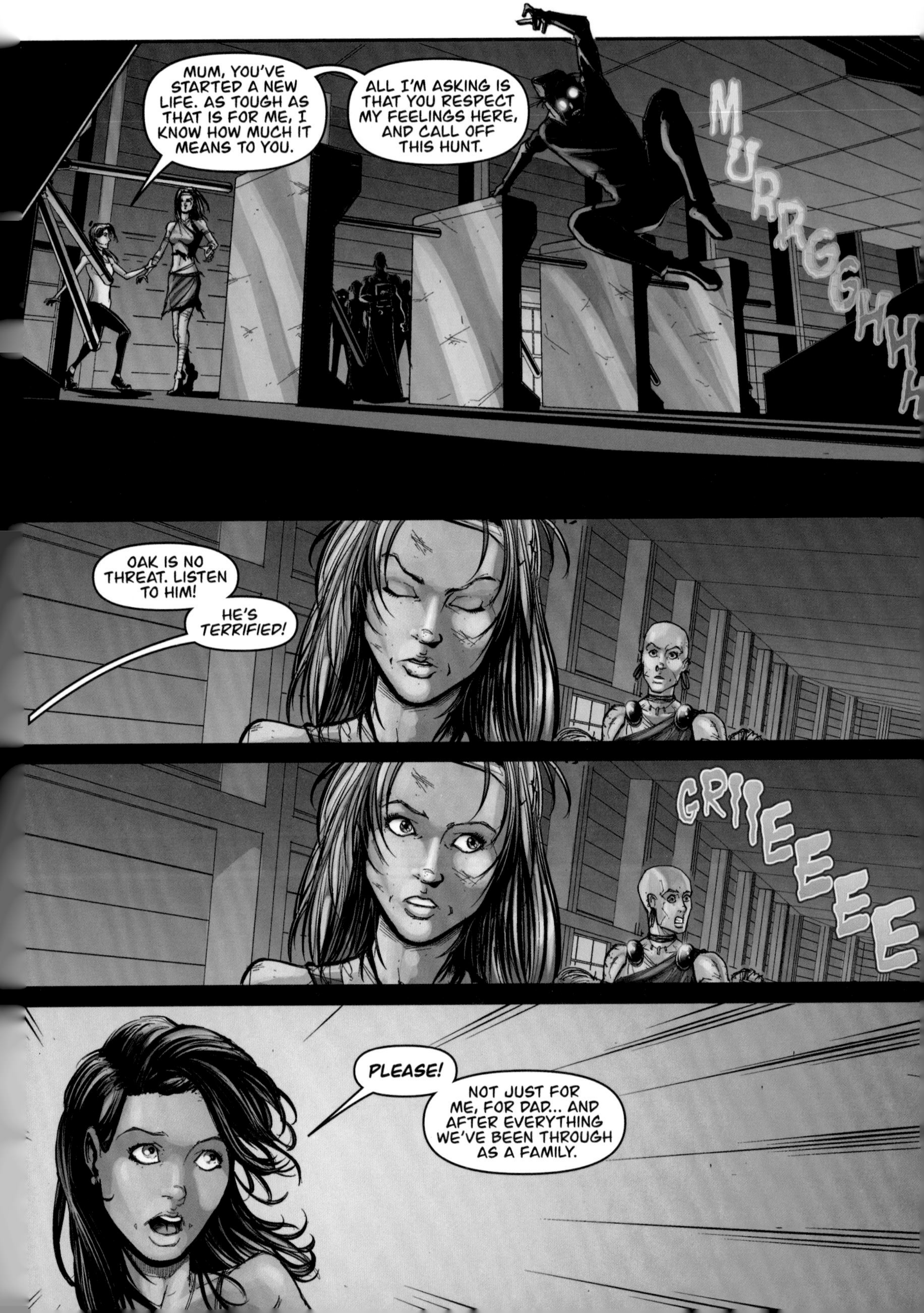
MUM, YOU'VE STARTED A NEW LIFE. AS TOUGH AS THAT IS FOR ME, I KNOW HOW MUCH IT MEANS TO YOU.
ALL I'M ASKING IS THAT YOU RESPECT MY FEELINGS HERE, AND CALL OFF THIS HUNT.
MURRGGHHHH
OAK IS NO THREAT. LISTEN TO HIM!
HE'S TERRIFIED!
GRIIEEEEE
PLEASE!
NOT JUST FOR ME, FOR DAD... AND AFTER EVERYTHING WE'VE BEEN THROUGH AS A FAMILY.

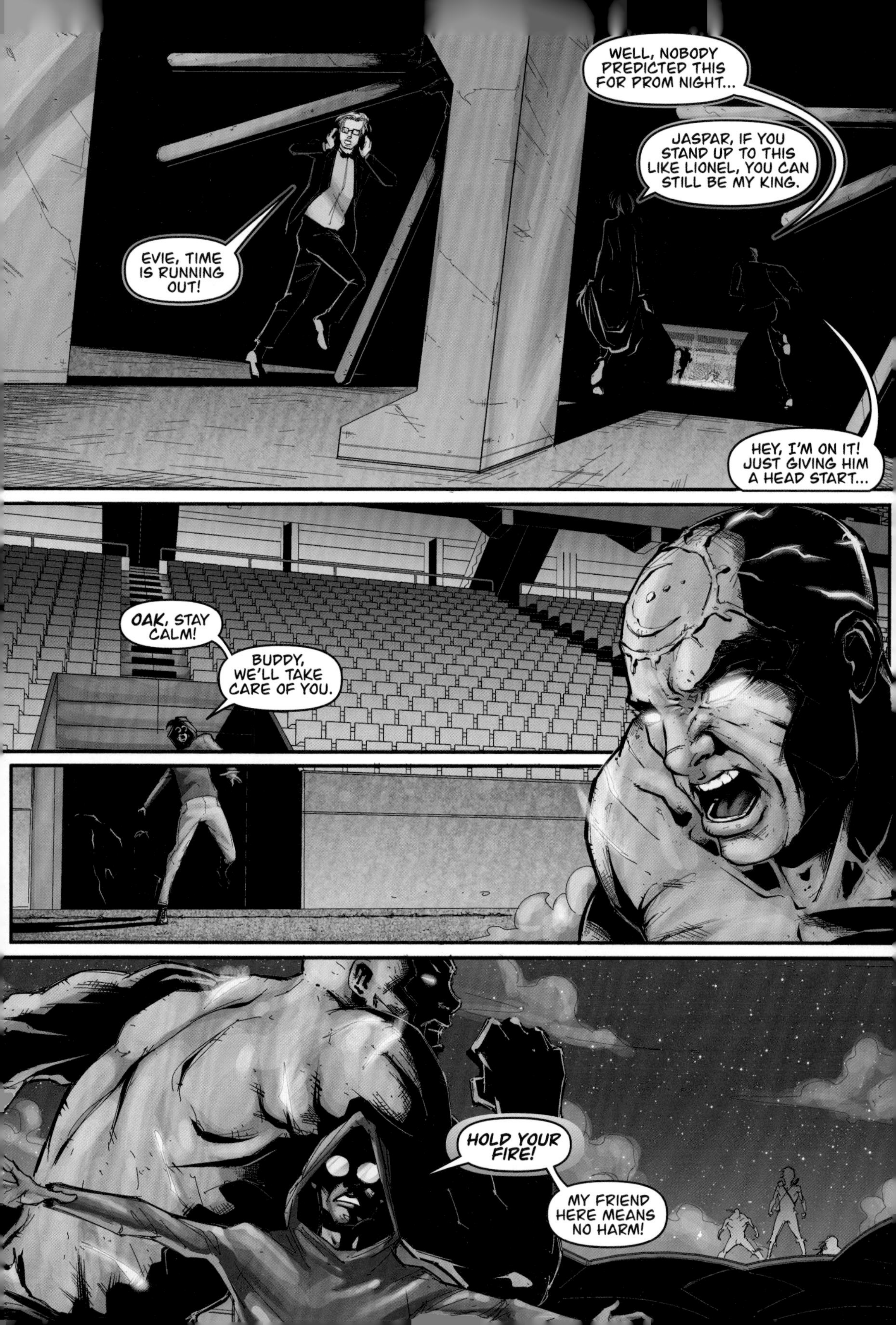
EVIE, TIME IS RUNNING OUT!
WELL, NOBODY PREDICTED THIS FOR PROM NIGHT...
JASPAR, IF YOU STAND UP TO THIS LIKE LIONEL, YOU CAN STILL BE MY KING.
HEY, I'M ON IT! JUST GIVING HIM A HEAD START...
OAK, STAY CALM!
BUDDY, WE'LL TAKE CARE OF YOU.
HOLD YOUR FIRE!
MY FRIEND HERE MEANS NO HARM!

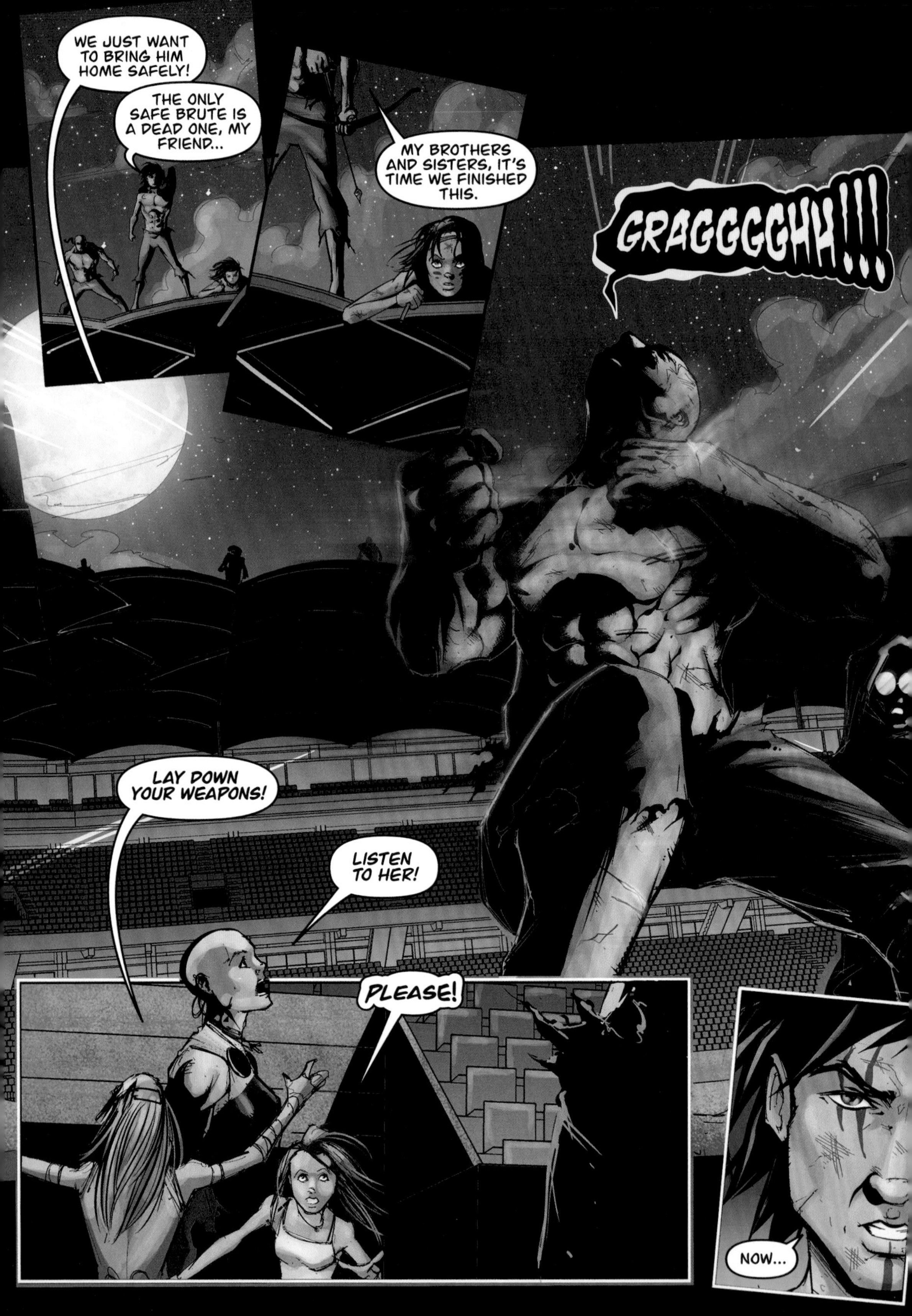
WE JUST WANT TO BRING HIM HOME SAFELY!
THE ONLY SAFE BRUTE IS A DEAD ONE, MY FRIEND...
MY BROTHERS AND SISTERS, IT'S TIME WE FINISHED THIS.
GRAGGGGHH!!!
LAY DOWN YOUR WEAPONS!
LISTEN TO HER!
PLEASE!
NOW...

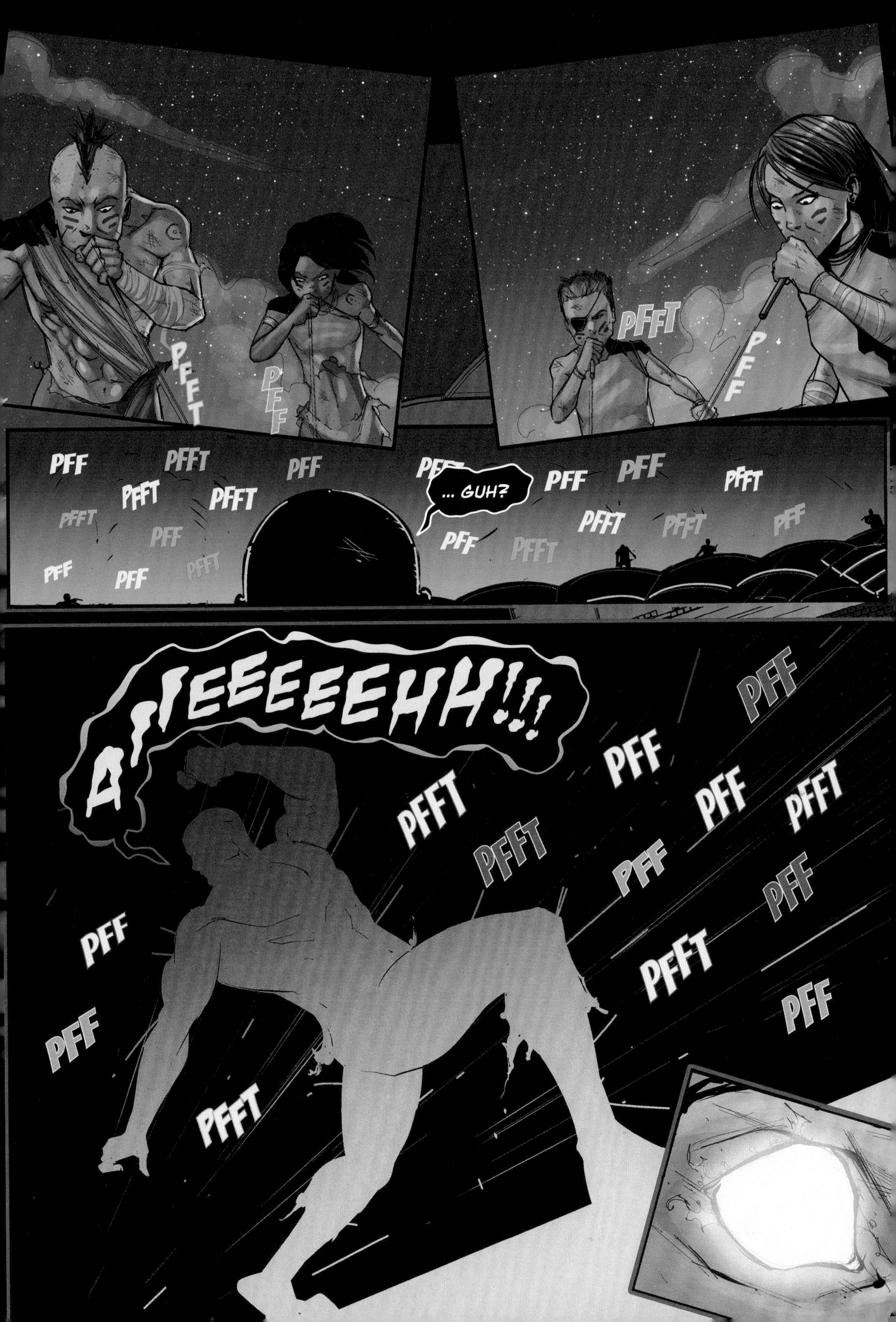

PFFT
PFF
PFFT
PFF
PFF
PFFT
PFF
PFFT
PFFT
PFFT
PFF
PFF
PFF
PFF
PFFT
... GUH?
PFF
PFF
PFFT
PFFT
PFFT
PFFT
PFF
AIIEEEEEEHH!!!
PFF
PFF
PFFT
PFF
PFFT
PFFT
PFF
PFF
PFF
PFFT
PFF
PFF
PFFT

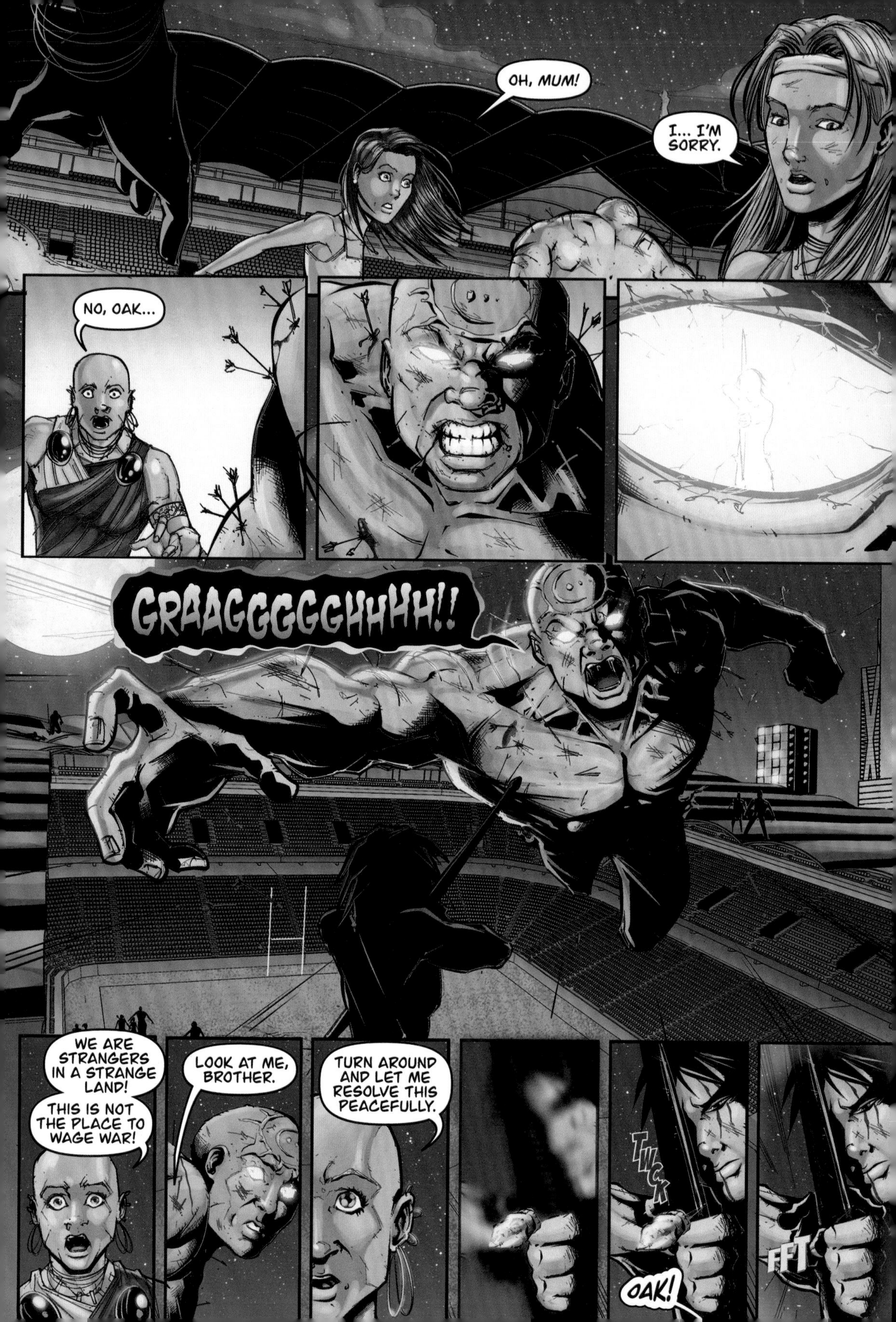
OH, MUM!
I... I'M SORRY.
NO, OAK...
GRAAGGGGGHHHH!!
WE ARE STRANGERS IN A STRANGE LAND!
THIS IS NOT THE PLACE TO WAGE WAR!
LOOK AT ME, BROTHER.
TURN AROUND AND LET ME RESOLVE THIS PEACEFULLY.
THUCK
FFT
OAK!

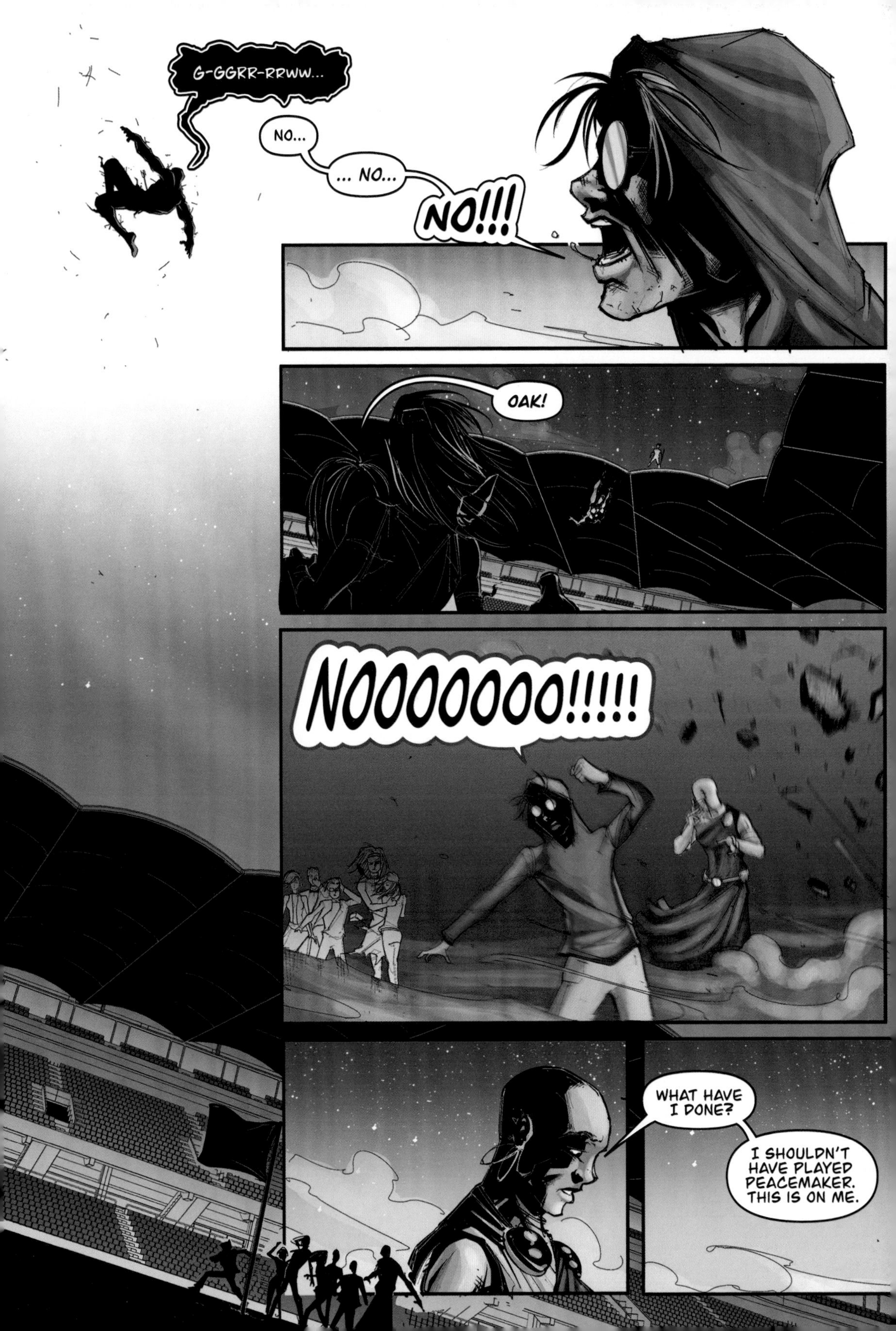
G-GGRR-RRWW...
NO...
... NO...
NO!!!
OAK!
NOOOOOOO!!!!!
WHAT HAVE I DONE?
I SHOULDN'T HAVE PLAYED PEACEMAKER. THIS IS ON ME.

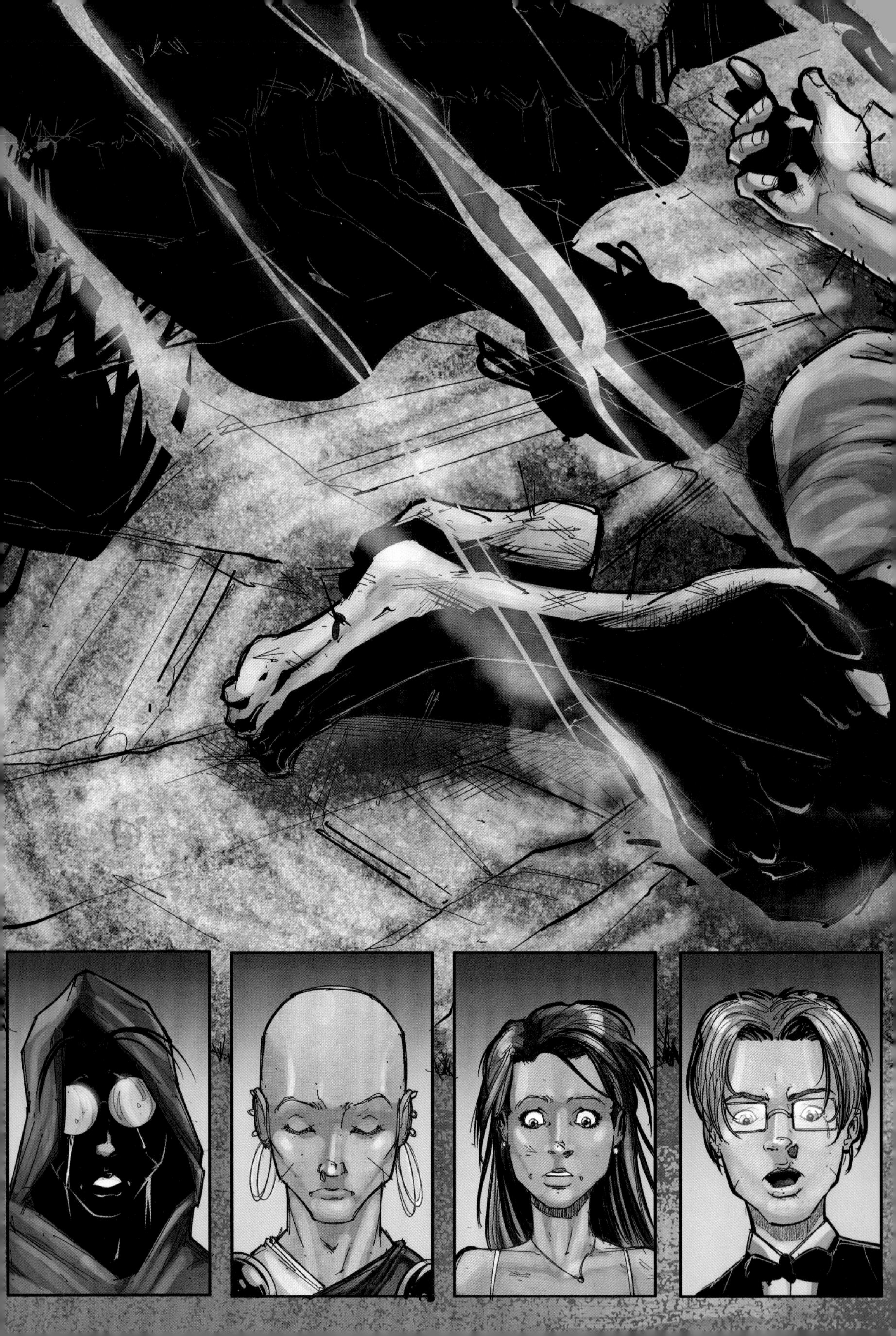

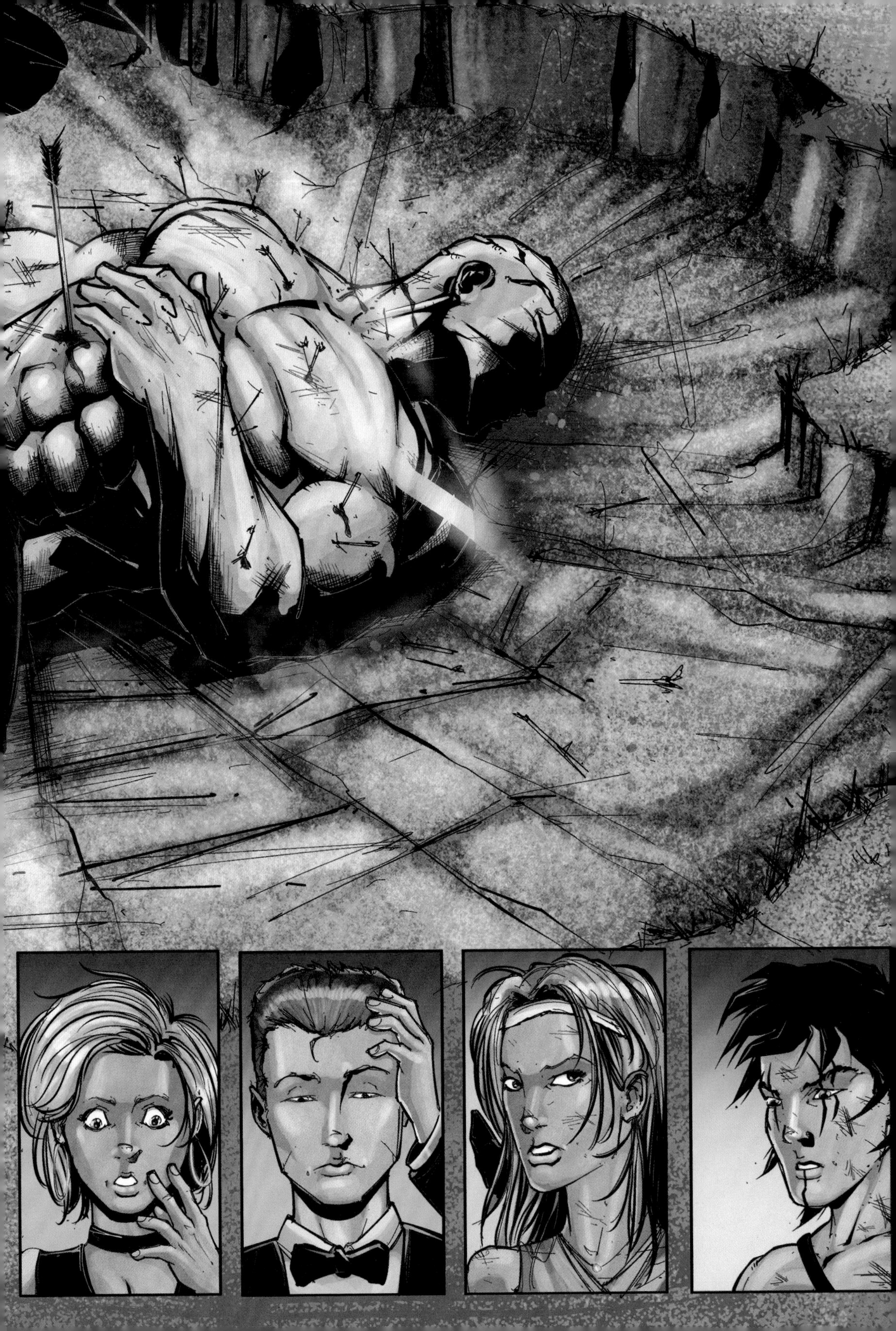

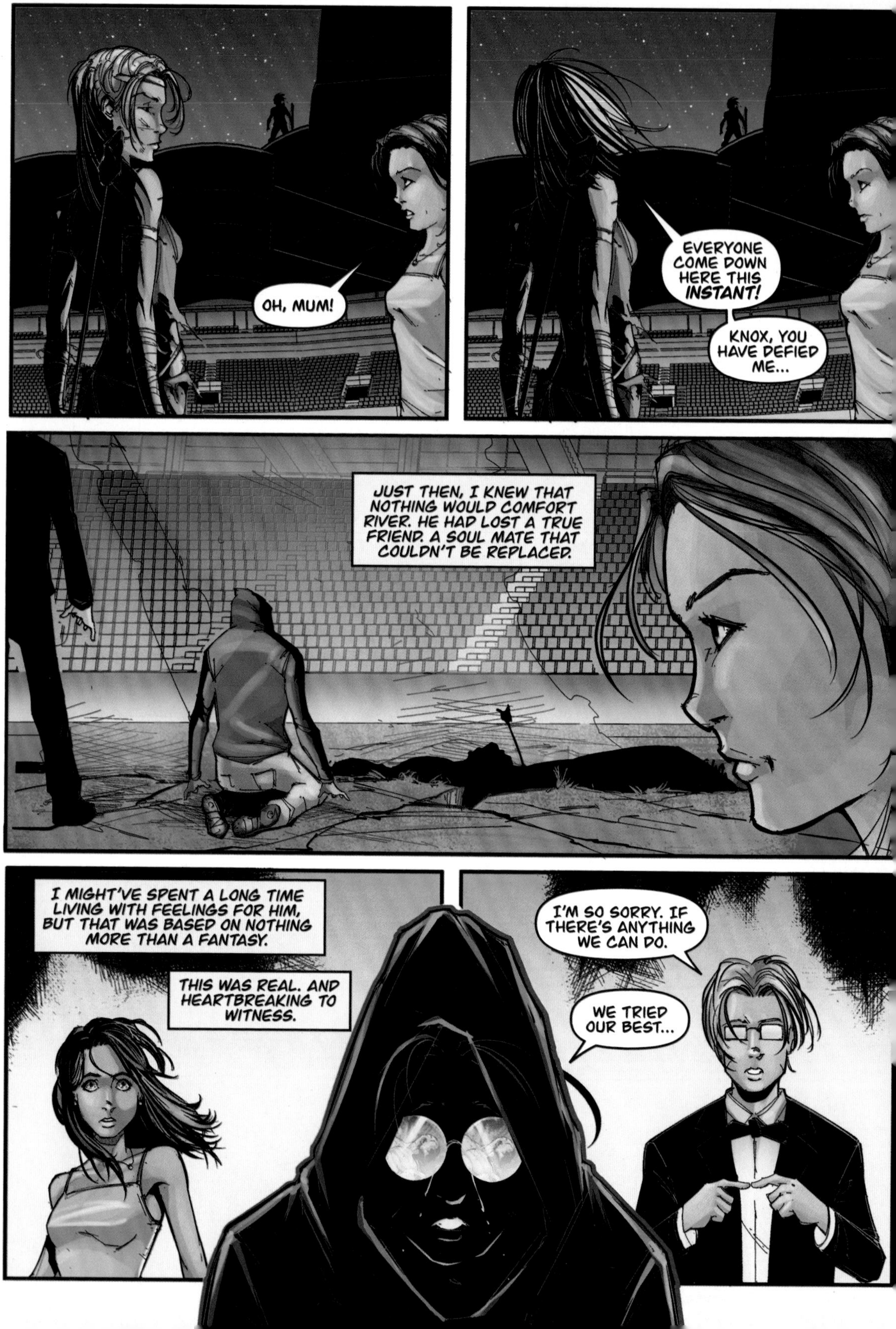
OH, MUM!
EVERYONE COME DOWN HERE THIS INSTANT!
KNOX, YOU HAVE DEFIED ME...
JUST THEN, I KNEW THAT NOTHING WOULD COMFORT RIVER. HE HAD LOST A TRUE FRIEND. A SOUL MATE THAT COULDN'T BE REPLACED.
I MIGHT'VE SPENT A LONG TIME LIVING WITH FEELINGS FOR HIM, BUT THAT WAS BASED ON NOTHING MORE THAN A FANTASY.
THIS WAS REAL. AND HEARTBREAKING TO WITNESS.
I'M SO SORRY. IF THERE'S ANYTHING WE CAN DO.
WE TRIED OUR BEST...

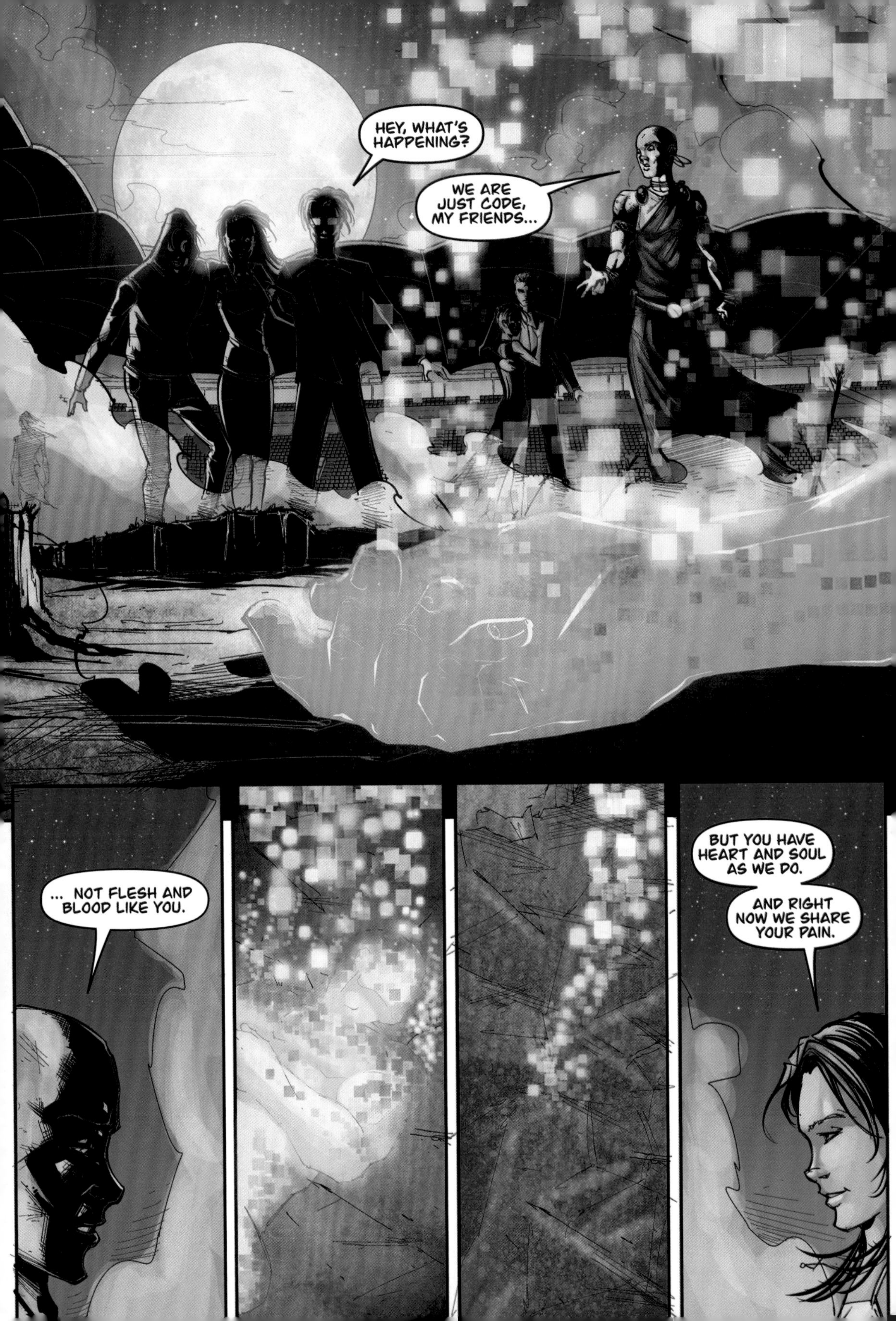
HEY, WHAT'S HAPPENING?
WE ARE JUST CODE, MY FRIENDS...
... NOT FLESH AND BLOOD LIKE YOU.
BUT YOU HAVE HEART AND SOUL AS WE DO.
AND RIGHT NOW WE SHARE YOUR PAIN.

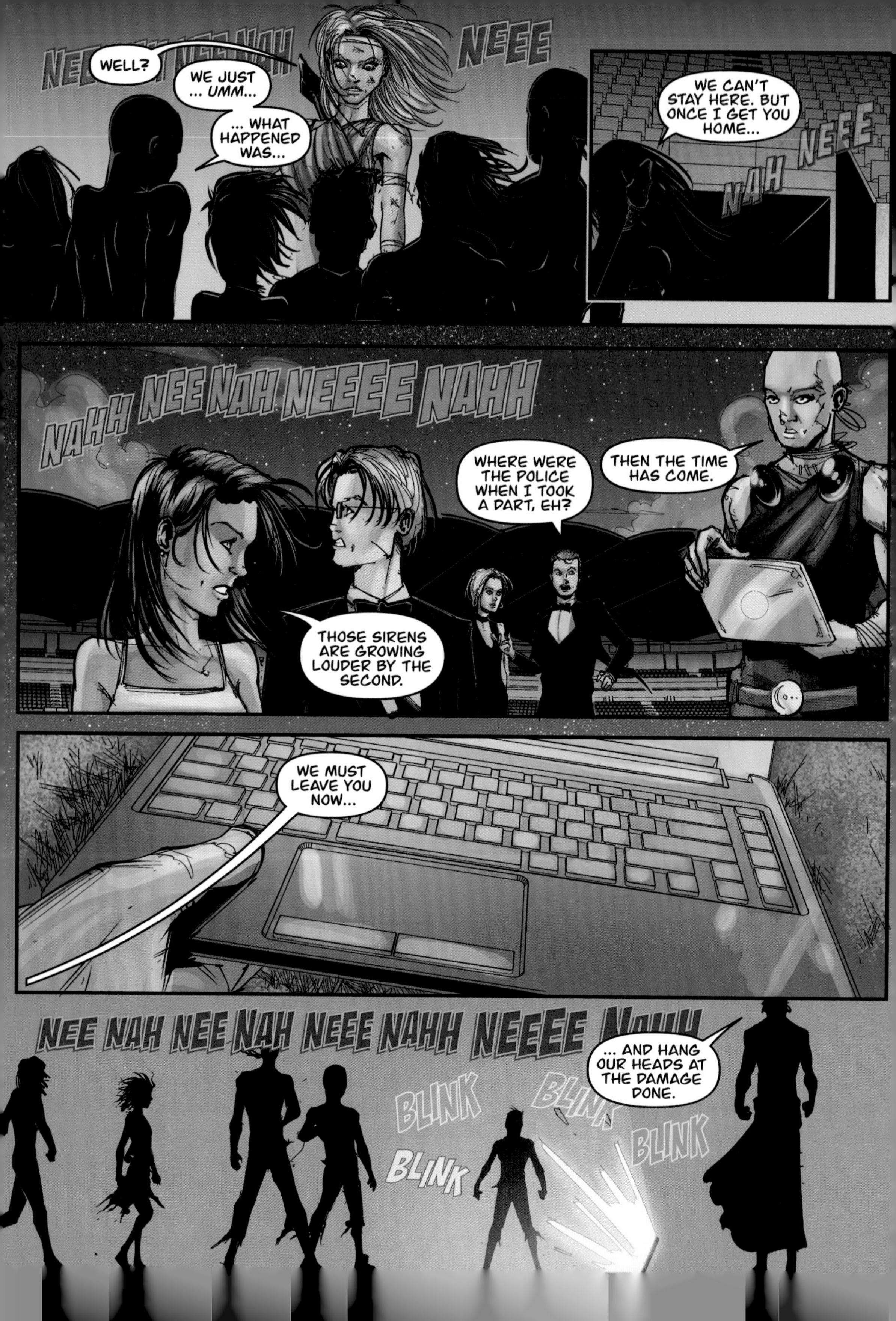
NEE NEE NAH
WELL?
WE JUST ... UMM...
... WHAT HAPPENED WAS...
NEEE
WE CAN'T STAY HERE. BUT ONCE I GET YOU HOME...
NAH NEEE
NAHH NEE NAH NEEEE NAHH
THOSE SIRENS ARE GROWING LOUDER BY THE SECOND.
WHERE WERE THE POLICE WHEN I TOOK A PART, EH?
THEN THE TIME HAS COME.
WE MUST LEAVE YOU NOW...
NEE NAH NEE NAH NEEE NAHH NEEEE
... AND HANG OUR HEADS AT THE DAMAGE DONE.
BLINK
BLINK
BLINK
BLINK

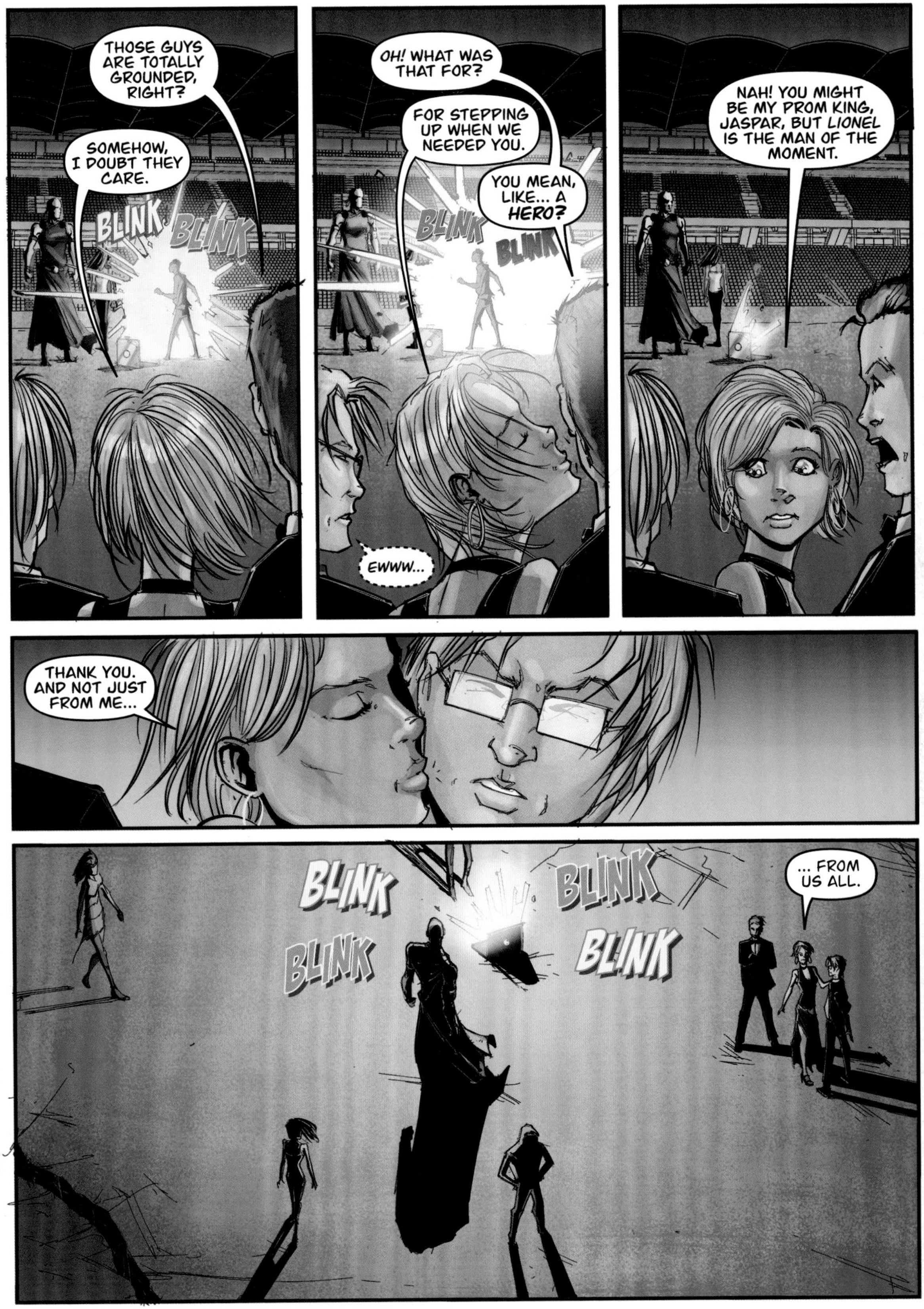
THOSE GUYS ARE TOTALLY GROUNDED, RIGHT?
SOMEHOW, I DOUBT THEY CARE.
BLINK
BLINK
OH! WHAT WAS THAT FOR?
FOR STEPPING UP WHEN WE NEEDED YOU.
YOU MEAN, LIKE... A HERO?
BLINK
BLINK
EWWW...
NAH! YOU MIGHT BE MY PROM KING, JASPAR, BUT LIONEL IS THE MAN OF THE MOMENT.
THANK YOU. AND NOT JUST FROM ME...
BLINK
BLINK
BLINK
BLINK
... FROM US ALL.

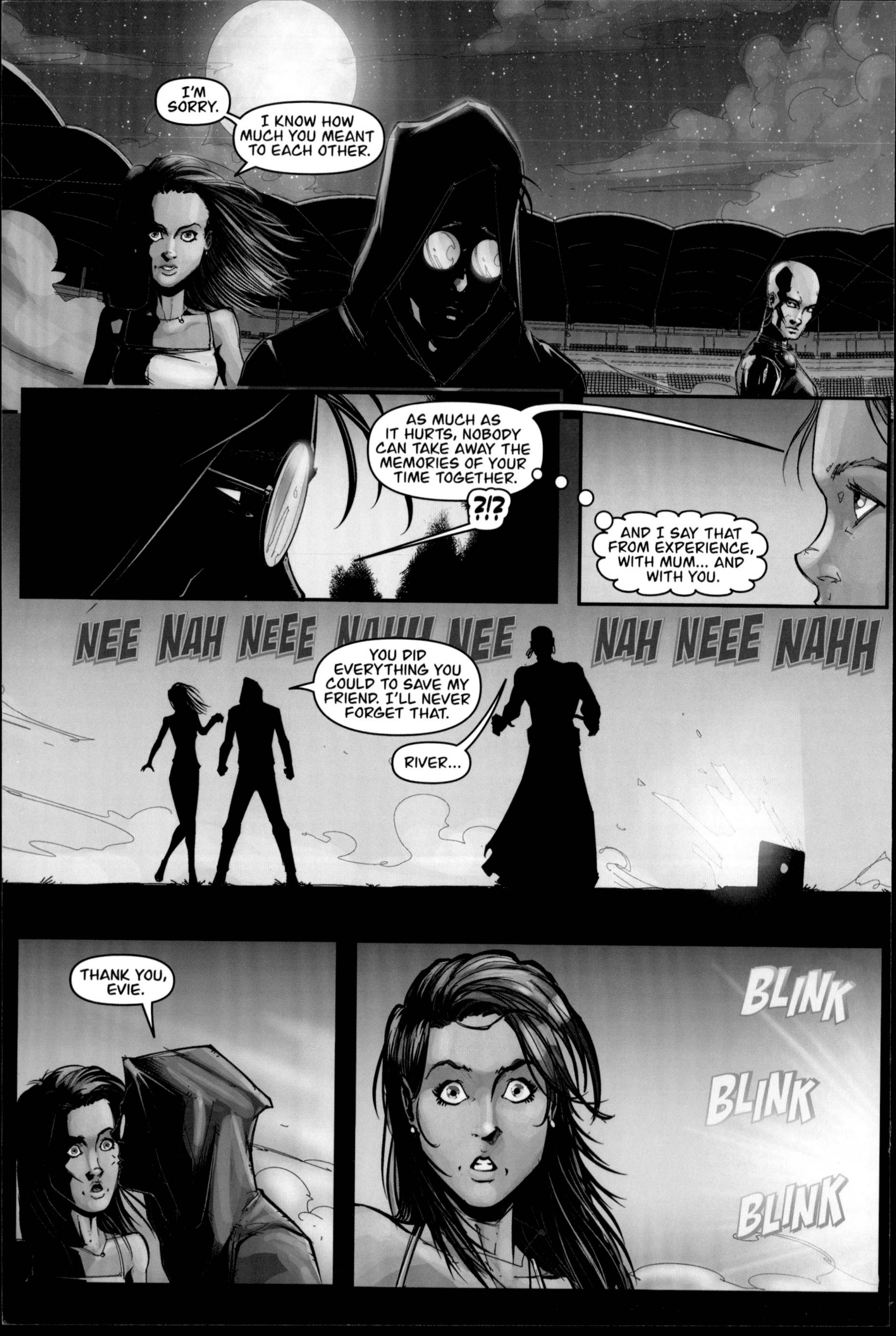
I'M SORRY.
I KNOW HOW MUCH YOU MEANT TO EACH OTHER.
AS MUCH AS IT HURTS, NOBODY CAN TAKE AWAY THE MEMORIES OF YOUR TIME TOGETHER.
?!?
AND I SAY THAT FROM EXPERIENCE, WITH MUM... AND WITH YOU.
NEE NAH NEEE NAHH NEE NAH NEEE NAHH
YOU DID EVERYTHING YOU COULD TO SAVE MY FRIEND. I'LL NEVER FORGET THAT.
RIVER...
THANK YOU, EVIE.
BLINK
BLINK
BLINK

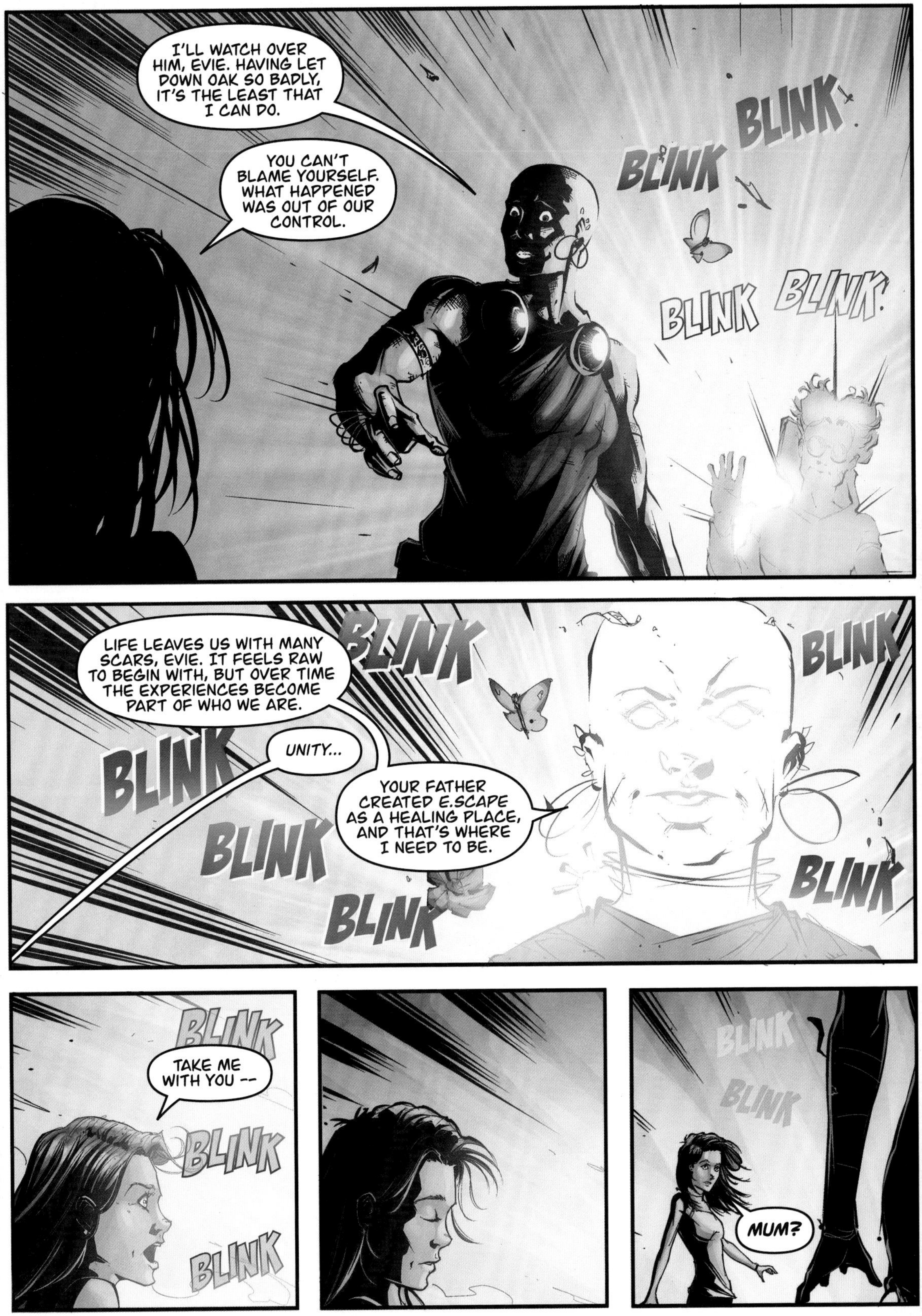

I'LL WATCH OVER HIM, EVIE. HAVING LET DOWN OAK SO BADLY, IT'S THE LEAST THAT I CAN DO.
YOU CAN'T BLAME YOURSELF. WHAT HAPPENED WAS OUT OF OUR CONTROL.
BLINK BLINK
BLINK BLINK
LIFE LEAVES US WITH MANY SCARS, EVIE. IT FEELS RAW TO BEGIN WITH, BUT OVER TIME THE EXPERIENCES BECOME PART OF WHO WE ARE.
UNITY...
YOUR FATHER CREATED E.SCAPE AS A HEALING PLACE, AND THAT'S WHERE I NEED TO BE.
BLINK BLINK BLINK BLINK BLINK BLINK
BLINK
TAKE ME WITH YOU --
BLINK BLINK
BLINK BLINK
MUM?

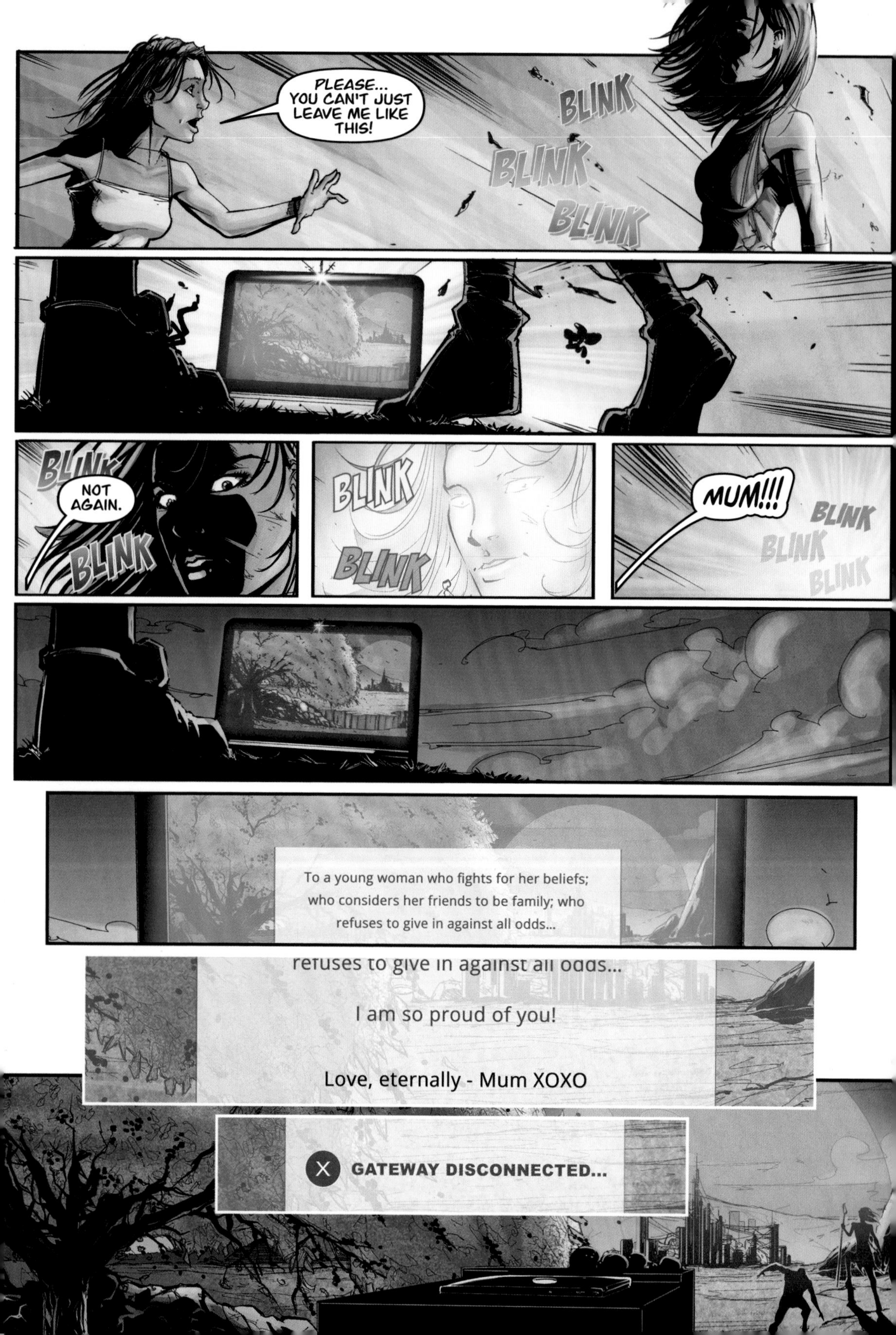
PLEASE... YOU CAN'T JUST LEAVE ME LIKE THIS!
BLINK
BLINK
BLINK
BLINK
NOT AGAIN.
BLINK
BLINK
BLINK
MUM!!!
BLINK
BLINK
BLINK
To a young woman who fights for her beliefs; who considers her friends to be family; who refuses to give in against all odds...
refuses to give in against all odds...
I am so proud of you!
Love, eternally - Mum XOXO
GATEWAY DISCONNECTED...

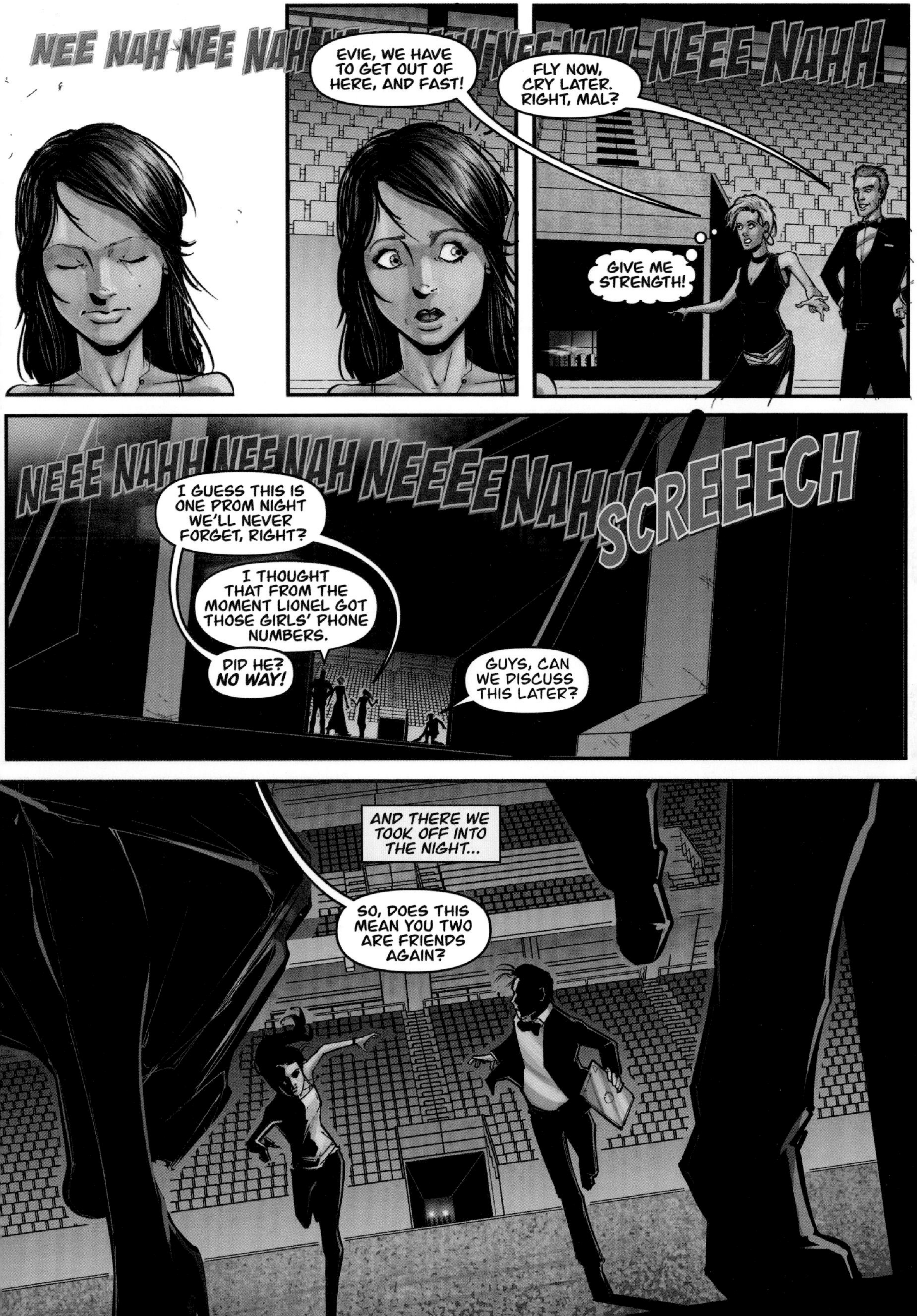
NEE NAH NEE NAH
EVIE, WE HAVE TO GET OUT OF HERE, AND FAST!
NEEE NAHH
FLY NOW, CRY LATER. RIGHT, MAL?
GIVE ME STRENGTH!
NEEE NAHH NEE NAH NEEEEE NAHH SCREEEECH
I GUESS THIS IS ONE PROM NIGHT WE'LL NEVER FORGET, RIGHT?
I THOUGHT THAT FROM THE MOMENT LIONEL GOT THOSE GIRLS' PHONE NUMBERS.
DID HE? NO WAY!
GUYS, CAN WE DISCUSS THIS LATER?
AND THERE WE TOOK OFF INTO THE NIGHT...
SO, DOES THIS MEAN YOU TWO ARE FRIENDS AGAIN?

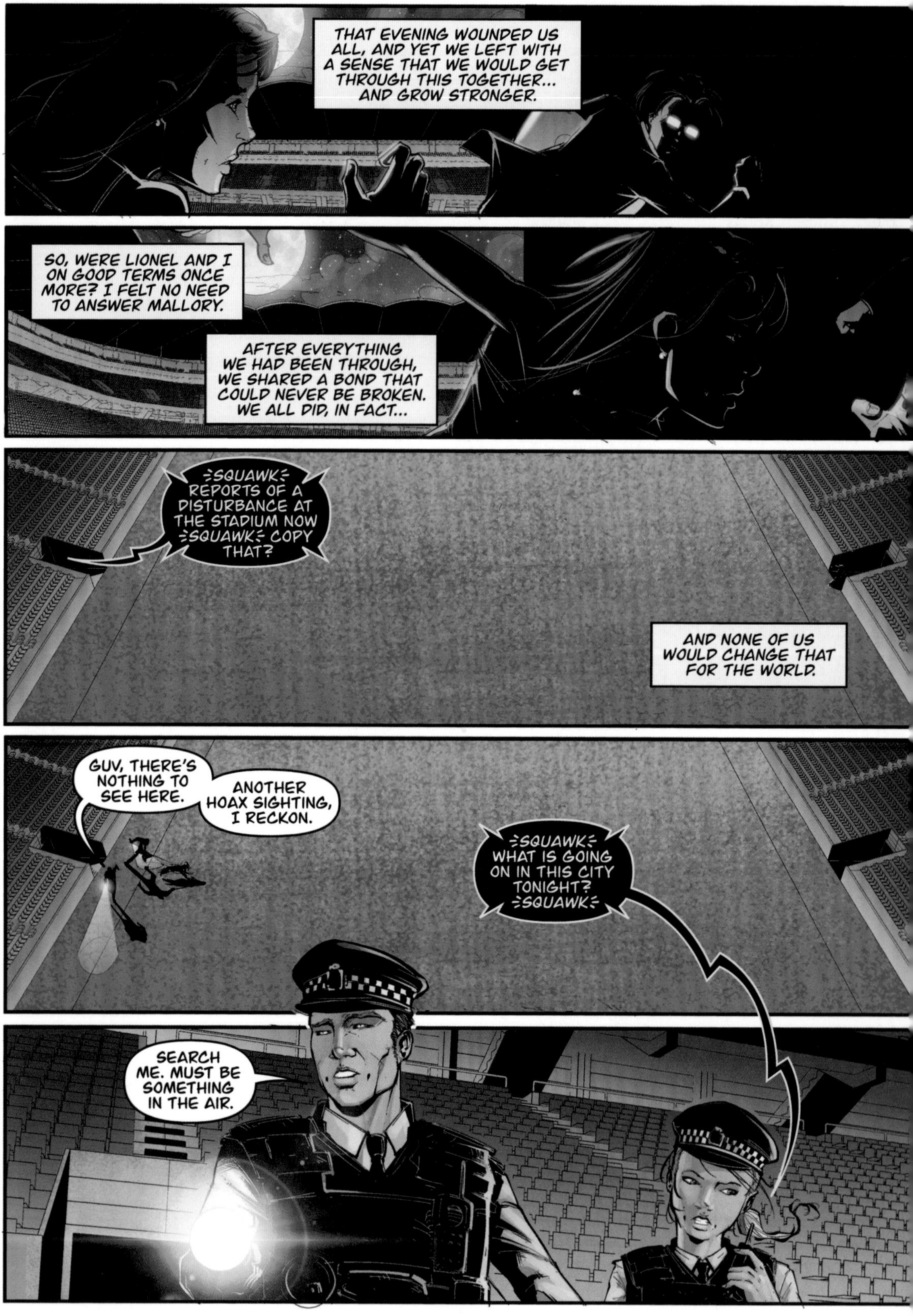
THAT EVENING WOUNDED US ALL, AND YET WE LEFT WITH A SENSE THAT WE WOULD GET THROUGH THIS TOGETHER... AND GROW STRONGER.
SO, WERE LIONEL AND I ON GOOD TERMS ONCE MORE? I FELT NO NEED TO ANSWER MALLORY.
AFTER EVERYTHING WE HAD BEEN THROUGH, WE SHARED A BOND THAT COULD NEVER BE BROKEN. WE ALL DID, IN FACT...
SQUAWK REPORTS OF A DISTURBANCE AT THE STADIUM NOW SQUAWK COPY THAT?
AND NONE OF US WOULD CHANGE THAT FOR THE WORLD.
GUV, THERE'S NOTHING TO SEE HERE.
ANOTHER HOAX SIGHTING, I RECKON.
SQUAWK WHAT IS GOING ON IN THIS CITY TONIGHT? SQUAWK
SEARCH ME. MUST BE SOMETHING IN THE AIR.

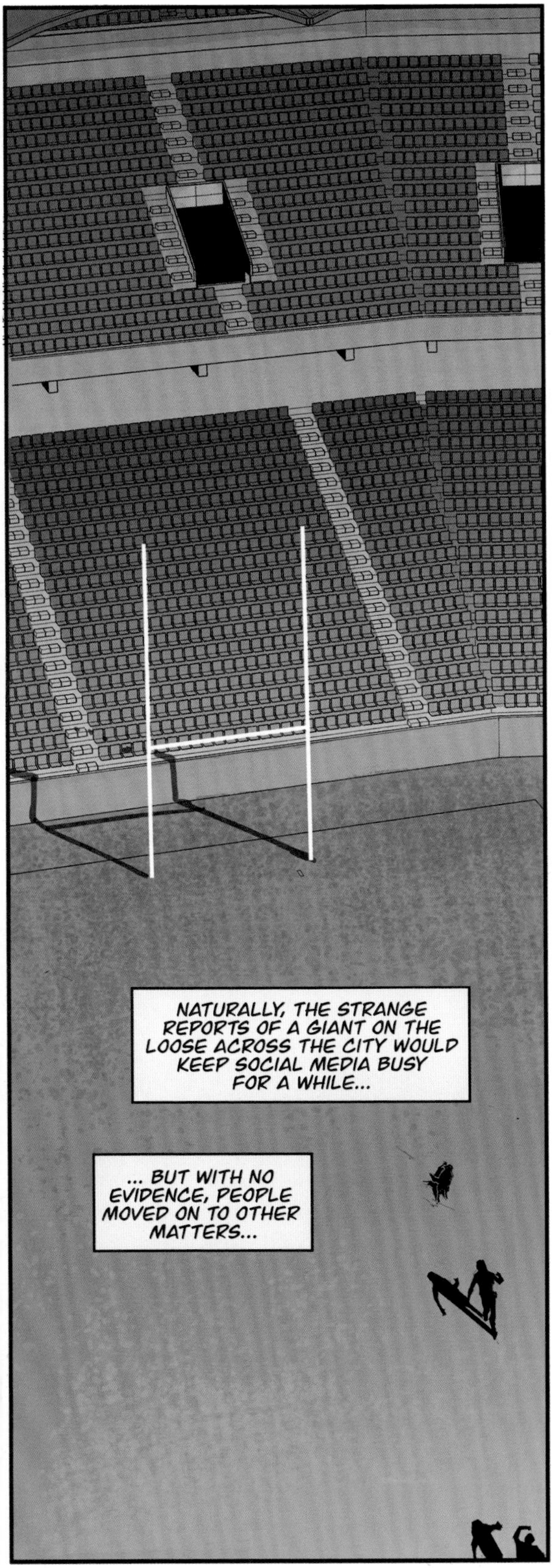
NATURALLY, THE STRANGE REPORTS OF A GIANT ON THE LOOSE ACROSS THE CITY WOULD KEEP SOCIAL MEDIA BUSY FOR A WHILE...
... BUT WITH NO EVIDENCE, PEOPLE MOVED ON TO OTHER MATTERS...

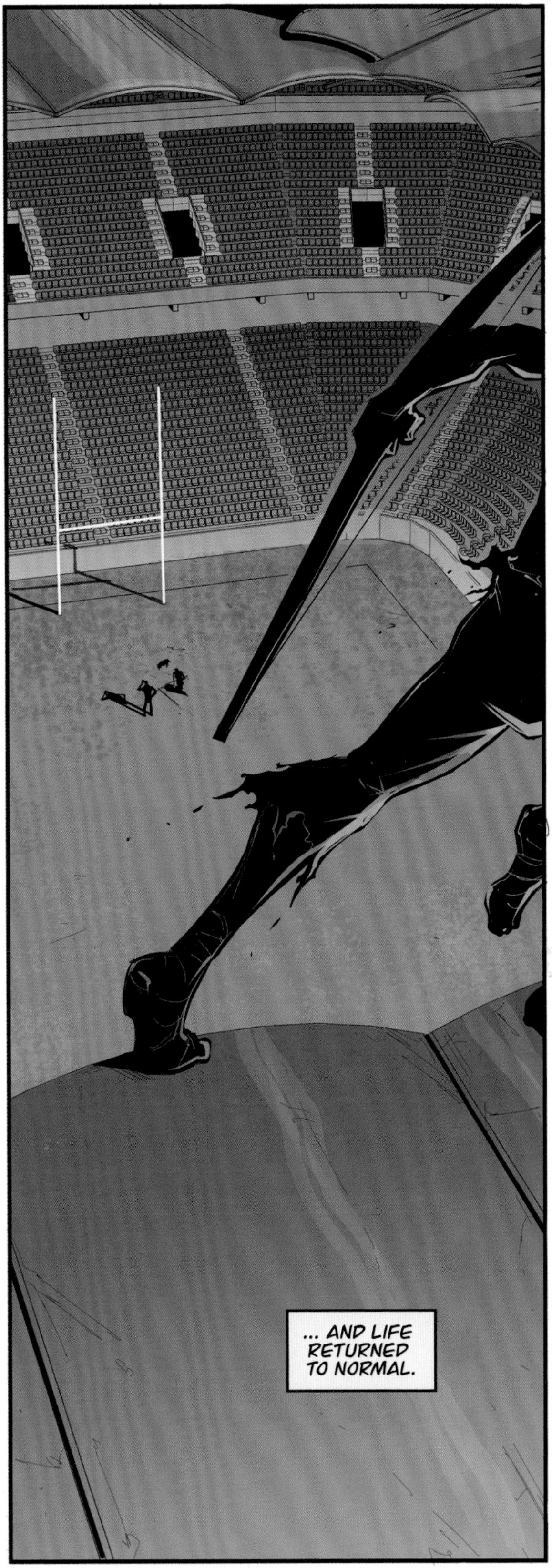
... AND LIFE RETURNED TO NORMAL.

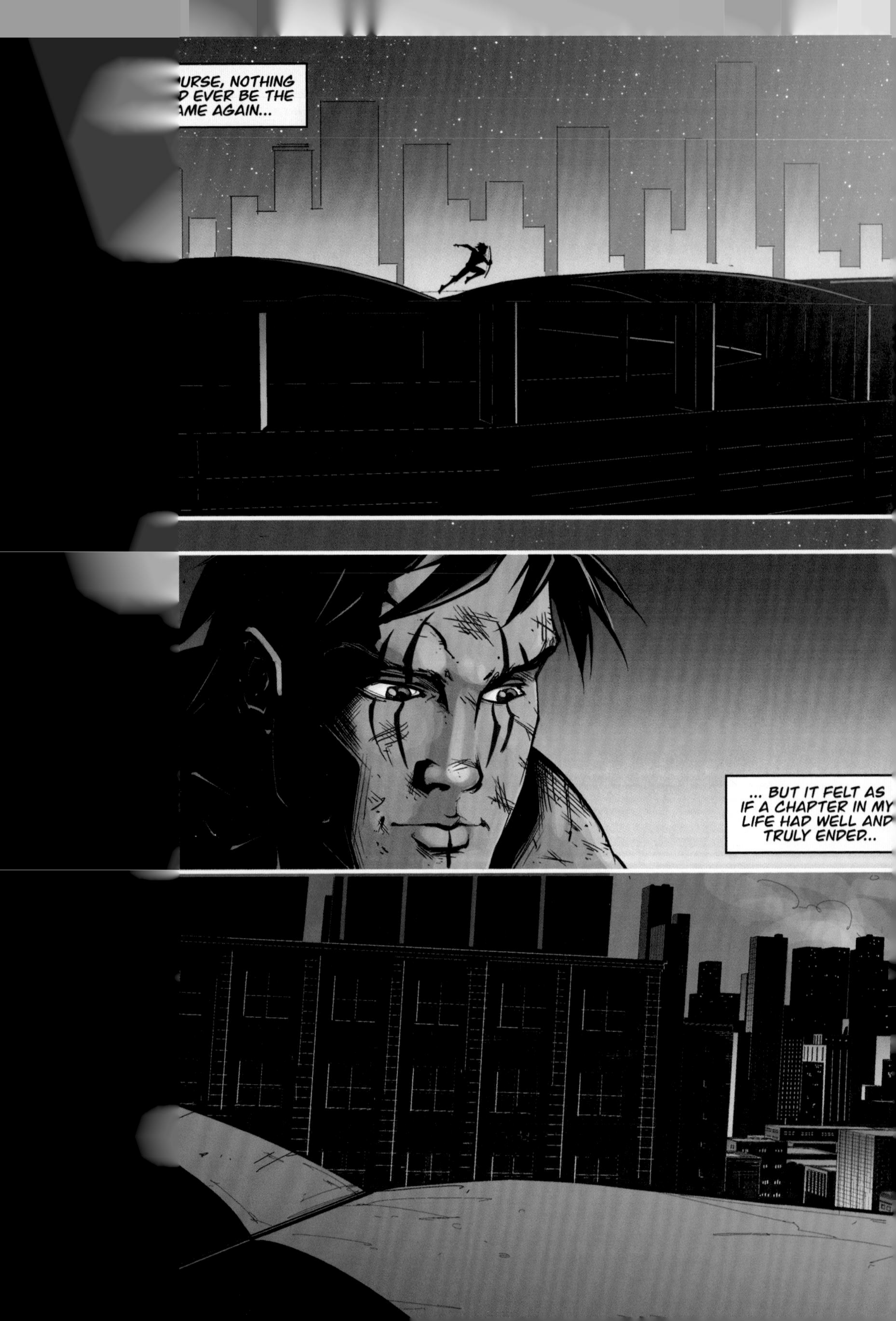

URSE, NOTHING
D EVER BE THE
AME AGAIN...
... BUT IT FELT AS IF A CHAPTER IN MY LIFE HAD WELL AND TRULY ENDED...

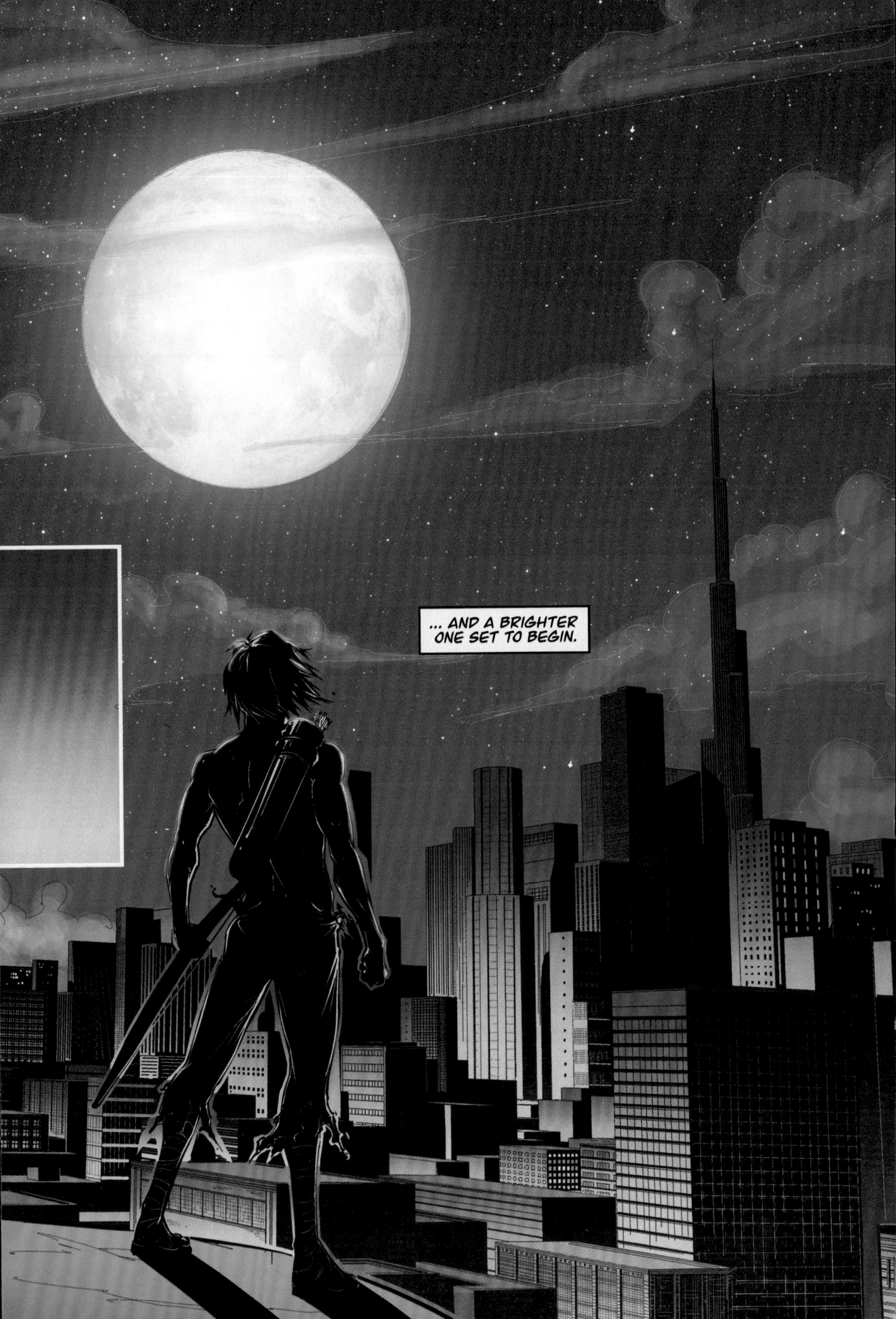
... AND A BRIGHTER ONE SET TO BEGIN.

THANK YOUs

ONCE AGAIN I'D FIRSTLY LIKE TO THANK YOU READING THIS. IT'S BECAUSE OF YOUR MASSIVE LEVELS OF SUPPORT ON THE FIRST GRAPHIC NOVEL THAT I HAVE BEEN GIVEN THE OPPORTUNITY TO CARRY ON WHAT I LOVE AND PRODUCE THIS SECOND ADVENTURE IN THE USERNAME SERIES. I REALLY HOPE YOU SHARE THIS STORY WITH FRIENDS AND FAMILY AND GET THEM INTO THIS AMAZING GENRE OF STORYTELLING.

THANKS SO MUCH TO BRIONY AND JAMIE AND THE REST OF HODDER. YOU HAVE HONESTLY BEEN SO AMAZING FROM START TO FINISH ON THIS BOOK. LIKE...ACTUALLY FAULTLESS, AND FOR THAT I'M VERY GRATEFUL. I'LL ALWAYS REMEMBER ATTENDING MY FIRST BOOK OF THE YEAR AWARDS WITH YOU AND BEING SO NERVOUS AND OUT MY COMFORT ZONE BUT YOU ALL MADE ME FEEL SO WELCOME AND PART OF THE FAMILY. ALSO...THE HOTEL STILL HASN'T CONTACTED ME ABOUT BREAKING THAT DOOR, OOPS.

THANK YOU TO THE SUGG SQUAD: AMRIT, MATT, JOAQUIN AND MINDY. ONCE AGAIN YOU HAVE ALL BEEN THE BEST TEAM I COULD POSSIBLY WISH FOR, GOING ABOVE AND BEYOND MY EXPECTATIONS OF HOW I IMAGINED THIS SECOND STORY TO BE.

THANK YOU TO LUCY, ALEX AND DOM FOR ALL THE HARD WORK AND PATIENCE...AGAIN. THANKS TO ALL MY FELLOW YOUTUBERS, THE BUTTERCREAM AND MY MATES FROM BACK HOME IN THE SHIRE. YOUR SUPPORT IS EVERYTHING TO ME.

LASTLY THANKS TO MY AMAZING FAMILY. KNOWING THAT YOU'RE ALL WATCHING ME GO ON THIS CRAZY RIDE AND SHARING THESE MOMENTS WITH ME MAKES ME SO HAPPY AND I HOPE (WELL I KINDA KNOW ALREADY AS YOU ALL TELL ME A LOT) THAT YOU'RE PROUD OF ME. YOU'VE ALWAYS ENCOURAGED ME TO BE CREATIVE THROUGHOUT MY LIFE AND FOR THAT I CAN'T THANK YOU ENOUGH. ALSO THANKS AGAIN ZOBO FOR THE BOOT UP THE ARSE TO START A YOUTUBE CHANNEL AND BEGIN THIS MAD LIFE I NOW LIVE. I'M A LUCKY SOD.

P.S. I STILL CAN'T DOWN A PINT.

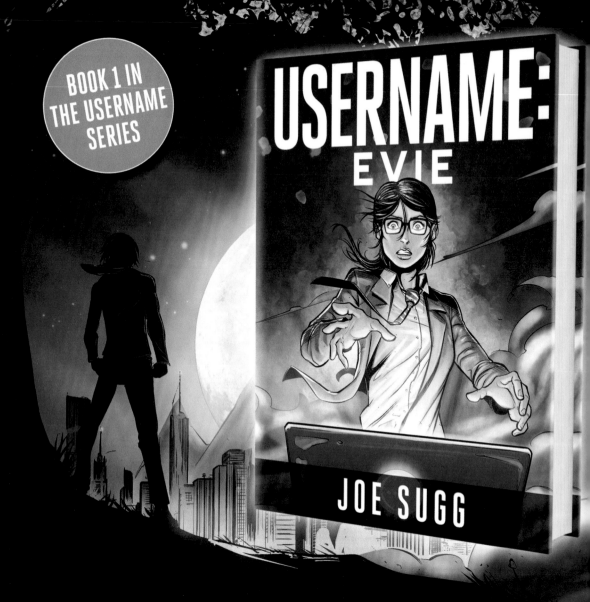

BOOK 1 IN THE USERNAME SERIES

USERNAME: EVIE

JOE SUGG

$17.95 | PAPERBACK | 978-0-7624-6010-6

THE BEGINNING OF THE ONLINE ADVENTURE

Like anyone who feels they don't fit in, Evie dreams of a place of safety. When times are tough all she wants is a chance to escape from reality and be herself.

But unknown to Evie her beloved father has been working tirelessly to create a virtual idyll just for her, and life as she knows it is about to be altered forever. Could this be the perfect world Evie has longed for? Or does the hardest journey still lie ahead . . .